Crime and Justice

Crime and Justice
A Review of Research

Edited by Michael Tonry

VOLUME 16

The University of Chicago Press, Chicago and London

This volume was prepared under Grant Number 89-IJ-CX-0013 awarded to the Castine Research Corporation by the National Institute of Justice, U.S. Department of Justice, under the Omnibus Crime Control and Safe Streets Act of 1968 as amended. Points of view or opinions expressed in this volume are those of the editors or authors and do not necessarily represent the official position or policies of the U.S. Department of Justice.

The University of Chicago Press, Chicago 60637
The University of Chicago Press, Ltd., London

ISSN: 0192-3234

ISBN: 0-226-80815-7

LCN: 80-642217

Contents

Preface

Six of the essays in this volume discuss sentencing and corrections issues, the seventh deals with motor vehicle crimes; there is no doubt that these topics will remain of central professional and public concern throughout the 1990s.

Rates of incarceration and the numbers of inmates have increased continuously and steeply in the United States since 1973. The number in prison and jail more than doubled between 1980 and 1990 and quadrupled between 1970 and 1990. The incarceration rate is four times that of any country with which most Americans would care to be compared. Yet there remains sharp conflict as to what should be done about this.

There are some who search for ways to reduce the use of prison and jail, to develop alternative sentencing strategies and alternative punishments, who suggest that reliance on imprisonment or probation as the basic punishments, with little in between, is a grave error. There are others who are not at all troubled by the numbers in prison, seeing their confinement as essential to the reduction of the scourge of crime.

In these often acrimonious debates, much is in doubt. For example, some see an obvious linkage between rates of imprisonment and rates of crime; others doubt that there is any such linkage at all. Some see the cost of imprisonment as prohibitive; others see it as less than the cost of the crime it prevents. There are victims advocates and advocates for safe and humane prisons, and between them discourse is rarely joined. What is so often missing in all three confrontations is the calm and close analysis of what is known and what is likely. That is, of course, the mission of this volume and of the other volumes in this series.

The development of a rational and fair sentencing policy will likely remain at the center of policy-making concern for many years to come. A revolution in sentencing practice began in the 1960s, with the pace of "reform" steadily increasing, but without any agreement on its efficacy or even on the wisdom of its direction. As an earlier editor of this series occasionally remarked: "Reform, Sir! Reform! Don't talk to me of reform; things are bad enough as they are."

The debate is most vehement concerning the federal sentencing guidelines and the work of the U.S. Sentencing Commission. But there are many other legislative and judicial conflicts concerning the sentencing of convicted criminals, not the least of which is the increasing legislative popularity of mandatory minimum sentences. This volume presents contributions to many of those debates. Topics range from philosophical first principles and public opinion through mandatory penalties and methods of structuring sentencing discretion to inmates' adjustments to prison and prison privatization. Andrew von Hirsch surveys recent writing in the philosophy of punishment. Julian Roberts examines the sizable, and growing, literature on public opinion about sentencing and punishment and concludes that much of the conventional wisdom—that the public is more punitive than are judges, that the public is uninterested in rehabilitation, that the public favors incarceration as the punishment of choice for most offenders—is wrong. A third essay examines the role and effects of mandatory minimum sentencing laws. Andrew Ashworth examines efforts throughout the English-speaking countries to structure sentencing discretion. Kenneth Adams and Douglas McDonald, respectively, examine the current state-of-the-art of knowledge concerning prisoners' adaptation to prison life and the ongoing debates about the costs and benefits of privately operated prisons.

For readers benumbed by so much punishment, Ronald Clarke and Patricia Harris tell us what is known about the patterns, perpetrators, and prevention of motor vehicle crimes.

Michael Tonry

Ronald V. Clarke and Patricia M. Harris

Auto Theft and Its Prevention

ABSTRACT

Auto theft makes a substantial contribution to the crime statistics of the
United States. Eleven percent of all Uniform Crime Report index crimes
in 1989 and 12 percent of crimes reported in the Victim Risk Supplement
to the National Crime Survey comprised thefts of and from vehicles.
Auto theft is even more prevalent in other developed countries,
particularly when theft rates are calculated per vehicles registered.
Marked urban/rural and intercity variations are only partly explained by
variations in overall levels of crime or in the availability of vehicles. Many
thefts involve cars parked in the street at night, and automobile models
vary greatly in their vulnerability to theft. Auto theft has not increased
more than other important property crimes in the United States during
the last thirty years but may have come increasingly under the domain of
more adult, organized offenders. Even so, thefts for temporary use and
joyriding outnumber professional thefts by at least two to one. In turn,
these forms of auto theft are outnumbered by thefts from vehicles
(including components) by about five to one. The most promising
preventive approach is through the manufacture of more secure vehicles.
Improved documentation of ownership and environmental modifications at
parking lots might also yield some gains.

According to crime surveys a substantial proportion of known crime—
12 percent in the Victim Risk Supplement to the National Crime Survey and about 18 percent in the British Crime Survey—consists of
thefts of or from vehicles. In addition, the British Crime Survey found

Ronald V. Clarke is dean of the School of Criminal Justice at Rutgers University;
Patricia M. Harris is assistant professor at the University of Texas at San Antonio.
Thanks are due for their help and advice to Simon Field and Pat Mayhew of the Home
Office Research and Planning Unit and to David Biles of the Australian Institute of
Criminology.

that, while the emotional upset for victims of car theft was less than for burglary, the financial losses and inconvenience were generally greater. These findings speak to a significant problem, yet one that has received little attention from criminologists. We were unable to find a single academic book on auto theft published in the English-speaking world during the last twenty years. The contrast with burglary is particularly striking even allowing for its more serious nature. In his recent *Crime and Justice* essay, Shover (1991) identifies at least ten criminological books on burglary published in the 1970s and 1980s and many more articles and government reports.

The unusually wide scope for criminological inquiry afforded by auto theft makes neglect of this offense all the more surprising. Theft of vehicles is perhaps the best reported of all property crimes, while the offenders most usually involved, juveniles, are among the most accessible groups for study. There can be few other theft targets for which there is so much available information about numbers at risk, age, value, and location, which makes auto theft particularly fertile ground for opportunity theories of crime. While the ubiquity of automobiles, their inadequate protection, and their attractiveness to a variety of offenders makes it easy to understand the high levels of theft, some other facts about auto theft demand explanation. For example, why has this offense increased less in the United States during the past thirty years than have some other property crimes, and why are rates of auto theft in the United States lower than in the United Kingdom, Scandinavia, and some other countries, particularly when expressed in relation to the number of vehicles registered? Why are there such large urban/rural and intercity variations in rates of auto theft? And why is there so much variation among models of automobile in their vulnerability to different kinds of theft? Aside from these largely unanswered questions, there are others that remain contentious. For example, it is unclear to what extent auto theft has evolved in recent years from a problem of juvenile joyriding into a more serious problem of thefts for profit committed by more organized, adult offenders. Nor is it clear, as some opportunity theorists have argued, to what extent levels of auto theft increase in direct proportion to the number of vehicles on the road, or whether a point is reached when more cars no longer mean more thefts.

The principal reason for paying more criminological attention to auto theft, however, relates to the tangible prospects for prevention and the associated opportunity for making a substantial dent in the nation's crime statistics. We have therefore chosen to structure our review by considering what is known about auto theft (and what needs to be discovered) from a policy-oriented, preventive perspective. While this narrowed focus still permits a discussion of the main findings and theories, it raises a number of particular research issues. For example, because the different forms of auto theft may need to be separately addressed, it becomes important to refine estimates concerning their prevalence and costs so as to determine priorities in a rational manner. At present, only a rough division can be made among the three main forms of auto theft, suggesting that 85 percent of offenses comprise thefts from vehicles (including components), 10 percent comprise joyriding and other temporary use, and 5 percent are thefts for resale of the vehicle or its disassembled parts. Our review of preventive options suggests that, in general, there is greater scope for increasing the difficulties of auto theft than for increasing the risks or reducing the motivation. To prevent thefts from being displaced from protected to unprotected targets, security improvements should be built in at manufacture. Since the vehicle fleet is renewed every fifteen years or so, this means that improvements in security could be introduced across-the-board in a comparatively brief space of time. However, it remains unclear how consumers, manufacturers, and politicians can be persuaded that this may be the best way of dealing with the problem.

The literature covered in this essay is of somewhat uneven quality, and the focus on prevention is intended to lend it greater coherence as well as providing an agenda for further research, beyond the scholarly pursuit of knowledge. Section I deals with the extent and nature of auto theft in preparation for the analysis, in Section II, of the policy options. These are seen as falling into three categories, discussed separately in further sections of the review: reducing the motivation for auto theft (Sec. III), increasing the risks (Sec. IV), and increasing the difficulties (Sec. V). The final section summarizes the research needed to advance the goal of prevention.

I. The Extent and Nature of the Problem

In this section we review information concerning trends in the scale and nature of the problem in the United States and elsewhere, the costs of auto theft, and its distribution within the United States. We also summarize research findings concerning the most vulnerable vehicles and the highest-risk locations and times for auto theft.

A. Varieties of Auto Theft

The definition of motor vehicles in the Uniform Crime Reports (UCR) includes trucks, buses, motorcycles, and other surface vehicles, but most incidents falling under the UCR index crime of "motor vehicle theft" (79 percent in 1989) involve automobiles, and much of the research is focused on these. Indeed, motor vehicle theft is frequently referred to as auto theft, which practice is followed here.

No accepted classification of the various auto theft offenses exists, though a distinction is frequently made between theft from a motor vehicle (when items are removed but not the vehicle itself) and theft of a motor vehicle (when the vehicle is removed whether or not subsequently recovered). Variations on this distinction are employed in all four major sources of published data on auto theft—the UCR, the Victim Risk Supplement of the National Crime Survey (NCS), the British Criminal Statistics, and the British Crime Survey.[1] The UCR, for example, distinguishes between "motor vehicle theft," one of eight index crimes, which is defined as the theft or attempted theft of a motor vehicle, and two subcategories of the index crime of larceny-theft, "theft from motor vehicles (excluding any accessories)" and "theft of motor vehicle accessories."

A second common distinction, which reflects wide agreement that levels of sophistication vary considerably among car thieves, is between opportunistic thefts by juveniles for "joyriding" and thefts for profit by more "hardened" offenders (e.g., Home Office 1988). In keeping with this, the British Criminal Statistics long presented statistics for "taking and driving away" (defined by recovery of the car within a period of thirty days) and "thefts of motor vehicles" (incidents in which cars were not generally recovered). However, this distinction increasingly proved unworkable in practice since many cars were found intact after the thirty-day period whereas others, recovered after a day or two, might be found stripped of valuable components.

Attempts to develop more detailed classifications of auto theft reflect a consistent difference in viewpoint between criminologists and the law enforcement community. Criminologists tend to regard vehicle theft as principally involving temporary appropriation of the vehicle for "joyriding" and other purposes by juveniles (Schepses 1961; McCaghy, Giordano, and Henson 1977; Higgins and Albrecht 1981). For exam-

---

[1] These four data sets have recently been described for *Crime and Justice* in Shover (1991).

ple, in their criminological analysis of auto thefts in Toledo, McCaghy, Giordano, and Henson (1977) found that three classes of temporary use—joyriding, short-term transportation, and longer-term transportation—accounted for about 90 percent of all thefts.

For the police, the involvement of "professionals" in auto theft assumes greater salience, as exemplified by the testimony of law enforcement officials—offered only two or three years after the publication of McCaghy et al.'s research—in hearings leading to the passage of the Motor Vehicle Theft Law Enforcement Act of 1984 (98 Stat. 2754). This testimony (see, e.g., Permanent Subcommittee on Investigations 1979; and Subcommittee on Consumer Protection and Finance 1980) focused almost exclusively on varieties of professional theft—"chopping" (the disassembly of stolen vehicles and the subsequent sale of their parts), "retagging" or "body switches" (in which stolen vehicles are given new identities by using documents from wrecked vehicles), and theft for export to other countries (principally Mexico for the United States).

One useful classification of auto theft (see fig. 1) has been developed by Challinger (1987). Building on earlier work by McGaghy, Giordano, and Henson (1977), Challinger makes a threefold distinction between thefts for recreation, for transport, and for financial gain. Under recreation, he groups thefts for fun ("joyriding"), for status seeking, and for meeting the challenge of successfully stealing a car. Thefts for transport may be to obtain a car to complete a single trip, to use in another crime such as a bank robbery, or to keep for extended personal use. Thefts for profit include "stripping" of radios and other valuable parts by amateurs; "chopping," "retagging," and thefts for export by professionals; and crimes by owners more properly regarded as insurance frauds. He considers that "opportunity makers," that is, individuals who do not simply take advantage of opportunities they stumble on, are found in increasing proportions in progressing through his three main categories of theft.

While Challinger's classification may provide a useful starting point for more detailed research, it serves less well as the basis for a review of current knowledge because so little information is available for each of the different categories of theft that he identifies. Indeed, most research into auto theft involves theft of the vehicle itself, and our review will inevitably reflect this focus. Nevertheless, because of some important differences in offender motivation and levels of skill, and consequently in the likely explanatory variables (cf. Tremblay, Clermont,

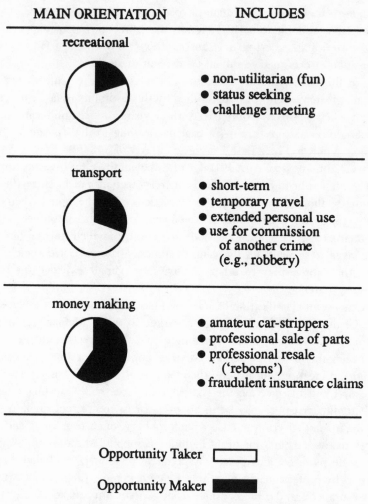

MAIN ORIENTATION   INCLUDES

recreational
- non-utilitarian (fun)
- status seeking
- challenge meeting

transport
- short-term
- temporary travel
- extended personal use
- use for commission
   of another crime
   (e.g., robbery)

money making
- amateur car-strippers
- professional sale of parts
- professional resale
   ('reborns')
- fraudulent insurance claims

Opportunity Taker ▭

Opportunity Maker ▬

Fig. 1.—Orientations of car thieves. Source: Adapted from Challinger (1987).

and Cusson 1991), we attempt to differentiate whenever possible between three main categories of auto theft: thefts for temporary use (including joyriding and short-term transportation); professional thefts (thefts intended to deprive the owner permanently of the vehicle, including for extended personal use by the thief, for resale, for export, and for chopping); and thefts from vehicles (including small components such as the radio or battery as well as theft of personal possessions).

It may sometimes be simply a matter of convenience whether a car is moved before it is stripped and thus largely a matter of chance whether it is counted as a stolen car. This provides one reason for including theft from vehicles in a review of auto theft. More important, given the policy focus of this review, is that theft from vehicles makes a substantial contribution to the crime statistics. Rational assignment of priorities among preventive measures requires information about the costs and prevalence of specific subcategories of auto theft. Moreover, while preventive measures often need to be precisely tailored to highly specific categories of offense (e.g., basic improvements in automobile security may reduce joyriding by juveniles but may have little effect on thefts of automobiles for chopping by organized criminals), some measures can be expected to have an impact on more than one category of offense and need to be assessed in this light. For instance, making it difficult to gain entry to the car may reduce not only joyriding but also incidents of theft from the vehicle.

B. Scale of Auto Theft

Whether measured by official statistics or crime surveys, vehicle-related thefts constitute a substantial proportion of the criminal incidents that come to light. For example, thefts of and from vehicles accounted for about 18.5 percent of all offenses reported in the 1988 British Crime Survey (Mayhew, Elliott, and Dowds 1989) and 12 percent of all crimes revealed in the Victim Risk Supplement to the NCS (Lynch and Biderman 1984). Similarly, these offenses constituted 11 percent of all index crimes in the UCR for 1989. This figure is likely to underestimate the prevalence of vehicle thefts in a small but growing number of cases involving thefts at gunpoint (Dean 1991; Freid 1991), which are subsequently counted in the UCR as robberies. From the perspective of the individual member of the public, there is little doubt that simply owning a vehicle greatly increases his or her chances of becoming a victim of crime.

In 1989, the two UCR categories of theft from vehicles between them outnumbered thefts of vehicles by nearly two to one (respectively, 2,554,785 and 1,370,766). For a variety of reasons (including the high value of vehicles, insurance requirements, the assistance needed from police to recover stolen and abandoned cars, and, indeed, the high probability that cars reported stolen will be located and returned), theft of a motor vehicle has much higher reporting rates (90 percent or better; e.g., Harlow [1988]) than other thefts. This means that the UCR undoubtedly underestimates the size of the difference in the incidence of thefts of and thefts from. Indeed, the 1989 International Crime Survey found that the rate of theft from a car in the United States was nearly five times as high as the rate of theft of a car (Mayhew 1990a; van Dijk, Mayhew, and Killias 1990).

The much larger proportion of crimes accounted for by auto theft in the British Crime Survey than in the NCS Victim Risk Supplement suggests that the problem may be greater elsewhere than in the United States. This is generally confirmed by international comparisons based on crimes reported to the police (e.g., Kalish 1988; Motor Trades Association of Australia 1990; NRMA Insurance, Ltd. 1990). Table 1, derived from Interpol data, is illustrative of these results and shows rates of auto theft per capita and per registered automobiles of nineteen industrialized countries for two pairs of years: 1977 and 1978, and 1987 and 1988.[2] The per capita rate for the United States, which increased only slightly during the ten-year period, was lower in 1987/88 than for five other countries: Norway, Denmark, Sweden, England and Wales, and Australia.

Part of the explanation for the lower per capita rates in the United States may be the generally high levels of vehicle ownership. These mean that more people, perhaps especially the young, have legitimate access to a car. Mayhew (1990a) has shown that countries such as the United States, with the highest levels of ownership, have rates of theft somewhat lower than countries with intermediate levels (though still higher than countries with low levels of ownership). It is because of high ownership levels that the United States appears in an even more favorable light in the comparison in table 1 of thefts per 1,000 registered automobiles, with a rate in 1987/88 (8.9), for example, less than half that for England and Wales (20.3), and lower than those of nine of the countries listed.

C. Costs

The costs of auto theft can be considered from two main perspectives: direct costs to victims and other social costs. Existing estimates

[2] Not all countries reporting to Interpol give figures for auto theft, and for some countries automobile registration figures were also unavailable. Some technical points of comparability also mean that care must be exercised in interpretation (Mayhew 1990a). These relate mainly to the treatment of attempts and the vehicles covered in the theft reports. Countries where the coverage was known to be different were excluded (e.g., Switzerland, which includes bicycle thefts). In some countries a distinction is made between incidents in which it is thought the thief intends "to permanently deprive" the owner and other incidents often called "unauthorized takings"; it is not always clear which are counted.

TABLE 1

International Comparison of Thefts of Cars Recorded by the Police, 1977/78 and 1987/88

	Per Thousand Persons		Per Thousand Cars	
	1977/78	1987/88	1977/78	1987/88
Austria	.2	.2	.6	.4
Japan	.3	.3	1.1	.7
Portugal	.7	.5	5.2	2.7
West Germany	1.0	1.2	2.6	2.3
Netherlands	1.0	1.6	2.6	3.8
Belgium	.6	2.0	1.6	5.1
Finland	.4	2.3	1.3	6.0
Canada	3.6	3.4	8.4	6.9
Italy	3.7	3.6	10.2	6.9
Spain	2.3	3.7	11.4	12.7
France	3.7	4.3	8.4	9.3
Northern Ireland	.7	4.9	3.1	17.2
Scotland	6.7	5.2	31.4	18.3
United States	4.6	5.6	8.3	8.9
Norway	1.8	6.2	5.7	14.1
Denmark	4.1	7.0	12.9	19.2
Sweden	5.0	7.0	14.5	16.8
England and Wales	6.4	7.6	21.8	20.3
Australia	3.8	7.7	6.0	13.4

SOURCES.—Crime data: Interpol (various years); populations: *UN Demographic Yearbook* (various years); vehicles: *UN Statistical Yearbook* (various years).

NOTE.—Rates are per 1,000 persons and per 1,000 registered cars for nineteen industrialized countries. (1) Rates are ranked in order of 1987/88 rates per person. (2) The vehicles covered were passenger cars and motorcycles. (3) Crime data were not available for all the years in question for Canada and the Netherlands and, with the help of Patricia Mayhew of the Home Office Research and Planning Unit, were obtained from publications of those countries. Similarly, some of the population and vehicle data were obtained from other official publications for particular countries and years.

of the former are more satisfactory than for the latter. According to National Crime Survey data for 1973–85, the net cost to victims of a theft or attempted theft of a vehicle (after taking account of recoveries and insurance reimbursements) averaged $242 in 1985 dollars (Harlow 1988). The 1984 British Crime Survey found that net losses (after insurance payouts) were greater for theft of a vehicle than for a residential burglary; 23 percent of burglaries involved losses of more than £250 compared with 54 percent of vehicle thefts (Hough and Mayhew 1985).

Moreover, while a few victims will be better off when insurance claims have been met (Hough and Mayhew 1985, p. 28), the financial costs identified by victim surveys may not include indirect costs incurred such as loss of earnings, the rental of a temporary replacement vehicle, or the cost of retrieving the vehicle from the police lot. National Crime Survey data reveal that 13 percent of victims of a completed theft lost at least one day from work (Harlow 1988), while the British Crime Survey (Hough and Mayhew 1985) shows that many more victims of theft of a vehicle (49 percent) reported inconvenience and practical problems than did victims of a burglary (19 percent). However, only 4 percent of the victims of car theft in the British Crime Survey reported emotional distress compared with 37 percent of the victims of burglary (Hough and Mayhew 1985). The recent emergence of vehicle thefts at gunpoint (in Los Angeles, armed robberies made up 6 percent of vehicle thefts in 1990 [Dean 1991]) could require modification of conclusions about the relatively nontraumatic nature of auto theft.

The direct costs to victims are, however, only a part, almost certainly the smaller part, of the full costs of auto theft to society. Other social costs will include the cost of insurance, the cost of measures taken by car owners to reduce their risks of auto theft, the cost of accidents incurred in joyriding and in attempting to evade arrest, and the criminal justice costs of auto theft. A portion of all car insurance premiums covers the risk of theft and the associated higher accident rates for stolen vehicles (Weglian [1978] reports that joyriders are between 47 and 200 times more likely than other drivers to be involved in accidents). All cars are equipped at manufacture with door and ignition locks in the interests of security, and some owners seek to reduce their risks further by purchasing security devices and paying to park in garages. It has been claimed (Brill 1982) that costs of vehicle theft fall disproportionately on the less affluent motorists who live in higher-risk areas, who cannot park their cars in garages, and who cannot afford to purchase preventive devices or comprehensive insurance. Finally, taxpayers at large have to foot the bill for the increased burden due to auto thefts (and the crimes sometimes facilitated by stolen cars such as bank robberies) falling on the police and the criminal justice system.

In 1981, the total cost of vehicle theft for the United States was estimated to be at least $3.3 billion (Brobeck 1983). Criminal justice costs, estimated by multiplying the total cost of the criminal justice system by the proportion of all auto-theft-related arrests contributed about 20 percent of Brobeck's total, while victimization costs and preventive expenditures constituted another 30 percent. The largest contribution, accounting for the remaining 50 percent, came from insurance premiums.

Crude as such costings may be, they shed additional light on the scale of the auto theft problem and are useful in providing a guide as to how much might be spent on prevention. Knowing where the costs fall also provides an indication of where the incentives for prevention might lie.

D. Auto Theft Trends in the United States

Prior to the advent of the NCS, the authoritative data on crime trends for the United States were provided by the Uniform Crime Reports. Data on thefts of vehicles are available from 1933 and despite small changes in definition in 1933, 1960, 1972, 1973, 1976, and 1986, what has been counted seems reasonably constant.[3] These data show increases in rates of auto theft since the inception of the UCR in the 1930s. Figure 2 presents data from 1958 (the year the FBI began using more accurate population estimates) until 1989. It shows an increase of about 400 percent, slightly more than the increase in burglaries and somewhat less than the increase in robberies in the period.

According to the UCR, there was little change in rates of auto theft during the period for about fifteen years from the early 1970s until the mid-1980s; after then, rates began to increase again. This recent rise is confirmed by data from the National Crime Survey, which reports a 23 percent increase in auto thefts between 1985 and 1988, much greater than for any other crime covered in the survey (Flanagan and Maguire 1990). The general conclusion to be drawn about trends in auto theft since 1958 is that this offense has generally increased at a similar rate to that of other important categories of crime, such as burglary and robbery, but with an unusually steep increase in very recent years.

Leslie Wilkins (1964) showed that the increase of vehicle thefts during 1938–61 closely paralleled the rise in the numbers of vehicles on the road, and opportunity theorists generally would hold that rates of auto theft should be based on the number of vehicles (cf. Cohen and Felson 1979; Clarke 1984). Rates for the index crime of motor vehicle

---

[3] For example, while attempts were introduced into the definition in 1973, the rates do not exhibit marked inclines in the year.

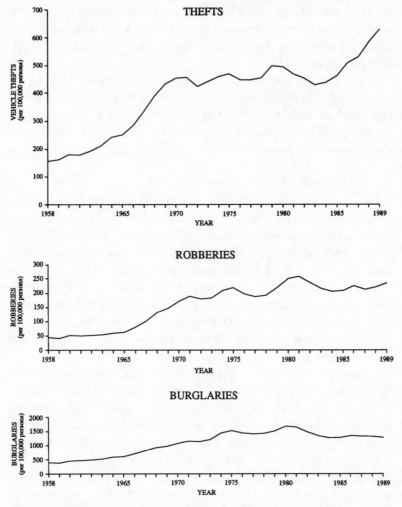

Fig. 2.—Vehicle thefts, robberies, and burglaries per 100,000 population, United States, 1958–90. Sources: Federal Bureau of Investigation (1959–90).

theft have been calculated in this way by the UCR since 1966 and show greater fluctuations during the period than would be predicted on the basis of opportunity theory (fig. 3). The greater rise in theft rates calculated on a population base (also shown in fig. 3) may reflect an increase in population that has been substantially less than the increase in cars in the period.

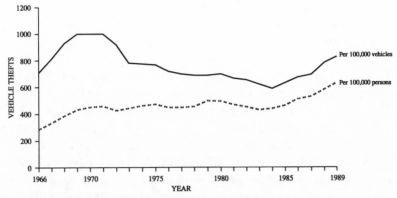

Fig. 3.—Vehicle thefts per 100,000 population and per 100,000 vehicles registered, United States 1966–89. Sources: Federal Bureau of Investigation (1967–90).

E. Trends in the Nature of Auto Theft

Until recently, persons under the age of 18 constituted the majority of those arrested for vehicle theft. Through 1977, more than 50 percent of arrests involved juvenile thieves. The proportion of juveniles arrested fell to 35 percent in 1983, though it rose again slightly to 40 percent by 1988. This trend is frequently cited by law enforcement officials and auto industry personnel in support of contentions that auto theft has evolved from a mundane activity monopolized mainly by juvenile joyriders to a lucrative profession dominated by members of organized crime engaged in a black-market body parts industry (Subcommittee on Telecommunications, Consumer Protection, and Finance 1982).

Two further facts are adduced in support of this proposition. First, auto theft clearance rates have dropped from a high of 27.8 percent in 1961 to 15 percent in 1988, which suggests the increasing involvement of more skilled offenders. Second, recoveries of stolen vehicles are widely thought to have declined, which might suggest an increase in the profit motive. However, data on the decline are not entirely consistent. Since 1958 the UCR has included information about the percentage of the value of stolen vehicles recovered (not the percentage of vehicles recovered), which declined from a high in that year of 92.2 percent of the total value stolen to a low of 51.7 percent in 1981, with a subsequent increase to 66.4 percent by 1988 (Federal Bureau of Investigation 1959–89). These figures certainly suggest an overall decline in recoveries—a trend which has also been observed in other countries such as Canada (Tremblay, Clermont, and Cusson 1991)— and they are supported by NCS data that indicate that 62 percent of stolen vehicles were recovered during 1973–85, with little year-to-year variation (Harlow 1988). However, recently published data (National Highway Traffic Safety Administration 1991) from the FBI's National Crime Information Center (NCIC) indicate that 78 percent of stolen vehicles were recovered in 1988, a much higher proportion than is suggested by the UCR and NCS figures.

Comparisons between the NCS and the UCR are fraught with difficulty, and the consistency on recoveries may be due to no more than chance. As for the apparent discrepancy between the two FBI data sources (UCR and NCIC), part of the explanation may lie in the stricter verification procedures followed by the NCIC, which automatically purges any auto theft report for which the vehicle identification number (VIN) has not been supplied within thirty days. The UCR data showed 6.7 percent more vehicle thefts in 1988 than did the NCIC, and a disproportionate number of cases purged from the NCIC might have related to vehicles that were never recovered (National Automobile Theft Bureau 1990a). A more important reason for the discrepancy between the two FBI sources, however, may be a difference in what is being measured in each case. For the NCIC, this is the proportion of vehicles recovered, and for the UCR it is the value recovered. While UCR figures for value recovered and proportion of vehicles recovered (Federal Bureau of Investigation 1936–59) were almost identical between 1935 and 1958 (which may have been the reason for discontinuing the publication of both), they could have diverged since then. For example, the value recovered could have declined much faster than the proportion recovered for a variety of reasons, including more stripping of valuable components from vehicles principally taken for temporary use, more accidental damage to stolen vehicles, and higher repair costs.

Whatever the explanation for the difference between the recovery figures yielded by the UCR and NCS, and by the NCIC, the apparent discrepancy weakens the argument that auto theft has come increasingly under the domain of more professional and organized adult offenders. The other findings supporting this position are also capable of alternative explanation. Thus, both the growth in the proportion of adults arrested and the decline in clearance rates for auto theft might reflect changes in enforcement priorities. In the face of increasing rates

of violent crime, auto theft overall may be attracting less police attention, which would help to account for declining clearance rates. Further, the establishment of specialized vehicle theft investigation units
by both police and insurance agencies nationwide may reflect a greater
concentration on professional thefts. While these may cause greater
losses to victims than do thefts by juveniles, they may also be harder
to detect and prosecute.

F. Variations within the United States

Nationwide vehicle theft rates obscure substantial variation within
the United States. According to the National Crime Survey (Harlow
1988), vehicle theft risk varies with proximity to the center city, with
inner-city residents experiencing the highest risks and residents of rural
areas the lowest.[4] Official data concur with this picture of auto theft
as predominantly an urban phenomenon. In 1989, vehicle theft rates
per 100,000 persons were 770.5 for Metropolitan Statistical Areas but
only 117.3 for rural counties. This disparity (a ratio of 6.6 to 1) is
much higher than for all other index crimes (arson is excluded, for lack
of information), save robbery, for which the ratio is nearly 19 to 1.
For example, the ratio of urban to rural larceny rates is only 3.6 to 1,
and it is 2.1 to 1 for burglary (Federal Bureau of Investigation 1990).

This urban/rural difference is reflected in the variation in vehicle
theft rates between states. In 1989, for example, the jurisdictions with
the five lowest rates per 100,000 population—South Dakota (109.0),
North Dakota (113.0), Iowa (158.0), Maine (183.0), and Vermont
(198.9)—were all rural, whereas those with the five highest rates—the
District of Columbia (1,372.7), California (1,026.9), New York (952.7),
Rhode Island (924.1), and Massachusetts (910.7)—all consisted of, or
encompassed, large conurbations (Federal Bureau of Investigation
1990).

Consistent with Gould (1969) and Mansfield, Gould, and Namenwirth (1974), who argued that illegitimate demand for vehicles will be
greater when vehicles are less plentiful, Mayhew (1990b) concluded
from her analysis that variation in vehicle thefts among U.S. states
depended, not just on urban/rural differences or on opportunities for
theft as indicated by vehicle density, but also on percentage of households without an automobile; there was a greater likelihood of thefts

---

[4] Hope (1987) reports similar findings from the British Crime Survey (BCS) for England and Wales.

where legitimate access was lowest. Some of the variation between states may also be explicable in terms of relative ease of export of stolen vehicles. Each of the ten highest theft-risk states in 1987 either had seaports or bordered on the Great Lakes (*National Underwriter* 1988). In that year, these ten states accounted for 69.3 percent of all vehicle thefts.

Both UCR and insurance industry data show that much variation also exists across cities. For example, in a report issued by the Highway Loss Data Institute (1990*b*) on theft claim experiences (which include thefts from and of vehicles) of the 30 largest U.S. cities (excluding Boston, for which data were not available), claims ranged from 27.2 per 1,000 insured vehicle years in New York City, to 8.3 in Minneapolis.

The nature of targets at greatest risk of theft also appears to vary markedly from city to city. For example, in 1989, the Chevrolet Caprice was among the five most frequent targets of theft in New York City, but not in Los Angeles or Chicago. In Los Angeles, the Suzuki Samurai and Toyota pickups were specially at risk and, in Chicago, the Cadillac De Ville and Brougham models (Highway Loss Data Institute 1990*b*). However, since no account was taken in this part of their analysis of the numbers at risk of each model, these differences in targets might primarily reflect differences in the popularity of the models in each city.

G. Timing and Location of Vehicle Theft

National Crime Survey data for the years 1973–85 (Harlow 1988) placed the largest proportion of vehicle thefts (37 percent) on the street outside the victim's home, followed by noncommercial parking lots (19 percent), and other street locations (16 percent). Completed and attempted thefts of vehicles parked in garages were rare (7 percent and 4 percent, respectively). British Crime Survey data also showed that the street immediately outside victims' residences was the most common location for "autocrimes" (thefts of and from vehicles and vandalism), with 38 percent of the incidents; households where cars were parked in garages integral to the dwelling had victimization rates one-third those of households where cars were parked on the street and one-half those of households using off-street private parking (Hope 1987).

Analyses of Australian auto thefts confirm the primacy of the street and other public locations as sources of accessible vehicles (Biles 1974;

NRMA Insurance, Ltd. 1990). Approximately one-half of autos are taken from streets and one-third from various parking lots open to the public (NRMA Insurance, Ltd. 1990). Using insurance data for the state of New South Wales for the year 1986, Liddy (1987) found evidence for car theft "hot-spots"—parking lots for railway stations and major shopping centers—where 40–50 percent of thefts in the high-risk districts occurred. Exactly what weight should be accorded to this evidence is unclear. Certain hot spots may be none other than locations where more desirable targets can be predictably found with higher frequency than elsewhere. For example, train stations, where affluent commuters are known to park, may contain larger concentrations of more expensive vehicles than would other car lots. However, other evidence of hot spots for auto theft comes from a Police Executive Research Forum study of problem-oriented policing in Newport News, where shipyard parking lots seemed highly vulnerable to theft from vehicles (Eck and Spelman 1988). Nevertheless, auto theft may not cluster to the same extent as some other predatory crimes, such as robbery (Sherman, Gartin, and Buerger 1989), which would be consistent with findings mentioned above that many incidents involve cars parked outside people's homes in the street.

That thefts frequently occur just outside victims' homes may seem inconsistent with the conclusion reached in all studies that risks of theft are greatest when there is least surveillance by owners or other guardians. This finding is more easily understood, however, when one considers that most vehicle thefts take place at night. Sixty-six percent of attempted and 59 percent of successful thefts were found in the NCS to occur at "night" (Harlow 1988). The BCS also places the time of greatest vulnerability to autocrimes between the hours of 6:00 P.M. and 6:00 A.M. (Hope 1987).

The importance of surveillance is suggested by a variety of other findings. First, Ley and Cybriwsky (1974) found that limited opportunity for surveillance and low territorial control (as characterized, e.g., by streets faced by windowless sides of buildings) facilitated the stripping of abandoned automobiles. Second, BCS data showed that risks of autocrime were greater in areas where more residents walked to work or took public transportation than where they drove, which might reflect the greater tendency of victims to leave their cars unattended for longer periods of the day (Hope 1987). Third, Saville and Murdie (1988) found that auto thefts in the Peel Region of Ontario for the year 1984 were most common in "areas of easy availability," which included those with the greatest number of car dealerships, unprotected parking lots, and mixed residential-industrial activity.

H. Target Vehicles

By either NCS or UCR accounts, passenger vehicles constitute slightly more than three-quarters of stolen vehicles (Harlow 1988). However, the rate of theft for passenger cars in 1988 (625 per 100,000 registered vehicles) was higher only than that for light trucks (564 per 100,000) and lower than the rates for heavy trucks and buses (1,853 per 100,000 vehicles) and motorcycles (1,414 per 100,000) (National Highway Traffic Safety Administration 1991, app. 1, B-8). It is unclear to what extent the high rate for motorcycles may be due to their greater attractiveness for joyriding and that for trucks and buses to a more developed criminal market. Trucks and motorcycles may also be less secure than automobiles as suggested by the greater involvement of the latter in thefts that are not completed (Harlow 1988).

According to Australian research (Biles 1974; Liddy 1987; NRMA Insurance, Ltd. 1987), the risk of theft also varies markedly with the *age* of the vehicle. For example, Liddy (1987, p. 12) found in his analysis of insurance data that rates of theft were higher among those models that had been out of production at least six years. Newer models also appear to be stolen for different reasons than older ones; an insurance industry study found that the motivation behind the theft of newer models was the removal of accessories, particularly audio equipment, while vehicles five years and older appeared to be stolen mainly for their body parts (NRMA Insurance, Ltd. 1987). The generalizability of these Australian findings is called into question, however, by recent data published by the National Highway Traffic Safety Administration (1991), which show no relationship between a vehicle's age and its risk of being stolen or its likelihood of recovery, at least up to seven years old. The reasons for this apparent discrepancy need to be clarified in further research.

Much variation in rates of theft is also present across vehicle *make*. In the first criminological study of this topic, Biles (1974) showed that Morrises and Holdens, particularly older models, were much more likely to be stolen than other cars in Australia. The preeminent position of Holdens was confirmed in Liddy's (1987) later study in New South Wales, but by then Morrises had been supplanted by Fords. Highest-risk makes were many times more likely to be stolen than others; the

Holdens, for example, were over eight times more likely to be stolen than the lowest-risk make. In the United States, the disproportionate theft of Ford models during the years 1969 and 1974 was attributed to notoriously poor ignition locks, a claim that was substantiated when thefts fell by one-quarter after the locks were upgraded in 1975 (Karmen 1981). But the relatively higher risks of the Australian Holdens and Fords could not be explained by differences in factory-installed security features across high- and low-risk makes (Liddy 1987).

Even greater variation in theft risk is present across *model* types. For example, the Vauxhall Cavalier is stolen at far greater rates than other models in Northern Ireland (McCullough, Schmidt, and Lockart 1990). Recently published data for England and Wales for 1989/1990 show that "higher performance cars are vastly more susceptible to theft than are other cars" (Home Office 1991, p. 5), and, because of their appeal to joyriders, Ford Laser Turbos experienced theft rates 22 times the average for vehicles in New South Wales (Liddy 1987, p. 12).

High risks of theft appear to be due to more than a model's attractiveness to joyriders. An early questionnaire survey conducted by the International Criminal Police Organization (1962, p. 8) of police authorities in several countries suggested that cars particularly at risk of theft were locally manufactured, were much in demand on the used car market, had poor security, and were powerful or sporty. One insurance industry report attributed the high theft rate of Volkswagens marketed in the United States to the desirability of their radios (Highway Loss Data Institute 1988, p. 2), while a substantial theft rate among pickup trucks was credited to the high interchangeability of their parts (New York State Senate Committee on Transportation 1978, pp. 22–23). Vehicles stolen for export to Mexico have been found to coincide with the type of autos that are produced there (Miller 1987, p. 21; Field, Clarke, and Harris 1992), because of either higher demand for such vehicles or reduced risks of detection.

In an attempt to elucidate further the reasons for the vulnerability of particular models, Clarke and Harris (1992) used model-specific vehicle theft data published annually in the *Federal Register* by the National Highway Traffic Safety Administration (NHTSA) together with data on claim frequency and average losses due to theft provided annually by the Highway Loss Data Institute to rank 121 new cars in 1983–85 on three indices of theft: stripping of parts; theft for temporary use; and theft for permanent retention, chopping, or resale. As expected, important differences were found among the top-ranking models in each index: those in the stripping index were predominantly German-made cars with good audio equipment (including a number of Volkswagens); in the temporary use index, American-made performance vehicles; and in the permanent retention group, a mix of very expensive high-performance cars and less expensive foreign cars (see table 2 for the top 10 percent of cars on each index). The range in risk was greatest for stripping and least for permanent retention; for example, the most-stripped vehicle, the Volkswagen Cabriolet, had an annual rate of stripping (141.18 per 1,000 cars) more than ten times the average for all 121 models (13.19 per 1,000), while the model at greatest risk of theft for permanent retention, the Mercedes 380SEL/500SEL (with 40 percent recovered), was less than twice as much at risk as the average for all 121 models (74.9 percent recovered). Clarke and Harris argue that, in general, these differences in risks of theft more likely reflected variations in the attractiveness of cars for joyriding or for profit than in their accessibility to thieves or in their levels of security.

II. Policy Options and Objectives

On the basis of the material reviewed in Section I, it is not difficult to understand the reasons for the large contribution made by auto theft to the total volume of crime. The targets of auto theft are widely available, they offer a variety of strong temptations to thieves, they are afforded little guardianship by their owners, and they seem comparatively easy to enter and steal. This interpretation is supported by a number of the findings reviewed above. The trends and distributions of auto theft fit quite well the numbers and distribution of vehicles. Individual vehicles are in neighborhoods most vulnerable at times and places of least surveillance and also where fewest people have legitimate access to them. Large differences in the vulnerability of individual models seem to be less due to variations in security than in their appeal to joyriders or their potential for profit.

This formulation of the problem may hold pointers to its solution since possibilities appear to exist for reducing the motivation for theft, increasing the risks, and increasing the difficulties of auto theft. Our review of preventive options is therefore organized under these headings.

Few if any preventive implications seem to flow, however, from another component of the problem concerning the relationship between the numbers of available vehicles and the numbers of thefts. This remains true even under the more complex hypothesis of Leroy

TABLE 2

Highest-Risk Models for Three Indices of Theft, United States, 1983–85

Make	Model	Stripping Rank	Temporary Use Rank	Permanent Retention Rank
Top-ranked cars for stripping:				
Volkswagen	Cabriolet	1	26	77
Volkswagen	Scirocco	2	77	15
Saab	900	3	74	26
Volkswagen	Jetta	4	110	25
Mercedes	190D/E	5	101	4
BMW	Series 3	6	60	17
Peugeot	505	7	108	32
Mercedes	380SEL/500SEL	8	100	1
Mercedes	300SD/380SE	9	99	6
BMW	Series 5	10	67	14
Volkswagen	Rabbit	11	53	12
Audi	4000	12	112	42

Make	Model	Temporary Use Rank	Permanent Retention Rank	Stripping Rank
Top-ranked cars for temporary use:				
Buick	Riviera	1	66	34
Toyota	Celica Supra	2	100	23
Pontiac	Firebird	3	52	37
Mazda	RX-7	4	87	42
Cadillac	Eldorado	5	55	22
Chevrolet	Camarro	6	54	32
Chevrolet	Corvette	7	13	93
Pontiac	Grand Prix	8	58	61
Chevrolet	Monte Carlo	9	50	59
Buick	Regal	10	47	68
Oldsmobile	Cutlass	11	49	91
Oldsmobile	Toronado	12	69	31

Make	Model	Permanent Retention Rank	Temporary Use Rank	Stripping Rank
Top-ranked cars for permanent retention:				
Mercedes	380SEL/500SEL	1	100	8
Porsche	911 Coupe	2	22	14
Porsche	944 Coupe	3	85	17
Mercedes	190 D/E	4	101	5
Nissan	300ZX	5	29	27
Mercedes	300SD/380SE	6	99	9
Lincoln	Mark VII	7	27	113
AMC/Renault	Fuego	8	119	36
BMW	Series 7	9	72	18
Mercedes	380SL Coupe	10	43	19
Lincoln	Town Car	11	18	86
Volkswagen	Rabbit	12	53	11

SOURCE.—Clarke and Harris (1992).

Gould and his coworkers (Gould 1969; Mansfield, Gould, and Namenwirth 1974), who argued that availability interacts with motivation
for theft, so that as cars become increasingly common, they attract
increasingly more amateurish groups of offenders. Eventually a point
would be reached when cars became so commonplace that the motivation for theft disappears because most people, even juveniles, would
have legitimate access to them.

While some support for this idea—called the "deprivation hypothesis" by Biles (1977)—can be found in the lower risks of theft in some
countries with high car ownership (Mayhew 1990b), the only preventive implication seems to be "Wait and hope for the best." But even
this may be too optimistic as suggested by other findings about the
"demand" for vehicle theft, in particular that joyriders are attracted to
powerful, sporty vehicles and professional criminals to expensive lux-
ury cars. These vehicles will never become truly commonplace and
may thus always present powerful temptations to certain groups of
offenders. Further, many joyriders are barred from legitimate access
to vehicles not simply for economic reasons but because they have no
license or are below the legal driving age. Finally, the excitement of
theft and the status gained among peers must not be discounted as
powerful sources of reinforcement for joyriding.

A. Ordering Priorities

This discussion of motives underlines the point that a variety of
preventive measures may be necessary to deal with the three main
forms of auto theft identified above: thefts from the vehicle, thefts of
the vehicle for temporary use, and professional thefts. Existing research suggests that juveniles are predominantly involved in the first
two categories of theft and that thrill seeking (McCullough, Schmidt,
and Lockart 1990) and easy opportunities play a large part in these
offenses (Challinger 1987). Simple improvements in the security of
windows and doors might therefore eliminate thefts by juveniles but
may have little impact on "professional thefts." These involve more
serious or committed adult offenders who can probably defeat most
security. However, levels of sophistication are likely to vary quite
markedly even among thefts in this category—for example, between
thefts for the thief's own extended use and theft for export—and may
thus require similar variety in the sophistication of preventive measures.

In assessing priorities for action, it is important to make some assessment of the respective contributions of the major categories of auto theft to the overall problem. Two bases for such assessments exist— volume and costs—that would yield different ordering of priorities. Professional thefts, for example, are more costly than thefts for temporary use but, judged by recovery data, are much less common. While some vehicles are abandoned by joyriders but not recovered (because they have been burned out or dumped in rivers or quarries), a rough estimate of the proportions of stolen cars taken by professionals may be given by the proportions recovered. As explained above, there is some inconsistency between the two FBI sources (UCR and NCIC) on this point. According to the UCR (Federal Bureau of Investigation 1990), about 66 percent of the value of stolen vehicles is recovered (a figure largely consistent with the NCS data on recoveries), while the NCIC suggests that 78 percent of stolen vehicles are recovered. Whatever the precise figure, it would appear that in the United States thefts for temporary use outnumber professional thefts by at least two to one. British Crime Survey data (Chambers and Tombs 1984; Mayhew, Elliott, and Dowds 1989) suggest that these two forms of theft are outnumbered by thefts from vehicles by a factor of five, and a similar ratio was found in a small sample for the United States by van Dijk, Mayhew, and Killias (1990).

On the basis of these figures it can be roughly estimated that thefts from the vehicle may account for about 85 percent of the total problem of auto theft in the United States, thefts for temporary use about 10 percent, and professional thefts at most about 5 percent. These proportions undoubtedly differ between regions of the United States and also among countries; for example, with 85 percent of stolen cars recovered (McCullough, Schmidt, and Lockart 1990), professional thefts may be less common in Northern Ireland. Whatever the precise proportions accounted for by each category of auto theft, it appears that successful action against professional theft (the most costly and serious form of auto theft) would have less effect on the scale of the overall problem than against thefts for temporary use and much less than against thefts from the vehicle.

B. Private versus Public Benefits

Before proceeding to the analysis of particular measures, an important distinction should be discussed between two objectives of prevention: assisting individuals to protect themselves from victimization and reducing the overall level of crime. The former is much easier to achieve than the latter. For example, a "lock your car" campaign might improve conformity among formerly neglectful motorists and may reduce their risks of victimization but may be unlikely to reduce overall levels of theft because there might still be enough unlocked cars around to provide easy pickings for the thief.

It might be said that helping concerned people to protect themselves from crime is a desirable aim for government action. However, a frequently unrecognized cost is that of the possibly increased risk of victimization for some other no less deserving individuals, less able to look after themselves. A well-documented example of such "displacement" can be found in the increased risks of theft for *older* cars that followed the introduction of steering column locks for *new* cars in Britain in 1971 (Mayhew et al. 1976).

It is sometimes argued that displacement will result from all such attempts to reduce opportunities for crime on the implicit grounds that criminal motivation has drivelike qualities that will inevitably be expressed in criminal action. But much crime can be more realistically seen not as behavior, which people are driven inexorably to perform, but as acts that they choose to commit for the benefits provided. This "rational choice" perspective (Clarke and Cornish 1985; Cornish and Clarke 1986) regards the probability of displacement as contingent on the ease or difficulty for offenders of modifying their usual practices. While numerous examples of displacement can be cited, such as that following the introduction of steering locks in Britain, there are also many instances of situational measures that have apparently achieved real reductions in crime (Clarke 1989; Barr and Pease 1990). For example, the introduction of helmet-wearing requirements for motorcyclists in West Germany in the early 1980s not only led to a substantial decline in the theft of motorcycles (presumably because the need to have a helmet ruled out spur-of-the-moment opportunistic thefts) but also resulted in little displacement of thefts to cars or bicycles (Mayhew, Clarke, and Elliot 1989). This probably was because neither bicycles nor cars provided thieves with the particular combination of opportunities and benefits formerly provided by motorcycles.[5]

While not inevitable, displacement is still the likely consequence of many measures to reduce auto theft. Helmet-wearing laws, easy to enforce, appear to have greatly limited the opportunities for impulsive

[5] Mayhew (1991) has subsequently attempted to reconcile this conclusion with a finding from the 1989 International Victim Survey (van Dijk et al. 1990) of an inverse relationship between vehicle and bicycle thefts in the countries surveyed.

thefts of motorcycles in Germany. The introduction of steering column locks only for new cars in Britain, by contrast, would have had little immediate effect on thefts for temporary use because most cars were still unprotected. While some redistribution of risks may be desirable in certain cases (e.g., to achieve a reduction in the risks of repeated victimization of the same person or group; cf. Barr and Pease [1990]), it has been assumed in this review that public policy should seek to reduce the overall scale of auto theft, rather than merely to promote measures whose primary value is to assist individuals in reducing their own risks. Promotion of these latter measures should be left to the private sector.

III. Reducing the Motivation for Theft

Trend data on arrests and vehicle recoveries discussed above suggest that older and more determined offenders may be committing an increasing proportion of auto thefts. Other than by manipulating risks and opportunities, it is difficult to conceive of ways to reduce the motivation of these offenders. In particular, there seems little scope for increasing the severity of punishments without compromising sentencing penalties for more serious crimes and unacceptably increasing criminal justice costs. In any case, the problem seems less one of the severity than of the imposition of penalties. Federal prosecutions for violations of the Dyer Act, which prohibits the interstate transport of stolen vehicles, have plummeted from thousands in the mid-1960s to little more than a few hundred in 1990 (fig. 4). While the proportion of federal offenders receiving prison terms has remained fairly consistent (roughly 70 percent of persons convicted for auto theft have been sentenced to prison every year during this period), these sentences now affect only a small group of offenders. Moreover, the risk to auto thieves convicted by state courts is far lower. One survey of penalties administered to eighty felons convicted of auto theft in New York found that only six individuals actually served any time (Permanent Subcommittee on Investigations 1979, p. 231). Aside from the formidable problems associated with the detection and apprehension of auto thieves, prosecutors feel pressured to deal with more serious offenders. They also point to the "hassle factor" associated with the prosecution of thieves who take vehicles across state lines (New York State Senate Committee on Transportation 1978), a problem which the first federal legislation concerned with vehicle theft—the Dyer Act of 1919—was designed to combat.

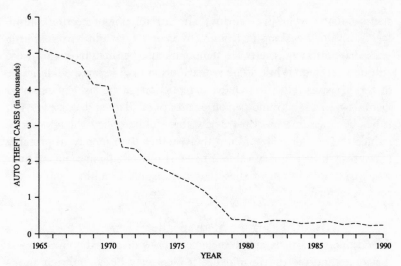

Fig. 4.—Auto theft cases commenced in U.S. District Courts, 1965–90 (includes only cases in which auto theft was major offense). Sources : Administrative Office of the U.S. Courts (1969–90).

For juveniles, however, who still commit most of the auto thefts (particularly those involving joyriding and casual thefts from the vehicle), measures directed at the fundamental social and psychological causes of delinquency can be considered. While some early research suggested that juvenile car thieves more frequently came from advantaged homes, known as the "favored group" hypothesis (Wattenberg and Balliestri 1952; Savitz 1959; Schepses 1961), later research has suggested that they differ little if at all from other delinquents (McCaghy, Giordano, and Henson 1977; Higgins and Albrecht 1981). In other words, they tend to be young males, living in the inner cities, and socially and psychologically deprived. If effective means of prevention or rehabilitation could be devised, therefore, and applied to the individuals most at risk, car theft and other forms of property theft would decline.

While interest in delinquency prevention is once again increasing (Farrington, Ohlin, and Wilson 1986), criminologists are not agreed on the required measures. Some of the important "causes" of delinquency, such as inconsistent discipline or lack of parental affection, are inherently difficult to manipulate (Wilson 1975), and intensive research over a long period has furnished little optimism that significant crime control benefits are likely to be achieved through rehabilitative treatments

(Martinson 1974; Brody 1976; Sechrest 1987). Nevertheless, a recent Home Office Working Party identified so-called motor projects as a promising initiative in Britain. These schemes, generally operated by probation departments for juveniles who have committed vehicle thefts, "provide facilities for driving, vehicle maintenance, training in safe driving techniques etc." (Home Office 1988, p. 17).

There seems little new in the philosophy underlying these schemes in terms of teaching juveniles respect for law or their responsibilities as citizens, but it is possible that the opportunities provided to learn about and drive cars may remove some of the motivation for theft. This was the conclusion reached by the Home Office Working Party on the basis of questionnaire replies received from twenty-five projects. There also seems to be consensus in Northern Ireland that the motor projects operated there by voluntary agencies have been successful in reducing recidivism (Chapman and Pinkerton 1987; McCorry and Morrisey 1989; McCullough, Schmidt, and Lockart 1990, p. 34). While none of these sources present evaluative data, Chapman and Pinkerton quote unpublished government research as crediting the motor projects with being "more successful and cost-effective than the alternative custodial response." This is encouraging enough to suggest that the effectiveness of motor projects should be subjected to closer study.

As for deterrence, there is a presumption, on good penal grounds, that juveniles should be treated leniently while there is also little evidence that more severe punishments are effective. The abolition for juveniles of cautioning for a first offense and the introduction of a new law dealing specifically with car theft was credited by the New South Wales' authorities with a 7 percent decline in car thefts in 1988. Introduction of the law coincided with some additional police surveillance and a large, well-organized "lock-your-car" publicity campaign (Monaghan 1989), and Geason and Wilson (1990) consider there is little supporting evidence for the claimed deterrent efficacy of the harsher penalties. Parker (1984) claims that, judged by rates of auto theft in the community and the reconviction rates of those sentenced, the greater use of custodial sentences for juvenile car thieves in a Merseyside court was a "dismal failure." This may be hardly surprising given that punishment shootings and kneecappings of joyriders by the Irish Republican Army (IRA) in Belfast failed to reduce the overall scale of the problem (McCullough, Schmidt, and Lockart 1990, p. 4).

IV. Increasing the Risks

Most cars can be entered and driven away illegally in a matter of seconds, and the chances of police intervening at the scene are small. Nor do evaluations of neighborhood watch programs provide much hope that the police surveillance role can usefully be extended by involving the public (e.g., Bennett 1989). Unless being driven dangerously or erratically, stolen cars will not usually be detected by police patrols and, in some American cities such as Newark and Jersey City, police are now constrained in their ability to detain the drivers of stolen vehicles by "hot pursuit" policies designed to reduce the dangers of collision. (According to a California Highway Patrol study cited by Fyfe [1990] and one in Florida undertaken by Alpert [1987], about one-third of hot pursuits end with an accident and one percent in a death.) The chances of any single theft of a vehicle resulting in arrest are thus small, and the reasonably respectable clearance rate for this offense of about 15 percent is primarily a reflection of the number of other offenses admitted to on arrest.[6]

Measures being tried in an attempt to improve arrest rates include informant hotlines, curfew decals, and vehicle tracking devices. There is little evaluation of these, and there are reasons for doubting their value, but they enjoy wide support and are therefore discussed in some detail below. Some other measures, such as "gotcha" cars, sting operations, and automatic number plate readers, seem little more than gimmicks. Gotcha cars trap thieves once they have entered the vehicle by automatically locking doors and windows. Waiting police can then move in swiftly to make an arrest. Given the very small risk of any one car being stolen on a particular day, it is difficult to avoid the conclusion that simple surveillance of "hot spots" would be a less costly and equally effective means of achieving the same end—though admittedly not as enjoyable for the police. Sting operations, in which the police set up "shop" as dealers in stolen property, have sometimes targeted auto thieves with apparently useful results (e.g., Crawford 1988). However, Klockars (1988) has concluded on the basis of a general survey of experience in the United States that sting operations do not reduce levels of property crime or have high rates of successful prosecutions. Automatic number plate (or tag) readers are roadside cameras linked to computerized records of stolen vehicles. Manned by

---

[6] "In court, many (joyriders) have had over 100 car thefts taken into consideration" (McCullough, Schmidt, and Lockart 1990, p. 12).

police, these can be used to detect vehicles that have been reported stolen and thus facilitate arrests. A Home Office trial of one such device on the Severn Bridge in 1976 (Stevens 1976) netted three stolen cars out of more than 20,000 checked in a continuous 48-hour period (a rate of 1.5 per 10,000). On these figures, police would have to be waiting a long time indeed to detect a stolen car. Moreover, if widely deployed, one might expect that the devices would become vulnerable to the use of false plates.

A. Informant Hotlines

Insurance companies are increasingly collaborating with state authorities and the police to offer rewards for information leading to the arrest of car thieves. The essential elements of such schemes are a twenty-four-hour toll-free hotline, protection of informants' identities, and cash rewards (these have averaged $500, but may be as much as $10,000 for a tip leading to the break up of a car theft ring). The best-known scheme of this kind, "Help Eliminate Auto Theft" (HEAT), was recently credited by an insurance industry spokesman as leading in Michigan to "the recovery of 909 vehicles with a value of nearly $11 million" and the arrest of 647 persons (Zarate 1990).

There has been no published evaluation of HEAT, though informant schemes in general are "highly productive" (Rosenbaum, Lurigio, and Lavrakas 1986, p. 4) in terms of successful prosecutions and the recovery of stolen property. However, their crime prevention value is unclear and, given the comparatively petty nature of most car theft and the predominance of juveniles as offenders, HEAT in particular seems a somewhat heavy-handed approach. It is also hard to see how it could be successfully targeted more specifically on professional car theft.

B. Curfew Decals

Curfew decals are the central component of the "Combat Auto Theft" (CAT) program instituted in 1988 in New York City and now being adopted in other American cities. A fluorescent decal is placed in the rear passenger window of participating cars. This indicates that the car is not normally driven between the hours of 1:00 A.M. and 5:00 A.M. and authorizes the police to stop anyone driving the car during these hours and inspect documents.

A *New York Times* article (1990) reports that, within two years of the scheme's introduction, more than 52,000 vehicles were registered.

Uncontrolled comparisons made in the article with other vehicles suggested that cars with decals were much less likely to be stolen. In the words of the state senator who initiated the scheme, this was because thieves "are anxious to get into the car quickly . . . they don't want to spend time with a razor blade taking the decal off." Decals could probably be made even more resistant to removal, thereby increasing the protection to participating cars, but it appears that this program suffers from the general limitation of any measure applied only to some cars in the vehicle pool; the diminished risk for protected cars is likely to be at the expense of increased risks for other cars. Moreover, a great many vehicle thefts are made in the afternoon and at other times when cars are given no protection by the decals.

Despite these criticisms, the scheme should be subjected to closer evaluation; whatever its preventive value, it appears to provide public relations benefits for the police at comparatively low cost.

C. Vehicle Tracking Devices

LOJACK is the best developed of a variety of vehicle tracking devices being offered for sale to the public in some areas of the United States. For a cost of $600–800, a small transmitter is concealed in the body of the car and the vehicle identification number is entered into the local police computer. On being notified of the vehicle's theft, the police activate the transmitter that, by means of LOJACK tracking devices installed in police cruisers, enables them to pinpoint the stolen car's position and move in quickly to make an arrest.

Once again, no evaluations have yet been conducted of these devices, but, according to company officials, 95 percent of stolen vehicles equipped with LOJACK are recovered (Romano 1991). As an aid to arrest, however, LOJACK is limited in that thefts have to be quickly discovered and reported—in many instances (e.g., when the car is taken while the owners sleep) thefts will be discovered only after the vehicles have been abandoned, perhaps stripped of valuable parts. Some other tracking devices are triggered by the thief failing to use a cut-off switch when driving away, but even with this refinement, and with perfectly functioning equipment, the preventive value of the devices may be inherently limited (as suggested by the small percentage of vehicles with LOJACK that are never recovered [McGurrin 1988]). First, it can be expected that professional thieves will develop ways of locating and disabling the transmitters or jamming the signals. Second, the high cost means that only a minority of motorists could afford to participate (in some cases owners will, in addition to installment costs, be charged monthly fees to cover the costs of monitoring equipment), and those who have invested such comparatively large sums in protecting their cars will want to advertise the fact on the vehicle itself. Thieves who cannot disable the transmitter will therefore take unprotected vehicles instead.

Finally, these devices could divert police resources from dealing with the broad range of auto thefts, affecting all members of the public, increasingly toward thefts committed against wealthier people. These social costs would give rise to less concern were tracking and recovery to be operated on a private basis. Indeed, as more of these devices come onto the market, the vendor companies may need to take over this responsibility since it is unclear whether local police agencies could accommodate all of the competing systems, with the variety of tracking equipment required, in the way that they are able at present to accommodate LOJACK (Romano 1991).

An alternative scenario would be to mandate vehicle tracking devices for all cars, old and new, in which case economies of scale should decrease costs and the social inequities would also be reduced. However, it seems unlikely that legislators would prefer these devices, whose main value is in recovering stolen vehicles, over some less costly measures that would prevent cars being taken in the first place. In general, it therefore seems that promotion of vehicle tracking should be left to the private sector.

V. Increasing the Difficulties of Auto Theft
The means of increasing the difficulty of vehicle thefts are quite varied, and all require the involvement and cooperation of groups and agencies outside the criminal justice system; for example, motorists themselves, the insurance industry, vehicle licensing and customs authorities, vehicle manufacturers, and parking lot operators.

A. "Lock Your Car" and Other Publicity Campaigns
"Blaming the motorist" (Karmen 1984) is a common response to theft, partly because quite high proportions of stolen cars seem to be left unlocked. According to the 1988 British Crime Survey, about 10–15 percent of vehicle thefts involved unlocked cars (Mayhew 1990c), though this figure may be an underestimate because people may not accurately remember whether they locked their car securely on a particular occasion or may be reluctant to admit negligence.

Whatever the precise figure, such carelessness contributes to the scale of the problem, and it is tempting to see more people locking their cars as providing the best solution. Indeed, this has been the objective of many publicity campaigns, though generally without much success. Two studies conducted by the Home Office evaluated a police-directed campaign in one city that relied on local radio and leaflets (Burrows and Heal 1979) and a government-sponsored campaign in the North of England that used television and national newspaper advertising (Riley and Mayhew 1980). In neither study was any evidence found that auto thefts had declined or that more motorists had locked their cars. For example, virtually identical proportions of vehicles (around 80 percent) were found to be locked in police checks after the North of England campaign as before.

Similar results have been found for other crime prevention publicity campaigns (Riley and Mayhew 1980; Silverman and Sacco 1980), though more success has been reported (Monaghan 1989) for a campaign conducted in New South Wales by the National Roads and Motorists' Association (NRMA). This disseminated leaflets with detailed information to the NRMA membership of 1.5 million about high-risk locations and vulnerable models. The campaign was reinforced by extensive media coverage and through NRMA-sponsored discussions with neighborhood watch groups to concentrate awareness at the local level. Most significant, perhaps, was that it took place during a period of mounting political concern about the problem and was endorsed by both the state government, which, at the same time, introduced a new law abolishing juvenile cautioning for car theft, and the New South Wales Police, who stepped up their surveillance of high-risk locations.

The campaign was followed by a drop of about 20 percent in the number of thefts as measured by police statistics and insurance claims (Monaghan 1989). However, car thefts have recently begun to rise again (NRMA Insurance, Ltd. 1990), so that any effect may have been temporary. The publicity generated may also have achieved its effect, not by galvanizing the motorist, but by warning off offenders. Indeed, it is hard to see how such publicity can exert much influence compared with some other factors determining security behavior. Thus, people frequently leave their cars insecure for reasons of convenience rather than simple carelessness. Without central locking, which few cars now have, it can also be difficult to ensure that all doors and windows are securely closed. In addition, the risks in many places are such that lax security behavior is repeatedly reinforced when owners return to find their cars intact. When combined with prevailing "it can't happen to me" attitudes, it may be very difficult significantly to improve the public's security behavior. Some countries have responded by making it a criminal offense for owners to leave their cars unlocked (e.g., West Germany; Sherman 1991). Nothing has been published about the effectiveness of such laws, and, whatever their "declaratory" value, it seems doubtful that they would do much to improve security behavior. The costs of falling victim to auto theft are already quite substantial, and it is unlikely that the additional legal punishment resulting from leaving the car unlocked would be more than symbolic. It also seems doubtful that such legislation would receive much public support.

But this discussion begs the fundamental question of what proportions of vehicles would need to be properly secured to achieve an overall reduction in auto theft. The proportion of cars left secure seems to have increased substantially in the United States since the 1940s (Karmen 1984), and surveys in Britain in the late 1970s suggested that the large majority of vehicles (about 80 percent) are left properly locked (Riley and Mayhew 1980). Even if this proportion could be somewhat increased, it may be asked whether this would be sufficient to reduce significantly the opportunities for vehicle theft. Rather, it may be that most cars are so easy to break into that, even if thieves found a significantly greater proportion of cars locked, they could still readily find a suitable target. In other words, efforts to persuade more people to lock their cars, park off street or in garages, purchase additional locks and alarms, or even to avoid purchasing cars attractive to joyriders, may all fall prey to the usual problem: while these measures may reduce the individual's chance of victimization, they may do little to reduce the overall scale of the problem.

In summary, there may be little to be gained by crime prevention campaigns of this kind beyond keeping the issue of car theft before the public and demonstrating government concern about the problem. Even these benefits have to be weighed against campaigns' possible costs in unnecessarily increasing the public's fear of crime (Home Office 1989).

B. Protecting Parking Lots

Large parking lots, particularly those in some housing projects (Poyner and Webb 1987) and ones used by rail commuters (Liddy 1987; Mancini and Jain 1987; NRMA Insurance, Ltd. 1987; Saville and Murdie 1988), are "hot spots" for theft. This may not be surprising given the large numbers of cars that can be found together in a publicly accessible place, left unguarded by their owners for long periods of the day.

While attention to parking lot security might therefore bring benefits, it is necessary to consider again whether increased security at a particular lot would not simply displace thefts elsewhere. This cannot be discounted, but the opportunities for obtaining lucrative pickings in these settings may be so great that this of itself generates theft. Offenders prefer not to travel far (Brantingham and Brantingham 1984), and while they may be prepared to walk a few extra minutes to find an unprotected vehicle, they may not be willing to go the much longer distances sometimes needed to reach another parking lot. Local theft "industries,"[7] centered on particular lots, might therefore be put out of business if security were improved.

An example is provided by action taken at the Port of Newark to stop juveniles from stealing recently imported cars by driving them through the wire fence of the lot where they were stored. A concrete barrier was put around the fence, which reduced car thefts from 179 cases in one year to zero in the next (Geason and Wilson 1990). Two further examples come from Britain (Poyner 1991). The first involved a multistory parking garage in the town center of Dover, serving a nearby hotel and the needs of holiday makers using the cross-channel ferry to France. The long-term nature of the parking produced a particular problem of theft that was addressed through a package of measures, including improved lighting, wire mesh on the ground floor to stop youths climbing into the garage, restriction of pedestrian access from the street, and the leasing of an office by the garage entrance to a twenty-four-hour taxi company. There was little reduction in thefts from cars, but an 85 percent reduction was achieved in thefts of cars (with no displacement to two nearby open-air parking lots). Poyner concluded that the latter thefts were committed by people with no

---

[7] Eck and Spelman (1988) provide anecdotal evidence of two such local "industries" focused on a large shipyard parking lot in Newport News. At the northern end of the lot, a "loosely knit gang of white, working class youths" operated who were principally after drugs. "They especially looked for 'muscle' cars, cars with bumper stickers advertising local rock and roll radio stations, or cars with other evidence that the owner might be a marijuana or cocaine user." At the southern end, a group of young black adults operated, who, while they knew each other, operated independently. They were "after money rather than drugs; as a result they concentrated on car stereo equipment, auto parts, guns, and other goods that could be fenced easily."

legitimate business in the parking lot, whereas many thefts from cars were committed by legitimate users of the lot tempted by opportunity.

Poyner (1991) also evaluated efforts made to reduce vehicle thefts at the open-air parking lots of Surrey University. Because entrances were manned and parking permits were required, there was little opportunity for theft *of* cars; however, there was a considerable problem of thefts *from* cars. The measures introduced included improved lighting, trimming of hedges bordering the lots, and the installation of closed-circuit television (CCTV) cameras. Poyner's analysis suggested that the CCTV, in particular, was responsible for a large reduction of about 50 percent in the numbers of thefts from vehicles.

While promising, these results do not provide sufficient basis for recommending ways of modifying parking lots. In particular, it is not clear what measures work best against which forms of theft. Nevertheless, the results justify further experimentation to explore the likely benefits of more widespread preventive action involving parking lots.

C. Improved Vehicle Registration and Documentation of Ownership

The introduction of vehicle registration requirements in the United States during the 1920s and 1930s produced very significant declines in auto theft. One of the last states to require registration was Illinois in 1934 when, according to Hall (1952), vehicle thefts declined to about 13,000 from a total of nearly 28,000 in the previous year and, by 1950, annual thefts had further declined to about 3,000. An unfortunate consequence of the absence of federal leadership in introducing vehicle registration, despite intense lobbying by insurance companies and other interest groups for nationwide registration and titling provisions (Hall 1952), was that vehicle registration documents, bills of sales, and manufacturer's certificates of origin now differ from state-to-state and sometimes within states (Lee and Rikoski 1984). The resulting confusion creates many opportunities for fraud. Thieves produce counterfeit documents or alter genuine documents, knowing that motor vehicle agency and insurance personnel will be unfamiliar with many of the submitted forms, particularly those from other states. Fraudulent or altered documentation enables thieves to acquire proof of ownership for stolen vehicles. In addition, it assists the thief in purchasing insurance for nonexisting vehicles (called paper cars) that are subsequently reported as stolen (National Highway Traffic Safety Administration 1980).

Related opportunities for theft exist during the sale of salvage vehicles. In many jurisdictions valid ownership documents and VIN plates are provided to the purchasers of wrecks. Thieves buy the wrecks to legitimate matching, stolen vehicles, which are readily sold for large profits (Permanent Subcommittee on Investigations 1979, p. 40).

In 1980, the National Highway Traffic Safety Administration issued a set of guidelines to improve state-level titling practices. Recommendations included a call for uniform documentation across states, physical inspections of VINs during vehicle registration, and surrender of salvage documentation to a central agency (National Highway Traffic Safety Administration 1980). Perhaps because compliance with the guidelines was voluntary, opportunities for vehicle theft created by lax and disparate ownership documentation practices continue into the present. Although some states have enacted legislation to eliminate inconsistencies in vehicle ownership processes (Lee and Rikoski 1984; Crepeau 1989), achievement of a substantial impact on vehicle thefts due to lax documentation procedures will likely require laws that are national in scope.

Exports of stolen vehicles out of the country are facilitated by inadequate customs procedures. As many as 20,000 stolen vehicles per year may be exported to Mexico (National Automobile Theft Bureau 1990b). Recovery of stolen vehicles has not been greatly assisted by treaties signed for this purpose between the United States and Mexico (Miller 1987), while the volume of traffic relative to the numbers of inspectors is said to make the checking of VIN numbers at border crossings prohibitively expensive (New York State Senate Committee on Transportation 1978). Stolen vehicles are also transported worldwide by ship. Although the U.S. Customs Service recently revised its procedures to require presentation of a certified copy of the certificate of ownership three days prior to departure from the country (Friedland 1989), detection of stolen vehicles is difficult due to the use of containerized shipments that are usually only inspected by law enforcement agents acting on probable cause (National Automobile Theft Bureau 1988–89).

Problems posed by border crossings are formidable, but it is likely that changes in certain customs procedures can deter some auto thieves. Random but frequent inspection of containerized shipments to verify the match of content to title would provide some deterrent, while offering no greater threat to constitutional liberties than is now presented by searches of luggage and random inspections of vehicles at border crossings and elsewhere. Improved customs procedures in Britain, which required the printing of export documents on security paper and which limited their release to unauthorized parties, have minimized fraudulent export practices there (Smith and Burrows 1986).

Unlike the suggestions below for better built-in security, which will generally produce benefits only in the longer term, changes in customs and registration procedures have the potential to bring about immediate reductions in auto theft.

D. "Built-in" Security at Manufacture

As *Which?* the British consumer magazine, recently concluded following an examination of 56 new cars: "The ease with which locked cars can be broken into would be laughable if it weren't so serious. Our security tester has got into nearly all cars he has checked in a matter of seconds, using the unsophisticated tools of the car thief's trade" (*Which?* 1988, p. 118).[8] Similar conclusions were reached in an Australian test of the security of new cars, though more variation among models was found than in Britain (NRMA Insurance, Ltd. 1990).

These findings point to considerable scope for building more secure cars. As most vehicles last for only about fifteen years, the security of the whole vehicle fleet could be greatly improved in a comparatively short time, and, indeed, visions of the "crime free" car may not be so illusory (Ekblom 1979; Svensson 1982). Measures to this end fall into two main groups: those that increase the difficulties of entering and starting the vehicle and those that increase the difficulties of disposing of the vehicle or its parts.

1. *Entering and Starting the Vehicle.*   Measures to impede entry into a vehicle may be seen as logically separate from those to prevent its being driven away, but the former might assist the latter, and it may therefore be more efficient to consider the vehicle's security as a whole. This point has been argued by Southall and Ekblom (1985) who, on the basis of a detailed study undertaken for the Home Office by the Institute of Consumer Ergonomics at Loughborough University, have identified a number of standard factory-fitted features as necessary to reduce the risks of theft for the typical car. These include properly installed high-security locks for the steering column, doors, and hood;

---

[8] All cars were entered within twenty-five seconds, though the same tester failed to bypass the new deadlocks on the Vauxhall Cavalier after an eight-hour attempt (Geason and Wilson 1990).

flush sill buttons and strengthened window glass; protected internal door-latching components and hood-release catches; and an audible reminder to remove keys from the ignition. More expensive cars should also have alarms,[9] central locking, and immobilization of the engine through its electronic management system.

One electronic system now fitted routinely on Chevrolet Corvettes (at one time the most stolen car in the United States) involves a small resistor embedded in the ignition key. The key will work only if its resistance matches that of the car's decoder; otherwise, the decoder cuts off the fuel injectors and starter motor, disabling the car for some minutes. Jump starting cannot bypass the system, though an electronically sophisticated thief could defeat it in about fifteen minutes (Newton 1987). Whether or not due to these measures, the Corvette no longer heads the list of stolen cars.

The security concepts car, produced by the British Rover Company, also employs advanced electronic measures, including elimination of external door locks (the doors being opened by an infrared transmitter), immobilization of the ignition system if windows are smashed, security coding of the in-car entertainment system (which makes it necessary to key-in a secret personal identification number [PIN] if it is removed), and its dispersal into a number of modular units spaced around the interior of the car (Geason and Wilson 1990).

Measures relating to the in-car entertainment system are especially needed since radios frequently attract juvenile thieves (Parker 1974). Volkswagen has attempted to deal with the extraordinarily high rates of theft for their Heidelberg radios (Highway Loss Data Institute 1986) by introducing security coding. Australian data suggest that theft rates of models fitted with such radios have recently declined (NRMA Insurance, Ltd. 1990).

2. *Parts Marking and Disposal of Stolen Vehicles.*   Most measures to prevent illegal entry and starting are aimed at opportunist thieves, on the assumption that professionals will be able, given a little time and ingenuity, to find ways round most forms of inbuilt security. (It should be noted, however, that professional criminals sometimes appear to

---

[9] Despite this endorsement, a recent *New York Times* article suggests that the value of car alarms is doubted by many experts in the United States (Tierney 1991). For example, Professor Lawrence W. Sherman is quoted as follows: "Car alarms are a terrible urban blight with obvious social costs—noise pollution, increased stress, wasted police manpower dealing with broken alarms—and it's not clear there are any benefits in return. No study has demonstrated that they reduce auto theft."

use juveniles to steal a targeted vehicle [Macdonald 1990]). A different approach has therefore been pursued by the federal government in its most recent effort to address the problem of auto theft.[10] Under the provisions of the Motor Vehicle Theft Law Enforcement Act of 1984 (MVTLEA), this involves the marking of all major body parts with the VIN. The MVTLEA's sponsors believed that parts marking, when combined with closer regulation and inspection of the crash repair trade, would substantially increase the difficulties of "chopping" and "retagging," forms of theft that were widely thought to have substantially increased in the 1970s and 1980s (Permanent Subcommittee on Investigations 1979, p. 55). In fact, the evidence on the effectiveness of parts marking was somewhat equivocal. When General Motors discontinued marking of the engines of Chevrolets, thefts of these vehicles increased (Karmen 1981), and substantial success also attended limited parts marking experiments in Kentucky and Chicago (Subcommittee on Surface Transportation 1983, pp. 63, 77) and Australia (Perricord 1987). However, both General Motors and Ford concluded after experimental parts-marking schemes involving just a few models that there was little evidence of much impact on thefts (Subcommittee on Surface Transportation 1983, pp. 88, 312).

Indeed, it was manufacturers' opposition to parts marking, particularly to the costs, that has resulted in potential difficulties for the Motor Vehicle Theft Law Enforcement Act of 1984. This is because, in the interests of cost saving, its parts marking-provisions were limited to "high-risk" cars. Leaving aside the dangers of displacement to unmarked cars, the definition of "high risk" is problematic. Included under this category are all models manufactured in 1987 and thereafter with first-year theft rates above the median theft rates reported for 1983 and 1984 year models in their first year of operation. But thefts for temporary use are not excluded, and it seems unlikely that many "high-risk" models, as defined under the MVTLEA, are stolen by

---

[10] Following passage of the Dyer Act of 1919 (which prohibited the transportation, sale, and receipt of stolen vehicles across state lines), federal-level involvement in auto theft prevention resumed only in 1966 with passage of the Highway Safety Act. This led to the development of two Federal Standards, standard number 114, which required that steering column locks be included in most vehicles manufactured after this date and increased the number of combinations of vehicle key-locking systems, and standard number 115, which mandated the placement of VINs on new vehicles. In 1978, an amended version of this regulation standardized VINs to inhibit frauds (National Highway Traffic Safety Administration 1978). In 1971, a section of the Postal Reorganization Act of 1971 prohibited the distribution of motor vehicle master keys through the mail.

professional criminals (Clarke and Harris 1992). Harris (1990) has also
shown that first-year theft rates are unreliable, and, in any case, the
theft experience of new models may not be an accurate guide to rates
as they age (Biles 1974; Liddy 1987; NRMA Insurance, Ltd. 1987).
Finally, Harris and Clarke (1991) could find no evidence that new cars
with higher collision rates, and for which there should therefore be a
greater demand for spare parts (including stolen ones), were those with
high theft rates.

In view of these difficulties, it may not be surprising that two recent
evaluations of the MVTLEA have been unable to provide consistent
evidence of the value of its parts marking provisions. The first of these
evaluations, undertaken by the Highway Loss Data Institute (1990*a*)
and based on insurance industry data, found slightly reduced theft
rates for marked vehicles especially in urban areas, but the second,
undertaken by the Federal government using NCIC data, could find
no similar evidence (National Highway Traffic Safety Administration
1991). These evaluations have been called premature since only very
small proportions of all vehicles on the road had been marked, and it
has also been claimed that considerable confusion exists among law
enforcement officials about which cars should or should not carry
markings (National Automobile Theft Bureau 1990*a*).

It seems unlikely that a conclusive evaluation of the MVTLEA will
be produced in the near future, and, in any case, it is important that
the MVTLEA's flaws do not lead to the rejection of parts marking.
Not only does parts marking seem a logical way of making life difficult
for the professional thief, but it has received some support in earlier
studies mentioned above. The manufacturers' concerns about costs,
which were the root of the MVTLEA's difficulties, seem to have been
misplaced as the cost of marking the average car has proved to be only
about $4 (National Highway Traffic Safety Administration 1991). This
strengthens the argument for marking all new cars at manufacture
rather than just a proportion of them as under the MVTLEA.[11]

E. Limitations of Built-in Security

Despite the potential of many of the measures discussed in this
section, which appears to make better built-in security the policy option most worth pursuing, the difficulties should not be underesti-

[11] It would also seem sensible, though this was not done under the MVTLEA, to
include windows under the parts marking.

mated. Not the least of these is that automakers have generally been resistant (Karmen 1981). Indeed, after incorporating serial numbers and ignition locks into most models in the early 1920s (Smith 1923), motor vehicle manufacturers took no new security initiatives until the 1960s. Their renewed interest in prevention at this time was probably no coincidence since standard improvements mainly involved modifications that were soon to be mandated by federal regulations or changes that were cost-efficient to the auto industry. For example, most of the manufacturers installed public VINs, increased the number of key codes, and introduced steering column locks prior to the effective dates of Federal Standards 114 and 115 that were promulgated under the Highway Safety Act of 1966. It is questionable whether these improvements would have been made in the absence of new federal regulations. Manufacturers also began to place VINs on engines and transmissions of all vehicles, but largely because compliance with the salvage laws of a few states was more economical when all vehicles were marked versus only vehicles to be shipped to the states in question (Permanent Subcommittee on Investigations 1979; Subcommittee on Consumer Protection and Finance 1980). General Motors Corporation only committed itself to a major redesign of the steering column used in numerous GM models (Riefe 1990) when this was demanded by sixty-three police chiefs from the United States and Canada; until then, the company had maintained that its vehicles were stolen with greater frequency because there were more of them on the road (Bryan 1990).

This resistance is not simply because of conservatism or, as argued by Karmen (1981) and Brill (1982), because manufacturers benefit from the increased sales resulting from theft. Brand loyalty has declined to such an extent that a motorist may be likely to replace his stolen automobile with one manufactured by a competitor. Rather, it appears that increased security is not considered a selling point by manufacturers (Karmen 1981), despite the fact that many motorists spend considerable sums on the fitting of sophisticated alarms to their cars.[12] Manufacturers also resist any increase in the price of their cars because of resulting lower sales (Brill 1982). This problem is compounded by the international character of the automobile industry; for example, the proposed British Standard (BS AU209) on vehicle security is likely to

---

[12] 1988 British Crime Survey evidence (Mayhew 1990c) also showed that 64 percent of consumers would be prepared to pay extra for better security when buying a new car and that over a third of these would be willing to pay between the equivalent of $200–$500 at present exchange rates.

be resisted so long as it is seen to disadvantage domestic manufacturers (Home Office 1988).

The great variety of possible measures, their technical nature, and the related engineering and cost issues constitute a second group of obstacles to pursuing improved built-in security. It is not hard to see that policymakers may have difficulty in knowing which measures to endorse and difficulty in evaluating the arguments of resistant manu- facturers. Given the pace of developments in electronics, it is equally easy to see that decisions about measures to promote may be delayed in the belief that something better may be imminent.

One way of dealing with these problems may be to place the respon- sibility for finding feasible and effective preventive measures on a fed- eral authority with access to appropriate technical, economic, and criminological expertise. The assignment would be to produce perfor- mance-based standards (e.g., steering column locks that could not be defeated in less than ten minutes) which, if necessary, could be en- forced through legislation.

Last, any reductions in overall levels of theft due to improved built- in security may only become substantial when the proportion of newer, better-protected cars on the road is sufficiently large. Three factors limit the initial impact of such measures, the first of which is the lower risk of theft for newer cars (Biles 1974; NRMA Insurance, Ltd. 1987). Whether due to their being less frequently found in areas where car thieves operate (e.g., in the poorer suburbs of large cities; NRMA Insurance, Ltd. 1987) or their less frequently constituting a source of spare parts for vehicles that have been on the road for a number of years, this lower risk for new cars means that any reduction in thefts will be incommensurate with the numbers of cars protected. Second, some thefts are likely not to be prevented by the improved security but displaced from new to older cars (Mayhew et al. 1976). Third, the gradual introduction of improved security may provide for a learning period during which thieves can find ways around the new measures, while still continuing to steal older, unprotected cars. In the mean- while, the new equipment may begin to wear out and become easier to defeat.

These points may help to explain why the introduction of steering column locks in Britain, Australia (Biles 1987), and other countries where they were put only on new cars has been a failure compared with their introduction in Germany where they were installed at the same time on old cars. In Germany, the drop in car thefts was not only immediate and substantial (about 40 percent) but sustained (Mayhew 1990*b*). This further suggests that the greatly reduced opportunities for theft contributed to the destruction, almost overnight, of a car theft "culture" among juveniles; the theft techniques learned on the street may no longer have been applicable and thus no longer worth passing on to other, younger delinquents. Speculative as this may be, it serves to reinforce the point that some security improvements required for new cars, such as parts and window marking, might also be worth mandating for older ones.

VI. Summary and Conclusions

Our review of research on auto theft has been undertaken from a policy-oriented, preventive perspective. In this concluding section we summarize the main conclusions about prevention and outline research needed to clarify policy directions.

A. *Summary of Preventive Implications*

Numerous measures are open to individuals to reduce their risks of auto theft, including use of off-street parking, purchase of alarms or additional locks, and avoidance of vulnerable models. Many of these measures are of doubtful value for public policy because they increase the risks for other motorists who do not or cannot take them. Measures not subject to this limitation, whose promotion by government will reduce auto theft risks overall, are more difficult to identify. That risks are concentrated in particular locations or on specific models might suggest that prevention should be similarly focused, but any reduction in the opportunities achieved may be insufficient to deter offenders. For example, by walking only a little bit further than to the parking lot where they may previously have operated, joyriders may still be able to obtain access to a large pool of suitable targets. And making Chevrolet Camaros impossible to steal, for example, might have little effect on joyriding so long as it is still possible to take the more widely available and only slightly less enticing Chevrolet Monte Carlo.

This may seem a counsel of despair, but the costs of auto theft, which constitute a large proportion of all crime, make it imperative to find solutions. Our review has considered potential solutions of three main kinds (involving reductions in motivation and increases in risks and difficulty), and we have suggested that, to be effective, measures will need to be tailored to each of three important categories of auto theft: thefts from vehicles, thefts for temporary use of the vehicle, and professional thefts. While lack of evaluative research precludes firm conclusions, few promising ways for reducing the motivation for any of these offenses seem to exist, though the need for an evaluation of "motor projects" in reducing the involvement of juveniles in auto theft was identified. There also seemed little to be done to increase the risks of auto theft. Schemes currently enjoying support such as informant hotlines, vehicle tracking devices, and curfew decals are of little demonstrated value, though the latter may hold some low-cost public relations benefits. Most of the preventive potential we identified seemed to reside not in measures to reduce motivation or increase risks but to increase the difficulties of auto theft.

Reductions in *thefts from the vehicle* (which may account for about 85 percent of auto thefts and which are thought to be mainly the province of opportunist, juvenile offenders) may be achievable by improved parking lot security, but more research is needed. Greater potential is afforded, though in the slightly longer term, through better built-in security. Tests continue to show that the quality of locks on new cars is abysmal. Effective means of impeding entry to cars, including deadlocks, central locking, slam-lid boot locks, and the protection of door-opening levers, are still not routinely provided at manufacture. Security coding of radios and dispersal in modules of the in-car-entertainment system should also be undertaken for all new cars.

Impeding entry will also reduce joyridings and *temporary use of the vehicle* (frequently committed by juveniles and accounting for perhaps a further 10 percent of the overall problem), but other built-in measures are also needed. Electronics promise some powerful systems, but the most urgent requirement is for routine installation of stronger steering column locks. Considerable experience has accumulated of ways in which steering locks can be defeated by thieves, and it should not be beyond the ingenuity of designers to eliminate their vulnerability.

One limitation of better built-in security is that gains will usually become apparent only when a sufficient proportion of the vehicles on the road have been protected. Other difficulties include manufacturers' resistance and the need to secure international cooperation. Nevertheless, vehicle manufacturers have as much a public duty to provide secure cars as to provide safe and nonpolluting ones. Acceptance of this principle might eventually lead to a more radical approach in which opportunities are "designed out" for a range of other vehicle-related offenses, such as drunken driving, speeding, and driving without a license (Svensson 1982).[13] Better security for new vehicles may have some small deterrent effect on *professional thefts* committed for resale of cars or their parts, though more might be achieved by tightening and standardizing insurance, registration, and customs procedures. It may be particularly important to tighten regulations governing the sale of vehicles written off in accidents, which should be sold without their documents; if rebuilt, documentary proof of their origins should be required before reregistration. The potential of parts marking to reduce thefts for "chopping" and related purposes might be greater if *all* new cars were to be included under the parts marking provisions of the MVTLEA, rather than just a proportion as at present.

B. Research Needs

Despite the prevalence of "enlightenment" models of policy-relevant research in which any improved knowledge about a problem is held to be of value to policymakers (Weiss 1977), we believe that deeper understanding of auto theft will not necessarily enlarge policy options. Some important determinants of auto theft such as the proportion of the population living in big cities and, in many places, the numbers of people parking on streets overnight, cannot be manipulated. It is also unlikely that public transport would be improved, for example, by running more late-night buses, simply in the interests of reducing thefts for temporary use (Clarke 1987). In any case, some kinds of preventive action require little knowledge of motivational or social factors contributing to crime. The introduction of speed bumps on a particular stretch of road will eliminate speeding whatever the motives.

The same might be said of security devices that make it impossible for joyriders to start cars. But auto theft is not simply a matter of joyriding, and the development of effective prevention will require a specific agenda of research. The need for evaluations of "motor projects" and experiments in parking lot security has been discussed above. There is need also for a coordinated program of work to evaluate the impact of antitheft devices and automobile designs on vehicle theft rates. Studies of the effectiveness of alarms and other devices should control for model-specific and region-specific theft and recovery rates and should attempt to assess the nature and extent of displacement of theft.

---

[13] The opportunity to commit suicide by inhalation of automobile exhaust gases has already been greatly reduced in the United States by emission controls (Clarke and Lester 1989).

Effectiveness studies ought to include an assessment of the costs of prevention. But such assessments will only be helpful if better information is available about the costs of the different forms of auto theft. Useful start as it provides, Brobeck's (1983) work is capable of considerable refinement. For example, it includes no attempt to quantify the inconvenience and loss of earnings resulting to victims. Nor does it attempt to estimate some of the benefits said to flow from auto theft to insurers in the form of increased investment income, to manufacturers in sales of replacement vehicles, or to some sections of the population who benefit by the trade in stolen cars and their parts (Karmen 1981; Brill 1982). While more refined cost estimates would assist in identifying potentially cost-effective solutions, knowing where these costs fall might assist in designing incentives for action.

Better information about the relative contributions made by juveniles and adult professionals to the overall problem of auto theft would also assist the setting of priorities. Data bases are also needed that would permit finer classifications of auto theft along lines suggested by Challinger (1987). For this, more data should be collected about the circumstances of recovery, including when and where recovered and in what condition. Because of the costs and start-up time associated with improvements in public agency crime reporting systems, insurance companies must be persuaded by the research community to share their own more detailed data bases that contain information about numbers of models at risk, recoveries, and items stolen.

Interviews with offenders would assist in determining the degree of specialization among auto thieves and the extent to which juveniles are involved in what we have called "professional thefts." Interviews could also contribute to an understanding of the development of car theft "cultures" among juveniles (Parker 1974) and the means of "recruitment" to auto theft. Which designs, security features, and accessories attract thieves to some models but not others, and the reasons for local variations in this attractiveness, ought to be clarified. Especially helpful would be more information about thieves' perceptions of variations between models in their potential for profit and, in the light of discrepancies between Australian and U.S. findings mentioned above, about the relationship between a vehicle's age and its desirability for different forms of theft. Finally, such interviews could help researchers to explore the perceived deterrent effects of various antitheft devices and the worrying possibility that, as cars become more secure, criminals may more frequently resort to seizing cars at gunpoint (Dean 1991; Freid 1991).

In conclusion, we return to the point made at the beginning of this essay: that auto theft presents many opportunities for fascinating studies. Some of these, such as the relationship between availability of cars and illegal demand, or the decision-making processes of auto thieves, would have wider relevance for general criminological theory. Victimology, which has tended to focus on the personal characteristics of victims, might also be enriched by study of how greatly ownership of particular automobiles can increase an individual's risks of crime. We continue to believe (see Cornish and Clarke 1986), however, that the main value of an increasingly crime-specific focus for research lies not in enhanced theoretical understanding but in improved specification of preventive policy. Without detailed knowledge for highly specific forms of crime of the situations giving rise to the offense, the nature of the offenders, the levels of skill and organization required, and the methods employed, it can be very difficult to formulate effective and efficient countermeasures.

REFERENCES

Administrative Office of the U.S. Courts. 1969–90. *Annual Reports of the Director of the Administrative Office of the United States Courts*. Washington, D.C.: Administrative Office of the U.S. Courts.

Alpert, Geoffrey P. 1987. "Questioning Police Pursuits in Urban Areas." *Journal of Police Science and Administration* 15:298–306.

Barr, Robert, and Ken Pease. 1990. "Crime Placement, Displacement, and Deflection." In *Crime and Justice: A Review of Research*, vol. 12, edited by Michael Tonry and Norval Morris. Chicago: University of Chicago Press.

Bennett, Trevor. 1989. "The Impact of Neighborhood Watch on Residents and Criminals." *Journal of Security Administration* 11:52–59.

Biles, David. 1974. "The Victims of Car Stealing." *Australian and New Zealand Journal of Criminology* 7:99–109.

———. 1977. "Car Stealing in Australia." In *Delinquency in Australia*, edited by Paul R. Wilson. St. Lucia: University of Queensland Press.

———. 1987. "Some Questions That Need Answers." Paper presented at the Australian Automobile Association Car Theft Symposium, Canberra, November.

Brantingham, Paul J., and Patricia L. Brantingham. 1984. *Patterns in Crime*. New York: Macmillan.

Brill, Harry. 1982. "Auto Theft and the Role of Big Business." *Crime and Social Justice* 18:62–68.

Brobeck, Stephen. 1983. "The Consumer Costs of Automobile Theft." Unpublished manuscript. Washington, D.C.: Consumer Federation of America, October 14.

Brody, Stephen R. 1976. *The Effectiveness of Sentencing*. Home Office Research Study no. 35. London: H.M. Stationery Office.

Bryan, Bill. 1990. "Thefts Spur Police Chiefs' Visit to GM." *St. Louis Post Dispatch*. April 4.

Burrows, John, and Kevin Heal. 1979. *Crime Prevention and the Police*. Home Office Research Study no. 55. London: H.M. Stationery Office.

Challinger, Dennis. 1987. "Car Security Hardware—How Good Is It?" In *Car Theft: Putting on the Brakes, Proceedings of Seminar on Car Theft, May 21*. Sydney: National Roads and Motorists' Association and the Australian Institute of Criminology.

Chambers, Gerry, and Jaqueline Tombs. 1984. *The British Crime Survey Scotland*. Scottish Office Social Research Study. Edinburgh: H.M. Stationery Office.

Chapman, Tim, and John Pinkerton. 1987. "Contradictions in Community." *Probation Journal* 34:13–16.

Clarke, Ronald V. 1984. "Opportunity-based Crime Rates." *British Journal of Criminology* 24:74–83.

———. 1987. "Crime Prevention—Car Theft Strategies." In *Car Theft: Putting on the Brakes, Proceedings of Seminar on Car Theft, May 21*. Sydney: National Roads and Motorists' Association and the Australian Institute of Criminology.

———. 1989. "Theoretical Background to Crime Prevention through Environmental Design (CPTED) and Situational Prevention." In *Designing Out Crime: The Conference Papers*, edited by Susan Geason and Paul Wilson. Canberra: Australian Institute of Criminology.

Clarke, Ronald, V., and Derek B. Cornish. 1985. "Modeling Offenders' Decisions: A Framework for Policy and Research." In *Crime and Justice: An Annual Review of Research*, vol. 6, edited by Michael Tonry and Norval Morris. Chicago: University of Chicago Press.

Clarke, Ronald V., and Patricia M. Harris. 1992. "A Rational Choice Perspective on the Targets of Automobile Theft." *Criminal Behavior and Mental Health* 2:25–42.

Clarke, Ronald V., and D. Lester. 1989. *Suicide: Closing the Exits*. New York: Springer-Verlag.

Cohen, Lawrence E., and Marcus Felson. 1979. "Social Change and Crime Rate Trends: A Routine Activity Approach." *American Sociological Review* 44:588–608.

Cornish, Derek B., and Ronald V. Clarke. 1986. *The Reasoning Criminal*. New York: Springer-Verlag.

Crawford, Alan Pell. 1988. " 'Operation Greenlight' Made Car Thieves See Red." *Insurance Review* 49:50–54.

Crepeau, Philip J. 1989. "Photo Inspection Helps Deter Auto Fraud." *National Underwriter (Property and Casualty Division)* 93:18–20, 40–42.

Dean, Paul. 1991. "Guns Add Horror to Car Thefts." *Los Angeles Times* (May 21), pp. A1, A24–A25.

Eck, John, and William Spelman. 1988. *Problem Solving: Problem-oriented Policing in Newport News*. Washington, D.C.: Police Executive Research Forum and the National Institute of Justice.

Ekblom, Paul. 1979. "A Crime Free Car?" *Research Bulletin* 7:28–30. London: Home Office Research Unit.

Farrington, David P., Lloyd E. Ohlin, and James Q. Wilson. 1986. *Understanding and Controlling Crime: Toward a New Research Strategy.* New York: Springer-Verlag.

Federal Bureau of Investigation. 1936–90. *Uniform Crime Reports: Crime in the United States.* Washington, D.C.: U.S. Department of Justice.

Field, Simon, Ronald V. Clarke, and Patricia M. Harris. 1992. "The Mexican Vehicle Market and Auto Theft in Border Areas of the United States." *Security Journal* 2:205–10.

Flanagan, Timothy J., and Kathleen Maguire, eds. 1990. *Sourcebook of Criminal Justice Statistics—1989.* Washington, D.C.: U.S. Department of Justice, Bureau of Justice Statistics.

Freid, Joseph P. 1991. "Police Warn Luxury-Car Drivers." *New York Times* (March 8), p. B3.

Friedland, Jennifer. 1989. "Customs Tightens Up Vehicle Export Rules: Stolen Cars Strain System." *Journal of Commerce and Commercial* (April 26), p. 1A.

Fyfe, James J. 1990. "Controlling Police Vehicle Pursuits." In *Police Practice in the 90's: Key Management Issues,* edited by James J. Fyfe. Washington, D.C.: International City Management Association.

Geason, Susan, and Paul Wilson. 1990. *Preventing Car Theft and Crime in Car Parks.* Canberra: Australian Institute of Criminology.

Gould, Leroy C. 1969. "The Changing Structure of Property Crime in an Affluent Society." *Social Forces* 48:50–59.

Hall, Jerome. 1952. *Theft, Law and Society.* New York: Bobbs-Merrill.

Harlow, Caroline Wolf. 1988. *Motor Vehicle Theft.* Washington, D.C.: U.S. Department of Justice, Bureau of Justice Statistics.

Harris, Patricia M. 1990. "Targeting the High Theft Risk Automobile." *Security Journal* 1:164–68.

Harris, Patricia M., and Ronald V. Clarke. 1991. "Car Chopping, Parts Marking and the Motor Vehicle Theft Law Enforcement Act of 1984." *Sociology and Social Research* 75:228–38.

Higgins, Paul C., and Gary L. Albrecht. 1981. "Cars and Kids: A Self-Report Study of Juvenile Auto Theft and Traffic Violations." *Sociology and Social Research* 66:29–41.

Highway Loss Data Institute. 1986. *Insurance Theft Report: Passenger Cars, Vans, Pickups, and Utility Vehicles.* Arlington, Va.: Highway Loss Data Institute.

———. 1988. *Insurance Theft Report: Passenger Cars, Vans, Pickups, and Utility Vehicles.* Arlington, Va.: Highway Loss Data Institute.

———. 1990a. *Insurance Special Report A-31: The Effect of Vehicle Component Parts Marking on Theft Losses.* Arlington, Va.: Highway Loss Data Institute.

———. 1990b. *Insurance Special Report A-35: Automobile Losses in Selected Cities and Border Regions.* Arlington, Va.: Highway Loss Data Institute.

Home Office. 1988. *Report of the Working Group on Car Crime.* Standing Conference on Crime Prevention. London: Home Office.

———. 1989. *Report of the Working Group on Fear of Crime.* Standing Conference on Crime Prevention. London: Home Office.

————. 1991. *Car Theft Index*. London: Home Office.

Hope, Tim. 1987. "Residential Aspects of Autocrime." *Research Bulletin* 23:28–33. London: Home Office Research and Planning Unit.

Hough, Mike, and Patricia Mayhew. 1985. *Taking Account of Crime: Key Findings from the British Crime Survey*. Home Office Research Study no. 85. London: H.M. Stationery Office.

International Criminal Police Organization. 1962. *The Prevention of Thefts of Automobiles*. Report submitted by the General Secretariat to the thirty-first general assembly session of the International Chiefs of Police, Madrid, September.

Interpol. Various years. *International Crime Statistics*. Saint Cloud, France: Interpol.

Kalish, Carol B. 1988. *International Crime Rates*. Washington, D.C.: U.S. Department of Justice, Bureau of Justice Statistics.

Karmen, Andrew A. 1981. "Auto Theft and Corporate Irresponsibility." *Contemporary Crises* 5:63–81.

————. 1984. *Crime Victims: An Introduction to Victimology*. Belmont, Calif.: Brooks/Cole.

Klockars, Carl B. 1988. "Police and the Modern Sting Operation." In *Controversial Issues in Criminal Justice*, edited by Joseph E. Scott and Travis Hirschi. Beverly Hills, Calif.: Sage.

Lee, Beverly N. W., and Giannina P. Rikoski. 1984. *Vehicle Theft Prevention Strategies*. Washington, D.C.: U.S. Department of Justice, National Institute of Justice.

Ley, David, and Roman Cybriwsky. 1974. "The Spatial Ecology of Stripped Cars." *Environment and Behavior* 6:53–68.

Liddy, D. T. 1987. "Car Theft—a Strategy Needed." Paper presented at the annual meeting of the Australian Automobile Association, Canberra, November.

Lynch, James P., and Albert Biderman. 1984. "Cars, Crime and Crime Classification: What the UCR Doesn't Tell Us That We Should Know." Paper presented at the annual meeting of the American Society of Criminology, Cincinnati, November.

McCaghy, Charles H., Peggy C. Giordano, and Trudy Knicely Henson. 1977. "Auto Theft: Offender and Offense Characteristics." *Criminology* 15:367–85.

McCorry, Jim, and Mike Morrisey. 1989. "Community, Crime and Punishment in West Belfast." *Howard Journal of Criminal Justice* 28:282–90.

McCullough, Dave, Tanja Schmidt, and Bill Lockart. 1990. *Car Theft in Northern Ireland*. CIRAC (Extern Centre for Independent Research and Analysis of Crime) Paper no 2. Belfast: Extern Organization.

Macdonald, John. 1990. "Car Theft: The Thieves' Thoughts." Unpublished paper. New South Wales Police Department, Sydney.

McGurrin, Lisa. 1988. "The Lowdown on Lo-Jack." *New England Business* 10:48–53.

Mancini, Alan N., and Rejendra Jain. 1987. "Commuter Parking Lots—Vandalism and Deterrence." *Transportation Quarterly* 41:539–53.

Mansfield, Roger, Leroy C. Gould, and J. Zvi Namenwirth. 1974. "A Socioeconomic Model for the Prediction of Societal Rates of Property Theft." *Social Forces* 52:462–72.

Martinson, Robert. 1974. "What Works?—Questions and Answers about Prison Reform." *Public Interest* 35:22–54.

Mayhew, Patricia. 1990a. "Experiences of Crime across the World." *Research Bulletin* 28:4–13. London: Home Office Research and Statistics Department.

———. 1990b. "Opportunity and Vehicle Crime." In *Policy and Theory in Criminal Justice: Contributions in Honour of Leslie T. Wilkins*, edited by Don M. Gottfredson and Ronald V. Clarke. Aldershot: Gower.

———. 1990c. Personal communication with authors, November 15, 1990.

———. 1991. "Displacement and Vehicle Theft: An Attempt to Reconcile Some Recent Contradictory Evidence." *Security Journal* 2:233–39.

Mayhew, Patricia, Ronald V. Clarke, and David Elliot. 1989. "Motorcycle Theft, Helmet Legislation and Displacement." *Howard Journal of Criminal Justice* 28:1–8.

Mayhew, Patricia, Ronald V. Clarke, Andrew Sturman, and Mike Hough. 1976. *Crime as Opportunity*. Home Office Research Study no. 34. London: H.M. Stationery Office.

Mayhew, Patricia, David Elliott, and Lizanne Dowds. 1989. *The 1988 British Crime Survey*. Home Office Research Study no. 111. London: H.M. Stationery Office.

Miller, Michael V. 1987. "Vehicle Theft along the Texas-Mexico Border." *Journal of Borderlands Studies* 2:12–32.

Monaghan, Laurie. 1989. "Anatomy of a Crime Prevention Publicity Campaign." *Journal of Security Administration* 11:60–69.

Motor Trades Association of Australia. 1990. *A National Strategy to Reduce Car Thefts*. Canberra: Motor Trades Association of Australia.

National Automobile Theft Bureau. 1988–89. "Stolen Vehicles Exported to Central America." *National Automobile Theft Bureau Journal*, pp. 1–3.

———. 1990a. "Comments on 'Auto Theft and Recovery: Effects of the Motor Vehicle Theft Law Enforcement Act 1984, Preliminary Report—July 1990.'" Paper submitted to National Highway Traffic Safety Administration [Docket No. 90-15; Notice 1], September 7.

———. 1990b. *Annual Report*. Palos Hills, Ill.: National Automobile Theft Bureau.

National Highway Traffic Safety Administration. 1978. "Amendment to Federal Motor Vehicle Safety Standard Number 115, Vehicle Identification Number." *Federal Register* 45:36.

———. 1980. *A Manual of Anti-theft Guidelines for State Motor Vehicle Titling Programs*. Washington, D.C.: U.S. Department of Transportation.

———. 1991. *Auto Theft and Recovery. Effects of the Motor Vehicle Theft Law Enforcement Act of 1984*. Washington, D.C.: U.S. Department of Transportation.

National Underwriter. 1988. "Thieves 'Hit' One of Every 44 Cars in 1987." *National Underwriter (Property and Casualty Edition)* 92:29.

Newton, Bob. 1987. "Is a Thief-proof Car Possible?" In *Car Theft: Putting on the Brakes, Proceedings of Seminar on Car Theft, May 21*. Sydney: National

Roads and Motorists' Association and the Australian Institute of Criminology.

New York State Senate Committee on Transportation. 1978. *National Workshop on Auto Theft Prevention: Compendium of Proceedings, October 3–6*. Albany: New York State Senate.

New York Times. 1990. "Car Theft Decal Program Will Spread to All New York State" (August 19).

NRMA Insurance, Ltd. 1987. *Car Theft in New South Wales*. Sydney: NRMA Insurance, Ltd.

———. 1990. *Car Theft in New South Wales*. Sydney: NRMA Insurance, Ltd.

Parker, Howard J. 1974. *View from the Boys*. Newton Abbott: David & Charles.

———. 1984. "Locking Up the Joyriders." *Youth in Society* (November), pp. 11–13.

Permanent Subcommittee on Investigations. 1979. *Professional Motor Vehicle Theft and Chop Shops*. Hearings before the Permanent Subcommittee on Investigations, Senate Governmental Affairs Committee, November 27–30, December 4.

Perricord, Andrew. 1987. "Ripped Off." *Bike* (June), pp. 16–23.

Poyner, Barry. 1991. "Situational Prevention in Two Parking Facilities." *Security Journal* 2:96–101.

Poyner, Barry, and Barry Webb. 1987. *Successful Crime Prevention: Case Studies*. London: Tavistock Institute of Human Relations.

Riefe, R. K. 1990. Correspondence to Robert Sheetz, St. Louis, Missouri, chief of police, from the Steering Columns and Controls Business Unit of General Motors Corporation, May 7.

Riley, David, and Pat Mayhew. 1980. *Crime Prevention Publicity: An Assessment*. Home Office Research Study no. 63. London: H.M. Stationery Office.

Romano, Jay. 1991. "Device to Track Stolen Cars Raises Questions." *New York Times* (June 30).

Rosenbaum, Dennis P., Arthur J. Lurigio, and Paul J. Lavrakas. 1986. *Crime Stoppers—a National Evaluation*. Research in Brief. Washington, D.C.: U.S. Department of Justice, National Institute of Justice.

Saville, Gregory, and Robert Murdie. 1988. "The Spatial Analysis of Motor Vehicle Theft: A Case Study of Peel Region, Ontario." *Journal of Police Science and Administration* 16:126–35.

Savitz, Leonard D. 1959. "Automobile Theft." *Journal of Criminal Law, Criminology and Police Science* 50:132–43.

Schepses, Erwin. 1961. "Boys Who Steal Cars." *Federal Probation* 25:56–62.

Sechrest, Lee. 1987. "Classification for Treatment." In *Prediction and Classification*, edited by Don Gottfredson and Michael Tonry. Vol. 9 of *Crime and Justice: A Review of Research*, edited by Michael Tonry and Norval Morris. Chicago: University of Chicago Press.

Sherman, Lawrence W. 1991. Personal communication with authors, May 27, 1991.

Sherman, Lawrence W., Patrick R. Gartin, and Michael E. Buerger. 1989. "Hot Spots of Predatory Crime: Routine Activities and the Criminology of Place." *Criminology* 27:27–56.

Shover, Neal. 1991. "Burglary." In *Crime and Justice: A Review of Research*, vol. 14, edited by Michael Tonry. Chicago: University of Chicago Press.

Silverman, Robert A., and V. F. Sacco. 1980. *Crime Prevention through Mass Media: An Evaluation*. University of Alberta, Centre for Criminological Research.

Smith, Edward H. 1923. "Your Automobile and the Thief." *Scientific American* 128:366–67.

Smith, Lorna J. F., and John Burrows. 1986. "Nobbling the Fraudsters: Crime Prevention through Administrative Change." *Howard Journal of Criminal Justice* 25:13–24.

Southall, Dean, and Paul Ekblom. 1985. *Designing for Vehicle Security: Towards a Crime-free Car*. Home Office Crime Prevention Unit Paper no. 4. London: Home Office.

Stevens, J. R. 1976. "The Usage of Stolen Cars—a Trial on the Severn Bridge." Technical Memorandum 30/76. London: Home Office, Police Scientific Development Branch.

Subcommittee on Consumer Protection and Finance. 1980. *Motor Vehicle Theft Prevention Act*. Hearings before the Subcommittee on Consumer Protection and Finance, House Interstate and Foreign Commerce Committee, and the Subcommittee on Inter-American Affairs, House Foreign Affairs Committee, June 2, 10, and 12.

Subcommittee on Surface Transportation. 1983. *Motor Vehicle Theft Law Enforcement Act of 1983*. Hearings before the Subcommmittee on Surface Transportation, Senate Commerce, Science and Transportation Committee, July 19.

Subcommittee on Telecommunications, Consumer Protection, and Finance. 1982. *Motor Vehicle Theft Law Enforcement Act*. Hearings before the Subcommittee on Telecommunications, Consumer Protection and Finance, House Energy and Commerce Committee, February 4.

Svensson, Bo. 1982. "A Crime-Prevention Car." In *Crime Prevention*, edited by Eckhart Kulhorn and Bo Svensson. Stockholm: National Swedish Council for Crime Prevention.

Tierney, John. 1991. "Laws Encourage Car Alarms. But Din May Not Be Worth It." *New York Times* (February 19).

Tremblay, Pierre, Yvan Clermont, and Maurice Cusson. 1991. *Jockeys and Joyriders: Changing Patterns in Car Theft Opportunity Structures*. Working Papers in Social Behaviour, no. 91-1. Montreal: McGill University.

UN Demographic Yearbook. Various years. New York: United Nations.

UN Statistical Yearbook. Various years. New York: United Nations.

van Dijk, Jan J. M., Patricia Mayhew, and Martin Killias. 1990. *Experiences of Crime across the World: Key Findings from the 1989 International Crime Survey*. Deventer, Netherlands: Kluwer Law and Taxation.

Wattenberg, William W., and James Balliestri. 1952. "Automobile Theft: A 'Favored Group' Delinquency." *American Journal of Sociology* 57:575–79.

Weglian, Steven. 1978. "Testimony." Mimeographed. New York State, Committees on Transportation and Consumer Protection. Washington D.C.: U.S Department of Justice.

Weiss, Carol H. 1977. *Using Social Research in Public Policy-making.* Lexington, Mass.: Lexington.
Which? 1988. "Your Car at Risk." (March), pp. 116–21.
Wilkins, Leslie T. 1964. *Social Deviance.* London: Tavistock.
Wilson, James Q. 1975. *Thinking about Crime.* New York: Basic.
Zarate, Vincent R. 1990. "State Putting 'Heat' on Car Thieves." *Star-Ledger* (October 30).

Andrew von Hirsch

Proportionality in the Philosophy of Punishment

ABSTRACT

The principle of proportionality—that penalties be proportionate in their severity to the gravity of the defendant's criminal conduct—seems to be a basic requirement of fairness. Traditionally, penal philosophy has included a utilitarian tradition (dating from Bentham), which disregarded proportionality concerns, and a retributive tradition (dating from Kant), which did not supply a readily intelligible account of why punishment should be deserved. Recent philosophical writing has focused on penal desert, explained in terms of a just allocation of the "benefits" and "burdens" of law-abidingness, or as a way of expressing blame or censure of criminal wrongdoing. Expressive theories can explain the rationale of the proportionality principle and also account for the distinction between ordinal and cardinal proportionality. Desert models fully abide by the principle of proportionality. Alternative models might be devised that give proportionality a central role but permit limited deviations for other ends.

The last two decades have witnessed continuing debate over the rationales for allocating sanctions among convicted offenders. Various guiding theories or strategies have been put forward: "just deserts," "limiting retributivism," "selective incapacitation." The choice among them is sometimes treated as a matter of deciding allegiances: one adheres to "just deserts" or not, just as one decides to be a Democrat or a Red Sox fan or not. If one opts for just deserts, then one must worry about the scaling of penalties. If one does not, then perhaps one can disregard such issues.

Andrew von Hirsch is professor at the School of Criminal Justice, Rutgers University, and research fellow at the Law Faculty at Uppsala University, Sweden. The help of Andrew Ashworth, Carolyn Cass, Nils Jareborg, Lisa Maher, Uma Narayan, Don E. Scheid, and Michael Tonry is gratefully acknowledged.

Such a perspective is, I think, misleading. Sanctioning rationales differ from one another largely in the emphasis they give the principle of proportionality—that is, the requirement that sanctions be proportionate in their severity to the seriousness of offenses. A desert rationale is one that gives the principle a dominant role. Other viewpoints permit proportionality to be trumped, to a greater or a lesser degree, by ulterior concerns such as those of crime control.

If the choice among sanctioning rationales is, in important part, a choice about how much weight to give to proportionality, then any theory must address the proportionality principle. The prediction theorist—who wishes to stress incapacitation in deciding severity of sentences—will differ in his or her conclusions from a desert advocate. That theorist, however, still must worry about how much concerns about desert—about the seriousness of crimes—should limit the scope of predictive judgments (see, e.g., Morris and Miller 1985). And he or she can devise workable limits of this kind only with an understanding of the logic underlying the proportionality principle.

Why should the principle of proportionality have this crucial role—as a principle that any sanctioning theory needs to address? It is because the principle embodies, or seems to embody, notions of justice. People have a sense that punishments scaled to the gravity of offenses are fairer than punishments that are not. Departures from proportionality—though perhaps eventually justifiable—at least stand in need of defense.

Yet how can one tell, beyond simple intuition, that the principle is a requirement of fairness? And how can one discern the principle's criteria for application? These are, ultimately, questions of moral philosophy.

Criminologists are unaccustomed to dealing with philosophical questions, but an impressive body of writing on punishment does exist in the literature of analytical philosophy. That literature is occasionally referred to in penological writing, but a more complete exposition of the recent philosophical debate may be helpful.

In this essay, I undertake two tasks. The first is to show how the philosophical literature provides an understanding of the principle of proportionality and its rationale. The second is to suggest how various penal strategies—ranging from a pure "desert model" to more mixed schemes—can be analyzed in terms of the role they give to the proportionality principle.

Here is how this essay is organized. Section I sketches briefly the philosophical tradition on punishment: Bentham's penal utilitarianism, Kant's retributivism, and H. L. A. Hart's 1959 synthesis of utilitarian and retributive ideas. Section II addresses the contemporary philosophical discussion: current utilitarian theories are discussed, as are two different versions of penal desert theory. Section III deals with the rationale for the principle of proportionality, drawing on the themes of the preceding sections. Section IV describes the distinction between cardinal and ordinal proportionality and its significance. Sections V–VII sketch three different kinds of sentencing models that differ from one another in the degree of emphasis they give to the principle of proportionality. These are the desert model, Paul Robinson's suggested hybrid (1987) that permits departures from deserved sentences to prevent certain extraordinary harms, and more thoroughly mixed schemes that regularly would permit a certain degree of departure from ordinal desert constraints. Section VIII, finally, draws some conclusions.

I. The Philosophical Tradition

Traditionally, theories of punishment have been either consequentialist (i.e., concerned with the supposed effects of punishment) or deontological (i.e., concerned with moral considerations other than consequences). Consequentialist theories have tended to focus on the crime-preventive benefits of punishment. The most influential of these have been utilitarian and attempt to "weigh" those preventive benefits against punishment's human and financial costs. The most salient deontological theories have been concerned with penal desert. Until the last two decades or so, utilitarianism largely held sway, at least in English-speaking countries.

The great formulator of penal utilitarianism was Jeremy Bentham, writing two centuries ago. His contemporary and critic, Immanuel Kant, supported retributive sanctions. Two centuries later, in the 1950s, H. L. A. Hart attempted a synthesis of utilitarian and desert-based approaches.

A. *Utilitarianism*

Jeremy Bentham's account of punishment rests on the broader social ethic that he also developed: the principle of utility. Social measures are to be judged, he maintains, according to the degree to which they promote aggregate satisfaction (Bentham 1982, chap. 1). The satisfactions and dissatisfactions that a given course of action produces in each person affected are to be considered. The preferable policy or course of action is that which optimizes satisfaction, considering the number of persons affected, as well as both the intensity and duration of satisfaction or dissatisfaction for each person.

The justification and use of punishment, in Bentham's view, is to be determined according to the principle of utility. Punishment is an evil: it brings harm or dissatisfaction to those punished. Therefore, it can be justified only to the extent that it produces, in aggregate, other benefits or satisfactions to a greater degree. Because the principle of utility is wholly consequentialist, punishment cannot be warranted by the ill deserts of those punished. In gauging punishments' net social benefits, general deterrent effects are deemed of particular importance. Punishment is thus warranted only to the extent that its beneficial effects in discouraging criminal behavior outweigh the harm it produces (Bentham 1982, chap. 13).

To this general account of punishment, Bentham appends a number of "rules," or subprinciples. The most notable of these, perhaps, is the following: "Where two offenses come in competition, the punishment for the greater offense must be sufficient to induce a man to prefer the less" (p. 168). This points to a tariff of penalties, according to which the higher punishments would ordinarily be reserved for the more harmful acts.

Bentham's views have had great influence ever since, even on penologists who did not attempt to apply his utilitarian formula systematically. Testimony to that influence has been the strongly crime-preventive thrust of penal theory, especially in English-speaking countries. Penologists disputed whether general deterrence, incapacitation, or rehabilitation was the most effective preventive technique. Seldom (until recently) was it doubted, however, that the assessment of preventive effects, in some form, is the key to sanctioning policy. (What has too often been forgotten, alas, has been Bentham's restraining principle—that against the preventive benefits of punishing must be weighed the pains to those punished.)

Philosophers, however, have long expressed nervousness about some of the implications of penal utilitarianism. Those doubts crystallized around the punishment-of-the-innocent issue (see Pincoffs 1966, pp. 33–40). If the criterion for punishing is utility, what is to prevent the punishment of a few innocent persons—if their pains are outweighed by the aggregate benefits in deterring crime and reassuring the public? Utilitarians' suggested answers to this query—that the sacrifice of innocents will produce long-run ill effects, or that a practice of punishing innocents cannot easily be supported in utilitarian terms[1]—seem unconvincing. For what is being demanded is acknowledgment that it is categorically wrong to punish the innocent and, hence, not permissible to do so even if socially useful in some imaginable scenario. This acknowledgment utilitarian penal theory has difficulty giving.

B. The Retributivist Tradition

The most significant challenge to penal utilitarianism came from Kant. That challenge emerges from his general theory of justice—in particular, his injunction (expressed as the Second Categorical Imperative): "Act in such a way that you always treat humanity, whether in your own person or in the person of any other, never simply as a means, but always at the same time as an end" (Kant 1964, p. 96). This injunction requires each person to be treated as being of value in him- or herself, and not merely as one among many whose benefits and sufferings may be aggregated for the common good. Penal utilitarianism seems troublesome precisely because it so manifestly treats persons as means. The actor is to be punished in order to induce others to desist from crime, and the severity of his punishment depends on its degree of preventive impact.

Kant did not develop a theory of punishment of his own in any systematic fashion. He makes it plain that he prefers a retributive account—one that would make the person's punishment depend on his own deserts rather than on the penalty's societal benefits. However, the details are left unelucidated. Some passages give the initial impression of a starkly retributive theory of punishment, where only the offender's demerit, and no social utility, can be considered for any purpose. A closer look, however, suggests this is not necessarily so.

Kant's account provides valuable themes for discussion. It serves to remind us that retributive criteria for punishing are or appear to be grounded in notions of justice, and that sanctions based purely in utility may treat the punished person unjustly, as someone having no intrinsic value. However, he scarcely develops the arguments for his views, and an inadequately explained talionic criterion may have done penal desert theory disservice, in associating it with harsh sanctions.

---

[1] For discussion of so-called rule utilitarianism—according to which the principle of utility is to be applied to rules or social practices, rather than to individual decisions—see Rawls (1955); Mackie (1977, pp. 136–40).

Kant's most famous statement on punishment is the following passage from his *Rechtslehre:*

> Juridical punishment can never be administered merely as a means for promoting another good either with regard to the criminal himself or to civil society, but must in all cases be imposed only because the individual on whom it is inflicted has committed a crime. For one man ought never to be dealt with merely as a means subservient to the purpose of another. . . . Against such treatment his inborn personality has a right to protect him, even though he may be condemned to lose his civil personality. He must first be found guilty and punishable before there can be any thought of drawing from his punishment any benefit for himself or his fellow-citizens. The penal law is a categorical imperative; and woe to him who creeps through the serpent-windings of utilitarianism to discover some advantage that may discharge him from the justice of punishment, or even from the due measure of it, according to the Pharisaic maxim: "It is better that one man should die than the whole people should perish." For if justice and righteousness perish, human life would no longer have any value in the world. [Quoted in Pincoffs 1966, pp. 2–3]

This passage speaks of the "serpent-windings of utilitarianism," but its focus seems narrower: on punishment of the innocent. It is insistent that punishment may be visited fairly only on offenders and gives a reason why: that doing otherwise would treat punished persons solely as a means to the larger social good and not as beings having value in themselves. Another well-known statement runs as follows:

> Even if a civil society resolved to dissolve itself with the consent of all its members—as might be supposed in the case of a people inhabiting an island resolving to separate and scatter themselves throughout the whole world—the last murderer lying in prison ought to be executed before the resolution was carried out. This ought to be done in order that every one may realize the desert of his deeds, and that bloodguiltiness may not remain upon the people; for otherwise they will all be regarded as participators in the murder as a public violation of justice. [Quoted in Pincoffs 1966, p. 4]

This quotation speaks of a situation where the criminal sanction has already been established, and the question is of its allocation among convicted offenders. Relieving the last murderer of punishment may, indeed, raise problems of equity if previous murderers have been punished for comparable misdeeds. Some commentators (Scheid 1983; Byrd 1989) have thus interpreted Kant as being a retributivist primarily in the "distribution" of punishments (namely, who should be punished and how much), and not necessarily in his view of why the criminal sanction should exist in the first place.

A third passage of Kant's runs as follows:

> But what is the mode and measure of punishment which public justice takes as its principle and standard? It is just the principle of equality, by which the pointer of the scale of justice is made to incline no more to the one side than the other. It may be rendered by saying that the undeserved evil which any one commits on another, is to be regarded as perpetrated on himself. Hence it may be said: "If you slander another, you slander yourself; if you steal from another, you steal from yourself; if you strike another, you strike yourself; if you kill another, you kill yourself." This is the Right of RETALIATION (jus talionis); and properly understood, it is the only principle which in regulating a public court, as distinguished from mere private judgment, can definitely assign both the quality and the quantity of a just penalty. All other standards are wavering and uncertain; and on account of other considerations involved in them, they contain no principle conformable to the sentence of pure and strict justice. [Quoted in Pincoffs 1966, p. 3]

This statement is more troublesome. Kant simply asserts that talionic equality should be the criterion for deserved punishment, ruling out less draconian criteria such as the principle of proportionality. However, it is not easy to follow his reasons why this should be so.

From Kant's era until the decades after World War II, a number of other philosophical retributivists have written on punishment—most notably, Hegel (see Pincoffs 1966, pp. 9–14). However, their accounts also tended to lack an intelligible explanation of what is to be understood by "deserved punishment" and why it should be imposed. It is thus not surprising that penal retributivism remained somewhat restricted in its influence during this period.

C. Hart's Clarification

After World War II, interest in punishment grew among English and American analytical philosophers. The most significant clarification, perhaps, came in 1959, with the publication of H. L. A. Hart's "Prolegomenon to the Principles of Punishment" (Hart 1968, chap. 1).

Hart wrote his essay in response to the influence of penal rehabilitationism in the 1950s and early 1960s—particularly, the writings of Barbara Wootton, who contemplated a treatment-oriented scheme in which moral considerations would play relatively little role and in which penal desert as a normative matter would disappear entirely.[2] Hart was struggling to develop an account of punishment that rested ultimately on concerns of crime prevention, but in which liability was limited to offenders (typically those to whom fault can fairly be imputed) and in which the amount of the sanction was constrained, at least to a degree, by considerations of proportionality. To this end, he distinguishes the "general justifying aim" of punishment (namely, why the criminal sanction should exist at all) from the criteria for penalties' "distribution" (namely, the criteria governing who should be punished and how much). Relying on crime prevention as the general aim—that is, as the reason for existence of criminal sanction—still leaves room, he suggests, for placing nonutilitarian limits on the distribution of penalties, so long as the latter can be justified independently.

Hart proposes an independent justification for an important retributive limit on the substantive criminal law: the restriction of liability to conduct involving the actor's fault (1968, pp. 22–24). His argument rests on notions of choice. In a free society, citizens should have full opportunity (through their choice to remain law abiding) to avoid the impositions of the criminal law; this they can do only if criminal liability requires volition and fault, because otherwise even purely accidental breaches could trigger criminal liability. (Similar considerations militate against vicarious and strict liability.) This kind of reasoning, however, does not hold when one moves from substantive law to sentencing policy and considers the latter's most important retributive constraint, the principle of proportionality. That principle cannot be based on the idea of a fair opportunity to avoid the criminal law's impositions—since it concerns the quantum of punishment levied on persons who, in choosing to violate the law, have voluntarily exposed themselves to the consequences of criminal liability. Hart therefore supplies an alternative explanation for proportionality: disproportionate sanctions pose the "risk . . . of either confusing common morality

---

[2] Wootton wrote extensively in this vein during the period cited, but her views are most clearly stated in Wootton (1963).

or flouting it and bringing the law into contempt" (1968, p. 25). That, however, is scarcely a satisfactory explanation. Maintaining respect for law seems, plainly, a consequentialist concern. Laws that are not respected may be less likely to be obeyed, but if obedience is the touchstone, might it not otherwise be achieved—for example, through disproportionate sanctions that are sufficiently intimidating? Finding better reasons to show why the principle is a requirement of fairness is thus a challenge that Hart has left to other penal philosophers.

II. The Modern Philosophical Debate

During the past two decades, the philosophical debate over punishment has become more intense. Some reformulations of penal utilitarianism have been attempted. Still more has been written on deserved punishment and its possible justifications. This new interest in desert theory has been mirrored by a greater emphasis, in practical penal policy, on proportionate sanctions.[3]

This section summarizes this recent philosophical debate, starting with utilitarian and neo-utilitarian theories and proceeding to two recent versions of retributivism: one concerned with the fair allocation of benefits and burdens, the other with the expressive and censuring features of punishment.

A. Utilitarian Accounts

Modern followers of Bentham, such as Richard Posner (1977, chap. 7), have attempted to make Bentham's formulations more useable by interpreting "utility" in economic terms. Posner thus subjects punishment to a cost/benefit analysis—a matter of estimating the costs of punishment and weighing them against penalties' crime preventive yield. The criminal sanction prevents harm by discouraging criminal behavior but also creates harm by making punished offenders suffer and by incurring various expenses of administration. Those various harms incurred and prevented are quantified as costs, and how much to punish is decided by considerations of optimum cost reduction.

Such a formula, however, raises problems of justice. It can support

---

[3] A number of state sentencing guidelines—most notably those of Minnesota, Washington State, and Oregon—give considerable emphasis to requirements of proportionality; see von Hirsch, Knapp, and Tonry (1987, chaps. 2 and 5). The new English Criminal Justice Act, enacted in 1991, also gives an explicit central role to proportionality (Wasik and Taylor 1991), as does the 1988 Swedish sentencing law (von Hirsch and Jareborg 1989b).

drastic, even disproportionate interventions against the few if the net benefits to the many are great enough. Posner supplies his own vivid illustration. Because deterrent effects depend on the likelihood as well as severity of punishment, the same preventive effect can be achieved by punishing a few offenders very severely or more offenders less harshly. Given that choice, he argues, one should prefer the severe punishment of the few because it is more cost efficient (Posner 1977, p. 170).

Could the utility principle be reformulated to avoid such uncomfortable conclusions? One suggested reformulation has been forwarded recently by two Australian writers, one a sociologist and the other a philosopher (Braithwaite and Pettit 1990). Their proposed solution is to retain the forward-looking and aggregative features of the utilitarian calculus but to change the measure of utility. That measure would no longer be satisfaction or cost-reduction *simpliciter* but the promotion of personal autonomy. The best course of action, on this theory, is one that gives the most people voice in how they live. A harsh system of punishment, they argue, might be efficient in preventing harm, but it will not facilitate choice. Fear-provoking sanctions would diminish, not enhance, citizens' sense of control over their own lives.

Does Braithwaite and Pettit's redefinition of utility help? In certain contexts outside the criminal law, it might. One is in paternalistic interventions—for example, the restraint and treatment of persons with self-destructive tendencies. Conventional utilitarianism might support sweeping powers of compulsion for such persons' own good: it need merely be argued that they benefit more from the intervention than they lose by having their decisions disregarded. A shift to an agency-oriented measure of utility would restrict such interventions because they interfere so much with individual actors' choices.

In the criminal law, however, this redefinition of utility is less helpful. It is true that punishment interferes with the choices of those punished. But it also, to the extent of its preventive efficacy, fosters other persons' choices by protecting them from victimization. When more people are safeguarded than intruded on, why not proceed? The Braithwaite-Pettit theory thus would not necessarily restrict the use of harsh sanctions, provided that only the few suffer and the many have their choices better protected. Such punishments (unlike punishment of innocents) would not necessarily diminish citizens' sense of control over their own lives—because the sanctions would apply only to those who have chosen to offend and not to anyone in general (see von Hirsch and Ashworth [1992] for fuller discussion).

What remains troublesome about penal utilitarianism, therefore, is its aggregative and purely forward-looking features. The preoccupation with prevention of future offending makes it difficult to explain why the gravity of the crime of conviction is morally relevant to how much punishment is warranted. The theory's aggregative character—its concern with the net balance of benefits over costs—makes it insensitive to how these benefits are distributed: it allows some to suffer, possibly to a disproportionate degree, for the good of others. A penal theory may (as Hart has suggested and as I argue below) contain crime prevention as an important element. But it is doubtful that it can, with even a modicum of fairness, make crime prevention the only criterion.

B. Desert Theories

Traditional retributive theories, such as Kant's, were sketchy. While contending that justice calls for deserved punishments, they seldom explored the grounds of penal desert claims: namely, *why* wrongdoers deserve punishment. Recently, philosophers have been looking for explanations. The two leading accounts today are, respectively, the "benefits and burdens" theory and "expressive" desert theories.

1. *Benefits and Burdens.* The benefits and burdens theory originated in the writings of two contemporary philosophers, Herbert Morris (1968) and Jeffrie Murphy (1973). Both have recently questioned the theory (Morris 1981; Murphy 1985), but a number of other philosophers continue to support it (Gewirth 1978, pp. 294–98; Finnis 1980, pp. 263–64; Davis 1983; Sadurski 1985, chap. 8; Sher 1987, chap. 5).

The theory offers a retrospectively oriented account of why offenders should be made to suffer punishment. The account focuses on the law as a jointly beneficial enterprise: it requires each person to desist from predatory conduct; by desisting, the person not only benefits others but is benefited by their reciprocal self-restraint. The person who victimizes others—while still benefiting from their self-restraint—thus obtains an unjust advantage. Punishment's function is to impose an offsetting disadvantage.

The theory has some attractions. It goes beyond fuzzy notions of "paying back" wrongdoing or "righting" the moral balance. It points to a particular unwarranted advantage the wrongdoer obtains: namely, that of benefiting from others' self-restraint while not reciprocally restraining himself. The rationale for the penalty is retrospective in focus, as a desert-oriented account should be: to offset, through punishment, the unjustly obtained benefit.

The theory has difficulties, however. One problem is that it requires a heroic belief in the justice of the underlying social arrangements. Unless it is true that our social and political systems succeed in providing mutual support for all members, including criminal offenders, then the offender has not necessarily benefited from others' law-abiding behavior (Bedau 1978).

The theory also becomes awkward when one uses it to try to decide the quantum of punishments. One difficulty is assessing benefits and burdens (Scheid 1990; von Hirsch 1990a, pp. 264–69). The theory cannot focus on literal benefits the offender obtains—as some of the worst assaultive crimes can be quite unprofitable whereas other (apparently less serious) theft crimes may provide the offender with a considerable profit. What thus must matter, instead, is the additional degree of freedom the offender has unfairly appropriated. But notions of degrees of freedom are unhelpful in making comparisons among crimes. It is one thing to say the armed robber or burglar permits himself actions that others refrain from taking and thereby unfairly obtains a liberty that others have relinquished in their (and his) mutual interest. It is different, and far more obscure, to say the robber deserves more punishment than the burglar because, somehow, he has arrogated to himself a greater degree of unwarranted freedom than the burglar has.

The theory would also seem to distort the way the gravity of crimes is assessed. R. A. Duff (1986, pp. 211–17) has pointed out the artificiality of treating victimizing crimes, such as armed robbery, in terms of the "freedom-of-action" advantage the robber gains over uninvolved third parties, rather than in terms of the intrusion into the interests or rights of actual or potential victims. Perhaps, tax evasion can be explained in terms of unjustified advantage: the tax evader refuses to pay his or her own tax, yet benefits from others' payments through the services he or she receives. Tax evasion, however, is scarcely the paradigm criminal offense, and it is straining to try to assess the heinousness of common offenses such as robbery in similar fashion.

2. *"Expressive" Theories.* "Expressive" theories are those that base desert claims on the censuring aspects of punishment. Punishing someone consists of doing something painful or unpleasant to him, because he has committed a wrong, under circumstances and in a manner that conveys disapprobation of the offender for his wrong. Treating the

offender as a wrongdoer, Richard Wasserstrom (1980, pp. 112–51) has pointed out, is central to the idea of punishment. The difference between a tax and a fine, for example, does not rest in the kind of material deprivation imposed: it is money, in both cases. It consists, rather, in the fact that with a fine the money is taken in a manner that conveys disapproval or censure; whereas with a tax no disapproval is implied.

A sanction that treats conduct as wrong—that is, not a "neutral" sanction—has two important moral functions that, arguably, are not reducible to crime prevention. One is to recognize the importance of the rights that have been infringed. Joel Feinberg (1970, pp. 95–118) has argued that the censure in punishment conveys to victims and potential victims that the state recognizes they are wronged by criminal conduct, that rights to which they are properly entitled have been infringed.

The other role of censure, discussed by R. A. Duff (1986, chap. 9), is to address the wrongdoer as a moral agent, by appealing to his or her sense of right or wrong. This, Duff suggests, is not just a preventive strategy. While it is hoped that the actor will reconsider his actions and desist from wrongdoing in the future, the censure is not merely a means of changing his behavior—otherwise, there would be no point in censuring actors who are repentant already (since they need no blame to make the effort to desist) or who are seemingly incorrigible (since they will not change despite the censure). Any human actor, the theory suggests, is a moral agent, capable (unless clearly incompetent) of evaluating others' assessment of their conduct. The repentant actor has his own assessment of the conduct confirmed through the disapproval of others; the defiant actor is made to understand and feel others' disapproval, even if he refuses to desist. Such communication of judgment and feeling, Duff argues, is what moral discourse among rational agents is about. What a purely "neutral" sanction not embodying blame would deny—even if no less effective in preventing crime—is precisely that essential status of the person as a moral agent. A neutral sanction would treat potential offenders much as beasts in a circus—as beings that must be restrained, intimidated, or conditioned into submission because they are incapable of understanding that harmful conduct is wrong (see also von Hirsch 1990a, pp. 271–74).

Such censure-oriented desert theories have some potential advantages. They are less dependent on the supposition that the underlying social system is wholly just: an actor with cause for complaint against the social system may still be to blame, for example, if he knowingly injures those who have done him no wrong (von Hirsch 1990*b*, pp. 407–9). Moreover, the theory is more easily squared with notions of proportionality. If punishment is seen as an expression of blame for reprehensible conduct, then the quantum of punishment should depend on how reprehensible the conduct is. The punishment for typical victimizing crimes would depend on how much harm the conduct does, and how culpable the actor is for the harm—and no longer on how much extra freedom of action the actor has arrogated to himself vis-à-vis third parties.

III. The Principle of Proportionality: Its Justification

The principle of proportionality is said to be a requirement of fairness. But why is this so? Why are proportionate sanctions more just than disproportionate ones? To answer this question, the present section addresses the case for the principle—examining arguments based on general prevention and on censure.

A. *Arguments from "Positive" General Prevention*

Can the principle of proportionality be based on notions of crime prevention? Some European theorists have claimed it can—particularly on what they call "positive" general prevention (Roxin 1979; see also Ewing 1970).

"Positive" general prevention differs from simple deterrence in that it looks, not to the intimidating effect of criminal sanctions, but to their "positive" effect in reinforcing citizens' own moral inhibitions against predatory behavior (Andenaes 1974, pp. 111–28). The idea has been attractive to those wishing to combine a consequentialist penal philosophy with fairness constraints on the pursuit of crime prevention. A penalty structure in which sanctions reflect the relative gravity of crimes, arguably, would be perceived by citizens as more just—and being so perceived, would better reinforce citizens' sense of self-restraint (Roxin 1979). The argument thus resembles Hart's suggestion, discussed earlier, that proportionality promotes respect for law.

"Positive" general prevention, even if its existence is not easy to confirm empirically (Schumann 1987), is a plausible notion. It seems likely that the criminal sanction (in some direct or indirect way and at least to some degree) supports citizens' own moral qualms about victimizing others. The issue, however, is not whether positive general prevention exists, but whether it can serve as the basis for a principle of proportionate sanctions. That is far from clear, for a number of reasons.

First, the argument from positive general prevention assumes that the citizenry believes proportionate sanctions to be fairer. It is because of such supposed beliefs that the state, in order to safeguard the moral credibility of its sanctions, should levy punishments proportionately with crimes' gravity. But what if citizens care little about whether sanctions are proportionate? Or what if the state undertakes to persuade the citizenry that proportionality is unimportant? To the extent that proportionality is a matter of indifference to the public, disproportionate punishments would not undermine the penal system's credibility.

Second, "positive" general prevention is merely one of a variety of preventive strategies that must compete with others, such as deterrence and incapacitation. If crime prevention is the touchstone, then proportionality might be sacrificed in order to provide room for those other strategies for reducing crime. A system of penalties might be graded very roughly according to the gravity of offenses, but with broad exceptions to allow for deterrent or incapacitative sanctions. No sacrifice of principle would be involved in such a scheme because one is merely substituting among various possible crime-control techniques.

Third, the argument from positive general prevention fails also to account for the sense that proportionality is not just a prudential but an ethical principle. There seems to be something *wrong*, not just counterproductive in the long run, about punishing disproportionately. That sense of wrongfulness cannot be explained merely by arguing that proportionality influences citizens' attitudes in such a way as to reinforce inclinations to law-abidingness.

B. The Argument from Censure

The positive general prevention argument began with the censuring features of punishment, but then relied on arguments of preventive effectiveness to sustain the proportionality principle. It might be preferable to rely on the same censuring features—but then utilize fairness arguments, instead.

Punishment, as explained previously, consists of doing something unpleasant to an offender under circumstances and in a manner that conveys blame or disapprobation. Not only does punishment thus indicate disapproval, but the comparative severity of punishments connotes the degree of stringency of the implicit disapproval. If crime X is punished more severely than crime Y, this connotes the greater disapprobation of crime X.

When punishments are arrayed in severity according to the gravity of offenses, the disapprobation thereby conveyed will reflect the degree of reprehensibleness of the conduct. When punishments are arrayed otherwise, this is not merely inefficient (indeed, it might possibly be more efficient), but unfair: offenders are being visited with more (or with less) censure than the comparative blameworthiness of their conduct would warrant. Equity is sacrificed when the proportionality principle is disregarded, even when this is done for the sake of crime prevention. Suppose that offenders A and B commit and are convicted of criminal conduct of approximately equal seriousness. Suppose B is deemed more likely to re-offend and, therefore, is given a longer sentence. Notwithstanding the possible preventive utility of that sentence, the objection remains that B, through his more severe punishment, is being treated as more to blame than A, though their conduct has the same degree of blameworthiness (von Hirsch 1985, chap. 3; Duff 1986, pp. 277–79; von Hirsch 1990a, pp. 278–81).

This condemnation-based account of the principle of proportionality makes clear that the principle does not depend on hard-to-confirm factual claims that proportionality enhances the general preventive effect of the penal system. Suppose that new psychological evidence suggested that maintaining proportionality does little to enhance people's inhibitions against predatory conduct. Would such evidence mean that we properly could ignore the requirements of proportionality? Not according to this theory. As long as the state responds to violence, theft, and other noxious conduct through the institution of the criminal sanction, it is necessarily treating those whom it punishes as wrongdoers and condemning them for their conduct. If the state thus condemns, then the severity of the response ought to reflect the degree of blameworthiness, that is, the gravity, of the criminal conduct.

One commentator, Johannes Andenaes (1988), asks whether this argument is circular. Punishment entails blaming, he asserts, only in a system where the sentence is tied to moral judgments of the reprehensibleness of conduct. If the system's rules for allocating sentences were more utilitarian, would not the link between punishing and blaming disappear?

The link between punishment and blame, however, has much deeper roots than the sentencing rules of the particular jurisdiction.

Censure is integral to the very conception of punishing—as is apparent from the earlier-cited illustration of the difference between a fine and a tax. Punishment's blaming implications are also reinforced by the substantive criminal law. The core of the criminal law deals with acts commonly considered reprehensible: theft, violence, and the flouting of certain basic duties of citizenship (e.g., tax evasion or environmental crimes). The formal requirements of the substantive law, moreover, call not only for an unlawful act but for personal fault on the part of the offender—namely, intentionality (i.e., purpose, knowledge, or recklessness) or negligence. Harming through intention or negligence is typically reprehensible behavior, for which censure is an appropriate response. Conversely, one of the main reasons why the law should require intention or negligence is because the blame expressed through punishment is inappropriately applied to behavior that is not the actor's fault (von Hirsch and Jareborg 1989a).

C. Proportionality and the "Why Punish?" Question

The foregoing censure-based argument for proportionality assumes the existence of punishment. It assumes, that is, the existence of a sanction that connotes censure or blame. Why, however, have a sanction with blaming features? Conceivably, the criminal sanction could be replaced by a "neutral" sanction—one designed to visit material deprivation but convey no disapproval (i.e., be akin to a tax on behavior the state wished to discourage). Since such a sanction would not involve blaming, it perhaps would not have to be distributed according to the blameworthiness of the criminal conduct.

Could the censure element in punishment be explained on preventive grounds? Conceivably, it could. Here, the European notion of "positive" general prevention might be invoked. The preventive efficacy of punishment, the argument would run, operates in significant part through its "moral-educational" effect of stigmatizing predatory conduct and thereby making citizens more reluctant to offend. That effect can best be achieved when the sanction visits censure on violators (Mäkelä 1975). A "neutral" sanction would lack this educational effect. It thus would be either less effectual or require more draconian deprivations to achieve a similar effect.

Relying on "positive" general prevention in this fashion—to explain why the state's sanction should embody blame—still allows one to argue that proportionality is a requirement of fairness. One would be following Hart's strategy of argument—of distinguishing the general justification of punishment ("why punish?") from the principles of distribution ("how much?"). A preventive answer is being offered to the "why punish?" question—namely, that a blaming sanction has better preventive effects than a purely neutral one would. However, a fairness argument, not based on prevention, is being used to explain why punishments should be levied proportionately: namely, that once a blaming sanction is established, equity (not just crime prevention) requires that it be distributed consistently with its censuring implications. An analogy might be drawn to the prize. If one asks why prizes should exist, the answer might be consequentialist: the material benefit in a prize is an incentive, and the approbation conveyed by the prize constitutes an educational message that the conduct is desirable. Once a system of prizes has been established, however, the criteria for their distribution should be retrospective and desert oriented. Since the first prize symbolizes the best performance, justice—not social efficiency—demands that it be awarded to the best contestant.[4]

One might, however, be skeptical of the foregoing prevention-based account—that the censure element in punishment can be derived purely from the aim of reinforcing citizen self-restraint. Suppose it were proposed that the state should penalize adult criminal conduct in as morally "neutral" a way as possible. What objection is there to such a proposal? The preventionist would have to object that it would lead to more criminal behavior: once the state no longer censured the prohibited conduct, people's moral inhibitions would weaken, and they would become readier to commit crimes. Any such slackening of inhibitions would not be likely to take place right away, however, since people's moral attitudes would for a time remain supported by social institutions other than the criminal sanction. The preventionist would have to argue that, although the measure was not immediately objectionable, it would have long-run ill effects in diluting punishment's preventive efficacy.

One might well be inclined to assert, however, that the proposal is immediately obnoxious (regardless of its long-run ill effects). The behavior with which the criminal law mainly deals is wrongful conduct—

---

[4] Some writers (e.g., Walker 1991, pp. 3–4) argue that comparison between punishments and rewards or prizes is inappropriate because the former are inflicted on an unwilling recipient and the latter are not. However, there are some significant similarities—most notably, these institutions by their nature convey blame or praise. The punishment/prize analogy, in any event, is meant merely to be illustrative—and is not essential to the argument for proportionality.

culpable violation of the rights of other persons. If the state is to carry out the authoritative response to such behavior (as it must if it visits any kind of sanction on perpetrators), then it should do so in a manner that testifies to the recognition that the conduct is wrong. To respond in a morally neutral fashion is objectionable, not merely because it might lead to more crime in the long run, but because it fails to provide that recognition. A sanction that treats the conduct as wrong—that is, not a "neutral" sanction—has, arguably, certain important functions not reducible to crime prevention. Which functions? One might refer here to Feinberg's and Duff's views of censure that are discussed above. The censure in punishment recognizes the wrong done to victims (Feinberg's view). It is also a way of addressing the wrongdoer himself as a rational agent (Duff's).[5]

A committed general preventionist might try to subsume these functions of censure under positive general prevention. A society has better cohesion, he might assert, if the wrong done to victims is recognized, and if offenders are treated as moral agents. But that involves trying to reduce claims such as Feinberg's or Duff's to difficult-to-confirm hypotheses about social cohesion. While one might have some confidence in the ethical judgment that offenders should be treated as agents capable of choice, one can hardly verify that so treating them will lead to a better-integrated or more smoothly functioning society.

So far, I have been discussing the censure element in punishment. But what of the criminal sanction's "hard treatment" element? Can the pain or deprivation visited on offenders be justified in similar fashion, or need it rest on preventive arguments? Here, the expressive desert theorists disagree among themselves. Some, such as Duff and Kleinig, argue that some degree of hard treatment is needed to make the censure credible (for a summary of their arguments, see von Hirsch [1990a], p. 275). On this view, censure—at least in certain social contexts—cannot be expressed sufficiently in purely verbal terms; some imposition is needed to convey the intended disapprobation adequately. An academic department does not show its disapproval of a serious lapse by a colleague merely through verbal admonition; to convey the requisite disapproval, some curtailment of privileges is needed. A legal system, it is argued, is still less capable of conveying censure purely in words or symbols without action.

[5] For fuller statement of this argument, see von Hirsch (1985, chap. 5; 1990a, pp. 271–74).

Other expressive theorists (including the present author) disagree, and contend that the hard-treatment element in punishment rests on preventive grounds (von Hirsch 1985, chap. 5; Jareborg 1988, chap. 5; von Hirsch 1990a, pp. 275–78). On this view, the reason for punishing (i.e., expressing disapproval through hard treatment) instead of merely censuring has to do with keeping predatory behavior within tolerable limits. Had punishment no usefulness in preventing crime, then one would not need to visit material deprivation on those who offend. True, we might still wish to devise another way of issuing authoritative judgments of censure, for such predatory behavior as occurs. However, those judgments, in the interests of keeping state-inflicted suffering to a minimum, would no longer be linked to the purposeful visitation of deprivation.

A possible objection to this latter view runs as follows: if the deprivation element in punishment rests on consequentialist grounds of crime prevention but the censure element does not, then why cannot one allocate the deprivations on preventive grounds? The reply is that punishment's deprivations and its reprobative connotations are inextricably intermixed. If the deprivations visited for a given type of crime are altered, even for preventive reasons, this changes the severity of the punishment. But changing the severity, relative to other penalties, alters the implicit censure—which would not be justified when the seriousness of the conduct has remained unchanged.

The reader must decide which of these various accounts for the existence of punishment—the one based on general prevention, the one based on censure, or the mixed explanation just discussed—is preferable. Each account, however, calls for a sanction that is condemnatory in character. Given such a sanction, it becomes (for the reasons explained) a matter of equity, not preventive efficacy, that penalties should be proportionate, that is, distributed consistently with their blaming implications.

One can take the question back a step further and ask, whence do such ideas of equity derive? Such a question would draw us deeper into philosophical ethics than we can venture here. Recent Anglo-American analytical moral philosophy has by and large become skeptical of attempts to reduce ethical claims to those of social utility (see, e.g., Smart and Williams 1973, pp. 75–150), albeit there have been some philosophers who still support such attempts (see Smart and Williams 1973, pp. 1–74).

Proportionality in sentencing doctrine, however, does not stand or fall on the outcome of such debates over the foundations of ethics. The suggested basis of the principle of proportionality is that a censuring sanction must in fairness be allocated according to the blameworthiness of the conduct. That requirement of fairness has to do with moral consistency: with treating people in accordance with ascriptions made of their praise- or blameworthiness; it has nothing necessarily to do with installing inhibitions against predatory conduct more efficiently. Could a committed philosophical consequentialist identify other social utilities that are ultimately served by such a fairness requirement? Perhaps he or she might. Those would have to be complicated utilities, however, connected with the idea that the canons of fairness ultimately help people to lead more fulfilled and self-respecting lives (see Mackie 1977). Philosophical consequentialism of this more sophisticated sort—that attempts to derive justice or ethical imperatives from what is eventually useful to a good existence—is not reducible to ideas of short or long-run crime prevention.

IV. Ordinal and Cardinal Proportionality

What does the principle of proportionality require? Does the principle yield only broad outer bounds of punishment? If so, it is rather easily satisfied, by avoiding extremes of severity or leniency. Could the principle yield definite quanta of punishments—and if so, how could those quanta possibly be ascertained? Or is there some third possibility?

The first view, which might be termed the "range only" theory, holds that proportionality, by its logic, can only be a limiting principle. It cannot possibly tell us how much an offender deserves, but can only suggest certain upper and lower limits, beyond which punishment would be manifestly undeserved. Within these broad limits, the sentence would have to be decided on other grounds, say, the likelihood of the defendant's committing other crimes. Notice that this claim is one about the logic of desert: it is that proportionality cannot supply more than broad ranges. It thus differs from "hybrid" views to be discussed in Section VII, according to which—in order to achieve ulterior ends of one kind or another—desert requirements are to be relaxed to yield ranges.

The "range only" view is open to a fundamental objection, which becomes evident when one tests this view by the censure rationale for proportionality just suggested. Suppose one decides, for a particular offense involving a given degree of harmfulness and of fault on the part of the actor, that less than X quantum of sentence is undeservedly lenient and more than Y quantum is undeservedly severe. Suppose that, pursuant to the "range only" view, one treats the proportionality principle as supplying only these outer limits—that the sentence must fall somewhere between X and Y—and then allows the disposition to be decided within these bounds on preventive grounds. This would allow two offenders, whose conduct is equally reprehensible but who are considered (say) to present differing degrees of risk, to receive different punishments. One could receive a punishment close to the lower limit, X, and the other may receive a sentence at the upper limit, Y. Through these different penalties, the two defendants would be subject to differing degrees of censure or condemnation, although the reprehensibleness of their criminal conduct is *ex hypothesi* the same. In fact, a defendant who commits a less serious crime can receive comparatively the greater penalty if preventive concerns so dictate.

The opposite view, that the proportionality principle furnishes specific quanta of punishments, seems still less plausible. Taken literally, it would presuppose an heroic kind of intuitionism: that if one only reflects enough, one will "see" the deserved quanta of punishment for various crimes. No one, however, seems to have intuitions that are so illuminating.

Is there a way out of this apparent dilemma—that neither outer bounds nor a fixed point seems a plausible interpretation of the proportionality principle? It has been suggested that there is, once the crucial distinction is recognized between the internal structure of a penalty scale and the scale's overall magnitude and anchoring points (Bedau 1984; von Hirsch 1985, chap. 4; von Hirsch 1990a, pp. 282–86).

A. Internal Structure

How are punishments to be scaled relative to each other? Here, the requirements of *ordinal*, or relative, proportionality apply. Persons convicted of crimes of comparable seriousness should receive punishments of comparable severity (special circumstances altering the harm or culpability of the conduct in the particular case being taken into account). Persons convicted of crimes of differing gravity should suffer punishments correspondingly graded in their onerousness. These requirements of comparative proportionality are no mere limits, and they are infringed when equally reprehensible conduct is punished unequally in the manner that the "range only" view calls for. The requirements are readily explained on the censure rationale discussed earlier. Since punishing one offense more severely than another expresses greater disapproval of the former conduct, it is justified only to the extent it is more serious.

B. Anchoring Points

If the penalties for some other crimes have been decided, then the penalty can be fixed for (say) a robbery by comparing its seriousness with those other crimes. But such judgments require a starting point, and there is no quantum of punishment that can be identified as the uniquely deserved penalty for the crime or crimes with which one begins constructing the scale. Why not? The censure theory again provides the explanation. The amount of disapproval conveyed through penal sanctions is a convention. When a penalty scale has been devised to reflect the comparative gravity of crimes, altering the scale's overall punishment levels by making pro rata increases or decreases in all penalties would represent just a change in that convention.

Not all conventions are equally acceptable, however. There should be limits on the severity of sanction with which a given amount of disapproval may be expressed, and these constitute the limits of *cardinal*, or nonrelative, proportionality. Consider a scale in which penalties are graded to reflect the comparative seriousness of crimes, but in which overall penalty levels have been so much inflated that even the lowest-ranking crimes are visited with prison terms. Such a scale would embody a convention in which even a modest disapproval appropriate to low-ranking crimes is expressed through drastic intrusions on offenders' liberties. Such a convention would be objectionable on grounds that it depreciates the importance of the rights of which the defendant is being deprived. There might be a comparable lower limit against deflating overall punishment levels so much that even the most serious crimes are visited only with small intrusions.

This ordinal/cardinal distinction appears to provide the solution to the dilemma just mentioned. The leeway that the proportionality principle allows in deciding the anchoring points of the scale explains why we cannot perceive a single right or fitting penalty for a crime. Whether X months or Y months, or somewhere in between, is the appropriate penalty for a given offense depends on how the scale has been anchored and what punishments have been prescribed for other crimes of greater and lesser gravity. Once the anchoring points of the scale have been fixed, however, the more restrictive requirements of ordinal proportionality begin to apply. These explain why the proportionality principle would not authorize giving shorter prison terms to some and longer terms to others convicted of the same offense (even within supposed outer bounds of desert), on the basis of factors not reflecting its gravity.

The parallel that comes readily to mind is that of university grades. The anchoring points of a grading system cannot precisely be set. We know that first-class honors should be reserved for high-quality work, but just how high that quality should be cannot precisely be fixed and may depend on the character and traditions of the educational institution. Once the anchoring points of the grading scale are fixed, however, students' comparative ratings should be determined by the quality of their academic performance.

Where do these distinctions leave us? They suggest the following conclusions. First, there are no uniquely deserved punishments. Whether X is the appropriate, proportionate sanction for a given crime depends on how the penalty scale is anchored and how other crimes are punished. Second, in anchoring the scale and deciding the overall punishment levels, the proportionality principle provides at most only certain outer limits: that the scale as a whole may not be justly inflated above certain levels of punitiveness, and possibly (but more debatably)[6] that it may not be deflated below certain (rather low) levels. So here— in speaking of "cardinal," or nonrelative, proportionality—it makes sense to speak of imprecise outer limits. Third, once the anchoring points have been decided, however, the requirements of ordinal, or relative, proportionality apply, and these are more restrictive. To maintain ordinal proportionality, comparative severities of punishment would need to be decided according to the relative gravity of the criminal conduct involved.

Does this mean that sentences must always be ordered according to these requirements? Of course not. I am considering here what the proportionality principle calls for. Proportionality, however, is not the only value involved—there may be countervailing reasons of various sorts for departing from proportionality. Indeed, I suggested at the outset that sentencing theories can be classified by the extent to which they treat proportionality requirements as binding. I next examine a variety of sentencing models, distinguishable chiefly by the role and weight they assign to proportionality. One such view—or perhaps, spectrum of views—aims at abiding by proportionality requirements in full: the desert model. A second type of view (e.g., Robinson 1987) generally adheres to desert principles but allows departures to prevent

---

[6] For the questions involved, see von Hirsch (1990*a*, pp. 285–86, 1993, chap. 4).

exceptional types of harm. A third would relax proportionality constraints more regularly in setting punishments.

V. The Desert Model

A desert model is a sentencing scheme that observes the proportionality
principle: punishments are scaled according to the seriousness of
crimes. While speaking of a "desert model" might suggest a unique
scale, that is not the intent. A variety of scales of differing overall
severity and differing sanctions might satisfy the requirements of this
model. It is the core elements of a desert model that are sketched here.
Fuller accounts of the model and its rationale are available elsewhere
(von Hirsch 1985, chaps. 3–8; Ashworth 1989), as are discussions of
the use of the model in scaling noncustodial sanctions (von Hirsch,
Wasik, and Greene 1989; von Hirsch 1993, chap. 6).

A. Ordinal Proportionality

Ordinal proportionality is the requirement that penalties be scaled
according to the comparative seriousness of crimes. Two main sub-
requirements are involved. First, parity. The proportionality principle
permits differences in severity of punishments only to the extent these
differences reflect variations in the degree of blameworthiness of the
conduct. Accordingly, when offenders have been convicted of crimes
of similar seriousness, they deserve punishment of similar severity—
unless special circumstances (i.e., of aggravation or mitigation) can be
identified that render the offense, in the particular context, more or
less deserving of blame than would normally be the case. Second,
rank ordering. Punishing one crime more than another expresses more
disapproval for the former crime, so that it is justified only if that crime
is more serious. Punishments thus are to be ordered on a penalty scale
so that their relative severity reflects the seriousness rankings of the
crimes involved. This restricts the extent to which the arrangement of
penalties on the scale can be varied internally for crime preventive
purposes. Imposing exemplary penalties for a given type of offense to
halt a recent upswing in its incidence, for example, would throw the
ranking of offenses out of kilter unless other penalties are adjusted
accordingly.

While these two requirements of parity and rank ordering seem
straightforward enough, there have been a number of issues raised
concerning ordinal proportionality that are worth mentioning.

1. *"A Year Is Not a Year."* It has sometimes been objected that

parity can never be achieved because of the difficulty of comparing onerousness of penalties among individuals (Morris and Tonry 1990, pp. 94–95). Each person will suffer differently from any penal deprivation, depending on his or her age, personal sensitivities, and so forth. The reply is that law generally deals with standard cases—and should do so here as well. Notwithstanding the fact that individuals experience penalties differently, it still is possible to gauge and compare the characteristic onerousness of various sanctions. Deviations from those standard judgments could then be warranted in special situations, such as illness or advanced age, that give the penalty a manifestly uncharacteristic punitive impact (von Hirsch 1991a). Taking this approach, of course, means aiming at approximate rather than exact parity, but that seems a reasonable concession to the realities of legal classification.

2. *Substitution and Interchangeability.* How much interchangeability among penalties would a desert model permit? The proportionality principle addresses only the severity of penalties, not their particular forms. This permits substitution among penalties, provided those substituted are of comparable severity. If A is the sanction assumed ordinarily to be applicable to crimes of a given degree of seriousness, and B is another type of sanction of approximately equal onerousness, then B can be substituted for A without infringing ordinal desert requirements. This means one might even substitute between short stints of confinement and the more substantial noncustodial sanctions—provided the severity-equivalence test has been met (von Hirsch 1991a).

Where the test of severity equivalence is met, it would also be permissible to substitute among penalties on crime-preventive (e.g., predictive) grounds. Day fines could be given to most offenders convicted of a given middle-level crime, but probation to those offenders especially in need of supervision, provided the two sanctions are of comparable severity. Ordinal proportionality is infringed only if invoking probation substantially alters the comparative severities for those involved (von Hirsch, Wasik, and Greene 1989).

3. *Prior Convictions.* Another issue concerns the appropriateness of considering prior convictions. Some desert theorists (Fletcher 1978, pp. 460–66; Singer 1979, chap. 5) maintain that the presence or absence of prior convictions is irrelevant to offenders' deserts. Others (von Hirsch 1985, chap. 7; Wasik 1987; von Hirsch 1991b) support a penalty discount for the first offense—as a way of recognizing human fallibility in the criteria for punishment. By giving the first offender

a somewhat scaled-down punishment, their argument runs, the first offender is censured for his act but nevertheless accorded some respect for the fact that his inhibitions against wrongdoing appear to have functioned on prior occasions and some sympathy or tolerance for the all-too-human frailty that can lead to such a lapse. With repetition, however, this extenuation diminishes and eventually is lost. To the extent that first offending is seen as extenuating, it modifies the parity requirement: among those convicted of comparably serious offenses, some differentiation would be made on the basis of the prior record. The operative word, however, is "some": only a modest adjustment would be permitted on the basis of the record. This view thus would emphasize the gravity of the present offense of conviction.

4. *Grading Crimes' Seriousness.* The rank-ordering requirement presupposes a capacity to grade crimes according to their seriousness. As a practical matter, ranking crimes' gravity has not been an insuperable problem—as witness the experience of some state sentencing commissions, particularly those of Minnesota, Washington State, and Pennsylvania. These bodies were able to fashion systematic rankings of seriousness for use in their numerical guidelines. The commissions established seriousness gradations from, say, 1 (the least serious) to 10 (the most serious), and then assigned the various statutory crime categories or subcategories to one or another of these gradations. While the grading task proved time-consuming, it did not generate much dissension within the commissions, and the resulting seriousness rankings were not among the features that attracted public controversy when the guidelines were published (von Hirsch, Knapp, and Tonry 1987, chap. 5). One might debate the particular rankings these bodies adopted, but their experience does suggest that a rule-making agency is capable of agreeing on the seriousness ranking of crimes.

Less satisfactory, however, has been the state of the theory. What criteria should be used for gauging crimes' gravity? That question is only beginning to be addressed.

The seriousness of crime has two main elements: the degree of harmfulness of the conduct and the extent of the actor's culpability (von Hirsch 1985, chap. 6). The problem is to develop criteria for harmfulness and culpability that are more illuminating than simple intuition.

If we began with culpability, the substantive criminal law could provide considerable assistance—because its theories of fault have their analogs for sentencing. The substantive criminal law already distinguishes intentional (i.e., purposive, knowing, or reckless) conduct from negligent conduct (see, e.g., Model Penal Code 2.02 [American Law Institute 1962]). For sentencing purposes, however, more attention could be paid to the degree of the actor's purposefulness, knowledge, indifference to consequences, or carelessness. The substantive doctrines of excuse could also be relied on to begin to develop analogies of partial excuse: for example, partial duress and provocation (Wasik 1983; von Hirsch and Jareborg 1987).

With harm, the problem is to compare the harmfulness of criminal acts that invade different interests. How is car theft to be compared with burglary, when the former involves a substantial property loss, and the latter typically involves a smaller financial setback but an invasion of privacy as well? Making such comparisons would seem to require a common criterion for assessing the importance of the interests involved. One criterion that has been suggested is that interests are to be compared in importance according to the degree to which they characteristically affect choice—that is, people's ability to direct the course of their own lives (Feinberg 1984; von Hirsch 1985, chap. 6). Violence and certain economic crimes, on this view, would qualify as particularly harmful because persons who suffer serious bodily injury or are rendered destitute have their choices so drastically curtailed. A choice-based standard, however, seems somewhat artificial: mayhem obviously involves grievous harm, but is that merely because the person's choices have been curtailed? It might seem more natural to assert that the quality of the maimed person's life has been drastically set back. Accordingly, it has recently been suggested (von Hirsch and Jareborg 1991a) that interests should be ranked in importance according to how they typically affect a person's standard of living—understood in Amartya Sen's (1987) broad sense of that term, including noneconomic as well as economic concerns.[7]

5. *Spacing*. Ordinal proportionality includes a spacing requirement. Suppose that crimes X, Y, and Z are of ascending order of seriousness, but that Y is considerably worse than X but only slightly less serious than Z. Then, to reflect the conduct's comparative gravity, there should be a larger space between the penalties for X and Y than for Y and Z. Spacing, however, would depend on how precisely com-

---

[7] This analysis is proposed for crimes such as robbery or burglary that involve natural persons as victims. Crimes affecting societal interests primarily, such as tax evasion, may require a different and more complex treatment (see von Hirsch and Jareborg 1991a, pp. 32–35).

parative gravity can be calibrated, and serious gradations are likely to be matters of inexact judgment (von Hirsch and Jareborg 1991a). In any event, the spacing issue has scarcely been addressed by desert theorists.

Ordinal proportionality thus presents a number of theoretical questions, some of considerable interest and difficulty. None of these issues, however, would prevent a rule maker, using his or her best commonsense judgment, from ranking crimes according to their apparent gravity; deciding what weight is to be given prior offenses; and scaling comparative severities of sanction accordingly (see von Hirsch 1985, pp. 74–76; von Hirsch, Knapp, and Tonry 1987, chap. 5).

B. Scale Anchoring and Cardinal Proportionality

Cardinal proportionality requires that a reasonable proportion be maintained between overall levels of punitiveness and the gravity of the criminal conduct. The scale should not, for example, be so inflated that even lesser criminal conduct is penalized with substantial deprivations.

Since cardinal proportionality places only broad—and imprecise—constraints on how much the penalty scale can be escalated or deflated, substantial leeway remains for locating the scale's anchoring points. What other factors would be relevant?

The penal traditions of the jurisdiction would be a starting point. Since the censure expressed through punishment is a convention, it, like any other convention, will be influenced by tradition. Normative considerations, however, may justify altering this convention. One such consideration is the goal of reducing the suffering visited on offenders (Ashworth 1989; von Hirsch 1990a, pp. 286–88).

Should crime prevention also be considered in setting the anchoring points? Certain preventive strategies would alter the comparative rankings of punishments and thus infringe ordinal proportionality. Selective incapacitation, for example, calls for the unequal punishment of offenders convicted of similar offenses on the basis of predictive criteria that do not reflect the seriousness of the criminal conduct (von Hirsch 1985, chap. 11).

Other preventive strategies, however, would not necessarily be open to this objection. Consider general deterrence. Were the penalties for particular offense categories to be set by reference to those penalties' expected deterrent effects, it would infringe ordinal proportionality, as it would no longer be the seriousness of crimes that determined the ordering of sanctions. Suppose, instead, that deterrence were used differently: penalties might be ordered according to the crimes' seriousness on the scale, with the scale's overall magnitude being decided (in part) by its expected net impact on crime. Were the requisite empirical knowledge available (which it is not today),[8] it might be possible to compare the overall deterrent impacts of alternative scale magnitudes. That information could then be used to help anchor the scale, without disturbing the ordering of penalties. Moreover, this approach would not necessarily lead to increases in severity. Penalties might be cut back below their historical levels, on grounds that no significant loss of deterrence would occur (von Hirsch 1990a, pp. 286–88).

Were deterrence data available, could an optimum solution for setting anchoring points be found? Why not invoke the utilitarian calculus here? The objection to straightforward penal utilitarianism, we saw, is that it can violate proportionality requirements. Here, this would not be so, since utility would be relied on to decide between two alternative possible scales, either of which satisfy ordinal and cardinal proportionality constraints. Why not, then, decide between the two scales by comparing their deterrent yields against their human and financial costs? The answer is that, even here, the aggregative character of the calculus remains troublesome. Suppose that penalty scale A is considerably more severe overall than penalty scale B, that both scales have about the same impact on the more serious crimes, but that scale A is much more efficient than scale B in preventing lesser offenses. When aggregate impacts are considered, scale A might prove to yield higher net utilities. This would mean making convicted offenders suffer considerably more in order to provide modest but widespread benefits to the rest of the citizenry. It is at least debatable whether this should be the preferred result (see von Hirsch 1993, chap. 4).

Where does this leave us in fixing anchoring points? Almost certainly without a unique solution. Crime-prevention (particularly deterrent) concerns may furnish no single answers even if there were the requisite knowledge of the comparative preventive effects of different scales— and that knowledge is largely lacking today. Setting anchoring points will be a matter of judgment—in which concerns about reducing overall penal suffering need to be considered, along with the jurisdiction's penal traditions (see Ashworth 1989).

[8] For the difficulty of making estimates of deterrent impact, see, e.g., Blumstein, Cohen, and Nagin (1978).

A desert-based scheme is necessarily somewhat confining—in its requirement that offense seriousness, and not a variety of possible other considerations, should decide comparative punishments. Its confining character makes it easier to scale penalties in a coherent fashion, but it also limits the possibilities of achieving various other goals or objectives. Moreover, the proportionality principle rests on a particular value—that of equity. Other values of various sorts might be thought to override equity considerations, in at least some situations. Hence, we need to consider the "hybrid" models: those that, to a lesser or greater extent, allow departures from ordinal desert requirements in order to achieve other purposes.

VI. Desert Scaling with Exceptional Departures

In examining hybrid models, Paul Robinson's (1987) offers a good starting point, as it is perhaps the simplest—as well as being the nearest to a desert model. Under Robinson's scheme, penalties ought ordinarily to be scaled according to crimes' seriousness, consistent with the principle of proportionality. Departures from ordinal desert requirements would be permitted, however, in exceptional circumstances—if needed to prevent an "intolerable level of crime." However, Robinson would impose a further limitation on such departures: that even when the prevention of major criminal harm is at issue, gross deviations from proportionality would not be permitted.

How could one argue for such a model? The case in its favor can be stated schematically as follows (Robinson 1987; see also von Hirsch 1987).

First, ordinal proportionality is a requirement of fairness. This fairness constraint ought therefore to restrict the pursuit of crime-prevention policies. If desert may be disregarded routinely for the sake of crime prevention, it is no constraint at all. If desert is an important fairness constraint, moreover, then it should be observed up to the point of a major loss of utility.

Second, desert principles may be overridden, at least to some extent, when such major losses of utility occur. The idea is that fairness requirements may exceptionally be trumped if the stakes are high enough—that the world need not perish so that justice is done. Punishment policy scarcely involves the end of the world, but, Robinson suggests, avoiding a very large increase in seriously harmful conduct may be an important enough goal (assuming one had the requisite knowledge) to warrant at least some sacrifice of fairness. This position differs, nevertheless, from plain penal utilitarianism in that departures from desert requirements could be invoked only exceptionally, when extraordinary losses of prevention would otherwise occur.

Third, beyond a certain point, moreover, the disregard of desert would become unconscionable; hence, Robinson's suggested limitation that gross departures from ordinal desert should not be permitted. Such manifestly disproportionate sanctions would misrepresent wholly the degree of the person's blameworthiness and thus would be inappropriate in a system that purports to hold citizens answerable and subject to censure for their actions.

How much guidance does Robinson's model supply? For most situations, it calls for penalties that are graded to reflect ordinal desert requirements. The escape clauses, however, are couched in general terms: a decision maker may depart from desert exceptionally to avoid an "intolerable" increase in crime, but the departure itself may not visit intolerable injustice on the defendant. What is tolerable is a matter of judgment, and Robinson is not so much offering a criterion as a way of thinking of departures. However, the following two illustrations (von Hirsch 1987) suggest how the model might be applied.

Sweden's new sentencing statute, enacted in 1989, ordinarily bases the sentence on the gravity of the criminal conduct (Swedish Penal Code, chaps. 29 and 30, discussed in von Hirsch and Jareborg [1989b]). However, an exception was made to continue Sweden's policy of jailing, for a period of weeks, drivers who were found with more than a stated (rather substantial) blood alcohol level. From a desert perspective, such a penalty was problematic because many who drink and drive suffer from chronic alcoholism, and their culpability may be diminished. The penalty was imposed, however, as a deterrent. This exception might be arguably sustainable under Robinson's theory because heavy drinking and driving seems so especially hazardous. The amount of deviation from desert, moreover, is not very great: offenders were to receive a short period of confinement in lieu of the somewhat less rigorous noncustodial penalty that the less culpable drinking drivers would otherwise be deemed to deserve.

Selective incapacitation advocates in the United States proposed giving convicted robbers who are classified as high risks lengthy extensions of their prison terms: as much as eight years' imprisonment for allegedly high-risk robbers, as contrasted with as little as one year's confinement for lower-risk robbers (Greenwood 1982). Large preventive benefits have been claimed for such a strategy (Greenwood 1982;

Wilson 1983, chap. 8), although these claims are now in dispute (Blumstein et al. 1986; von Hirsch 1988). Smaller disparities between high-risk and lower-risk robbers would cause the projected preventive effects largely to disappear. Even if such a policy had the preventive effects its advocates claim, however, it would seem questionable under Robinson's model because it would involve routinely imposing a very large penalty increase on grounds wholly ulterior to the seriousness of the conduct. That would seem to constitute the kind of gross infringement of proportionality that is ruled out under the Robinson scheme.

Robinson would restrict departures to the most drastic kind of case—namely, where the conduct involved is not only very harmful to those affected, but a significant incidence of that conduct is also involved. In the Swedish drunk-driving policy, for example, it is not merely the rare victim but many victims that potentially may be affected. This, however, sharply limits the scope of the exception since it is so seldom that sound empirical grounds exist for believing that a departure from desert would reduce the incidence of the conduct involved. While there is some reason to believe that Sweden's policy of penalizing drinking and driving has achieved some preventive impact, it is far from clear that it requires presumptive resort to imprisonment for those with over a stated quantity of blood alcohol (see Ross 1982). It is thus worthy of note that in 1991 the Swedish parliament repealed the presumptive imprisonment exception, so that those who drink and drive are now treated according to general desert principles of the 1989 sentencing law.

If the requirement of traceable aggregate effects presents these difficulties, might it be dropped? Anthony Bottoms and Roger Brownsword (1983) have suggested so, using reasoning somewhat (albeit not entirely) comparable to Robinson's. In Bottoms and Brownsword's view, persons who constitute a "vivid danger" of seriously injuring others could be given a period of extra confinement, even if such a policy has no measurable impact on overall violence levels. However, these authors emphasize that such an exception should be invoked only when there is a high and immediate likelihood of the most serious injury otherwise occurring. "Vivid danger," in other words, must truly be vivid.

The Robinson model has undeniable attractions. While abiding by desert constraints ordinarily, it permits departures where the case for them seems the most plausible. What, then, are the potential problems? Three come to mind.

First, are the stakes high enough? The basic idea is that justice requirements may be overridden when the stakes are high enough. Consider the quarantine of persons with deadly and easily communicable diseases. Quarantined persons surely do not deserve to lose their liberty, for it is not their fault that they have become disease carriers. They lose their liberty, perhaps indefinitely, solely in order to protect the health of others. The reason for tolerating quarantine—despite its unfairness to those confined—is that community survival is considered paramount. Similar considerations are supposed to sustain Robinson's model, but do they? Punishing offenders as much as they deserve might sometimes entail loss of crime prevention, but seldom if ever would it cause harm comparable to epidemic diseases. Moreover, punishment, unlike quarantine, involves blaming. It would be obnoxious to treat quarantined individuals as bad persons who deserved their confinement. David Wood (1988) has thus suggested that the quarantine analogy could support only the civil detention of still-dangerous offenders after completion of their deserved term of punishment.

Second, are the factual inferences reliable enough? If prevention of extraordinary harm is to warrant departing from fairness constraints, there need to be reliable grounds for confidence that the departure is capable of preventing the harm. For quarantine, that confidence may exist, given what is known about certain communicable diseases. But can it exist today in relation to sanctioning policy? How reliable are estimates that an individual, or group of individuals, is likely to commit serious harm that can be prevented by imposing extended sentences? Even if such estimates have some degree of empirical support, it is open to debate whether that support is unequivocal enough for the present purpose.[9] Someone who concurred in principle with Bottoms and Brownsword's idea of extending sentences in cases of "vivid danger" might still doubt our present capacity to assess "vivid danger" (with its requirements of immediacy and high likelihood) with the requisite assurance.

Third, can a narrow departure standard be maintained? Critical to Robinson's model is a narrow departure standard: that desert requirements may be overridden only to prevent the most serious criminal harms. Eroding that standard, so as to admit lesser harms, compromises his whole idea that desert constraints, as important requirements

---

[9] For problems of estimating incapacitative effects, e.g., see von Hirsch (1985, chap. 10; 1988); Blumstein et al. (1986).

of justice, may be disregarded only in exigent circumstances. Yet how realistic is it to be confident (given the political dynamics of crime legislation in most jurisdictions) that narrow departure standards can be maintained? May not a narrow exception be expanded too easily in the name of more efficient crime prevention? Someone might support the Robinson model in theory if its narrow departure limits could be sustained and still be worried about implementing the model because of that "if."

VII. "Range" Models

Robinson's hybrid allows departures from ordinal desert only in exceptional cases. An alternative would be to allow relaxation of ordinal desert constraints more routinely. Desert considerations would be treated as setting an applicable range of punishments, but within that range the penalty could be fixed on consequentialist grounds. There are two different versions of such a model, both having different rationales and different practical implications.

A. "Limiting Retributivism"

This view is identified with the writings of Norval Morris (1982, chap. 5). Desert, according to his suggested model, is to be treated as providing no more than broad ranges of permissible punishment. Within these broad ranges, the "fine tuning" (as he calls it) is to be decided on the basis of other reasons. German penologists have urged a comparable view, termed the "Spielraumtheorie" (e.g., Bruns 1985, pp. 105–9).

In some passages, Morris suggests that his model is required by the logic of desert itself. Desert, he argues, is indeterminate: it suggests only how much is undeserved in the sense of being excessive or manifestly too lenient. Within these bounds, reliance on nondesert grounds is appropriate because the claims of desert have been exhausted (see Morris 1982, pp. 198–99).

The difficulty of this argument has been suggested earlier in Section IV. It overlooks the requirements of ordinal proportionality, particularly, the requirement of parity. When two defendants commit comparably culpable robberies, giving one a larger sentence than the other for the sake of (say) crime prevention visits more blame on one for conduct that is *ex hypothesi* no more reprehensible than that of the other. To say that desert, by its very logical structure, imposes mere limits disregards this demand for parity.

In other passages, Morris seems to concede that desert supplies not only outer bounds but also ordering principles including a parity requirement. This latter requirement, however, is said to be weak and easily overridden: it is no more than a "guiding principle" (1982, pp. 202–5). Parity concerns may thus be trumped by competing values—some preventive (deterrence, incapacitation) and some humanitarian (reduction of penal suffering). This version seems somewhat more credible, but it still does not address the commonly held intuition that there is something important—not just marginal—about punishing similarly those who have committed comparably serious offenses.

Abandoning or watering down comparative desert requirements also leaves little guidance on how the only remaining desert constraints—Morris's supposed desert limits—are to be ascertained. Not surprisingly, neither Morris nor the German advocates of the "Spielraumtheorie" have been able to suggest, even in principle, how those limits might be located (see von Hirsch 1985, chap. 12; Schünemann 1987; von Hirsch and Jareborg 1991*b*). It is thus unclear whether "limiting retributivism" would make desert or crime prevention the principal determinant of the sentence.

B. *"Range" Models Recast as a Hybrid*

There is, however, another way of conceptualizing a "range" model: one that would make it explicitly a hybrid theory. This version concedes that ordinal proportionality does require comparably severe punishments for comparably reprehensible conduct—that unequal punishment involves a sacrifice of equity. The extent of that sacrifice, however, depends on how great the inequality is. Why not, then, allow preventive (or other consequentialist) considerations to override desert, but only within specified, fairly modest limits? Variations in punishment for a given offense would be countenanced, provided the specified limits were not exceeded. The idea is to permit the pursuit of those objectives without "too much" unfairness (von Hirsch 1987).

This model differs from Morris's "limiting retributivism" in that it requires closer scrutiny of inequalities in punishment. Since parity is regarded as an important constraint, not just one of marginal significance, it matters how much deviation from parity is involved—and how strong the ulterior reasons are. Only fairly modest deviations, to achieve fairly pressing other objectives, would be permissible.

Under such a model, two major questions arise. The first concerns specifying the limits: how much variation from parity is to be permitted? The second is the identification of the ulterior ends: for what goal (crime prevention or what else) should such variations be warranted?

1. *Specifying the Limits.*   One objection to "limiting retributivism," just noted, has been the difficulty of delineating the applicable desert limits. On the alternative model of an explicit hybrid, the fixing of limits becomes conceptually easier. A specified degree of deviation from ordinal desert constraints is simply set as the applicable limit. Since the governing idea is that there should be only modest derogations of ordinal desert, those limits would have to be reasonably constrained. Perhaps a 15–20 percent deviation might be permissible, but not a 50–60 percent one. In such a model, the gravity of the criminal conduct would thus substantially shape (albeit not fully determine) the gradation of punishment severity. Penalties might be classified into several bands according to their degree of onerousness. Substitutions would be permitted within a band—even if the penalties differ somewhat in punitive bite—but would be restricted among different bands involving substantially differing severities. Thus, short prison terms and home detention might be substituted for one another as both are fairly onerous (albeit not necessarily of equal severity), but such prison terms could not be interchanged with lesser financial penalties because the disparity in punitiveness would be too large (von Hirsch 1991*a*).

2. *Identifying the Ulterior Ends.*   For what purpose should such moderate deviations from ordinal desert be allowed? In the literature to date, the end usually mentioned is that of crime control, particularly, incapacitation (compare Morris and Miller [1985] with von Hirsch [1988]). Applying this to the hybrid would permit reliance on offender risk, provided the applicable limits on deviation from ordinal desert were not exceeded. The end, then, is enhanced crime prevention.

This strategy encounters, however, a fairness-effectiveness dilemma. A substantial incapacitative effect is achievable only when the sentence differential between low- and high-risk individuals is large (see, e.g., von Hirsch 1988). Large differentials, however, mean infringing ordinal desert constraints to a great degree—and not the limited degree that the model contemplates. Keeping the differentials modest, moreover, means restricted preventive benefits. That, in turn, raises a further question. If ordinal proportionality is a demand of fairness, even limited deviations become justifiable only by a showing of strong countervailing reasons. It is questionable whether merely modest preventive benefits could qualify as such strong reasons.

Another possible ulterior end is "parsimony," that is, reduction in severity of punishments. Advocates of "limiting retributivism" claim that relaxing desert constraints permits milder sanctions (Morris and Tonry 1990, pp. 104–8). Suppose that penalties are scaled on a desert model and that the prescribed penalty for a given, fairly serious offense is X months' imprisonment. Suppose one were to allow a 20 percent penalty reduction for nondangerous offenders. Then, some high-risk offenders will receive X months, and the remainder only 80 percent of that period. Has not a penalty reduction been achieved?

The alternative, however, is to reset the anchoring points of the scale so as to reduce the prescribed penalty for the crime by 20 percent and to reduce the penalties for other offenses correspondingly.[10] Then, proportionality is not sacrificed. Moreover, parsimony is better achieved—because all, not just some, of those convicted of the crime get the benefit of lesser penalties. So why cannot parsimony be sought while adhering to, rather than departing from, desert principles? One possible response is that across-the-board reductions would increase the risk to the public—because even the higher-risk individuals will have shorter periods of confinement. This, however, would reduce the departure rationale to the just-discussed one of crime prevention.

Alternatively, political considerations might be invoked: rule makers in most jurisdictions, it is argued, may be more willing to accept penalty reductions for nondangerous offenders than across-the-board reductions. If politics are to be taken into account, however, is it realistic to expect the deviations to be in a downward direction? The demand is likely to be not merely for less punishment for the low risks, but also added punishments for the supposed high risks. Then, the question becomes "parsimony for whom?" Some offenders may well receive significantly more punishment than they would have had parity been observed (see von Hirsch 1984, pp. 1105–7). Political claims are also not easy to generalize. If such a strategy ever can lead to reduced punishments, it will only be in a particular jurisdiction where the political constellation happens to be propitious.

What other reasons might there be for deviating from desert constraints? One might be to facilitate the scaling of noncustodial penalties. Under a desert rationale, substitution among sanctions is permitted only where the penalties are about equally onerous. In order to give day-fines to some offenders convicted of a given intermediate-level offense, and probation to others, the penalties must have equivalent

---

[10] This assumes that the initial, desert-based penalties have not been set so low that further pro rata reductions would infringe cardinal proportionality.

penal bite, and this condition is not so easy to satisfy. Relaxing desert constraints a bit would allow these substitutions to be made more easily. It might also make it somewhat easier to devise back-up sanctions for offenders who violate the terms of their punishments (e.g., refuse to pay their fines). (For problems of devising back-up sanctions on a desert rationale, see von Hirsch, Wasik, and Greene [1989].) This approach may have the attraction of requiring only quite modest departures.

VIII. Conclusion

This essay has examined the principle of proportionality and its rationale, drawing on recent philosophical writing. Particular attention has been paid to the "expressive" account of proportionality, according to which penalties should, in fairness, be distributed depending on their blaming implications.

Three models for scaling punishments have also been sketched (Secs. V–VII). Each gives the principle of proportionality a central role in structuring penalties, and they differ from one another in whether, and to what degree, departures from ordinal proportionality are permitted to achieve other ends.

Are these the only possible sanctioning models? Of course not. Were the role of proportionality reduced, alternate schemes could be constructed, giving prominence to other aims—most notably, crime control. Such schemes, moreover, may differ from one another, depending on which preventive strategy is invoked. A deterrence-based model would produce a different array of penalties than one emphasizing restraint of potential recidivists (cf. Posner [1977, chap. 7] with Wilson [1983, chap. 8]).

Any such larger shift away from proportionality, however, would raise problems of justice. Proportionality is (if the arguments discussed in this essay are believed) an important requirement of fairness. If so, reducing its role in the determination of penalties would make the resulting scheme less just. To sustain such a scheme, it would be necessary to contend that proportionality is a less important fairness demand than has here been suggested; or that its criteria are weaker; or that other aims, such as crime prevention, are ethically paramount. Such questions relate, ultimately, to what values are to be upheld.

There is also the question of the degree of guidance a theory provides for the scaling of penalties. The proportionality principle, we have seen, offers no unique solutions, particularly because of the leeway it allows in the setting of a scale's anchoring points. However, the principle does offer considerable structure (although not unique solutions) for the comparative ordering of penalties. If proportionality is dislodged from this central, organizing role, it may not be easy to develop alternative (e.g., prevention-based) rationales that can provide much guidance.[11] While a considerable body of theory exists concerning the principle of proportionality, lacunae remain. More thought needs to be given to the following topics, among others.

The Criteria for Gauging the Seriousness of Crimes, Particularly the Harm Dimension of Seriousness. A "living-standard" conception of harm (see Sec. V) may be a start, but it requires further scrutiny and elaboration.

Spacing. Proportionality calls not only for penalties ranked according to the gravity of crimes but also for spacing among penalties that reflects degrees of difference in crime seriousness. The spacing question, however, has received little attention.

Anchoring the Scale. If penalties are graded according to offense seriousness and the scale as a whole is not inflated or deflated unduly, the requirements of ordinal and cardinal proportionality have been satisfied, and one must look elsewhere for grounds for anchoring the scale. What these grounds might be remains largely to be explored.

There are also a number of practical issues needing further thought. One concerns back-up sanctions. Under any punishment theory emphasizing proportionality, noncustodial sanctions (rather than the severe penalty of imprisonment) should be employed for crimes other than serious ones (von Hirsch, Wasik, and Greene 1989). Using such sanctions raises the question of what should befall defendants if they violate the terms of the penalty—for example, if they refuse to pay a fine or complete a stint of community service. How much added punitive bite may the back-up sanction legitimately entail?[12]

---

[11] One such alternative might be Posner's utilitarian, deterrence-based scheme (see Sec. II). This purports to provide optimum sentence levels, once punishment costs and deterrent benefits are known. Aside from any ethical objections, the requisite empirical information about the magnitude of deterrent effects is largely lacking. See n. 8 above. Another might be Norval Morris's "limiting retributivism." Morris and Miller (1985) have suggested relying on offender risk, within broad desert limits. However, these proposed desert limits are indeterminate. Morris has offered no account of how wide or narrow the desert limits should be, or of what principles should be employed for setting them. (See discussion in Sec. VII and also von Hirsch [1985, chap. 12]). Without a rationale for fixing the limits, it is not clear whether such "limiting retributivism" would make desert or predictions the main determinant of the sentence.

[12] It has been suggested (von Hirsch, Wasik, and Greene [1989, pp. 609–10]) that incarceration would ordinarily be disproportionately severe as a back-up penalty and that only a moderate increase in severity would be appropriate. The topic, however, requires further exploration.

The principle of proportionality continues to attract the attention of legal philosophers as well as penologists. Thus, some of these unresolved issues may well receive more scrutiny. Whether they can satisfactorily be resolved remains to be seen.

REFERENCES

American Law Institute. 1962. *Model Penal Code*. Proposed official draft. Philadelphia: American Law Institute.

Andenaes, Johannes. 1974. *Punishment and Deterrence*. Ann Arbor: University of Michigan Press.

————. 1988. "Nyklassisisme, proporsjonalitet och prevensjon." *Nordisk tidsskrift for kriminalvidenskab* 75:41–48.

Ashworth, Andrew. 1989. "Criminal Justice and Deserved Sentences." *Criminal Law Review*, 1989, pp. 340–55.

Bedau, Hugo A. 1978. "Retribution and the Theory of Punishment." *Journal of Philosophy* 75:601–20.

————. 1984. "Classification-based Sentencing: Some Conceptual and Ethical Problems." *New England Journal of Criminal and Civil Confinement* 10:1–26.

Bentham, Jeremy. 1982. *An Introduction to the Principles of Morals and Legislation*, edited by J. H. Burns and H. L. A. Hart. London: Methuen. (Originally published 1780.)

Blumstein, Alfred, Jacqueline Cohen, and Daniel Nagin, eds. 1978. *Deterrence and Incapacitation: Estimating the Effects of Criminal Sanctions on Crime Rates*. National Research Council, Assembly of Behavioral and Social Sciences, Committee on Research on Law Enforcement and Criminal Justice, Panel on Research on Deterrent and Incapacitative Effects. Washington, D.C.: National Academy Press.

Blumstein, A., J. Cohen, J. A. Roth, and C. A. Visher, eds. 1986. *Criminal Careers and "Career Criminals."* Washington, D.C.: National Academy Press.

Bottoms, Anthony E., and Roger Brownsword. 1983. "Dangerousness and Rights." In *Dangerousness: Problems of Assessment and Prediction*, edited by John W. Hinton. London: Allen & Unwin.

Braithwaite, John, and Phillip Pettit. 1990. *Not Just Deserts: A Republican Theory of Criminal Justice*. Oxford: Clarendon.

Bruns, Hans-Jürgen. 1985. *Das Recht der Strafzumessung*, 2d ed. Cologne: Carl Heymanns.

Byrd, A. Sharon. 1989. "Kant's Theory of Punishment: Deterrence in Its Threat, Retribution in Its Execution." *Law and Philosophy* 8:151–200.

Davis, Michael. 1983. "How to Make the Punishment Fit the Crime." *Ethics* 93:726–52.

Duff, R. A. 1986. *Trials and Punishments*. Cambridge: Cambridge University Press.

Ewing, A. C. 1970. *The Morality of Punishment*. Montclair, N.J.: Patterson Smith. (Originally published 1929.)

Feinberg, Joel. 1970. *Doing and Deserving: Essays in the Theory of Responsibility.* Princeton, N.J.: Princeton University Press.

———. 1984. *Harm to Others.* New York: Oxford University Press.

Finnis, John. 1980. *Natural Law and Natural Rights.* Oxford: Clarendon.

Fletcher, George. 1978. *Rethinking Criminal Law.* Boston: Little, Brown.

Gewirth, Alan. 1978. *Reason and Morality.* Chicago: University of Chicago Press.

Greenwood, Peter W. 1982. *Selective Incapacitation.* Santa Monica, Calif.: RAND.

Hart, H. L. A. 1968. *Punishment and Responsibility.* New York: Oxford University Press.

Jareborg, Nils. 1988. *Essays in Criminal Law.* Uppsala: Iustus.

Kant, Immanuel. 1964. *Groundwork of the Metaphysics of Morals,* translated by H. J. Paton. New York: Harper Torchbooks. (Originally published 1797.)

Mackie, J. L. 1977. *Ethics: Inventing Right and Wrong.* Harmondsworth: Penguin.

Mäkelä, Klaus. 1975. "Om straffens verkningar." *Jurisprudentia* 6:237–80.

Morris, Herbert. 1968. "Persons and Punishment." *Monist* 52:475–501.

———. 1981. "A Paternalistic Theory of Punishment." *American Philosophical Quarterly* 18:263–71.

Morris, Norval. 1982. *Madness and the Criminal Law.* Chicago: University of Chicago Press.

Morris, Norval, and Marc Miller. 1985. "Predictions of Dangerousness." In *Crime and Justice: An Annual Review of Research,* vol. 6, edited by Michael Tonry and Norval Morris. Chicago: University of Chicago Press.

Morris, Norval, and Michael Tonry. 1990. *Between Prison and Probation: Intermediate Punishments in a Rational Sentencing System.* New York: Oxford University Press.

Murphy, Jeffrie G. 1973. "Marxism and Retribution." *Philosophy and Public Affairs* 2:217–43.

———. 1985. "Retributivism, Moral Education and the Liberal State." *Criminal Justice Ethics* 4:3–10.

Pincoffs, Edmund L. 1966. *The Rationale of Legal Punishment.* New York: Humanities Press.

Posner, Richard A. 1977. *Economic Analysis of Law.* Boston: Little, Brown.

Rawls, John. 1955. "Two Concepts of Rules." *Philosophical Review* 64:3–32.

Robinson, Paul. 1987. "Hybrid Principles for the Distribution of Criminal Sanctions." *Northwestern Law Review* 82:19–42.

Ross, A. Laurence. 1982. *Deterring the Drinking Driver: Legal Policy and Social Control.* Lexington, Mass.: Lexington Books.

Roxin, Claus. 1979. "Zur Jüngsten Diskussion ber Schuld, Prevention und Verantwortlichkeit im Strafrecht." In *Festschrift für Paul Bockelmann,* edited by Arthur Kaufmann, Günter Bemmann, Detlev Krauss, and Klaus Volk. Munich: C. H. Beck.

Sadurski, Wojciech. 1985. *Giving Desert Its Due.* Dordrecht: Riedel.

Scheid, Don E. 1983. "Kant's Retributivism." *Ethics* 93:262–82.

————. 1990. "Davis and the Unfair-Advantage Theory of Punishment: A Critique." *Philosophical Topics* 18:143–70.

Schumann, Karl. 1987. *Positive Generalprävention*. Heidelberg: C. F. Müller Juristischer Verlag.

Schünemann, Bernd. 1987. "Plädoyer für eine neue Theorie der Strafzumessung." In *Neuere Tendenzen der Kriminalpolitik*, edited by Albin Eser and Karin Cornils. Freiburg: Max-Planck Institut.

Sen, Amartya. 1987. *The Standard of Living*. Cambridge: Cambridge University Press.

Sher, George. 1987. *Desert*. Princeton, N.J.: Princeton University Press.

Singer, Richard G. 1979. *Just Deserts: Sentencing Based on Equality and Desert*. Cambridge, Mass.: Ballinger.

Smart, J. J. C., and Bernard Williams. 1973. *Utilitarianism: For and Against*. Cambridge: Cambridge University Press.

von Hirsch, Andrew. 1984. "Equality, 'Anisonomy,' and Justice: A Review of 'Madness and the Criminal Law.'" *Michigan Law Review* 82:1093–1112.

————. 1985. *Past or Future Crimes: Deservedness and Dangerousness in the Sentencing of Criminals*. New Brunswick, N.J.: Rutgers University Press.

————. 1987. "Hybrid Principles in Allocating Sanctions: A Reply to Professor Robinson." *Northwestern Law Review* 82:64–72.

————. 1988. "Selective Incapacitation Reexamined: The National Academy of Sciences Report on Criminal Careers and 'Career Criminals.'" *Criminal Justice Ethics* 7(1):19–35.

————. 1990a. "Proportionality in the Philosophy of Punishment: From 'Why Punish?' to 'How Much?'" *Criminal Law Forum* 1:259–90.

————. 1990b. "The Politics of 'Just Deserts.'" *Canadian Journal of Criminology* 32:397–413.

————. 1991a. "Scaling Intermediate Punishments: A Comparison of Two Models." In *Smart Sentencing: Expanding Options for Intermediate Sanctions*, edited by James M. Byrne, Arthur J. Lurigio, and Joan Petersilia. Newbury Park, Calif.: Sage.

————. 1991b. "Criminal Record Rides Again." *Criminal Justice Ethics*, 11(1):2, 55–56.

————. 1993. *Censure and Sanctions*. Oxford: Oxford University Press (forthcoming).

von Hirsch, Andrew, and Andrew Ashworth. 1992. "Not Not Just Deserts: A Response to Braithwaite and Pettit." *Oxford Journal of Legal Studies*, 12:83–98.

von Hirsch, Andrew, and Nils Jareborg. 1987. "Provocation and Culpability." In *Responsibility, Character, and the Emotions: New Essays in Moral Psychology*, edited by Ferdinand F. Schoeman. Cambridge: Cambridge University Press.

————. 1989a. "Straff och proportionalitet—replik." *Nordisk tidskrift for kriminalvidenskab* 76:56–63.

————. 1989b. "Sweden's Sentencing Statute Enacted." *Criminal Law Review*, 1989, pp. 275–81.

————. 1991a. "Gauging Criminal Harm: A Living-Standard Analysis." *Oxford Journal of Legal Studies* 11:1–38.

————. 1991*b*. *Strafmass and Strafgerechtigkeit: Die deutsche Strafzumessungslehre und das Prinzip der Tatproportionalität*. Bad Godesberg: Forum Verlag.

von Hirsch, Andrew, Kay A. Knapp, and Michael Tonry. 1987. *The Sentencing Commission and Its Guidelines*. Boston: Northeastern University Press.

von Hirsch, Andrew, Martin Wasik, and Judith A. Greene. 1989. "Punishments in the Community and the Principles of Desert." *Rutgers Law Review* 20:595–618.

Walker, Nigel. 1991. *Why Punish?* Oxford: Oxford University Press.

Wasik, Martin. 1983. "Excuses at the Sentencing Stage." *Criminal Law Review*, 1983, pp. 450–65.

————. 1987. "Guidance, Guidelines and Criminal Record." In *Sentencing Reform: Guidance or Guidelines?*, edited by Martin Wasik and Ken Pease. Manchester: Manchester University Press.

Wasik, Martin, and Richard D. Taylor. 1991. *Blackstone's Guide to the Criminal Justice Act of 1991*. London: Blackstone.

Wasserstrom, Richard. 1980. *Philosophy and Special Issues: Five Studies*. South Bend, Ind.: University of Notre Dame Press.

Wilson, James Q. 1983. *Thinking about Crime*. Rev. ed. New York: Basic.

Wood, David. 1988. "Dangerous Offenders and the Morality of Protective Sentencing." *Criminal Law Review*, 1988, pp. 424–33.

Wootton, Barbara. 1963. *Crime and the Criminal Law*. London: Sweet & Maxwell.

Julian V. Roberts

Public Opinion, Crime, and Criminal Justice

ABSTRACT

Research on public knowledge has found that the public knows little about crime or the criminal justice system including crime-related statistics such as crime rates, recidivism rates, and average sentences. Members of the public have little familiarity with specific laws or with their legal rights. Although some research shows that most people favor the imposition of harsher sentences on convicted offenders, more refined research reveals that the public is not more punitive than the judiciary. Research on crime seriousness reveals substantial consensus between different groups and over time. Policymakers and criminal justice professionals believe attitudes to be harsher than they are. A priority for the criminal justice system is to dispel misperceptions of crime held by the public and misperceptions of public attitudes held by professionals and policymakers.

Crime—and the criminal justice system's response to crime—has long fascinated the public. In the past, this interest focused on the spectacle of punishments, both corporal and capital. Now that the penal system has forsworn the former, and confined the latter within prison walls, the public turns to the news media. Stories relating to criminal justice are never far from the front pages and from the collective consciousness. Many of the most-debated public questions of recent years derive from the criminal justice system. Was the fine of $100 million (approximately twenty-five days of profit for the company) levied against the owners of the Exxon Valdez sufficient punishment for polluting the

Julian V. Roberts is professor in the Department of Criminology at the University of Ottawa. I would like to acknowledge financial assistance of the Solicitor General of Canada's sustaining grant to the Department of Criminology at the University of Ottawa.

Alaska shoreline? Should the news media be allowed to attend executions? Should mass murderer Clifford Olson have received payments from the criminal justice system of $100,000 per victim to reveal where he had buried bodies? How could the "Guildford Four" and other innocent people have spent years in prison for crimes they never committed? Was John Hinckley really insane when he attempted to assassinate the President? To what extent are company executives responsible for *The Herald of Free Enterprise*, a ferry that capsized with great loss of life? Should Canada, a country without the death penalty, permit the extradition of murderers to the United States where, if convicted, they stand a good chance of being executed? Should juveniles convicted of murder be liable to the death penalty? Would more rigorous gun control legislation have prevented the massacre of women in Montreal in 1989? Was Bernard Goetz a law-abiding citizen provoked beyond reason, or a cold-blooded assassin? How much more than $100 million dollars should Ivan Boesky have paid in fines as a result of his conviction for insider trading? Was the assault on Rodney King by officers of the Los Angeles Police Department an isolated case of police brutality or does it happen all the time? Did Leona Helmsley get off easily? These and many other questions of relevance to crime and justice provoke discussions across our nations.

Researchers, too, have their questions. How well do members of the public understand crime and the criminal justice system? What kinds of opinions do the public hold about such critical issues as crime prevention, sentencing, and parole? Are the courts more lenient than the public? Is the criminal justice system affected by public opinion? Such questions have increasingly attracted the attention of criminologists since the inception of systematic opinion polls. Over the past thirty years there has been a surge of research and writing on this issue; one reason is the relationship between public opinion and criminal justice policy.

The past decade has witnessed significant increases in the prison populations of the United States and the United Kingdom. The incarceration rates of most American states more than doubled over this period. Both explicitly and implicitly, the rationale for this increase in prison population has been the ubiquitous perception that the public favors more vigorous law enforcement and more punitive sentencing. Few politicians can resist an appeal to "law-and-order" policies. In the last U.S. presidential election, advertisements for candidate Bush played on this theme, bringing attention to crimes committed by a furloughed felon in the opposing candidate's state of Massachusetts. The advertisements, and in the final analysis, the results of the election, suggest both that candidate Bush's public relations staff believed that the public would respond to such appeals and that they were right to hold such a belief. Thus a poll conducted in 1974 (Hindelang et al. 1976, table 2.95) found that four out of five respondents said that they would vote for a political candidate who advocated harsher sentencing. In jurisdiction after jurisdiction, judges claim to be responding to public sentiment when they impose harsher sentences than they otherwise might; legislators calling for more severe penalties, the passage of mandatory sentencing laws, and more restrictive parole release often claim to be responding to a public demand for a criminal justice system with more "bite."

The beliefs of public officials about public preferences for criminal justice policies affect political campaigns, decisions in individual cases, and criminal justice policy. Politicians' beliefs about the nature of public opinion probably derive from three sources: shared conventional wisdom, the perception of an association between electoral success and support for repressive criminal justice policies, and the publication of survey findings that seem to demonstrate public support for harsher sentencing.

It is clear then that public officials' beliefs about public opinion influence criminal justice policy. What is less clear is whether these officials are correctly interpreting opinion surveys regarding criminal justice issues. Conventional wisdom about public opinion is in some areas incorrect and, in other areas, while not incorrect, may be misleading because of problems concerning the ways in which public opinion surveys are conducted. An example of conventional wisdom that is incorrect is the widely held view that the public favor harsher sentences than those currently imposed. Evidence is accumulating from a variety of sources that suggests that the public (in the United States and elsewhere) is less punitive than the polls would suggest. Part of the problem is that the public generally believes that the sentences imposed are less severe than they in fact are.

A second problem affects officials' reliance on surveys of the public. Most opinion polls must of necessity use simple questions that invite— in fact may compel—simple answers. For example, if the general public, wrongly believing that sentences are less severe than they are, is asked whether sentencing is "too harsh, about right, or too lenient," the response by a substantial margin is "sentences are too lenient." In a variation on this problem, other opinion research shows that people often respond to questions about crime and crime control on the basis of stereotypes of "typical offenders." Unfortunately, these stereotypes (often involving violent offenders or even murderers) are often invoked when respondents answer questions pertaining to *all* offenders, including minor property offenders. Emphatic public rejection of the use of house arrest for "offenders," when people are thinking of violent offenders, does not imply that house arrest would be rejected for property offenders. Yet a poll finding that a large percentage of respondents do not favor house arrest may not distinguish between the kinds of offenders to whom this penalty would apply.

Pollsters have explored an ever-growing diversity of topics of relevance to the criminal justice system. This work reflects the recognition that policymakers need to be aware of public knowledge of, and attitudes toward, crime and criminal justice. Many states now conduct regular surveys of public opinion on criminal justice (e.g., Ohio—see Knowles 1979, 1980, 1982, 1984, 1987; Colorado—see Mande and Butler 1982; Mande and English 1989). Opinion polls are cited by legislators as evidence of public approval of their policies, by criminal justice professionals who seek to protect aspects of the system against calls for change, by the news media, and by many advocacy groups.

This essay provides a general introduction to polling and academic research on public opinion concerning criminal justice. Historical analyses are presented, where appropriate, but the emphasis is on recent research. For reviews of earlier work, see Sarat (1977) and Stinchcombe et al. (1980). Before reviewing research on public attitudes toward crime and criminal justice, I discuss the methods that have been used to measure public attitudes and touch on some of the problems and caveats that should be borne in mind when examining the research findings.

A discussion of all the salient polls and research would consume a monograph rather than an essay. Accordingly, some restrictions have been adopted. First, only polls or research conducted in North America, Great Britain, or Australia are reviewed. The emphasis is on North American research.[1] Second, the essay does not systematically explore cross-cultural comparisons of public opinion, although several

[1] For research pertaining to other jurisdictions see, e.g., Mäkelä (1966) (Finland); Podgorecki et al. (1973) (Scandinavia); van Dijk (1980) (Holland); Sebba (1983) (Israel); Ocqueteau and Perez-Diaz (1990*a*, 1990*b*) (France); Zimmerman et al. (1991) (Switzerland).

of these are also available (e.g., Lenke 1974). Third, issues dealing with juvenile justice have been omitted. Finally, the extensive literature on public fear of crime is not addressed here; it alone could sustain a separate essay (for recent findings, see Margarita and Parisi [1979]; Stinchcombe et al. [1980]; Research and Forecasts, Inc. [1983] [*The Figgie Reports*]; Lewis and Salem [1986]).

Section I of this essay provides an overview of the methods and methodological problems encountered in the area. The principal method of investigating public opinion data has been to survey a representative sample of respondents, but other strategies have also been employed, including focus groups and experimental designs with convenience samples of the public. The problems regarding much polling work include limited public knowledge of the criminal justice system, biased news media coverage of crime and justice, cognitive biases apparent in most laypersons, and specific problems with the surveys themselves. Section II discusses public attitudes toward crimes, offenders, and victims of crime. This section deals with the much-researched issue of crime seriousness. Section III examines public attitudes toward the criminal justice system. I discuss in particular the topic that is most often examined: sentencing, including the critical issue of whether the public is harsher than the courts. Section IV presents some suggestions for research in the area and a conclusion. A primary suggestion is that a dynamic data base be created to facilitate research and interpretation. At present, there is no single repository for public opinion data from around the world. A second recommendation is that researchers explore public reactions to crime that do not consist largely of punishment. Most pollsters provide respondents with a list of crimes and then ask them which punishment, or how many years imprisonment, is appropriate for each crime. The criminal justice systems in the countries surveyed now employ a variety of responses to offenders that do not involve simply determining the quantum of punishment. This reality should be reflected in future surveys of the public.

I. Methods and Methodological Problems

The methods researchers use are not perfect, and the public knows little about criminal justice; much of what it knows reflects an unrealistically negative perception of the criminal justice system, which in turn results in part from the ways the mass media cover crime issues. A comprehensive picture of public knowledge and opinion in the area of criminal justice can only be obtained by a multimethod approach. Representative opinion polls are necessary to set the approximate bounds on public attitudes and in order to identify issues requiring greater public education. Focus groups are needed in order to evaluate the depth of a particular opinion, and laboratory-based research is essential to test experimental hypotheses.

A. Methods

Research on public opinion falls into one of three principal methodological categories: quantitative analyses involving representative samples of the public; qualitative analyses deriving from small "focus groups"; studies employing nonrepresentative samples, usually college students. Attitudes and opinions have been measured or explored in other ways (e.g., Sarat 1977; Shoemaker and South 1978; Webb et al. 1981), but these alternate measures account for few studies in the area.

1. *Representative Surveys.*   Surveys of representative samples of the public account for most contemporary research (see Durham [1990] for a discussion of earlier polling work). Surveys are typically conducted by major polling companies (e.g., Louis Harris, Gallup) either as an independent survey for a specific client or as part of monthly or annual surveys; recently there has been an increase in the number of polls conducted by university-based polling centers. Both telephone and in-person interviews have been used, although researchers prefer mail surveys, as they cost less and result in comparable accuracy (Klecka and Tuchfarber 1978; Quinn, Gutek, and Walsh 1980).

National and statewide surveys use a probability sampling procedure that ensures a final sample that conforms to the characteristics of the population from which it was drawn. This entails oversampling respondents in certain categories that would be underrepresented by a simple "sweep" survey in which interviews are conducted with whoever happens to be at home when the interviewer calls. Different polling companies employ different sample sizes. The critical issue common to all is sampling error, which refers to divergences between results obtained from the sample and results that would have been obtained had a census of the entire population been conducted.

Consider a poll using a sample of 1,000 that finds 33 percent respondents in favor of abolition of parole. This means that the actual percentage of the population (from which the sample was drawn) that favors parole abolition lies somewhere between 29 and 37 percent, although 33 percent is more likely to be correct than a statistic located at the extremes. For most criminal justice issues, this degree of precision is probably adequate; whether the percentage favoring parole abolition is 30 percent or 34 percent is not a critical difference. In this respect, polls are a more useful tool to criminologists than to political scientists, who require greater precision. After all, a 5 percent difference in voting patterns can, when converted to parliamentary seats, mean a change in government.

In recent years the representative survey has evolved in some interesting ways, principally to incorporate the advantages of small-scale surveys. The general idea is to increase (and sometimes manipulate) the amount of information and the manner in which that information is conveyed. Two techniques in particular have proved fruitful. One is known as the factorial survey and was pioneered by Rossi and his colleagues (see Rossi and Anderson 1982; Rossi and Nock 1982; Rossi, Simpson, and Miller 1985). This technique permits researchers to explore the independent (and interactive) effects of several variables simultaneously. The simultaneous manipulation of multiple independent variables would typically be reserved for factorial experiments conducted in a laboratory using college students as subjects. In a factorial survey, computer-generated vignettes are presented to a large number of subjects in a way that ensures the statistical properties of a randomized factorial experiment. For example, Rossi, Simpson, and Miller (1985) explored the effects of several offense and offender characteristics on ratings of crime seriousness and punishment severity. Using this technique, researchers can see how different crimes (and different offender characteristics) affect judgments of the appropriate penalty in the case. The benefits of a factorial survey are clear: the design permits the researcher to run complex experiments with large numbers of subjects; the technique has become increasingly popular (e.g., Miller, Rossi, and Simpson 1986; Roberts and White 1986; Thurman 1989).

A second innovation is known as computer-assisted telephone interviewing (CATI). This is a computerized opinion poll that has several advantages in terms of cost saving and efficiency, but it also permits greater flexibility in the nature of the questions posed. Specifically, CATI permits the researcher to manipulate variables such as the wording of the question or the nature of the information that precedes the question. For example, in a survey about capital punishment, half the respondents may be given a small amount of information about the case, while the other half would be given a more complete account of the case. Both groups would then be asked to respond to the same dependent variable (e.g., "Is the death penalty appropriate in this case?"). This means that a randomized experiment is possible, using a representative survey of respondents. Of course, the technique can also go much further than this. The computer can easily provide further information to respondents, the exact nature of the information being contingent on the respondent's response to the preliminary question. Innovations of this kind will have considerable application in criminal justice, where, to date, polls have employed more traditional techniques (see Cantril [1980] and Bradburn and Sudman [1988] for further information).

2. *Focus Groups.* This kind of study is a relatively recent innovation in public opinion research, although the idea of intensive discussion, or "focused interviews," goes back many years (see Merton [1987] and Krueger [1988] for discussions of the historical antecedents of focus groups). The concept was bred from the dissatisfaction (see Bertrand 1982; Himmelfarb 1990) with polls in which the interviewer poses questions that require answers within seconds, usually entailing a simple choice among a small number of alternatives. Focus groups generate an environment in which respondents have the opportunity to reflect on the question posed, and can then discuss their reflections with other participants. These groups are designed to go beyond the reflexive (but far from reflective) responses elicited by surveys posing simplistic questions such as, "Are you in favor of, or opposed to, the use of the death penalty?"

Generally speaking, focus group studies consist of small groups (usually ten to fifteen) selected to represent (to the extent that this is possible with so small a number) major demographic categories. Several groups are conducted in different cities, with an attempt made at the end to synthesize the findings. In short, focus groups are a kind of public opinion jury, in which the task is not to render a verdict (in this case a single unanimous opinion) but to generate qualitative material that is recorded and later summarized for publication. Unlike juries, there is usually a moderator present who directs the discussion and who, in some cases, is responsible for introducing material to which group discussants are asked to respond. The focus group approach has become popular in North America; reports of recent studies employing this approach can be found in Doble (1987), Doble and Klein (1989), and Environics Research Group (1989*a*).

What exactly do focus groups contribute to the standard public opinion poll? They clearly generate information that cannot be derived from an opinion survey, but how far should such qualitative data be trusted, and to what extent are they a reflection of public opinion rather than the views of a particular moderator (or of the person who happens to summarize the group's discussion for publication)? Some empirical research into the way in which focus groups are conducted, with direct comparisons with other methodologies, would be informative; unfortunately, none appears to be available at the present.

At the very least, focus groups offer researchers an opportunity to explore the phenomenology of responses to questions posed on large-scale surveys. Thus a focus group discussion of the death penalty would quickly discover that many proponents of capital punishment have specific offenders in mind and are prepared to rule out capital punishment for many other offense/offender combinations. Focus groups also provide an opportunity to test the strength of attitudes by providing discussants with relevant information, counterarguments, and so on. This function of a focus group was explored with considerable success in recent analyses of public attitudes toward punishing offenders in Alabama (Doble and Klein 1989) and Delaware (Doble, Immerwahr, and Richardson 1991). Focus group participants were asked to sentence 23 offenders described in vignettes. At a later point the moderators provided information about alternative dispositions and asked discussants to resentence the offenders. The sentencing preferences of the group shifted significantly once they were made aware of the alternative sanctions. This kind of technique is not feasible in a large-scale survey.

A technique such as a focus group is open to criticism on several methodological grounds. In a study such as the sentence-resentence study in Alabama (Doble and Klein 1989), the "manipulation" must be apparent to subjects. This can lead to the presence of "demand characteristics" in the study. These are cues inadvertently given that then permit subjects to guess the hypothesis being tested. In some cases, the subjects then respond in ways to confirm the hypothesis they perceive is being tested. This phenomenon must be considered as a plausible alternative explanation of the findings. Subjects may have felt compelled to use the alternative sanctions simply because the moderator introduced them. And issues of external validity must also be addressed when one is attempting to make general statements about the residents of a state on the basis of a nonrepresentative sample of (in this case) 420 focus group participants. So long as broad generalizations are not made (and to date authors of reports based on focus group discussions have been scrupulous in setting the limits beyond which their data cannot be stretched), the focus group approach constitutes a valuable adjunct to surveys using larger, representative samples.

3. *Experimental Research with Purposive Samples.* This final category of research has proved to be at least as fertile as the others. It includes experimental, quasi-experimental, and correlational research, usually conducted on a university campus, but sometimes using more heterogeneous samples of subjects than university students. While precluding generalization to national, state, provincial, or county populations, these studies have permitted researchers to examine the effects of various experimental manipulations, the length of which precludes their use on representative surveys.[2] In a study by Doob and Roberts (1983), for instance, a sample of 115 members of the general public were randomly assigned to read either the newspaper description of a sentencing hearing or a description of the same hearing but based on the actual court documents. The purpose of the study was to see if subjects would rate the sentence differently depending on whether they read the news media account or an account based on court documents. A representative survey was not necessary to test this hypothesis; what was at issue was whether the two groups, statistically equivalent before the study began (due to random assignment), would react differently.

The distinction between large-scale traditional opinion polls and a more recent technique such as focus groups reflects the distinction proposed by Yankelovich (1991) between mass opinion and public judgment. According to Yankelovich, top-of-the-head responses to simple polls reflect mass opinion; they tend to be volatile, have little internal consistency, and indicate the respondent may be giving a response without accepting (or even considering) the consequences of the view. Public judgment is characterized by acceptance of the consequences of the opinion, by firmness (indicating the view changes little over time), and by consistency between this view and others held by the respondent.

To cite a concrete example, when people are asked, "Are you in favor of, or opposed to alternatives to prison?" they frequently express opposition. This reflects mass opinion more than public judgment. Why? Because the percentage opposing alternative measures fre-

---

[2] Examples can be found in Vidmar and Dittenhoffer (1981); Doob and Roberts (1983); Higginbottom and Zamble (1988); and Hilton (1989).

quently varies from poll to poll and because responses change dramatically when the consequences are made clear to respondents.[3] To date, surveys in criminal justice have all too often reflected mass opinion rather than public judgment. Recent developments such as CATI and focus groups are a step toward establishing the true nature of public opinion in the field.

B. Methodological Problems

Research on public opinions and judgments is affected by a variety of methodological problems, including limited public knowledge of the criminal justice system, the mass media's shaping of public knowledge, and psychological aspects of human knowledge acquisition.

1. *Limited Public Knowledge of Criminal Justice.* Public *knowledge* of crime and justice has been researched far less extensively than public *opinion* regarding these topics. This imbalance is curious, for as Quinney noted, "Reaction to all that is associated with crime rests initially upon knowledge about crime" (1975, p. 176). There are other reasons for wanting information about public knowledge. Some of these concern the efficacy of the criminal justice system: general deterrence, for example, is dependent on widespread public awareness of the consequences of lawbreaking. As well, the effectiveness of many criminal justice reforms is contingent on public knowledge of the reforms.

a. *Crime-related statistics.* Surveys have consistently found that the public has inaccurate, overly negative views of crime statistics. The following are some examples of misperceptions relating to crime statistics that are derived from national and statewide surveys conducted in the United States (e.g., Knowles 1984, 1987), Canada (e.g., Doob and Roberts 1982), and Australia (O'Connor 1978; Indermaur 1987).

—The public in the United States overestimates the victimization rate for violent crime. While the rate is fewer than four incidents per 100 residents (per year) in Ohio, only one citizen in twenty perceived the rate to be that low (Knowles 1984, table 6).[4]

—In Canada, approximately 5 percent of all reported crimes involve violence. However, when asked to estimate this percentage, three-

---

[3] The distinction between mass opinion and public judgment is not restricted to the methodological level. The former is the first stage toward the latter. On some issues in criminal justice, mass opinion has evolved to the stage of public judgment (see Yankelovich 1991).

[4] Estimates of property victimization rates were more accurate, implying, as Knowles notes, that the news media's emphasis on violent crime is responsible.

quarters of the public estimated that between 30 and 100 percent of crime involves violence (Doob and Roberts 1983; see also Gregg and Posner 1990). Similar results were found in Australia (Indermaur 1987). In Australia, O'Connor concluded: "When citizens' estimates of the numbers of thefts, violent crimes, rapes, and acts of vandalism, prostitution and fraud (both committed and convicted) were compared with official figures, it was found that estimates were higher than the official crime rates" (1978, p. 64).

—Most people overestimate the property crime victimization rate (Doob and Roberts 1982; Indermaur 1987).

—Most people overestimate the magnitude of the crime problem. Wilson and Brown noted that Australians had "very little idea of the numbers of crimes actually committed" (1973, p. 24).

—In Canada, most people believe (erroneously) that the murder rate has increased since capital punishment was abolished (Doob and Roberts 1982). In Australia, Indermaur (1987) found that 80 percent of the polled public thought that the murder rate had increased, when in fact there had been no change.

—The public tends to overestimate recidivism rates considerably. In Canada, a study by the Law Reform Commission found that between 13 and 17 percent of first-time violent offenders were reconvicted. When the public were asked to estimate this same percentage, four out of five respondents provided estimates between 30 and 100 percent. Almost half the public estimated the recidivism rate for this group of offenders to be between 60 and 100 percent (Doob and Roberts 1983).

—The tendency to overestimate recidivism rates is even greater when the question concerns mental patients. Pasewark, Seidenzahl, and Pantle (1981) found that community residents considerably overestimated arrest rates of mental patients.

—The Canadian public overestimates the recidivism rates of inmates released on parole. Thus while approximately 13 percent of inmates released on parole are reconvicted of a violent crime, over 60 percent of respondents estimated this percentage to be between 40 and 100 percent (Doob and Roberts 1982).

—Although crime rates have fluctuated over the past 50 years, people invariably respond when asked that crime rates are increasing. This is true when crime rates were increasing as well as during periods when police reports and victimization surveys indicated no change or a decline in crime rates. In 1972, 51 percent of the respondents to a

Gallup poll agreed that there was more crime in their area than a year earlier. In 1989, a poll found that the same number share this view (Flanagan and Maguire 1990, table 2.19). Moreover, the specific offenses they believe to be increasing fastest are those like murder that attract most media coverage and not those that are actually increasing in rate (Environics Research Group 1989*b*; see also McIntyre 1967).

Perceptions of the past are related to expectations for the future. When asked if the crime rate is going to increase over the next six months, two-thirds of the public responded affirmatively (Bertrand 1982; but see also Useem et al. 1990). Finally, these perceptions of crimes rates are shared by the public in other industrialized nations. In Sweden, for example, 80 percent of the polled public overestimated the number of homicides (Lenke 1974). And, while some demographic variation exists (principally in terms of education), these misperceptions are shared by diverse populations of respondents (Doob and Roberts 1982; see also Doleschal 1979; Bohm 1987*b*; Indermaur 1987).[5]

The myths and oversimplifications to which the public subscribe are not restricted to offenders or to the criminal justice system; they also include crime victims. Walker (1979) in discussing the battered woman syndrome notes the existence of a number of myths. Ewing and Aubrey (1987) conducted a survey of the general public and found that "many subjects . . . appeared to endorse the myths that a battered woman is at least partially responsible for her battering and is masochistic if she remains in a battering relationship. Moreover a clear majority of subjects appeared to subscribe to the myth that a battered woman can simply leave her batterer" (p. 261). Professionals working with spousal abuse cases are well aware of the dangerous inaccuracy of such opinions. As with other crime-related myths reviewed here, they have important consequences for the legal system. Jurors in cases of spousal homicide may be guided by such myths, and this would undermine claims of self-defense by the accused. Such myths may also be operative beyond the conviction stage. Weidner and Griffit (1983) found that sentencing decisions for the crime of sexual assault were significantly

---

[5] The exception to this pattern of inaccuracy regarding crime statistics is research conducted by Warr (1980, 1982), who compared public estimates of crime rates to crime data derived from self-report surveys (rather than criminal justice statistics). Warr found considerable agreement between public perceptions and self-reported crime patterns. We should, then, be wary of basing all tests of public knowledge on a picture of crime derived from official statistics. Nevertheless, the general conclusion still holds: the public's view of crime indicators is both inaccurate and biased toward a pessimistic view of the system.

affected by the degree to which the sentencer subscribed to rape myths, such as the notion that a woman cannot be raped against her will, and that she must have consented to the act.

b. *The criminal justice system.* Some polls have tested public knowledge of the structure of the criminal justice system. It would appear that the public are most familiar with the correctional stage and least familiar with policing (e.g., Fagan 1987). At first this may appear paradoxical; the mass media devote more attention to the police than to the courts or corrections. However, media coverage of policing (particularly fictional representations) is more stereotypical than coverage of other areas of criminal justice and focuses on aspects that do not represent the reality of policing. Most of the research on public knowledge of the criminal justice system has focused on sentencing and corrections.

c. *Sentencing.* Public awareness of sentencing is critical for a number of reasons. From the perspective of deterrence, potential offenders cannot be deterred by penalties of which they are unaware. Moreover, public knowledge of minimum and maximum penalties and actual dispositions provides the context against which people evaluate specific sentences. Whether a sentence of four years for robbery is regarded as lenient or harsh, depends, in part at least, on what the public believe the average sentence for robbery (and other offenses) to be. Estimates of maximum penalties may also be important in this respect. And finally, public *attitudes* in general toward the courts and the judiciary have been shown to be at least correlated with, and quite possibly determined by, *knowledge* of the sentencing process.

What then do the public know about the sentencing process and sentencing practices? The Canadian Sentencing Commission found widespread ignorance of sentencing trends: for three high-frequency offenses (assault, breaking and entering, and robbery) most people estimated sentences to be much more lenient than was the case. For example, in Canada, approximately 90 percent of offenders convicted of robbery are sent to prison. When the public were asked about the incarceration rate for this crime, fully three-quarters of the respondents estimated it to be under 60 percent (Canadian Sentencing Commission 1987). Similar results emerge from Great Britain (Hough and Mayhew 1985) and Australia (Indermaur 1987).

Similar disparities exist between public knowledge and reality in the area of statutory maxima. Williams, Gibbs, and Erickson concluded that "the overwhelming majority of respondents were unaware of the statutory maximums for all penalties and all crimes" (1980, p. 115; see also California Assembly Committee on Criminal Procedure 1975). In Canada, the maximum penalty for theft over $1,000 is ten years imprisonment. Two-thirds of the public estimated the maximum to be much lower (Canadian Sentencing Commission 1987). Even for a well-publicized offense such as impaired driving, three-quarters of the public could not identify the maximum penalty.

Minimum penalties raise a particularly telling example of public ignorance. Advocates argue that minimum penalties provide a general deterrent effect beyond that associated with a more discretionary sentencing framework. But do they? In California, shortly after the state legislature had increased the minimum penalties for certain offenses, this fact had escaped the attention of four-fifths of the population polled (California Assembly Committee on Criminal Procedure 1975). In Canada, when asked to identify one of the offenses carrying a minimum penalty, only 16 percent of the public were able to do so (Canadian Sentencing Commission 1987). As well, when given a list of five offenses, only one respondent in four correctly identified the offense carrying a minimum penalty.

d. *Parole and correctional trends.*   The public know as little about parole as they do about sentencing. When the Canadian Sentencing Commission (1987) provided respondents with three incorrect and one correct definition of parole, only 15 percent chose the right answer. And fully 85 percent were wrong when asked to identify the earliest point in a sentence at which inmates become eligible for parole.

They were also incorrect about actual release rates. Thus a representative sample of Canadians were asked the following question: "Have parole boards been releasing more inmates, have they been releasing fewer inmates, or has there been little change in the numbers of inmates released on parole?" Over two-thirds of the public thought that more inmates were being released on parole (Roberts 1988a). In fact, there had been no change in the percentage of inmates being granted release on full parole over the period preceding the survey (Hann and Harman 1986). Public estimates of parole release rates, then, are consistent with a broader view of a criminal justice system that responds to offenders with undue leniency.

The public also overestimate the parole revocation rate. In Canada, approximately one-quarter of the federal inmates released on full parole will have their parole revoked (Solicitor General Canada 1981). When asked to estimate the revocation rate, half the public sample estimated the rate to be higher. (In light of higher parole revocation rates in the

United States, this finding may well be restricted to the Canadian public.) In short, the public perception of parole, at least in Canada, reflects the belief that a large proportion of inmates are "getting out" early, and a substantial percentage are failing to complete their sentences in the community without further offending.

If the public know little about critical statistics relating to sentencing and corrections, they are also poorly informed about important changes in the nature of the correctional environment: the Alabama public appeared unaware of the recent, drastic increase in that state's prison population (only 14 percent of respondents to a statewide poll were accurate in their perceptions of the change in inmate populations—see Doble and Klein [1989]). Britons are equally in the dark about correctional trends: an early survey found that "less than 2% had even the haziest idea of the number of people in prison" (Silvey 1961). Gibbons (1963) also found little awareness of correctional matters (see also Banks, Maloney, and Willcocks 1975).

e. *Legal rights and criminal justice programs.* Residents of several American states have been surveyed about their legal rights and related issues such as police powers. Knowledge tends to be poor, particularly (as Sarat [1977] points out) for civil law issues, rather than criminal justice, but even for the latter, members of the public appear to know little (see Williams and Hall 1972; *Michigan Law Review* 1973; California Assembly Committee on Criminal Procedure 1975). In a recent survey of Canadians (Fletcher 1991), respondents were asked, "When someone is charged with a criminal offense, is that person required to testify in court or does that person have a right to remain silent?" Only a minority of the sample knew that accused persons are not compelled to testify. If over half the public are unaware of a right as central to our system of justice as this, there is little chance they will be familiar with other, lesser rights. A sample of Americans was asked (in 1977) if the following statement was correct: "In a criminal trial, it is up to the person who is accused of the crime to prove his innocence." Only a bare majority (56 percent) were aware of the presumption of innocence (Parisi et al. 1979).

Awareness of the powers of the state is no higher than awareness of the rights of the individual. In 1983, a sample of Americans were asked: "If someone is found innocent of a crime, the state can appeal the case. Is this true or false?" Less than a third responded correctly (McGarrell and Flanagan 1985, table 2.62). They were also asked if it were true that decisions taken by a state court could be reversed by the U.S. Supreme Court. Only 10 percent answered correctly (McGarrell and Flanagan 1985, table 2.66).

Legal aid programs provide a telling illustration of the extent to which the public lack adequate knowledge of the legal system. A survey in Great Britain found that half the respondents gave the wrong answer, or failed to answer, the simple question "Can people who don't have much money get free legal advice?" When asked specifically about the legal aid scheme functioning in their community, three-quarters of respondents did not know about the program (Abel-Smith, Zander, and Brooke 1973). More recently, in Canada, two-thirds of respondents to a nationwide poll were unsure of the nature of Legal Aid (Environics Research 1987). Most disquieting of all, awareness of Legal Aid tends to be poorest among those lower-income individuals for whom it was in large part created. This result has been found with other justice programs. Williams and Hall (1972) found that low-income groups performed only at chance level on a test of factual questions dealing with the law. Increasing public awareness of the law, and particularly of important programs such as Legal Aid, is clearly a priority if universal access to justice is to be achieved.

Edwards (1987) reports the findings of a telephone survey conducted in New Jersey that addressed the Domestic Violence Prevention program established in that state several years earlier. Results indicated that only 40 percent of the public (including, presumably, some victims of domestic violence) knew that there was a state law regarding domestic violence; fully one-third were not aware of any services available for the victims of violence.

f. *Legislative change.*   Awareness of legislative change is also far from universal. In 1990, the Ohio legislature passed Senate Bill 258, a major piece of legislation relating to drug offenses. A central aim was to crack down on illegal drug use by increasing the penalties for drug crimes; all drug offenses were moved up in seriousness, with a corresponding increase in the severity of penalties. However, months after passage of this much-debated, much-publicized piece of legislation, 89 percent of Ohio residents (including, presumably, some illegal drug users) had not heard anything about the changes (Schroot and Knowles 1990). A similar trend emerges in Colorado. In 1985, new legislation doubled the presumptive sentencing ranges. This had an important impact on sentence lengths in that state. And yet public surveys three years later showed that this change had had no effect on public perceptions of sentencing (Mande and English 1989).

In Canada, significant amendments were made a few years ago to the legislation covering drinking-and-driving offenses, including substantial increases in the severity of penalties. However, fully one-quarter of respondents to a nationwide poll were unaware of *any* changes to the law regarding impaired driving, even though this legislation was the object of a sustained public information campaign (see also Alford 1984). Comparable results emerged from a British study. Walker and Argyle (1974) found that a year after attempted suicide was decriminalized, fully three-quarters of the population believed it still to be a crime.

This gap between legislative reform and public awareness of the reforms is counterproductive. After all, legislation is frequently introduced for instrumental purposes related to the attitudes and behavior of the public. One of the goals of rape reform legislation in both the United States (Marsh, Geist, and Caplan 1982) and Canada (Roberts 1990) was to restore public confidence in the criminal justice system and thereby to promote the reporting of sexual assaults to the police. Likewise, concerning impaired driving, increasing the severity of penalties will only serve the desired goal of deterrence if the drinking and driving public is aware of the new, harsher penalties. Awareness of new laws or amendments to existing laws may not occur overnight, but if the public remain ignorant of such changes, many of the goals of law reform will prove unattainable.

2. *News Media Influences.*   There are two principal causes of public misperceptions of critical criminal justice statistics. First, the major sources of information, the news media, provide a biased view of criminal justice, one that stresses crimes of violence and leniency on the part of the system's response to such crimes. Second, members of the public fail to correct for the unrepresentativeness of the stories they encounter in the media and are subject to a number of cognitive errors that exacerbate differences between reality (as measured by criminal justice statistics) and public knowledge of that reality.

The news media are for most people the most important source of information about criminal justice. Knowles (1982) reports that 94 percent of U.S. residents cited the news media as their most important source of information. The same is true in Canada (Canadian Sentencing Commission 1987) and Australia (Broadhurst and Indermaur 1982). This finding is reflected in surveys dealing with direct experience with the system. For most questions relating to criminal justice, the percentage of respondents *without* an opinion is usually small. Smaller still, however, is the percentage with any direct experience with the system. For example, when asked what prisons are like, only 12 percent of Canadian respondents (Moore 1985) did not have an opinion. And yet only 2 percent had actually been to a prison. Likewise, when asked about courts, almost everyone had an evaluation to offer, although only one-third of the sample had ever attended court. Results such as these reveal the ease with which most of us form opinions (and sometimes strong ones) on the basis of indirect, presumably media-based reports. It is important therefore to know something about the images of crime and criminal justice that are projected by the news media, and the effects of these images on the public.

a. *Bias toward sensational crimes.* News media coverage of crime and punishment reflects a view of the criminal justice system that is biased toward serious and sensational crime. One of the most well-documented characteristics of news media treatment of crime is the emphasis placed on serious crimes of violence. Murder, for example, is highly overrepresented relative to its occurrence in crime statistics. Liska and Baccaglini (1990) found that homicide represented only .02 percent of Index crimes, but accounted for 30 percent of news stories in the United States. Doob (1984) found that over half the stories in a sample of Canadian newspapers dealt with violence. In fact, crimes of violence account in Canada for fewer than 5 percent of reported crimes (Solicitor General Canada 1984a). In short, the image of crime presented by the news media frequently involves violence (see also Sherizen 1978; Dussuyer 1979; Graber 1980; Gordon and Heath 1981; Mawby and Brown 1984; Surette 1984; Gabor and Weimann 1987). Moreover, this pattern is not restricted to the North American media: van Dijk (1978) reports that crime stories involving violence in parts of Europe were ten times more frequent than actual offenses involving violence. These results presumably explain why the public overestimate the amount of violent crime.

Criminal justice researchers may be aware of the deficiencies of news media coverage of crime, but the public are not. In fact, the public are inclined to believe crime is the same or even worse (i.e., more serious) than is indicated by the news media (Parisi et al. 1979, table 2.11). And, not surprisingly perhaps, those with most confidence in the news media are likely to be the respondents with the most distorted views of crime (Knowles 1984).

b. *Simplifying issues.* The news media seldom provide sufficient context and information for the public to make a reasoned evaluation of events; accordingly, opinions tend to form in the absence of substantive knowledge of the issues.

Illustration of this can be found in the trial of John Hinckley for the attempted assassination of President Reagan. Both the trial and subsequent acquittal (not guilty by reason of insanity) of Hinckley received widespread news media coverage. In a subsequent public survey (Hans and Slater 1983) almost 90 percent of respondents expressed their disapproval of the defense, yet a still higher percentage could not generate even an approximation of the legal definition of the insanity defense. The American public may not know much about the defense, but they know what they do not like.[6] (See also Steadman and Cocozza [1978] for further evidence of the news media's effects on public knowledge in this area.)

A second illustration of the media tendency to oversimplify concerns the sentencing process. The only systematic content analysis of news media coverage of sentencing stories examined newspapers in Canada (Canadian Sentencing Commission 1987). The results indicated that most sentencing stories were very brief, usually reporting little more than the offense category and the sentence.[7] In the newspaper stories analyzed by the Canadian Sentencing Commission, mention was seldom made of any sentencing purpose, and the structure of the sentencing system was completely ignored. In three-quarters of the stories no mention was made of the reasons for sentence. This is particularly important because many stories conveyed the impression that the sentence was lenient (Roberts 1988d).

Sentencing stories make ideal material for news media coverage, particularly cases in which the sentence appears to be lenient. The complexities of the sentencing system fall away, and the reader is left with a description of a crime, of which he or she can form a seriousness judgment, and a description of a sentence, the severity of which is apparent to all. When the two do not coincide, the perception of injustice is irresistible, hence the widespread view of inappropriate leniency in sentencing. The judicial reasoning underlying the sentence remains behind in the courtroom. A difficult case, in which there are complex

---

[6] This widespread disapproval of the verdict in this case led to many calls for the abolition of the defense of insanity (Hans and Vidmar 1986).

[7] This has always been the case. Over 100 years ago the celebrated jurist Stephen noted, "Newspaper reports are necessarily much condensed, and they generally omit many points which weigh with the judge in determining what sentence to pass" (1883, p. 90).

arguments both for and against a particular sentence, will be much simplified by the news media. It is far simpler to write, and read, that a rapist received the proverbial slap on the wrist.

c. *Effects of media on public knowledge.* The effects of the news media on public knowledge have been explored for many years now (e.g., Davis 1952). While the influence of the media has been demonstrated, its effects are not always strong or straightforward. A frequent research strategy consists of comparing some measure of public knowledge (e.g., estimates of crime rates) with some measure of media coverage (e.g., the distribution of crimes reported in the newspapers). Sometimes a third component is added: official rates of delinquency. Examples of this approach can be found in Davis (1952) and Hubbard, DeFleur, and DeFleur (1975). The results of this research suggest that, while public estimates of the distribution of crime do not directly reflect news media data, they are closer to the news media version of reality than to the official statistics. This is particularly true for violent crime.

A second line of research consists of comparing the perceptions of high and low media users (e.g., Gerbner and Gross 1976a, 1976b; Carlson 1985). This research finds that the high media users have particularly inaccurate perceptions of crime rates and the probability of victimization. However the research has been criticized on method-ological grounds because researchers have inferred a causal relationship on the basis of essentially correlational data (see Doob and MacDonald 1979; Hirsch 1980; Wober and Gunter 1982). One obvious difficulty in demonstrating media effects is that they are likely cumulative in nature, and may not be captured by short-term experiments, in which subjects are randomly assigned to read different materials. This rules out the use of randomized experiments, the most powerful research design available.

Nevertheless, three findings from the literature are inescapable: the public overestimate crime rates, particularly violent crime rates; the public cite the news media as their primary source of information about criminal justice; crimes of violence are considerably overrepresented in the news media. Taken together, these findings strongly suggest that the news media have an important influence on public knowledge of the distribution of crime.

d. *Effects of media on public attitudes.* Opinions regarding criminal justice issues also appear to be affected: the news media may influence opinion directly by covering aspects of the criminal justice system which encourage certain views (e.g., that the system is "soft" on offenders and ties the hands of law enforcement officials). But there may also be more subtle effects in which existing conceptions of criminal justice are maintained. Carlson (1985), for example, notes that crime programs on American television seldom if ever challenge mainstream views of criminal justice. The traditional, punitive responses to crime are the only ones reported in the news media. The relationship between the public, the media, and the ruling elite clearly needs further empirical exploration. Quinney (1973, pp. 149–55) asserts that the public are supportive of the criminal justice system not because that system is responsive to community values but because those values have been shaped by the elite. The validity of this assertion needs empirical exploration.

Attitudes toward sentencing is one area in which the influence of the news media is clear. In a series of studies, Roberts and Doob (1990) compared the reactions of groups of subjects randomly assigned to read either the news media account of a sentencing decision or a summary of the court documents from a sentencing hearing. In one study, 63 percent of the subjects assigned to read the news media account felt the sentence was too lenient, compared with only 19 percent of the subjects who read a summary of the actual court documents pertaining to the case. Thus, the same sentence can provoke very different reactions, depending on how it is presented. In addition there was also significant generalization of this attitude to other aspects of the case: subjects whose information derived from the news media had significantly more negative views of the judge, the offense, and the offender.

Several investigators have shown significant correlations between television viewing and attitudes toward criminal justice policies. For example, Barrile reports that "television viewing is related to a distorted and overly-violent view of crime" (1984, p. 153) and further that "the data strongly support the hypothesis that television viewing is related to a retributive attitude about punishment,[8] that harsher sentences deter or are deserved" (p. 154). As with all correlational research (and most of the research on media effects is of this kind), caution must

---

[8] One of the few studies that has explored the effects of the news media on public attitudes toward different sentencing purposes found no significant effects. Subjects were asked to read a series of newspaper articles, some of which described serious crimes, some of which described nonserious crimes. Afterward, all subjects were asked to rate the importance of various sentencing purposes in general, not relating specifically to the offenses that preceded the question. While the manipulation affected perceptions of the seriousness of other crimes (unrelated to the news stories), there was no effect on importance ratings assigned to different sentencing purposes (see Roberts and Edwards 1989).

be exercised in drawing the causal inference that exposure to television determines attitudes toward crime and punishment. Nevertheless, the volume and consistency of this research, along with other, short-term experimental studies makes the causal explanation at the very least highly plausible.

C. Psychological Aspects of Knowledge Acquisition and Attitude Formation

Eccentric coverage of criminal justice topics by the news media is not the sole reason that public knowledge is so poor. When responding to information, members of the public are prone to a number of cognitive errors that can give rise to beliefs such as those concerning sentencing patterns and recidivism rates. These cognitive failings have been studied by social psychologists (e.g., Ross 1977; Nisbett and Ross 1980; Fiske and Taylor 1984) and their research has important consequences for the area of public attitudes to crime and justice. How do cognitive errors explain public knowledge and attitudes? There are a variety of mechanisms at work.

1. *Overgeneralization.* Perhaps the most important is a tendency to generalize from a single instance of behavior. People are overly influenced by information about a single case (Tversky and Kahneman 1973) and this has consequences for many attitudes relating to crime and criminal justice. Hearing about one parolee committing a violent crime is likely to foster generalization to all parolees, with the result that most people will overestimate by a considerable margin the failure rates for parole. The same is true for sentencing; hearing of a particularly lenient sentence gives rise to the perception that *most* sentences are too lenient, and this may lead people to estimate sentence lengths that are considerably shorter than the periods of imprisonment actually imposed.

Scientific evidence of this phenomenon can be found in an experiment by Hamill, Wilson, and Nisbett (1980). Subjects were asked to watch a videotaped interview with a prison guard (in reality a confederate of the experimenter) who acted in one of two ways, either as a cold, inhumane person, or as a warm, caring individual. Half the subjects were told this individual was highly representative of prison guards, the other half were told he was atypical and unrepresentative. After watching the interview, subjects were asked to give their impressions of prison guards in general (not the particular individual they had seen being interviewed). The information regarding the representativeness of the guard being interviewed should have been critical to subjects. In fact, they were influenced only by the behavior of the specific individual in the interview. Those who had seen a brutal guard thought that most prison officers were inhumane; those who saw a warm individual believed that most guards were of a similar disposition.

Sentences reported in the news media are very unrepresentative of all sentences actually imposed. As Walker (1981) notes, "It is a very small percentage of sentences which is reported in the news media. National newspapers, radio and television are very selective, reporting only offenses which are in some way unusual" (p. 114). Generalizing on the basis of an unrepresentative sample of cases is clearly not a rational strategy, and yet the public do generalize, and tend to conclude that all sentences are too lenient. They also tend to regard high profile cases appearing in the media as representative of all offenders (see Walker 1985) and this may well have consequences for public attitudes and behavior toward offenders.

2. *Availability.*   Lenient sentences are easier to recall than "appropriate" ones because such sentences are more "available" to consciousness. Nisbett and Ross define cognitive availability as "accessibility in the processes of perception, memory or construction from imagination" (1980, p. 18). Estimates of the frequency or likelihood of an event are determined by the ease with which instances or examples come to mind. This bias—known as the availability heuristic—has been employed to explain the inaccuracy of public estimates of various events. For example, when asked to estimate the frequency of different causes of death, the public overestimated causes often covered by the media (e.g., homicide)[9] and underestimated causes of death not frequently covered (e.g., suicide). Lichtenstein et al. (1978, p. 577) concluded that "the media have important effects on our judgments, not only because of what they don't report . . . but because of what they do report to a disproportionate extent." In a similar way, the public are likely to overestimate the frequency of lenient sentences because they are highly available (see Diamond [1989] and Diamond and Stalans [1989] for further discussion of this issue).

3. *Confidence.*   Another line of research demonstrates the persistence of public attitudes, particularly attitudes that are held with confidence. There is evidence that many of the opinions held by the public

---

[9] Lichtenstein et al. (1978) found that homicide, while less frequent than suicide, was accorded approximately fifteen times more space in newspapers.

concerning criminal justice are held with a fair degree of confidence, particularly concerning sentencing. The theoretical complexities are not readily apparent to most people. Everyone has a view on what kind of sentence should be imposed on Ivan Boesky, Leona Helmsley, or Michael Milken, and these views are usually held with a high degree of confidence. Doob and Roberts (1983) provided members of the public with newspaper stories dealing with sentencing hearings. These subjects were asked to evaluate the sentences and to state how confident they were of their evaluations. Although the stories were very brief, and contained very little information, for almost 60 percent of the stories the subjects stated that they were "very confident" of their evaluations. Attitudes held with a high degree of confidence become resistant to change, and people who are very confident of their opinions tend to be more susceptible to cognitive errors, and respond less objectively to relevant information.[10]

4. *Biased Processing of Information.*   One final relevant finding from experimental social psychology concerns the way in which people process information relevant to their attitudes. This is particularly relevant to criminal justice opinions, because so many of them have an empirical component. Whether we support parole, or capital punishment, or electronic monitoring depends in part on what we know about their efficacy. How many parolees commit further crimes while on parole? Are homicide rates higher in states that execute offenders? What percentage of probation cases involving electronic monitoring are successful? Many people have strong views about these and other criminal justice issues, and the strength of the views may well hinder rational examination of relevant information. For example, people with strong views about capital punishment are likely to react to evidence relating to this issue in a biased manner. In short, we may well believe what we want to believe, namely, information that is congenial to our attitudes. This was demonstrated in an experiment conducted by Lord, Ross, and Lepper (1979).

Proponents and opponents of capital punishment were asked to read descriptions of two research studies, one of which confirmed the deterrent effect of the death penalty; the other showed evidence that capital punishment was not an effective deterrent for homicide. In short,

[10] See also Kessel (1966, p. 183) for evidence that attitudes to the U.S. Supreme Court determine what people read and hear about the court in the news media.

mixed evidence. After reading the studies, subjects in both groups were asked to evaluate them. Both proponents and opponents rated the research that supported their views to be more convincing and more scientific. (The researchers had prepared and pretested the two studies to ensure their equivalence from a scientific perspective.) In other words, the same study was rated very differently depending on the attitude of the person providing the rating. Even more remarkable was another finding from the same study. Even though they read essentially mixed evidence vis-à-vis the death penalty (which might give a rational observer pause), proponents became more strongly favorable to capital punishment, and opponents more extremely opposed. Both sides had looked for evidence to bolster their opinions, and views became more polarized.

This research suggests that other strongly held attitudes in the area of criminal justice are also likely to be resistant to change. A person convinced that parolees usually commit further crimes while on parole is likely to cling to this attitude even in light of disconfirming information. This tendency is most likely to be observed when the attitude is strongly held, and when relevant information is concrete (as in newspaper articles—see Anderson [1983]). Both conditions apply to many issues in criminal justice.

Despite—or perhaps because of—their keen interest in crime stories, the public appear to know little about the criminal justice system. Increasing public awareness of the purpose, structure, and practice of the criminal justice system is clearly a priority. Such a step is unlikely to encounter public resistance, if the reactions of Canadians are representative of all four countries. Fully 96 percent of respondents to a recent poll in Canada expressed the view that information about the law is important to them, and over two-thirds were of the view that governments should do more to educate the public in this area. Public interest was particularly high for information about legal rights and about procedures to follow after a crime had been committed (Environics Research Group 1989b). When asked to estimate various critical statistics, or to state the minimum or maximum penalties, the answers reflected a negative attitude to the problem of crime as well as to the system's response. Members of the public are largely unaware of the structure and function of the criminal justice system or the nature of specific laws. These results suggest that informing the public about the reality of crime rates, and punishment patterns, would reduce dissatisfaction (see Diamond 1989).

D. Problems with Surveys

The final area of concern from a methodological perspective concerns the nature of questions used in public opinion surveys. In many instances, complex questions of criminal justice policy are reduced to a simple yes/no/don't know trichotomy. The public's imperfect grasp of issues is also well illustrated by research in which additional information is provided to subjects prior to the survey. Under these conditions, opinions change radically.

1. *Simplicity of Questions.* Many polls pose questions that fail to do justice to the complexity of the issues addressed. Poll questions pertaining to sentencing are a case in point. A single, simple question ("Are sentences in general too harsh, about right, or too lenient?") encourages respondents to consider sentencing in a global context. And, as I have noted, public perceptions vary depending on the nature of the crime. Second, the questions assume that the hypothetical offender the person polled has in mind corresponds to the kinds of offenders being processed by the courts. This is seldom the case; Brillon, Louis-Guerin, and Lamarche (1984) asked respondents to describe the kind of offender they had had in mind when answering this question, and almost two-thirds (64 percent) were thinking of a violent or a "hardened" criminal. Another survey found that 38 percent of respondents were thinking of murderers (Solicitor General Canada 1980; see also Doob and Roberts 1983; Indermaur 1987). So the offenders that respondents have in mind are clearly unrepresentative of offenders being processed by the courts. But what of the punishments that come to mind when the public are asked if sentences are harsh enough? There is no research directly examining the question, but related work suggests that if respondents were asked what kind of *sentences* they had in mind, the answer would probably be *lenient* sentences, for these are most easily recalled: they are salient, and salience promotes recall (Fiske and Taylor 1984). And finally, as has already been shown, the public tend to underestimate the severity of actual sentencing trends as well as the duration of time actually served in prison. In short, if we want to know whether judicial practice is out of step with the views of the public, we need to do more than ask a simple question on a survey.

Relying on a single question to measure attitudes has obvious limitations that are particularly relevant to the issue of capital punishment (see also Zeisel and Gallup 1989). A number of investigators have found that support for capital punishment declines when respondents either are given information about the penalty (its effects on homicide rates; the nature of its administration) or are asked about specific cases rather than simply the appropriateness of the penalty in general (e.g., Ellsworth 1978). Sarat and Vidmar (1976) found that exposing subjects to information resulted in diminished support for capital punishment among almost half the sample (see also Vidmar and Dittenhoffer 1981; Zimmerman, Van Alstyne, and Dunn 1988). Finally, the nature of the specific questions posed on a survey also influences the percentage of respondents who support the death penalty (Williams, Longmire, and Gulik 1988). Durham (1989) found evidence that use of open or closed-ended questions affects the nature of the responses; closed-ended questions generated a greater degree of punishment in responses than did the open-ended version.

A final issue that should be borne in mind when evaluating opinion polls is that the response alternatives are sometimes provided by the pollster with little or no pretesting. The consequence is that information is lost about alternatives that might have arisen had there been extensive pretesting on the population sampled. The results may well reflect the choice of alternatives provided as much as the real views of the public. This may explain why over half the respondents to a 1975 poll in the United States identified "Communists" as a major contributor to violence in the country (Hindelang et al. 1976, table 2.17). It seems unlikely that over half the population in 1975 would have spontaneously identified this group as a major contributor to violence in America.

2. *Insufficient Information.* The last problem identified here concerns the amount of information provided to respondents. On most polls, very little information is provided. The result is an uninformed response that does not do justice to the public's views. This point can be illustrated by looking at studies that manipulate the amount of information provided to the respondents. For example, in the area of sentencing, several studies have varied the amount of information about the offender and the offense and the results are consistent: the more information respondents have, the less punitive they become. Doob and Roberts (1983) randomly assigned subjects to read either very brief or more complete descriptions of cases. Afterward, all subjects were asked to evaluate the sentences that were imposed. Subjects were far more punitive when they knew just a little about the case. For example, 80 percent of subjects exposed to a brief description of a manslaughter case thought the sentence was too lenient. Of those

subjects who read the more comprehensive account, only 15 percent evaluated the sentence as too lenient (see also Knight 1965; McIntyre 1967). This finding is important for, as noted earlier in this essay, most sentencing stories in the news media—which constitute the primary source of information for the public—are brief and devoid of much detail. It is not just information about the case that the public typically lack. They also lack information about different sentencing alternatives: when this kind of information is provided, opinions change, as the following study illustrates.

Focus group participants in Alabama were asked to sentence offenders in a number of cases. They responded by favoring incarceration for offenders in eighteen cases out of twenty-three. Subjects were then given information about alternative dispositions (e.g., house arrest). Afterwards they were asked to "resentence" the offenders. On the second occasion, respondents favored incarceration in only four out of the original twenty-three cases (Doble and Klein 1989). English, Crouch, and Pullen (1989) made similar findings with a representative survey of Colorado residents (see also Galaway 1984a, 1984b). Comparable results have been found by other researchers working with attitudes toward capital punishment (e.g., Sarat and Vidmar 1976; Vidmar and Dittenhoffer 1981). If members of the public were exposed to as much information as was available to the sentencing judge (in terms of the case and the different sentencing options available), public satisfaction with sentencing decisions would increase (see McIntyre 1967; Doleschal 1970; Thomson and Ragona 1987; Rossi, Simpson, and Miller 1985).

The more general point however is that interpretation of public opinion polls must take into account the extent of public knowledge of the criminal justice system. If comparisons are made between the views of the public and criminal justice professionals, researchers should ensure (to the extent that this is possible) that the two groups are equivalent in terms of knowledge of the issue. This implies that researchers should make greater use of computer assisted polling technology, a technique that permits the pollster to provide additional information and to evaluate its impact on responses.

II. Public Attitudes toward Crimes, Criminals, and Victims of Crime

The criminal justice system cannot function without public participation (see Sarat 1975). Legislation will frequently stand or fall on the degree of public support it attracts. As Sumner noted: "Legislation has to seek standing ground on the existing mores . . . to be strong [legislation] must be consistent with the mores" (1906, p. 55; see also Kutchinsky 1973). Kalven and Zeisel (1966) cite Prohibition in the United States as an example of a law that generated substantial conflict with public opinion. This conflict was apparent in the acquittal rate in trials by jury, and was instrumental in the repeal of the constitutional provision mandating Prohibition (see also Ehrmann 1976). Galiber (1990) cites the more recent example of widespread drug use in the United States which appears largely unaffected by drug legislation. A major reason for this is that attitudes toward drug use are discrepant with the position adopted by the legislation. As Galiber notes: "The prevalence of drug use in the U.S. tells us something about the public's true moral attitude towards criminalizing drugs . . . a universal consensus of immorality must precede, not follow, a penal sanction if that sanction is to be effective and enforceable . . . a penal proscription premised on anything less than a universal consensus will always prove unenforceable" (Galiber 1990, pp. 837–38).

A Canadian illustration can be found in the widespread opposition to the previous abortion laws, specifically the treatment of one physician who by his own admission had been performing illegal abortions. Repeatedly charged for performing abortions, Dr. Henry Morgenthaler was as repeatedly acquitted by juries sympathetic to his position. Eventually the acquittals cooled the Crown's enthusiasm for charging Morgenthaler to the point that further prosecution was abandoned. In effect, the law had become unenforceable. The trials of Henry Morgenthaler, and their effect as a catalyst for public opinion, contributed in large part to the eventual change in the Canadian abortion legislation.

It is also necessary to study public opinion because the views of the public are increasingly cited as a factor in determining criminal justice policies. Several writers have noted that responsibility for criminal justice policy has shifted (in the United States at least) from justice bureaucrats to legislators, who may well be more sensitive to public opinion (see Bynum, Greene, and Cullen 1986). If this is the case, understanding public opinion will help us understand the origins of recent criminal justice reforms.

If citizens hold strongly negative views about the criminal justice system, they will be less likely to report crimes or serve as witnesses.

Consider offenses of sexual aggression. Victims' attitudes toward the system have been shown to determine, in a substantial proportion of cases, whether they report incidents to the police (Solicitor General Canada 1984b). Similarly, the processing of rape and sexual assault cases will be affected by attitudes to the crime, and perceptions of victims and offenders, for many criminal justice professionals share stereotypes held by the public.

A. Crime as a Social Problem

Placed in the context of major public policy problems, crime does not assume a high profile in comparison with unemployment and inflation. The responses to the question, "What is the most important problem facing America today?" show little variation over the period 1980–87: crime was identified as the most important problem by between two and five percent of respondents. A 1989 poll (Gallup 1989) found that 6 percent of respondents identified crime as the most important problem facing the United States. But the preceding findings should not be interpreted to mean that crime does not concern the public. Blumstein and Cohen (1980), reporting the results of a mail survey, note that crime is identified as the most serious domestic problem after economic issues. Moreover, when asked a slightly different question, such as, "Is crime an important problem in your community?" most people state that it is. A recent poll in Canada, for example, found that one-third of respondents to a nationwide poll rated crime as a "very important" problem; a further 38 percent stated that it was "somewhat important." Only 7 percent expressed the view that crime was not an important problem (Environics Research 1989b). Furthermore, most Americans believe, and appear always to have believed, that crime has increased over the past year. Their expectations for the future are consistent with this view: almost two-thirds expect the crime problem to get worse. This exceeds the percentage who feel drug abuse or international terrorism are going to get worse (Flanagan and Maguire 1990, table 2.22). This is a striking finding in an era of epidemic drug abuse and proliferating international terrorism.

B. Causes of Crime and Responses to Crime

Public explanations of crime tend to be multidimensional in nature, but emphasize economic and environmental factors. The combination of specific factors varies from offense to offense and the public may have two explanatory models, one for "crime" in general and the other to explain specific individual offending (see also Doleschal 1970; Environics Research Group 1989a).

Lay views of the causes of crime determine, in large part, public enthusiasm for crime-control strategies. There will be little support for crime prevention through social development among those who view offending as an individual aberration rather than a consequence of adverse social conditions (Roberts and Grossman 1990). Likewise, target hardening will appeal to those who regard crime as the product of antisocial opportunism, while an emphasis on punishment clearly reflects a specific conception of the etiology of criminal behavior. As Cullen et al. (1985, p. 310) succinctly note: "How people explain crime will affect what they want done about it." And empirical research sustains this conclusion. Cullen et al. (1985) found that *explanations* about crime were consistently related to preferences for different criminal sanctions. Thus people who had a positivist orientation in terms of explaining crime tended to reject punishment in favor of treatment as a sentencing philosophy. And finally, understanding lay perceptions of the causes of crime (and the appropriate responses to crime) will also inform us about the behavior of criminal justice professionals who often share the same perceptions and prejudices (Carroll 1978).

While questions pertaining to crime causation have been posed repeatedly over the past 40 years, the wording of the questions, and changing response alternatives, preclude drawing exact historical comparisons. (See Flanagan [1987] for a thorough analysis of changes in public attributions of crime causation.) It seems clear however, that public perceptions of crime causation have undergone a change since 1950. There has been a shift in emphasis from factors reflecting individual culpability to factors associated with the offender's environment. By 1968, a Harris poll reported that 59 percent of respondents cited poor parenting as the main reason why people became criminals (Louis Harris 1968). By 1974, only a third of respondents attributed crime solely to individual motivation (Erskine 1974). Hindelang (1974) reports that when asked to assign blame to either the individual offender or society, the majority of respondents chose the latter. By the 1980s, gross economic factors predominate in public explanations of criminality. For example, in 1981, the most frequently cited response to the question "What is most responsible for the increasing rate of crime?" was unemployment (*Newsweek* 1981). Although it used a small, purposive sample, the study by Campbell and Muncer (1990) supports the view that the public see societal causes to be more important than personal factors. Finally, there is no single cause of crime identified consistently by a majority of the American public. The public appear to adopt a multidimensional view of the origin of crime.

Polls have sometimes posed questions about crime in general, and sometimes about the causes of individual offending. The results suggest that the public perceive economic factors to be responsible for increasing crime rates in general but view factors other than necessity as explaining a specific offender's decision to break the law. It may be that the poll respondents have two different kinds of offenses in mind when considering crime causation on a general or a specific level; this would explain the discrepancy in causal explanations for the two levels of question.

Public views of crime causation can be investigated by asking people what they believe the most effective response to crime to be. Views as to the most effective response presumably reflect perceptions of the underlying cause. The results of questions of this kind mirror those of a direct nature. The public adopt a multifactor approach, with heavy emphasis on social or economic interventions rather than on more repressive strategies of crime control. For example, a national survey in Canada found that the most popular solution to crime was to reduce the level of unemployment (supported by over 40 percent of respondents, see Canadian Sentencing Commission 1987).

Both Americans and Canadians appear willing to invest more money in nonpunitive, nonrepressive responses to crime. Thus when Canadians were given a choice between spending money on prison construction or on developing better alternatives to incarceration, fully 70 percent chose the latter (Canadian Sentencing Commission 1987). Only 23 percent favored building more prisons. When Americans were asked to choose between spending money on more prisons, police and judges, or on better education and job training, two-thirds endorsed education and job training (Gallup 1989).

There is also a perception—held by a significant number of Americans—that one of the causes of crime is the criminal justice system itself. In 1972, a survey asked the following question: "What's behind the high crime rate in the U.S.?" The option selected by the highest number of respondents (one in four) was "lenient laws; insufficiently harsh penalties" (Hindelang et al. 1976, table 2.22). This result reflects the public belief in deterrence (see later sections of this essay).

The picture of public beliefs about crime causation is further complicated by the finding that the public do not apply the same theory to all offenses. As Hollin and Howells (1987) point out, lay explanations of crime are offense-specific rather than global in nature. This was demonstrated in a study which compared lay explanations of burglary, robbery, and rape. Explanations for the first two offenses tended to be in terms of deficient child-rearing patterns, whereas rape was more often explained as a product of mental instability. Public views in this area are affected by current events, or at least news media representations of those events. One recent poll found that 60 percent of respondents regarded drugs as the greatest cause of crime in America. This is well in excess of the next most frequent alternative that was selected by only 5 percent (*Security* 1989). This is the first time drugs have been identified to this extent as a cause of crime and reflects the widespread public concern about drug use in America.[11]

C. Crime Prevention

Knowledge of crime prevention programs is high; participation rates tend to be low. The public are as enthusiastic in their support for the principle of crime prevention, as they are reluctant to participate in crime prevention programs. It is important, however, to note that the public regard crime prevention as a challenge for the community and not just as the responsibility of the criminal justice system. In Canada, over half the respondents to a recent poll endorsed the view that "society generally" was responsible (only 8 percent saw the police as mainly responsible—see Canadian Sentencing Commission [1987]).

Awareness of crime prevention programs exceeds active participation by a considerable margin. Knowles (1979) reports that two-thirds of respondents in a U.S. survey were aware of the principal crime prevention program in their area, although only 12 percent actually participated. In Canada, while over half the polled public were aware of *Operation Identification* (a property marking program), the percentage of households participating was only 15 percent. The participation rate in Toronto, Canada's largest city, was a mere 4 percent. In Britain, the discrepancy between awareness and active participation was even greater: over half were aware of *Neighborhood Watch*, but fewer than 1 percent reported participating (Hough and Mayhew 1985).[12] If com-

---

[11] Clearly sociological theories are more persuasive in the public's view: Only 5 percent of the polled public endorsed the existence of "born criminals" (see also Doble 1987, p. 19).

[12] The 1988 British Crime Survey (Mayhew, Elliott, and Dowds 1989) suggests that participation in Neighborhood Watch has increased in Great Britain since 1985.

munity-based crime prevention programs are to realize their potential fully, the criminal justice system will have to convert passive awareness and positive attitudes into active participation.

More positive attitudes are to be found when considering individual rather than collective crime prevention behaviors. In the U.S. poll just cited, while only 6 percent of respondents actively participated in a crime prevention program, almost half reported that they had taken some steps within the previous two years to prevent victimization. The most frequently cited was some form of target hardening. This figure is lower in Canada, where a recent survey found fewer than one-quarter of the public had recently changed their daily activities in this domain (Sacco and Johnson 1990).

D. Seriousness of Crimes

Considerations of proportionality underlie popular conceptions of justice. Sentencing theorists tend to represent either utilitarian (e.g., deterrence, rehabilitation, incapacitation) or nonutilitarian (e.g., just deserts) traditions. Both perspectives, however, tie the severity of punishments imposed to the seriousness of the offense committed (see Blumstein and Cohen 1980; Hamilton and Rytina 1980). Just deserts theorists advocate the imposition of a penalty commensurate with the seriousness of the offense, and, to a lesser extent, the culpability of the offender (von Hirsch 1985, 1986). This implies the necessity of establishing the seriousness of the offense. And even the most committed advocates of the utilitarian perspective also acknowledge considerations of proportionality.

The impetus for crime seriousness research came from experimental psychology. The early research by Thurstone (1927a, 1927b), Rose and Prell (1955), and Sellin and Wolfgang (1964) largely addressed the issue of consensus in perceptions of offense seriousness, usually measured by the degree of association between seriousness rankings derived from different groups. In two seminal works, Thurstone (1927a, 1927b) applied his law of comparative judgments to the problem of crime perception. Using a paired comparison technique, student subjects were required to state which of two crimes was the more serious. A literature has emerged on methodological issues surrounding the measurement of crime seriousness and punishment severity. Methodological issues that have been explored include assumptions of additivity (i.e., if robbery is assigned a score on a seriousness scale twice as great as that assigned to theft, does that mean robbery is twice as serious in the eyes of respondents?—see Pease, Ireson, and Thorpe

[1974]); issues relating to the nature of the scale used (Pease et al. 1977; Walker 1978); questions relating to subjects surveyed (Walker 1978); the impact of questionnaire form and item order (Sheley 1980); instructional or respondent biases (e.g., Miethe 1982; Travis et al. 1986); and the nature and amount of information contained in a seriousness questionnaire (Klein et al. 1983).[13]

In thinking about crime seriousness, it is important to distinguish between ordinal and cardinal magnitudes of seriousness. Ordinal seriousness refers to rankings of crimes in terms of their seriousness relative to all other crimes. Cardinal seriousness raises the related point of absolute seriousness: regardless of how two populations rank-order a series of crimes, do they assign comparable ratings of seriousness? If judges and members of the public assign rape to the same *rank* of seriousness, do both populations regard this offense as being equally serious? While most research has addressed ordinal seriousness, cardinal seriousness is also important. It may, for example, explain differences in punitiveness. If public ratings of crime seriousness are considerably higher than judicial ratings of the same crimes, this may explain (given the proportionality principle) divergences in punitiveness between the two groups. The findings of research conducted by Corbett and Simon (1991) is relevant here. These researchers found that rankings of seriousness derived from the police and the public were closely related but that differences emerged in terms of ratings of seriousness: those ratings derived from the public were significantly higher than ratings derived from the police.

1. *Some General Findings.*[14]   Substantial consensus exists across different groups in terms of the relative seriousness of different crimes (e.g., Coombs 1967; Wellford and Wiatrowski 1975; Thomas, Cage, and Foster 1976; Turner 1978; Rossi and Henry 1980; Miethe 1982; Indermaur 1990). A landmark study in 1977 surveyed over 60,000 respondents as a supplement to the National Crime Survey (Wolfgang et al. 1985). Seriousness ratings were generated for over 200 offenses. Crimes of violence were rated as being most serious, although there

[13] See Rossi and Henry (1980), Durham (1988), and Parton, Hansel, and Stratton (1991) for more general discussion of these issues.

[14] In this essay I have not, because of space limitations, explored the role of demographic variables in predicting responses to crime seriousness or sentence severity. There is a significant literature on this topic (e.g., Thomas and Cage 1976; Taylor et al. 1979; Hagan and Albonetti 1982; Brillon 1984; Flanagan, McGarrell, and Brown 1985; Skovron, Scott, and Cullen 1988; Secret and Johnson 1989).

was considerable awareness of the consequences (and hence seriousness) of white-collar crimes that result in death.

Greatest social consensus exists for offenses falling at the extremes; there is far less agreement on crimes of intermediate seriousness. In this respect the public are no different from judges: some offenses consistently generate a high degree of disparity in terms of perceptions of offense seriousness and the extremity of punishment; others generate a more consistent judicial response (Austin and Williams 1977; Palys and Divorski 1986). Most of the crime seriousness literature has addressed consensus issues by comparing the seriousness rankings within or across samples of the general public. A few studies have studied criminal justice professionals; Jones and Levi (1987) compared seriousness rankings and ratings derived from the public and police officers. Results indicated substantial concordance between the two populations, particularly for crimes of violence. Public and criminal justice professionals' perceptions do differ for offenses against the administration of justice. Crimes such as perjury and failing to comply with a judicial order are rated relatively low by the public. Judges, however, assign higher seriousness ratings to these crimes, and offenders convicted of them are accordingly punished severely (Canadian Sentencing Commission 1987). Differences also emerge when comparisons are made between offenders and nonoffenders. Figlio (1975) found that average crime seriousness ratings derived from offenders were significantly lower than those derived from nonoffenders.

Rankings of seriousness appear to be relatively stable over time, particularly for high-consensus offenses such as rape and homicide. Coombs (1967) replicated the 1927 Thurstone study and found great similarity in overall seriousness rankings, although some shifting had occurred: offenses against the person were judged to be more serious and crimes involving property as being less serious (see also Borg 1988). Cullen, Link, and Polanzi (1982) found that public perceptions of white-collar crime had changed; the public now regarded these offenses as more serious than earlier polls had suggested. This is also true in other countries such as Australia (Grabosky, Braithwaite, and Wilson 1987). Thus public perceptions of offense seriousness are far from being immutable.

Both crime seriousness and punishment severity have an intuitive appeal to the layperson that suggests consensus regarding their definitions. We all know what we mean when we say murder is more serious than assault. But this conceptual clarity is more apparent than real, as recent writings have shown (e.g., Rossi, Simpson, and Miller 1985; Warr 1989).

Several researchers have explored the conceptual basis of crime seriousness. What exactly does it encompass? Are definitions of seriousness common to different groups? To what extent do lay definitions of crime seriousness correspond to legal constructions? Warr (1989) identifies two dimensions underlying public views of seriousness: the extent to which an act is wrong, and the extent of harm inflicted. Using survey data, Warr shows the distinct nature of the dimensions and demonstrates that seriousness judgments are far more complex than assumed by earlier researchers (see also von Hirsch 1985; Hoffman and Hardyman 1986).

Public conceptions of seriousness appear to emphasize the consequences of the crime, and the harm inflicted, rather than the offender's intention and the offense's potential for harm. Thus inchoate crimes are not regarded as being very serious and are "punished" relatively leniently by members of the public. Riedel (1975) concluded that "there is little evidence to support the hypothesis that inferences of intent alter judgments of seriousness" (p. 207; see also Sebba 1980; Dejoy and Klippel 1984).

One question that has not been widely explored using large, representative samples concerns cross-cultural variation in perceptions of crime seriousness. The research that has been conducted has found consensus in terms of rankings of serious crimes against the person, but intercultural (and intracultural) differences emerge for less serious crimes, particularly ones that carry some local significance.

A typical study in the area is the survey conducted by Scott and Al-Thakeb (1977) in eight countries (United States, United Kingdom, Finland, Sweden, Norway, Denmark, Holland, and Kuwait). Respondents were asked about a list of common offenses (murder, rape, robbery, assault, burglary, theft, and auto theft). Specifically, they were asked to assign penalties; thus this was a study from which seriousness was inferred on the basis of severity (seriousness per se was not measured). Apart from the Kuwaitis, who assigned consistently harsher penalties, the patterns from the other countries show a substantial degree of concordance. Similar results have been found elsewhere, for example, in an Australian replication (Broadhurst and Indermaur 1982).

Local variation does influence rankings of lesser crimes however. A recent poll in France illustrates the point. Results showed that "fraudulent naming of wine" was regarded as being more serious than many other offenses, including having sexual intercourse with a minor (under fourteen) or sexual discrimination in the workplace. In fact this crime occupied a seriousness level only six ranks behind launching a terrorist attack against a public building (Ocqueteau and Perez-Diaz 1990a, 1990b). Regulatory offenses comparable to fraudulently selling wine occupy a rank much lower in seriousness scales derived from samples of North Americans.

2. *Influences on Perceptions of Crime Seriousness.* Little attention however has been paid to influences on public perceptions of crime seriousness. As noted above, crimes against the person are perceived as being more serious now than in the past. Can this be traced to the news media, which, as noted earlier, place great emphasis on crimes of violence? Some correlational evidence exists that suggests this is the case: ratings of the seriousness of several crimes were significantly correlated with news media use (Gebotys, Roberts, and DasGupta 1988). In addition, laboratory research (e.g., Pepitone and DiNubile 1976; Roberts and Edwards 1989) finds support for "anchoring" and "contrast" effects. It appears that the context that precedes a judgment of seriousness is important. Thus, if people read about a series of brutal crimes, subsequent judgments of other, unrelated crimes will be affected by this prior context. While the psychological mechanism for this contextual effect has yet to be determined by research, the finding is important. It suggests that the emphasis on violent crime in the news media may well affect public perceptions of crime seriousness.

Another area that remains to be explored is the effect of the judicial response on perceptions of crime seriousness. At this point, tricky questions of causality emerge. Is there a causal relation between the severity of sentences imposed by the courts and public perceptions of crime seriousness? Are sentences imposed a reaction to, or a determinant of, public perceptions of crime seriousness? Is the relationship causal at all? If causal, is the relationship bidirectional, with perceptions of seriousness changing the severity of sentences and vice versa? These and other questions remain to be addressed by research using representative samples of the public.

E. Public Perceptions of Offenders

Results from several studies suggest that the public hold stereotypes of offenders. The term "offender" is sufficient to provoke a concrete, negative stereotype, and this has consequences for the interpretation of all polls concerning offenders. In the eyes of the public, an offender is typically an outsider, a young, lower-class male, physically unattractive, who has been convicted of a crime involving violence (e.g., Simmons 1965; Reed and Reed 1973; Saladin, Saper, and Breen 1988). A number of investigators (e.g., Bull and Green 1970; Shoemaker, South, and Lowe 1973; Goldstein, Chance, and Gilbert 1984) have presented subjects with facial photographs and have asked those subjects to pick out the offender. The results reveal considerable consistency. Stereotypes apparently exist as to what an offender looks like, and these stereotypes are shared by diverse populations (see Shoemaker and South [1978] for a review of this literature). Brillon, Louis-Guerin, and Lamarche (1984) asked Canadians to describe what kind of individual came to mind when they thought about a "criminal." Most descriptions involved a violent individual, or someone who was mentally ill. In addition the offender would typically have several previous convictions for similar offenses; accordingly, the expectations of further offending are high. A single conviction is sufficient to generate the label of criminal in the mind of the public (Reed and Reed 1973; Roberts and White 1986).

Beyond the general stereotype, it appears that the public also indulge in more detailed social typing. O'Connor (1984) examined public reaction to violent crime versus fraud and found that the public held different perceptions of the two categories of offense. In a similar way, Sunnafrank and Fontes (1983) found that the American public had clear race-related stereotypes about offenders. The public ascribed certain crimes (e.g., auto theft, assault) to blacks and others (e.g., rape, child molestation) to whites. Moreover, these racial ascriptions did not correspond to actual racial patterns in crime rates. Public perceptions of offenders, then, are complex and far from unidimensional. Finally, there are also likely to be behavioral consequences of these attitudes. Louis Harris (1968) found that most people stated they would feel uneasy working with paroled inmates, and the majority would hesitate to hire ex-offenders. This was particularly true for people in the upper social strata (Simmons 1965; Kutchinsky 1968; Conklin 1975). Even more telling is a Canadian survey that showed that more people would feel at ease in the presence of an ex–mental patient than an ex-inmate (Bibby 1981).[15]

[15] Steadman and Cocozza (1978) studied public perceptions of the criminally insane. They found public views of this intersection of the two stereotypes (mental instability; criminality) to contain a highly negative image, one that reflects media coverage of a few, very unusual cases.

F. Victims of Crime

Fear and apprehension of offenders is associated with sympathy and support for victims of crime. This is reflected in public attitudes toward victims' rights. Most people favor reforms that speak to the needs of victims, particularly victims of violent crimes. Sixty percent of respondents to a recent survey in Canada (Environics Research Group 1987) felt the system was not doing enough for victims of crime. Moreover, 90 percent support the use of victim impact statements. Similar percentages support other victim-related initiatives such as victim assistance programs.

III. Public Attitudes toward the Criminal Justice System

The public do not evaluate all phases of the criminal justice system in the same way. While no national survey has systematically asked respondents to rate different stages of the criminal justice process, it is clear from a number of sources that the public have more positive attitudes toward front-end components, such as the police (see Decker 1981, p. 81; Fagan 1981). English, Crouch, and Pullen (1989) report the results of a Colorado poll in which respondents were asked to rate various components of the criminal justice process. The most positive ratings were accorded the police (two-thirds rated them as "excellent" or "good"). Judges received the poorest ratings (one-third rating them as "excellent" or "good"); district attorneys and public defenders received ratings between these extremes (see English, Crouch, and Pullen 1989, table 3-17; Mande and Butler 1982, chart 4; and Mande and Crouch 1984, table 5.1). After reviewing opinion poll data on attitudes toward the police, Thomas and Hyman (1977) concluded that levels of public support were high (see also Smith and Hawkins 1973; Margarita and Parisi 1979; Brillon 1984; Zamble and Annesley 1987). Since that review was completed, support for police has attenuated somewhat but remains higher than for judges, parole boards, or correctional officers. Thus Hindelang (1974) reports that 77 percent of respondents stated they had "a great deal" of respect for the police, while evaluations of judges were substantially more negative (see also Flanagan, McGarrell, and Brown 1985). The first reaction of most people to the police (three-quarters of respondents in one survey; Knowles [1982]) is one of warmth or support. Recent data from Canada sustain the positive image of the police held by the public: most people perceive the police to be doing a good job (Sacco and Johnson 1990).

To the extent that the public consider the criminal justice system responsible for controlling crime, these findings in the area of attitudes toward the police raise a paradox. The public believe crime rates are high, have been rising sharply, and will continue to rise in the future. Yet at the same time, the police are seen as doing a good job. Resolution of the paradox is twofold. First, the public hold the courts (and the correctional authorities) more responsible than the police for increases in crime. And second, the public seems to realize that controlling crime is a social not just a criminal justice problem.

Negative attitudes toward the courts focus on two concerns: perceptions that certain groups are treated inequitably, and a general view that the system is tilted in favor of the suspect, accused, or offender, rather than in favor of victims or agents of the criminal justice system. The public—particularly in the United States—have little patience for what they regard as minor legal technicalities such as the laws affecting the acquisition of evidence or wire-tapping. In the United States (McClosky and Brill 1983) and in Canada (Fletcher 1991) the populace overwhelmingly feels that stopping crime is more important than protecting the rights of suspects or accused persons. Fully 80 percent of respondents to a national poll in 1982 agreed with the statement "Most crimes go unpunished" (McGarrell and Flanagan 1985, table 2.34), and most people think that the vast majority of suspects charged are never convicted (Knowles 1987). A recent study in Canada found that respondents "overwhelmingly attributed the problems of the criminal justice system to too much concern with rights" (Environics Research Group 1989b, p. 9).

Recent legislation in Great Britain has eroded the accused's right to remain silent under interrogation. Some writers (as long ago as Bentham) have asserted that a defendant should not have the right to remain silent. Encroachments on the rights of suspects, defendants, and accused persons such as these are unlikely to provoke a hostile reaction from members of the public. For example, in Canada, most people feel that a suspect charged with a serious offense should be compelled to answer questions by the police (Fletcher 1991). This reluctance to extend rights does not end with the determination of guilt, it also applies to inmates; Knowles (1980) reports that over half the respondents in an Ohio poll endorsed the view that the criminal justice system has too much concern for inmates' rights.

Although attitudes toward the courts are consistently negative, there is an exception. The majority of the American public have retained, over the years, a positive view of the U.S. Supreme Court (Margarita and Parisi 1979). When asked to rate both the Supreme Court and "courts in general," the U.S. public provided much higher confidence ratings for the former. In 1989, the nation's highest court received a higher confidence rating than any other U.S. institution (including the executive branch of the federal government, Congress, organized labor) except the military and the universities. Moreover, confidence in the court has not diminished over the past twenty years (Flanagan and Maguire 1990, table 2.8). (For research on the basis of these attitudes, see Kessel [1966].) The Supreme Court of Canada receives similarly positive ratings from Canadians (see Ouellet 1991).

A. Perceptions of Inequity

The public appear to regard the criminal justice system as both unjust and inequitable: unjust in that guilty parties go unpunished, inequitable in that sanctions are unevenly distributed between equally culpable individuals. When asked to indicate whether people who commit sexual assault get caught "frequently" or "rarely," 90 percent of Canadians chose the latter (Environics Research Group 1987). Almost as many thought the same about other offenses such as impaired driving.

The perception of systematic inequity is most clearly associated with the courts. This is clear from many polls conducted in the United States, Canada, Great Britain, France, and Germany (see Ehrmann [1976] for a summary of the European findings). Wealthy offenders are perceived to receive preferential treatment by the police (e.g., Hylton 1985), the courts, and also by the nature of certain laws (Parisi et al. 1979). Brillon, Louis-Guerin, and Lamarche (1984) found that most Canadians agreed with the statement that "Justice favors the rich over the poor"; the locus of discrimination was seen to be the court system rather than the police. This is supported by other polls (e.g., Angus Reid 1984a, 1984b; Moore 1985; Environics Research Group 1989b). A recent survey conducted by the Canadian Sentencing Commission (Roberts 1988c) found that 77 percent of the public believed wealthy offenders received disparately lenient sentences.

The issue of inequity of treatment with relation to the courts raises the issue of sentencing disparity. Most people consider sentencing disparity to be a major problem with the judicial system. This view was shared by three-quarters of respondents to a recent poll in Canada (Canadian Sentencing Commission 1987).

B. Punishments

The first empirical study into public attitudes toward punishment, conducted in the United States over eighty years ago, begins in the following way: "The popular attitude towards retribution as a ground of punishment by the state, and as a motive for the infliction of loss or suffering by the individual, is a matter about which both the moralist and the student of political and social life need definite knowledge. Yet at present we have nothing better at our disposal than abstract and contradictory statements, the outcome of apparently mere impressions" (Sharp and Otto 1909, p. 341). Some of the contradictions remain, but if the authors were writing today there would seem ample reason to revise this evaluation of our knowledge.

Besides the research on crime seriousness, there has been a concomitant interest in public perceptions of punishment severity. As Sebba and Nathan (1984) point out, the idea of graduated severity is central to virtually all systems of punishment. And yet in most common-law jurisdictions, punishments are currently imposed in the absence of any formal scale or structure (other than a relatively crude ordering of maximum penalties). The need for an orderly scale of severity is particularly acute in sentencing systems following the principle of just deserts. In order to match increments in seriousness with corresponding increments in punishment severity, we need to have a scale of severity. The research on scaling of punishments also has considerable practical application. Uniformity in sentencing would be promoted if judges adhered to a common metric in terms of the severity of punishments they impose. This has led a number of researchers (e.g., Sebba 1978; Buchner 1979; Erickson and Gibbs 1979; Sebba and Nathan 1984; Tremblay 1988; Durham 1989) to explore what has become known as penal metric theory.

The results have revealed considerable reliability in public reactions to different sanctions and to increments in the severity of those sanctions. One weakness of this literature is that researchers sometimes describe their work as examining the "severity" of different penalties, when it is of course only *perceptions* of severity that are being explored. And these may vary depending on a number of factors, not the least of which is experience with the penalties themselves. This point is important because underlying the literature on crime seriousness is the assumption that rankings of seriousness derived from the public may serve to guide, or at least inform, sentencing practices. Von Hirsch (1985) rejects the argument that seriousness ratings for use in determining sentencing practices can be derived from public surveys. His point (see p. 65) is that harmfulness and culpability—the components of seriousness—have to be determined by their real, not perceived, im-

pact. The same is true for perceptions of punishment severity. Underlying research in this area is the assumption that public perceptions of
the severity of those punishments match their severity as experienced
by sentenced offenders. Severity ratings (and rankings) from the public
may differ from those derived from offenders. For example, the public
may over- (or under-) estimate the severity of a period of probation.
Perhaps researchers in the area of severity scaling should pay less attention to the views of the public and more to the perceptions of offenders
who have actually experienced the penalties being scaled.

C. The Purposes of Sentencing

Public preferences for various sentences cannot be understood without knowing something about the purposes of sentencing endorsed by
the public. Many public surveys deal with the purposes of sentencing.
One reason for this interest is that divergences between the courts and
the public in terms of punitiveness might be explained by differences
between the judiciary and the public in terms of the purposes sentencing is supposed to serve. There may not be great differences in terms
of punitiveness per se but rather in terms of the purposes perceived to
underlie sentencing. In any case, sentencing purposes will determine
in large part the nature and quantum of punishment imposed (e.g.,
Hogarth 1971; McFatter 1978). In sentencing as elsewhere in the criminal justice system, theory determines practice: if a judge adopts a reha-
bilitation-oriented sentencing theory, the sentences imposed will differ
from those imposed by a deterrence-oriented sentencer.

The findings of surveys in this area cannot be summarized neatly;
there is little consistency across polls or over time. A major cause of
this inconsistency is the diversity of approach in terms of methodology.
Some pollsters have elected a "menu-style" approach, in which respondents are allowed to choose a single purpose from a list provided by
the interviewer. In other surveys, subjects are asked to rank-order
purposes or to assign a numerical score reflecting the importance of
each purpose. And finally, some polls ask respondents to consider the
purposes of sentencing generally, while in others they are asked about
the relevance of specific purposes for specific offenses.

There are obvious deficiencies to the menu-style approach. Responses may be a function of respondents' relative familiarity with
different purposes. Deterrence, for example, may attract support because members of the public are more familiar with it than with a
sentencing goal such as incapacitation. General deterrence has a great

deal of intuitive appeal; most people see the principle of deterrence at work in everyday life and extrapolate to criminal behavior. Curiously though, people do not seem to generalize from their *own* behavior. When asked what prevents them from breaking the law, most people cite internal, personal factors, such as individual morality. When asked what prevents *others* from breaking the law, people cite external factors such as the threat of punishment (Banks, Maloney, and Willcocks 1975). This is an example of a broader psychological process known as the fundamental attribution error (Nisbett and Ross 1980): people tend to explain their own behavior in terms of internal dispositions, and others' behavior by means of external factors (such as the fear generated by the threat of punishment—see Ross [1977]). This phenomenon was noted by Aristotle, who wrote: "I do of my own accord what some are forced to do by their fear of the law" (cited in Cahn 1949, p. 14).

Most problematic however is the assumption made that responses reflect the actual purposes underlying sentencing decisions favored by the public. Nisbett and Wilson (1977) have shown that self-reports are often discrepant with reality. In the context of sentencing purposes, it is possible that people believe they are sentencing according to one principle (e.g., deterrence) and yet are in fact guided by another. McFatter (1982) found little concordance between the purposes judges rated as being important and the purposes that actually governed their sentencing decisions. For example, individuals who rated just deserts as the most important purpose were not the ones who followed this purpose when actually assigning penalties. Similarly Levin (1966) found that judges imposed sentences on the basis of a few purposes but were unaware of this. In short, direct questions may not be the optimal method of ascertaining public preferences regarding sentencing purposes.

With these limitations in mind, some general conclusions can be drawn. Members of the public appear to endorse many purposes (as do judges). A recent American poll (Jamieson and Flanagan 1989) found greatest support for special deterrence (79 percent rated it "very important"), but rehabilitation also received substantial support (rated "very important" by 72 percent of respondents). The public view punishment as serving multiple purposes: five sentencing purposes were rated as being very important by at least two-thirds of the sample.

While differing in emphasis from the responses of judges, public reactions are nevertheless as articulated and as complex. For example, support for different purposes varies from offense to offense. In a national survey conducted in the United States (Jacoby and Dunn 1987), rehabilitation was the purpose supported by most respondents (85 percent) for a crime such as arson and yet was supported by the fewest respondents (50 percent) for a crime such as forcible rape. Likewise in Canada, if the crime was relatively minor, the sentencing purpose endorsed by the greatest number of respondents was individual deterrence. When asked to consider instead serious crimes such as sexual assault or robbery, the percentage supporting individual deterrence fell from 34 percent to 11 percent, while support for incapacitation grew from 5 percent to 39 percent (Canadian Sentencing Commission 1987). It is hard therefore to make statements about sentencing purposes favored by the public since they endorse several aims simultaneously with support for any particular aim depending on the nature of the crime under consideration.

One issue that has not been fully explored concerns the relationship between public and professional sentencing philosophies.[16] The best data on the question come from polls conducted in several U.S. states, the results of which revealed significant concordance between the public and criminal justice professionals. For example, in Colorado, rankings of sentencing purposes derived from the public were remarkably similar to rankings of the same purposes derived from criminal justice officials (see Mande and English 1989, table 7).

D. Proportionality in Public Views of Sentencing

A central question addressed by researchers concerns the relationship between offense seriousness and punishment severity. The seriousness-severity relationship is, however, more complex than some have assumed. There can be little doubt about the strong association between public assessments of seriousness and severity in our culture. The notion that sentences should match in severity the seriousness of the crimes for which they are imposed permeates our culture and is frequently alluded to by policymakers and politicians. For example,

---

[16] Sebba and Nathan (1984) compared responses from a small ($N = 15$) sample of inmates with samples of students and criminal justice professionals. The results indicated consistency between the severity rankings of different penalties, but disagreements in terms of means. However, it would be imprudent to draw strong conclusions on the basis of so small a sample.

Margaret Thatcher, the former British prime minister, spoke of "the very real anxiety of ordinary people that too many sentences do not fit the crime" (*Economist* 1985).

Hamilton and Rytina (1980) conducted face-to-face interviews with 391 Boston residents who were asked to evaluate the seriousness of a list of crimes and also the relative severity of a list of punishments. On average, the degree of association between the seriousness of a particular crime and the severity of the assigned penalty was very high. The principle of just deserts was therefore strongly supported by the research. Blumstein and Cohen (1980) explored similar ground with a mail survey. Once again impressive correlations emerged to support the just deserts principle of proportionality (see White 1975; Gebotys and Roberts 1987).

More recently, Rossi, Simpson, and Miller, employing the factorial survey approach (see Sec. I of this essay), found that the relationship between crime seriousness and punishment severity was far from perfect: "There is no one-to-one direct relationship between the seriousness measures of crimes and desired sanctions" (1985, p. 89). Subjects were affected (not unlike judges) by characteristics of the offenders, the victims, and the consequences of the crime. Demographic characteristics of subjects played a statistically significant role.

Seriousness and severity are sometimes interchangeable terms in the literature; indeed, some researchers (e.g., Scott and Al-Thakeb 1977) have used punishment severity as a measure of crime seriousness, thereby assuming what other researchers have set out to prove. Thus rankings of seriousness are derived from rankings of the severity of accorded punishments. At one level of analysis, the two concepts are manifestations of the same underlying concept: harm, either inflicted or threatened. In the one case the harm is directed toward an individual victim or society, in the other the target is the convicted offender. However, it is important to separate on the empirical level the measurement of crime seriousness and severity of punishment.

Harm inflicted or threatened does not account for all the variation in scales of seriousness and severity. If scales measuring the two reflected exactly the same underlying dimensions, factors relevant to one would be equally applicable to the other. The age of the offender illustrates why this is not true. Age is frequently a mitigating factor that affects the severity of any punishment imposed, with youthful (and elderly) offenders receiving more lenient dispositions. The offender's age will have no such effect on perceptions of the seriousness of the offense committed. Thus the factors relevant to offense seriousness are not identical to the factors affecting the severity of the appropriate punishment.

E. Attitudes toward Sentencing

Are the courts more lenient than the public? This critical question has been addressed repeatedly over the past twenty years, and more than any other it exposes the limitations of public opinion surveys as an adequate measure of the views of the public. Although members of the public are generally believed to be harsher than judges, there is accumulating evidence that this is not always the case.

Several writers have affirmed that the public are harsher than judges. Ray (1982) for example, concluded: "There is very clearly a stark gap between actual sentencing practice and what the public see as appropriate sentencing practice . . . the gap between the judiciary and the public is so gross that nothing can disguise it" (p. 442). This perception is shared by many policymakers and criminal justice professionals. The corollary to this view is that any shift in sentencing practices toward the views of the public would result in the imposition of harsher punishments on convicted offenders. Discussion of this issue has tended to begin (and, until recently, also to end) with the results of polls in which respondents are asked the following question: "In your view, are sentences too harsh, about right, or not harsh enough?" The question has never failed to generate the result that the majority of the public in all countries covered in this survey expressed their desire for harsher penalties. In fact, the question concerning sentencing severity generates a more consensual response than any other issue in criminal justice, including capital punishment. Polls conducted in 1989 reveal that 84 percent of respondents in the United States (Flanagan and Maguire 1990, table 2.38) and 62 percent in Canada (Sacco and Johnson 1990) feel sentences are not harsh enough. Figure 1 presents the results of responses to this question over the past twenty-five years in the United States and Canada. This figure shows similar trends across the two countries, although the view that the courts are too lenient would appear to be more widespread in the United States than in Canada.

Similar trends emerge from polls conducted elsewhere. In Australia, 76 percent favored harsher sentences when responding to this question in 1987 (Indermaur 1987). Certainly, then, the public disapprove of perceived sentencing trends and on the face of it seem to want harsher sentences. For criminal justice researchers, the data presented in figure

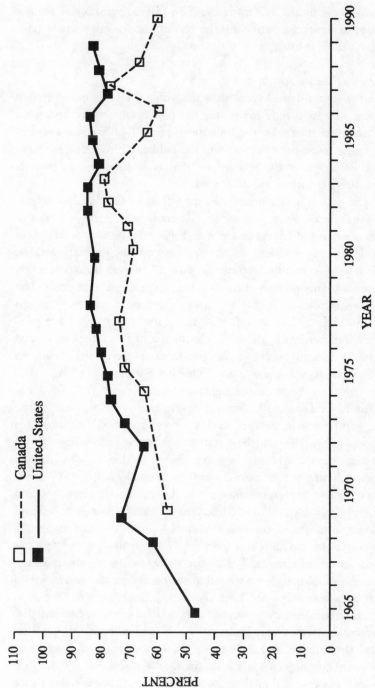

FIG. 1.—Percentage of public who state that sentences are too lenient. Sources.— *Sourcebook of Criminal Justice Statistics* (various years); Gallup Canada (1969–90). Note: Canadian data are not available for the years 1965–68, 1970–73, 1976, 1978, 1984, and 1989. United States data are not available for the years 1970–71, 1979, 1981, and 1990.

1 represent the point of departure. For many politicians and criminal justice policymakers, these data also represent the point of arrival. The poll findings have been interpreted to mean that sentencing cannot become more lenient, for fear of further alienating an already disenchanted public.

It is not just the sentencing decisions imposed by the courts of which the public disapprove. They also have a negative view of decisions that affect the sentencing process. In the United States, Knowles (1979) found the majority disapproved of plea bargaining. In Canada, Cohen and Doob (1989) found that 79 percent of respondents disapproved of the practice. There were clear links between disapproval of plea bargaining and disapproval of sentencing trends: those respondents who found plea bargaining to be unacceptable were also likely to disapprove of sentencing trends. While correlational in nature, this finding suggests disapproval of sentencing trends is part of a more global perception that the courts are not performing well.

But are the public in fact more punitive? Research refutes the conventional wisdom which portrays the public in this way.

F. Relative Punitiveness of the Public and the Courts

Two principal strategies have been adopted by researchers to compare public attitudes about punishing offenders to judicial attitudes and practices. In some cases sentences derived from surveys of the public have been compared to actual sentencing patterns (e.g., Gibbons 1969; Boydell and Grindstaff 1972; Grindstaff 1974; Warr, Meier, and Erickson 1983; Hough and Mayhew 1985; Hough and Moxon 1985; Zimmerman, Van Alstyne, and Dunn 1988; Diamond and Stalans 1989; Mande and English 1989; Roberts and Doob 1989; Diamond 1990; Zamble and Kalm 1990) or to sentences prescribed by penal codes (e.g., Samuel and Moulds 1986). Researchers have also compared public responses to attitudinal data derived from judicial officers such as judges and probation officers (e.g., Gottfredson and Taylor 1984; Fichter and Veneziano 1988; Ouimet 1990; Tremblay, Cordeau, and Ouimet 1991). Other studies have compared the public and the courts using a single case history (e.g., Doob and Roberts 1984) or a series of high-profile actual cases (e.g., Ray 1982). Contrary, perhaps, to expectation, the preponderance of evidence supports the view that the public are not harsher than the courts, or at least are not consistently harsher as the poll findings would suggest. Recent representative articles from the four countries surveyed for this essay are illustrative.

1. *United States.* Diamond and Stalans (1989) compared sentences derived from laypersons and from judges in Illinois. The sentences favored by the public were no more severe, or even less severe, than those imposed by the judges. Fichter and Veneziano (1988) compared the sentencing preferences of citizens to those derived from a sample of judges. In comparisons involving nineteen offenses, the public were harsher once (manslaughter); the judges were harsher than the public in the remaining eighteen cases. Mande and English (1989) also report convincing data that support a reversal of the accepted view of the public. In a series of cases, members of the public were more supportive of community corrections than were judges. It is often said that the public will support community-based sanctions, but only for minor offenses. The data from this Colorado study offer impressive refutation of this interpretation. Using aggravated robbery as the offense of comparison, these researchers found that only 14 percent of offenders convicted of this offense received a community-based sentence; 76 percent were imprisoned. Only 30 percent of the public endorsed incarceration for this kind of offense; almost half of the public sample favored a community based alternative to incarceration. This finding—of a public that is not harsher than the courts—is to be found in other U.S. studies as well (Rose and Prell 1955; Parker 1970; Williams, Gibbs, and Erickson 1980; Warr, Meier, and Erickson 1983; Gottfredson and Taylor 1984; Samuel and Moulds 1986; Thomson and Ragona 1987; Diamond and Stalans 1989; English, Crouch, and Pullen 1989; Mande and English 1989). Two exceptions to this pattern are studies by Blumstein and Cohen (1980), in which public sentences were one-half to two times longer than time actually served, and by Zimmerman, Van Alstyne, and Dunn (1988).

2. *Canada.* Roberts and Doob (1989) compared incarceration rates derived from a national sample of the public with the actual incarceration rate for ten high-frequency offenses. For some offenses the public were harsher than the courts; for others the courts were harsher. Overall, the results showed considerable similarity between public opinion and judicial practice. If the sentencing decisions of the public had actually been applied to the offenses in question, the result would have been 81,863 admissions to custody. In fact, 92,415 offenders were actually sent to prison over the period.[17] Similar results have been

---

[17] The offenses included in this study were high-profile crimes of the kind with which the public are most familiar (e.g., breaking and entering). These offenses are also the

found in other Canadian studies (see Doob and Roberts 1984; Roberts 1988*b*; Zamble 1990; Zamble and Kalm 1990). The counterexample to this trend in Canada is a study by Tremblay, Cordeau, and Ouimet (1991).

3. *Great Britain.* Analysis of data from the British Crime Survey (BCS) shows that for a series of crimes, the wishes of the public in terms of dealing with offenders coincided with the actual treatment of offenders by the courts (Hough and Moxon 1985). For example, 85 percent of the BCS respondents favored incarceration as the sentence for robbers, and 92 percent of sentences in cases of robbery were in fact terms of imprisonment. Hough and Moxon conclude: "These findings suggest that policy-makers and courts can treat with a degree of skepticism the claims often made by the media that public opinion demands a tougher line with offenders. The BCS offers no evidence to suggest widespread punitive attitudes among the public" (1985, p. 171).

4. *Australia.* A representative sample of Australians in a recent study were asked to assign the most appropriate sentence for a series of offenses. The authors note: "The average response shows broad agreement with typical court decisions" (Walker, Collins, and Wilson 1988, p. 150). For some offenses the public responses were more punitive than the courts', although not to the extent that one might expect on the basis of the poll results showing that the vast majority of the public feel sentences are too lenient. Thus for armed robbery, 88 percent of the public favored incarceration, while 80 percent of actual convictions resulted in imprisonment.

Finally, further light is shed on the alleged punitiveness of the public by research exploring alternatives to incarceration. If the public are as punitive as suggested by polls, we are not likely to find much support for alternative sanctions such as restitution. In fact, several studies have found widespread public acceptance of this concept. In a typical study, respondents (and sometimes criminal justice professionals) are presented with a case study and are asked if restitution should be considered as a disposition. Research in several countries (e.g., Galaway 1984*a*, 1984*b*; Boers and Sessar 1989; Bae 1991) has demonstrated

---

ones for which the public are most likely to demand harsh penalties. If the researchers had selected other crimes (such as offenses against the administration of justice), discrepancies between the public and the courts might well have been even greater. In short, the offenses chosen for this study were ones on which most agreement would be found, thus making it a conservative test of the public punitiveness hypotheses.

that the public endorse the use of restitution in a fairly wide range of cases, and that they are at least as accepting of restitution as are criminal justice professionals such as judges and prosecutors. In the most recent study conducted in the United States (Bae 1991), the researchers found that criminal justice officials in Minnesota were much less likely to accept restitution as an alternative punishment to imprisonment for property offenders than was the public (see Bae [1991] for a review of this literature).

These studies all involved comparisons between responses or sentences from groups of judges and responses from samples of the public. Another way of assessing the public and the judiciary consists of comparing lay versus professional magistrates. When this is done, the outcome is no different. Diamond (1990) examined the sentencing preferences of these two groups in England and found the lay magistrates to be at least as lenient as their professional counterparts on both simulated cases and actual decisions.

In addition to these studies finding few differences between sentences favored by the public and by the criminal justice system, there are others in which dramatic differences are found, with the public being markedly less punitive. Mande and Crouch (1984) for example compared public and professional reactions to a case of aggravated robbery in which the offender had a criminal record. Over 85 percent of the criminal justice professionals favored imprisonment. The comparable statistic from the public was 67 percent. Differences in terms of median sentence lengths were even more striking: sixty months from the criminal justice sample, only thirty-six months from the public. In a related study (Mande and English 1989), median sentence lengths recommended by criminal justice professionals exceeded median sentence lengths favored by the public in ten out of fourteen comparisons.

Taken together, these studies do not sustain the conclusion that the public is overwhelmingly more punitive than the courts.[18] This issue has been dealt with at length here because, of all the topics considered, it is in this area that the impact on criminal justice policy is most likely to have effects on offenders' lives. It has long been argued that criminal justice reforms that involve noncarceral options are likely to encounter resistance from the public. Ryan notes: "The construction of public opinion should be of more than passing interest to civil servants and

---

[18] See Mäkelä (1966) for similar findings in countries other than the four included in this essay.

politicians. . . . It is, after all, they who are constantly arguing that reforms, say shorter sentences or more alternatives to prison, are impractical because public opinion would not tolerate more 'soft options' " (1983, p. 120). As we have seen, when the public are given information about alternative dispositions, support for incarceration declines significantly (Doble and Klein 1989).

G. Residual Difficulties in Comparing Public and Courts

Some methodological problems persist in the studies discussed above. There remains the question of whether the public are responding with an accurate perception of the system. Do the public have a realistic idea, for example, of the extent to which early release on parole affects time served in prison? As noted earlier in this essay, the public have inaccurate ideas of what is happening in the system, and these misperceptions are biased in the direction that would lead the public to demand harsher penalties. Finally, as Thomson and Ragona (1987) have pointed out, public opinion polls of this kind do not provide respondents with information about the "punitive content" or "behavioral impact" of different sentences. Even when the public have the same sentences to consider as do the courts (and this is not always the case), the significance of these dispositions may well be very different. To return to Yves Brillon's (1984) research, almost 60 percent of respondents agreed with the statement that "prisons are veritable hotels." The public might well be more restrained in their support for incarceration if they knew what a sentence of imprisonment actually entailed (particularly at the maximum-security level). Support for this hypothesis comes from data gathered in that study. While it is only correlational, there was a clear relationship between attitudes toward prisons and perceptions of prisons: those agreeing with this statement were far more likely to endorse the use of punitive measures. In the United States, a surprisingly high percentage (40 percent) of respondents to several polls felt that prison was "not a harsh experience" (e.g., Mande and Butler 1982). Banks, Maloney, and Willcocks (1975) in Great Britain also found that people were generally very poorly informed about prisons and prison life. In short, comparisons between the public and the judiciary under the best of circumstances will remain imperfect.

The research summarized here qualifies, to a substantial degree, the perception that the public are exceedingly more punitive than the courts. But it would be a mistake also to think that judicial practice is consistently more severe than public opinion. In all likelihood, while the views of the public and the decisions of the courts are fairly close, generalizations are risky. It seems probable that for some offenses the public are harsher, and for other types of offenses the courts are harsher, but that overall significant differences between the two do not exist. The challenge to researchers now moves beyond the simple level of differences in punitiveness and into more complex questions relating to explaining why certain types of offenses attract a punitive response. Research has begun to address these questions (e.g., Diamond and Stalans 1989; Tremblay, Cordeau, and Ouimet 1991).

Pollsters will doubtless continue to conduct, and the news media will continue to report, polls in which the public are simply asked whether sentences are too harsh or too lenient. And in all probability the public will continue to state that the courts are too lenient. In light of this, it is important that the results of more refined research be made available to policymakers.

H. Attitudes toward Capital Punishment

Although surveys of public attitudes to the death penalty continue to be conducted in all four countries surveyed for this essay, the United States is the only country in which executions take place. As with attitudes to sentencing severity, a consensus exists: most Americans favor capital punishment as a penalty for some cases of homicide, and this has been true for as long as the question has been posed. In 1936, 61 percent were in favor; in a 1989 poll, the figure was 79 percent (Flanagan and Maguire 1990, table 2.47). Similar findings emerge from polls in Canada, the United Kingdom, and Australia. Support for capital punishment has increased over the past few years. Surveys of younger people suggest that support for abolition of the death penalty is at an all-time low among the next generation. The percentage of college freshmen endorsing abolition now stands at 21 percent. It has declined steadily since 1969 when over 54 percent of freshmen took this position (Flanagan and Maguire 1990, table 2.80).

In explaining the continued (and increasing) support for capital punishment, it is important to bear in mind the changing face of homicide over the fifty-year period. In the 1930s, the most highly publicized murders were gangland slayings involving professional assassins. Mass or multiple murders were rare, serial killers unknown. Both these forms of homicide have now been seen in all four countries over the past few years. To the public, it is cases such as these that spring to mind when asked about the death penalty, and the increase in the volume and seriousness of murders reported in the press may have the effect of increasing general punitiveness and, in turn, support for capital punishment. Many of the murders with the highest media profile also now involve randomly selected victims. This may also increase fear and thereby inflate public support for the death penalty.

1. *Proponents of Capital Punishment.* A central question addressed but not completely resolved by researchers concerns the grounds for public support for the death penalty. Is execution endorsed for utilitarian purposes such as deterrence or incapacitation, or more on retributive grounds? The answer appears to be a mixture of both, with neither perspective attracting wide support. Most recently, Zeisel and Gallup (1989) found 50 percent of respondents endorsed capital punishment on grounds of desert, while a further 22 percent did so for reasons relating to deterrence (see also Lotz and Regoli 1980; Bohm 1987a; Finckenauer 1988). But earlier research found more support for general deterrence (Vidmar 1974; Vidmar and Ellsworth 1974; Thomas and Foster 1975; Ellsworth and Ross 1983). Once again, the issue may rest on the nature of the specific cases: execution for a professional killer may be deemed necessary primarily (but not exclusively) on grounds of public safety (incapacitation and general deterrence). Public desire for capital punishment for a child killer may rest more on moral outrage and a desire for retribution.

2. *Opponents.* Moral considerations are preeminent among those who oppose the death penalty: excluding "don't knows," they account for 65 percent of responses (Zeisel and Gallup 1989). Skepticism regarding deterrent effects was cited by only 5 percent of respondents as the reason for opposing the death penalty.

3. *Knowledge of the Efficacy and Nature of Capital Punishment.* As with other issues reviewed in this essay, the strength of public feeling exceeds the depth of knowledge about the issue. Sarat and Vidmar (1976) found varying levels of public knowledge, depending on the specific question asked, but public awareness was particularly weak on the critical issue of the effectiveness of capital punishment as a deterrent. Most people assume that the presence of the death penalty acts as a deterrent against homicide. Zeisel and Gallup report that almost two-thirds of the public believe the death penalty to be an effective general deterrent for murder. Zeisel and Gallup (1989) also note that, if respondents were convinced of the inefficacy of execution as a general deterrent, the percentage supporting the death penalty would decline

from 71 percent to 55 percent. Knowles (1979) reports that over 70 percent of Ohio residents believed that capital punishment was effective in deterring crimes. Earlier polls by the Harris organization found widespread public confidence in the deterrent advantage of execution over life imprisonment (with or without parole—Hindelang et al. [1976]). The relative contribution of deterrence and desert to the pro–capital punishment statistics is clear from several Louis Harris polls. Sixty percent of the sample supported execution for offenders convicted of murder. This percentage dropped to 35 percent when respondents were asked: "Suppose it could be proven to your satisfaction that the death penalty was NOT more effective than long prison sentences in keeping other people from committing murder, would you be in favor of capital punishment or opposed to it?" (Margarita and Parisi 1979). Clearly, if the public were acquainted with the empirical research on the relative deterrent effect, the percentage of proponents would fall.

I. Attitudes toward Parole

Attitudes toward early release from prison have not been studied as often as attitudes toward sentencing. This is surprising in light of the widespread criticism parole attracts when the news media report that a serious crime was committed by a parolee. Polls that have explored opinion regarding parole show public dissatisfaction with the current administration of parole but at the same time strong support for the underlying principle that inmates be allowed to serve part of their prison sentences in the community under supervison. In reviewing this material, it should be recalled that the public hold several misconceptions of parole: they overestimate both release rates and recidivism rates.

In general, the U.S. public supports the concept of parole. For example, a poll conducted in 1984 (Jamieson and Flanagan 1987, table 2.12) found that 82 percent endorsed the view that "parole supervision is useful in deterring crime and in helping the individual to adjust to the community." The percentage of respondents who favor abolition is small. A poll conducted in Canada in 1986 found that less than one-quarter of respondents favored parole abolition as a possible criminal justice reform (Roberts 1988a).

Nevertheless, accompanying this positive reaction toward the notion of parole is the widespread perception that parole has become too easy to obtain, and should be granted later, and to fewer inmates. Of the

Canadian public, two-thirds see parole boards in that country as being too lenient (Roberts 1988a), approximately the same percentage as those who regard sentences as being too lenient (Sacco and Johnson 1990). Fully 70 percent of respondents to a 1987 poll in Canada supported the view that "parole boards release too many offenders on parole" (Canadian Criminal Justice Association 1987).

As with the questions dealing with sentencing, the public have a concrete image of an offender in mind when responding to the issue of parole. When asked, "When answering this question [about the release of offenders on parole] what kinds of offenders were you thinking of?" over half the sample were thinking exclusively of violent offenders (Canadian Criminal Justice Association 1987). There is significant correlation between the two attitudes, suggesting that people who perceive sentencing as being lenient also perceive parole as being lenient (Roberts 1988a). Most members of the public would favor restricting parole release to certain offenders. The same survey revealed that two-thirds favored restricting parole to inmates serving time for nonviolent crimes.

Following the views of the public on the issue of parole would seem to result in longer periods of imprisonment, with a greater percentage of sentences served in prison. However, it should be recalled that the public opposition to parole is largely founded on inaccurate perceptions of parole release rates. This suggests that correcting misperceptions about parole would result in greater support for community-based corrections, although this hypothesis remains to be tested empirically.

J. Criminal Justice Professionals' Misperceptions of the Public

Misperceiving the criminal justice system, the public is itself misperceived by criminal justice professionals. This is true for several issues, but two in particular stand out: alternative sanctions and the goal of rehabilitation. Gottfredson and Taylor (1984) provide some fascinating comparisons between policymakers and the public. They studied a sample of the criminal justice elite and the general public in Maryland. Contrary to expectation, dissensus was more likely to exist between policymakers and criminal justice professionals than between policymakers and the general public. Policymakers tended to underestimate the amount of public support for reform strategies in the area of criminal justice. This is not an isolated example: Immarigeon (1986), in a study of policymakers in Michigan, notes that this criminal justice elite believed that fewer than one resident in four would support the greater use of alternatives to imprisonment. In fact, two-thirds of the public supported this policy. Riley and Rose (1980) found the public in the state of Washington to be far less punitively oriented than criminal justice elites had anticipated. They note: "the elites' belief that their attitudes are very different from the public's does not seem to be substantiated" (p. 350). On a variety of practices in the area of corrections, the views of the public were close to the views of the elite. For example, 99 percent of the elite and 95 percent of the public supported "increased emphasis on vocational training"; 53 percent of both populations supported conjugal visits for inmates; 82 percent of the elite and 78 percent of the public favored greater use of group therapy for inmates (see Riley and Rose 1980, table 4). In a similar vein, Smith and Lipsey (1976) found high degrees of public support for conjugal visits. They concluded: "The research reported herein suggests that the appraisal of public concern by legislators, prison administrators and criminologists is often incorrect" (p. 122). As Cullen, Clark, and Wozniak (1985) note: "The public 'will,' in short, is much more complex and tolerant than politicians acknowledge" (p. 22). (See also Gandy [1978] for findings on restitution.)

Another misperception of public opinion concerns support for rehabilitation. Much has been made about a punishment-oriented U.S. public; however, one conclusion that can be drawn from surveying relevant polls over the past few years is that support for rehabilitation as a sentencing purpose and as a purpose of the correctional system remains substantial. To return to Immarigeon's report, while only 12 percent of policymakers believed the public would support rehabilitation as a criminal justice objective, in reality two-thirds of the public took this view. (This point has recently been made by Francis Cullen and others—see Cullen et al. [1990]). In fact, when rehabilitation goes head-to-head against punishment as a purpose of imprisonment, rehabilitation emerges with more public support—56 percent of those respondents who had an opinion (Flanagan and Maguire 1990, table 2.46). A Canadian survey also found more support for rehabilitation as a reason for imprisonment (compared to punishment—see Environics Research [1989b]). Communicating information to policymakers on the true mood of the public in these areas is therefore a priority for researchers.

IV. Directions for Future Research

The researcher who has followed public opinion surveys over the past few years may acquire a sense of déjà vu, as poll follows poll, repeating questions pertaining to the punishment of offenders. What percentage of offenders convicted of rape should be incarcerated? And for how long? Repetition of these questions may be useful, particularly for historical comparisons, and yet might it not be profitable to test public tolerance of reactions to deviance on a more ambitious level?

Questions pertaining to alternative punishments are sometimes posed, but this is always done within the framework of a criminal law whose raison d'être is punishment, whether that punishment is imposed to deter, to incapacitate, or for the purpose of just deserts. As noted earlier in this essay, public responses have produced some surprises in reaction to poll questions such as these. Researchers and pollsters might find still more surprising results were they to pose more provocative questions. For example, can the public conceive of a response to crime in which punishment does not play the primary role? Academics and some practitioners in criminal justice have proposed alternatives to the current criminal justice models employed in most Western nations. Some of these new paradigms involve placing more emphasis on restorative justice (see Bianchi and Swaaningen 1986; Galaway and Hudson 1990). Are we sure that the public simply cannot countenance such paradigm shifts? Or are there conditions under which the public, who, for the most part, harbor no illusions about the efficacy of the current system, might endorse some alternative response to deviance? One has to pose the question in order to know for sure.

Research on public knowledge and opinion in the area of criminal justice needs to be broader than it has been to date. The emphasis in polls on crime seriousness and punishments is understandable: these topics pique the interest of the media and the public alike. Nevertheless, we have little clear idea about public opinion in other, less well illuminated areas of criminal justice. What do the public know and think about topics such as diversion, electronic monitoring, the treatment of inmates (e.g., solitary confinement), community-based policing, to name but a few. For a comprehensive picture of public opinion these topics will have to be explored further.

A final note concerns the complexity of questions posed on surveys. In the overwhelming majority of polls conducted, the questions have been relatively straightforward, dealing with criminal justice issues in the same way as consumer preferences. This simplicity has been favored by pollsters in order to avoid confusing respondents. Evidence suggests, however, that researchers have underestimated the public's ability to comprehend and respond to questions of considerable subtlety and complexity. On those occasions that complex questions have been posed, the results have been encouraging.[19]

A. *Effects of Legislation and Legal Decisions on Public Opinion*

The influence of the criminal law on public opinion is an underresearched topic. The criminal law aims to influence the views of the public in a number of different ways. The criminalization (or decriminalization) of certain acts may influence public disapproval or the level of moral condemnation. Maximum penalties may determine (in part at least) public perceptions of crime seriousness: the public may infer the seriousness of crimes from the severity of the maximum punishments prescribed. This is one of the arguments made against lowering maximum penalties that in Canada and Great Britain at least are in many cases unrealistically high. And finally, individual sentencing decisions may influence public perceptions of specific offenses and offenders (see Cahn 1949; Walker 1985).

Empirical research on this question has been scarce; Walker and Argyle (1974) found that the decriminalization of attempted suicide had no significant effect on public attitudes toward this behavior. Berkowitz and Walker (1967) performed an experiment in which subjects were informed that various actions either were or were not criminal in nature. This manipulation had a weak effect. Being told that an action was criminal led to stronger disapproval on the part of subjects in the study. A similar result emerged from Walker and Marsh (1984), who capitalized on the impending criminalization of operating a motor vehicle without wearing a seat belt. Subjects were asked how much they disapproved of driving without use of a safety belt "at the moment" and later "when it becomes an offense." Mean disapproval scores were higher under the criminalization condition, suggesting an impact on public attitudes due to the criminal law (see also Nesdale 1980).

Concerning sentencing, a recent study in Canada examined the impact of information about maximum penalties on the views of a rep-

[19] Mellinger, Huffine, and Balter (1982) have shown that the public can understand and provide meaningful responses to complex questions. In the area of criminal justice, the Canadian Sentencing Commission posed a complex question dealing with exemplary sentencing (the imposition of exceptionally severe sentences in order to achieve general deterrence). Analysis of public responses indicated that respondents had clearly understood the question. By the same token, a greater use of open-ended questions rather than simply providing a limited number of alternatives is likely to elicit more valuable information about public attitudes (see Geer 1987). In short, while there are limitations to the length and complexity of questions employed in large-scale surveys, these limitations have perhaps been overstated.

resentative sample of the public (Canadian Sentencing Commission 1987). Having established that most people were unaware of the maximum penalty for impaired driving, researchers informed half the sample about the actual maximum penalty. The remainder were told nothing about the maximum. All respondents were then asked to rate the seriousness of this offense. The manipulation had no effect: the average seriousness ratings provided by the two groups were almost identical. It is possible, however, that perceptions of the seriousness of a familiar offense such as impaired driving are sufficiently fixed as to be impervious to the influence of the severity of the maximum penalty. Walker and Marsh (1984) asked members of the public to read news media accounts of sentencing decisions. These researchers were testing the "expressive" theory of punishment, namely, that sentences "lead" public opinion in that public views are likely to be affected by the sentence imposed. The nature of the sentence imposed had little effect on disapproval scores (of the offenses for which the sentences were imposed). Walker summarized the results of this line of research in the following way: "The results did not provide any support for the belief that disapproval levels of substantial numbers of adults were raised or lowered by information about the sentence or about the judge's views" (1985, p. 102). It appears then that the legal status of a behavior has an effect on public attitudes, but the nature of the specific penalty imposed does not. It should be noted, however, that there has not been a great deal of research on this topic; effects may yet be found under different conditions.

B. The Impact of Public Opinion on the Justice System

To this point this essay has dealt with the effects of the criminal justice system (albeit mediated by the news media) on public attitudes. It is important to reverse perspective and also study the effects of public opinion on the legal culture and the criminal justice system. Many write of the system's concern for the views of the public (e.g, Lenke 1974), but to what extent does this concern affect policy or practice? This is also an underresearched question. Lenke (1974) provides examples of legislative changes in Europe that may have been provoked by public opinion.[20] There is little hard evidence for the link

---

[20] For example, a provision of the English Criminal Justice Act of 1967 (involving the suspending of sentences of imprisonment) is cited as a law that was passed as a result of the direct influence of public opinion.

in these cases however, and as Lenke notes, many alternate explanations exist. In the United States, Rodgers (1969*a*, 1969*b*) reports a case history that demonstrates the impact of public opinion. In Iowa, a law required all children to attend schools where they would be taught by state-certified teachers. For most citizens such a law is relatively uncontroversial. However, the Amish refused to hire such teachers for their schools. In the end, the law was not applied to the Amish, and local authorities decided that it would not be enforced. Opposition from the public—in this case sympathy for the Amish—in effect defeated the law.

Public opinion may well exercise an important, although indirect, influence on the criminal justice system. It is likely to have most impact in the area of sentencing, where judges may well consider the views of the public (or what they perceive the views of the public to be). Almost two-thirds of the participants in one survey of judges in Canada indicated that the views of the public were important to consider when determining sentence (Hogarth 1971; see also Walker 1985, p. 64). Research evidence for a link between public opinion and sentencing trends is mixed, however. Glick and Pruet (1985) found little association between measures of public opinion and measures of judicial behavior. Earlier work (Kuklinski and Stanga 1979) in California, however, found that aggregate sentencing decisions had changed in the direction of prevailing opinion. The level of analysis performed may well explain the discrepancy between the two studies. In any case, the question deserves further research attention.[21]

C. Need for a Survey Data Base

The literature on public opinion research—particularly opinion surveys—is not to be found in any one field of social science. Some surveys eventually make their way into scientific journals, but frequently they remain in the archives of the institution that commissioned them or of the polling organization that carried them out. The researcher who wishes to assemble a picture of public opinion on crimi-

[21] One difficulty confronting researchers engaged in the issue is the complexity of the relationship between public opinion and judicial practice. If there is a causal relationship between the two, it may well be bidirectional: judges may be influenced by public opinion, but the sentences they impose may well (in some cases at least) change public views (see Walker 1985). Some kind of cross-lagged panel design may be able to disentangle the direction, nature, and magnitudes of effects (see Kenny 1975; Clegg, Jackson, and Wall 1979). The impact of public opinion on the behavior (and longevity in office) of elected officials is even harder to evaluate.

nal justice issues has to turn over a lot of different stones. And, as one opinion poll succeeds another, it becomes clear that little collective memory exists in the field. While the occasional article presents an historical analysis of results of polls that have repeatedly posed a particular question, most publications report the results of a specific poll and little else. And yet, in all the countries included in this survey, there has been a relentless accretion of historical data on public attitudes. What is needed is a central repository of opinion data to which all public opinion polls would be sent. Such a data base, once computerized, could then be accessed by users via telephone lines.

In addition to facilitating research, such a data base would also serve a substantive purpose. Policymakers contemplating criminal justice reforms (and possible public reaction to those reforms) frequently commission an opinion survey. With the results comes the question of interpretation: if 50 percent of the public favor the abolition of parole, is this high or low? Has support for parole declined over a given period? Only comparisons in a time-series design will permit informed interpretation of the results of any particular poll. Finally, a data base of this kind would permit researchers to conduct meta-analyses (see Smith and Glass 1977; Guzzo, Jackson, and Kutzell 1987) in which the results of many polls are aggregated with a view to hypothesis testing on a large scale.

The basis for such a data base already exists. The Roper Center, which is located at the University of Connecticut, already contains a wealth of opinion poll data going back to the beginning of systematic polling.[22] Many of these polls deal with criminal justice issues. All that is required is the necessary software to permit researchers ready access to the data (see Roberts 1989).

Notwithstanding the breadth and volume of research on public knowledge and opinion regarding crime and criminal justice, many issues remain to be explored. This is particularly true for public knowledge. We need to know more about public awareness in this area, not least because this information will promote understanding of public attitudes for which they are the foundation. This survey of public attitudes toward criminal justice has revealed that the people in all four countries are frequently hostile toward their criminal justice systems. However, part of this hostility springs from an inadequate grasp of the

---

[22] The reader interested in further information about the Roper Center at the University of Connecticut should contact Dr. Everett Ladd.

system and misperceptions of crime and criminals. A priority for the criminal justice systems of all four countries is therefore clear: public education in the area of crime and criminal justice. Research seems to demonstrate that, if the public had more accurate perceptions of the system, they would also be more satisfied (see Stalans and Diamond 1990). But as long as news media stories remain the public's primary source of information, dissatisfaction will be rampant.

While divergences between the public and the legal system will not be eliminated, they will be considerably attenuated by providing better information about the system to the public and better information about the views of the public to professionals working in the system. The existence of an uninformed and frequently hostile public poses an important problem for the criminal justice system and also raises questions about the democratic nature of our legal institutions.

REFERENCES

Abel-Smith, Brian, Michael Zander, and Rosalind Brooke. 1973. *Legal Problems and the Citizen*. London: Heinemann.

Alford, David. 1984. *Public Awareness of Impaired Driving Initiatives*. Ottawa: Department of Justice, Canada.

Anderson, Craig. 1983. "Abstract and Concrete Data in the Perseverance of Social Theories: When Weak Data Lead to Unshakeable Beliefs." *Journal of Experimental Social Psychology* 19:93–108.

Angus Reid Associates. 1984a. *Canadians' Attitudes toward the Justice System*. Toronto: Angus Reid Associates, Inc.

———. 1984b. *Canadian Unity Information Office Survey*. Toronto: Angus Reid Associates, Inc.

Austin, William, and Thomas A. Williams. 1977. "A Survey of Judges' Responses to Simulated Legal Cases: Research Note on Sentencing Disparity." *Journal of Criminal Law and Criminology* 68:306–10.

Bae, Imho. 1991. "A Survey on Public Acceptance of Restitution as an Alternative to Incarceration for Property Offenders in Hennepin County, Minnesota." Ph.D. dissertation, University of Minnesota.

Banks, C., E. Maloney, and H. D. Willcocks. 1975. "Public Attitudes to Crime and the Penal System." *British Journal of Criminology* 15:228–40.

Barrile, Leo. 1984. "Television and Attitudes about Crime." In *Justice and the Media*, edited by Ray Surette. Springfield, Ill.: Thomas.

Berkowitz, Leonard, and Nigel Walker. 1967. "Laws and Moral Judgments." *Sociometry* 30:410–22.

Bertrand, Francine. 1982. "Public Opinion about Criminal Justice Issues: Some Caution about Poll Data." *Impact* 1:11–20.

Bianchi, Herman, and Rene van Swaaningen, eds. 1986. *Abolitionism: Towards a Non-repressive Approach to Crime*. Amsterdam: Free University Press.

Bibby, Reginald W. 1981. "Crime and Punishment: A National Reading." *Social Indicators Research* 9:1–13.

Blumstein, Alfred, and Jacqueline Cohen. 1980. "Sentencing of Convicted Offenders: An Analysis of the Public's View." *Law and Society Review* 14:223–61.

Boers, Klaus, and Klaus Sessar. 1989. "Do People Really Want Punishment? On the Relationship between Acceptance of Restitution, Needs for Punishment, and Fear of Crime." In *Developments in Crime and Crime Control Research*, edited by Klaus Sessar and Hans-Jurgen Kerner. New York: Springer-Verlag.

Bohm, Robert M. 1987*a*. "American Death Penalty Attitudes. A Critical Examination of Recent Evidence." *Criminal Justice and Behavior* 14:380–96.

———. 1987*b*. "Myths about Criminology and Criminal Justice: A Review Essay." *Justice Quarterly* 4:631–42.

Borg, Ingwer. 1988. "Revisiting Thurstone's and Coombs' Scales on the Seriousness of Crimes and Offences." *European Journal of Social Psychology* 18: 53–61.

Boydell, Craig L., and Carl F. Grindstaff. 1972. "Public Opinion and the Criminal Law: An Empirical Test of Public Attitudes toward Legal Sanctions." In *Deviant Behaviour and Societal Reaction*, edited by Craig L. Boydell, Carl F. Grindstaff, and P. C. Whitehead. Toronto: Holt, Reinhart & Winston.

Bradburn, Norman, and Seymour Sudman. 1988. *Polls and Surveys*. San Francisco: Jossey-Bass.

Brillon, Yves. 1984. "Les attitudes punitives dans la population canadienne." *Canadian Journal of Criminology* 26:293–311.

Brillon, Yves, Christiane Louis-Guerin, and Marie-Christine Lamarche. 1984. *Attitudes of the Canadian Public toward Crime Policies*. Ottawa: Ministry of the Solicitor General Canada.

Broadhurst, Roderic, and David Indermaur. 1982. "Crime Seriousness Ratings: The Relationship of Information Accuracy and General Attitudes in Western Australia." *Australian and New Zealand Journal of Criminology* 15: 219–34.

Buchner, Deborah. 1979. "Scale of Sentence Severity." *Journal of Criminal Law and Criminology* 70:182–87.

Bull, R., and J. Green. 1970. "The Relationship between Physical Appearance and Criminality." *Medical Science Law* 20:103–25.

Bynum, T., J. Greene, and F. Cullen. 1986. "Correlates of Legislative Crime Control Ideology." *Criminal Justice Policy Review* 1:253–67.

Cahn, Edmund N. 1949. *The Sense of Injustice: An Anthropocentric View of the Law*. New York: New York University Press.

California Assembly Committee on Criminal Procedure. 1975. "Public Knowledge of Criminal Penalties." In *Perception in Criminology*, edited by Richard L. Henshel and Robert A. Silverman. Toronto: Methuen.

Campbell, Anne, and Steven Muncer. 1990. "Causes of Crime. Uncovering a Lay Model." *Criminal Justice and Behavior* 17:410–19.

Canadian Criminal Justice Association. 1987. *Attitudes toward Parole*. Ottawa: Canadian Criminal Justice Association.

Canadian Sentencing Commission. 1987. *Sentencing Reform: A Canadian Approach*. Ottawa: Ministry of Supply and Services Canada.

Cantril, Albert, ed. 1980. *Polling on the Issues*. Washington, D.C.: Seven Locks.

Carlson, J. M. 1985. *Prime Time Law Enforcement: Crime Show Viewing and Attitudes toward the Criminal Justice System*. New York: Praeger.

Carroll, John S. 1978. "Causal Theories of Crime and Their Effect upon Expert Parole Decisions." *Law and Human Behavior* 2:377–88.

Clegg, C. W., P. R. Jackson, and I. D. Wall. 1979. "The Potential of Cross-lagged Correlation Analysis in Field Research." In *Research in Organizations: Issues and Controversies*, edited by Richard T. Mowday and Richard M. Steers. Santa Monica, Calif.: Goodyear.

Cohen, Stanley A., and Anthony N. Doob. 1989. "Public Attitudes to Plea Bargaining." *Criminal Law Quarterly* 32:85–109.

Conklin, John. 1975. *The Impact of Crime*. New York: Macmillan.

Coombs, Clyde H. 1967. "Thurstone's Measurement of Social Values Revisited Forty Years Later." *Journal of Personality and Social Psychology* 6:85–91.

Corbett, Claire, and Frances Simon. 1991. "Police and Public Perceptions of the Seriousness of Traffic Offences." *British Journal of Criminology* 31: 153–64.

Cullen, Francis T., Gregory A. Clark, John B. Cullen, and Richard A. Mathers. 1985. "Attribution, Salience, and Attitudes toward Criminal Sanctioning." *Criminal Justice and Behavior* 12:305–31.

Cullen, Francis T., Gregory A. Clark, and John F. Wozniak. 1985. "Explaining the Get Tough Movement: Can the Public Be Blamed?" *Federal Probation* 9:16–24.

Cullen, Francis, Bruce Link, and Craig Polanzi. 1982. "The Seriousness of Crime Revisited." *Criminology* 2:83–102.

Cullen, Francis T., Sandra E. Skovron, Joseph E. Scott, and Velmer S. Burton. 1990. "Public Support for Correctional Treatment: The Tenacity of Rehabilitative Ideology." *Criminal Justice and Behavior* 17:6–18.

Davis, F. 1952. "Crime News in Colorado Newspapers." *American Journal of Sociology* 57:325–30.

Decker, Scott. 1981. "Citizen Attitudes toward the Police: A Review of Past Findings and Suggestions for Future Policy." *Journal of Police Science and Administration* 9:80–87.

Dejoy, David, and Judith Klippel. 1984. "Attributing Responsibility for Alcohol-related Near Miss Accidents." *Journal of Safety Research* 15:107–15.

Diamond, Shari S. 1989. "Using Psychology to Control Law: From Deceptive Advertising to Criminal Sentencing." *Law and Human Behavior* 13:239–52.

———. 1990. "Sentencing Decisions by Laypersons and Professional Judges." *Law and Social Inquiry* 15:191–221.

Diamond, Shari S., and Loretta J. Stalans. 1989. "The Myth of Judicial Leniency in Sentencing." *Behavioral Sciences and the Law* 7:73–89.

Doble, John. 1987. *Crime and Punishment: The Public's View*. New York: Public Agenda Foundation.

Doble, John, Stephen Immerwahr, and Amy Richardson. 1991. *Punishing Criminals: The People of Delaware Consider the Options*. New York: Edna McConnell Clark Foundation.

Doble, John, and Josh Klein. 1989. *Punishing Criminals: The Public's View. An Alabama Survey*. New York: Edna McConnell Clark Foundation.

Doleschal, Eugene. 1970. "Public Opinion and Correctional Reform." *Crime and Delinquency Literature* 2:456–76.

———. 1979. "Crime—Some Popular Beliefs." *Crime and Delinquency* 25:1–8.

Doob, Anthony. 1984. "The Many Realities of Crime." In *Perspectives in Criminal Law*, edited by Edward L. Greenspan and Anthony Doob. Aurora, Ontario: Canada Law Book.

Doob, Anthony, and Glen MacDonald. 1979. "Television Viewing and Fear of Victimization: Is the Relationship Causal?" *Journal of Personality and Social Psychology* 37:170–79.

Doob, Anthony, and Julian V. Roberts. 1982. *Crime and the Official Response to Crime: The Views of the Canadian Public*. Ottawa: Department of Justice, Canada.

———. 1983. *An Analysis of the Public's View of Sentencing*. Ottawa: Department of Justice, Canada.

———. 1984. "Social Psychology, Social Attitudes and Attitudes toward Sentencing." *Canadian Journal of Behavioural Science* 16:269–80.

Durham, Alexis M. 1988. "Crime Seriousness and Punitive Severity: An Assessment of Social Attitudes." *Justice Quarterly* 5:131–53.

———. 1989. "Judgments of Appropriate Punishment: The Effects of Question Type." *Journal of Criminal Justice* 17:75–85.

———. 1990. "Public Opinion regarding Sentences for Crime: Does It Exist?" Paper presented at the annual meeting of the American Society of Criminology, Baltimore, November.

Dussuyer, Inez. 1979. *Crime News: A Study of 40 Ontario Newspapers*. Toronto: University of Toronto, Centre of Criminology.

Economist. 1985. Untitled article. (July 20), p. 51.

Edwards, Cheryl. 1987. "Public Opinion on Domestic Violence: A Review of the New Jersey Survey." *Response to the Victimization of Women and Children* 10:6–9.

Ehrmann, Henry W. 1976. *Comparative Legal Cultures*. Englewood Cliffs, N.J.: Prentice Hall.

Ellsworth, Phoebe. 1978. "Attitudes toward Capital Punishment: From Applications to Theory." Paper presented to the Society for Experimental Social Psychology, Princeton, N.J.

Ellsworth, Phoebe C., and Lee Ross. 1983. "Public Opinion and Capital Punishment: A Close Examination of the Views of Abolitionists and Retentionists." *Crime and Delinquency* 29:116–69.

English, Kim, Joan Crouch, and Suzanne Pullen. 1989. *Attitudes toward Crime:*

A Survey of Colorado Citizens and Criminal Justice Officials. Denver: Colorado Department of Public Safety, Division of Criminal Justice.

Environics Research Group. 1987. "Survey of Public Attitudes toward Justice Issues in Canada." Toronto: Environics Research Group Limited.

———. 1989*a*. "A Qualitative Investigation of Public Opinion on Sentencing, Corrections and Parole." Final report. Toronto: Environics Research Group Limited.

———. 1989*b*. "The Focus Canada Report: 1989." Toronto: Environics Research Group Limited.

Erickson, Maynard J., and Jack P. Gibbs. 1979. "On the Perceived Severity of Legal Penalties." *Journal of Criminal Law and Criminology* 70:102–16.

Erskine, Hazel. 1974. "The Polls: Causes of Crime." *Public Opinion Quarterly* 50:288–98.

Ewing, Charles P., and Moss Aubrey. 1987. "Battered Women and Public Opinion: Some Realities about the Myths." *Journal of Family Violence* 2: 57–64.

Fagan, Ronald W. 1981. "Public Support for the Courts: An Examination of Alternative Explanations." *Journal of Criminal Justice* 9:403–17.

———. 1987. "Knowledge and Support for the Criminal Justice System." *Criminal Justice Review* 12:27–33.

Fichter, Michael, and Carol Veneziano. 1988. *Criminal Justice Attitudes— Missouri.* Jefferson City: Missouri Department of Corrections.

Figlio, Robert M. 1975. "The Seriousness Of Offenses: An Evaluation by Offenders and Non-offenders." *Journal of Criminal Law and Criminology* 66:189–201.

Finckenauer, James O. 1988. "Public Support for the Death Penalty: Retribution as Just Deserts or Retribution as Revenge?" *Justice Quarterly* 5:81–100.

Fiske, Susan, and Shelley Taylor. 1984. *Social Cognition.* Reading, Mass.: Addison-Wesley.

Flanagan, Timothy. 1987. "Change and Influence in Popular Criminology: Public Attributions of Crime Causation." *Journal of Criminal Justice* 15: 231–43.

Flanagan, Timothy J., Edmund F. McGarrell, and Edward J. Brown. 1985. "Public Perceptions of the Criminal Courts: The Role of Demographics and Related Attitudinal Variables." *Journal of Research in Crime and Delinquency* 22:66–82.

Flanagan, Timothy J., and Kathleen Maguire, eds. 1990. *Sourcebook of Criminal Justice Statistics—1989.* Washington, D.C.: U.S. Department of Justice, Bureau of Justice Statistics.

Fletcher, Joseph. 1991. "Policing, Police Culture and Race: Police Attitudes in the Canadian Cultural Context." Unpublished manuscript. Toronto: University of Toronto, Centre of Criminology.

Gabor, Thomas, and Gabriel Weimann. 1987. "La couverture du crime par la presse: Un portrait fidele ou deforme?" *Criminologie* 20:79–98.

Galaway, Burt. 1984*a*. *Public Acceptance of Restitution as an Alternative to Imprisonment for Property Offenders: A Survey.* Wellington: New Zealand Department of Justice.

————. 1984*b*. "Survey of Public Acceptance of Restitution as an Alternative to Imprisonment for Property Offenders." *Australian and New Zealand Journal of Criminology* 17:108–17.

Galaway, Burt, and Joe Hudson. 1990. *Criminal Justice, Restitution and Reconciliation*. Monsey, N.Y.: Criminal Justice Press.

Galiber, Joseph. 1990. "A Bill to Repeal Criminal Drug Laws: Replacing Prohibition with Regulation." *Hofstra Law Review* 18:795–853.

Gallup. 1989. *The Gallup Report. Number 285*. Princeton, N.J.: Gallup Poll.

Gallup Canada. 1969–90. *The Gallup Report*. Toronto: Gallup of Canada Ltd.

Gandy, John T. 1978. "Attitudes toward the Use of Restitution." In *Offender Restitution in Theory and Action*, edited by Burt Galaway and Joe Hudson. Toronto: Lexington.

Gebotys, Robert J., and Julian V. Roberts. 1987. "Public Views of Sentencing: The Role of Offender Characteristics." *Canadian Journal of Behavioural Science* 19:479–88.

Gebotys, Robert G., Julian V. Roberts, and Bikram DasGupta. 1988. "News Media Use and Public Perceptions of Crime Seriousness." *Canadian Journal of Criminology* 30:3–16.

Geer, John. 1987. "What Do Open-ended Questions Measure?" *Public Opinion Quarterly* 52:365–71.

Gerbner, George, and Larry Gross. 1976*a*. "Living with Television: The Violence Profile." *Journal of Communication* 26:172–99.

————. 1976*b*. "The Scary World of TV's Heavy Viewer." *Psychology Today* 9:41–45.

Gibbons, Don C. 1963. "Who Knows What about Correction?" *Crime and Delinquency* 9:137–44.

————. 1969. "Crime and Punishment: A Study in Social Attitudes." *Social Forces* 47:391–97.

Glick, Henry R., and George W. Pruet, Jr. 1985. "Crime, Public Opinion and Trial Courts: An Analysis of Sentencing Policy." *Justice Quarterly* 2:319–43.

Goldstein, Alvin, June Chance, and Barbara Gilbert. 1984. "Facial Stereotypes of Good Guys and Bad Guys: A Replication and Extension." *Bulletin of the Psychonomic Society* 22:549–52.

Gordon, M., and L. Heath. 1981. "The News Business: Crime and Fear." In *Reactions to Crime*, edited by D. A. Lewis. Beverly Hills, Calif.: Sage.

Gottfredson, Stephen, and Ralph B. Taylor. 1984. "Public Policy and Prison Populations: Measuring Opinions about Reform." *Judicature* 68:190–201.

Graber, Doris. 1980. *Crime News and the Public*. New York: Praeger.

Grabosky, P. N., J. B. Braithwaite, and P. R. Wilson. 1987. "The Myth of Community Tolerance toward White-Collar Crime." *Australian and New Zealand Journal of Criminology* 20:33–44.

Gregg, Allan, and Michael Posner. 1990. *The Big Picture: What Canadians Think about Almost Everything*. Toronto: McFarlane, Walter & Ross.

Grindstaff, Carl F. 1974. "Public Attitudes and Court Dispositions: A Comparative Analysis." *Sociology and Social Research* 58:417–26.

Guzzo, R. A., S. E. Jackson, and R. A. Kutzell. 1987. "Meta-analysis Analysis." In *Research in Organizational Behavior*, vol. 9, edited by B. M. Stans and L. L. Cummings. Greenwich, Conn.: JAI.

Hagan, John, and Celesta Albonetti. 1982. "Race, Class, and the Perception of Criminal Injustice in America." *American Journal of Sociology* 88:329–55.

Hamill, Ruth, Timothy Wilson, and Richard Nisbett. 1980. "Insensitivity to Sample Bias: Generalizing from Atypical Cases." *Journal of Personality and Social Psychology* 39:578–89.

Hamilton, V. Lee, and Steve Rytina. 1980. "Social Consensus on Norms of Justice: Should the Punishment Fit the Crime?" *American Journal of Sociology* 85:1117–44.

Hann, Bob, and Bill Harman. 1986. *Full Parole Release: An Historical Descriptive Analysis*. Ottawa: Solicitor General Canada.

Hans, Valerie P., and Dan Slater. 1983. "John Hinckley, Jr. and the Insanity Defense: The Public's Verdict." *Public Opinion Quarterly* 47:202–12.

Hans, Valerie P., and Neil Vidmar. 1986. *Judging the Jury*. New York: Plenum.

Higginbottom, Susan F., and Edward Zamble. 1988. "Categorizations of Homicide Cases: Agreement, Accuracy and Confidence of Public Assignments." *Canadian Journal of Criminology* 30:351–66.

Hilton, N. Zoe. 1989. "When Is an Assault Not an Assault? The Canadian Public's Attitudes towards Wife and Stranger Assault." *Journal of Family Violence* 4:323–37.

Himmelfarb, Alex. 1990. "Public Opinion and Public Policy." *Forum on Corrections Research* 2:20–22.

Hindelang, Michael. 1974. "Public Opinion regarding Crime, Criminal Justice, and Related Topics." *Journal of Research in Crime and Delinquency* 11:101–16.

Hindelang, Michael, Christopher Dunn, Paul Sutton, and Alison Anmick. 1976. *Sourcebook of Criminal Justice Statistics—1975*. Washington, D.C.: U.S. Department of Justice, Bureau of Justice Statistics.

Hirsch, Paul. 1980. "The 'Scary-World' of the Nonviewers and Other Anomalies: A Reanalysis of Gerbner et al.'s Findings on Cultivation Analysis, Part I." *Communication Research* 7:403–56.

Hoffman, Peter B., and Patricia L. Hardyman. 1986. "Crime Seriousness Scales: Public Perceptions and Feedback to Criminal Justice Policymakers." *Journal of Criminal Justice* 14:413–31.

Hogarth, John. 1971. *Sentencing as a Human Process*. Toronto: University of Toronto Press.

Hollin, Clive R., and Kevin Howells. 1987. "Lay Explanations of Delinquency: Global or Offence-specific?" *British Journal of Social Psychology* 26:203–10.

Hough, Mike, and Pat Mayhew. 1985. *Taking Account of Crime: Key Findings from the Second British Crime Survey*. Home Office Research Study no. 85. London: H.M. Stationery Office.

Hough, Mike, and David Moxon. 1985. "Dealing with Offenders: Popular Opinion and the Views of Victims." *Howard Journal of Criminal Justice* 24:160–75.

Hubbard, Jeffrey, Melvin DeFleur, and Lois DeFleur. 1975. "Mass Media Influences on Public Conceptions of Social Problems." *Social Problems* 23: 22–34.

Hylton, John H. 1985. "Public Attitudes towards Crime and the Police in a Prairie City." In *Law in a Cynical Society? Opinion and Law in the 1980s*, edited by Dale Gibson and Janet Baldwin. Calgary: Carswell.

Immarigeon, Russ. 1986. "Surveys Reveal Broad Support for Alternative Sentencing." *Journal of the National Prison Project* 9:1–4.

Indermaur, David. 1987. "Public Perception of Sentencing in Perth, Western Australia." *Australian and New Zealand Journal of Criminology* 20:163–83.

———. 1990. "Perceptions of Crime Seriousness and Sentencing: A Comparison of Court Practice and the Perceptions of a Sample of the Public and Judges." Canberra: Criminology Research Council of Australia.

Jacoby, Joseph E., and Christopher S. Dunn. 1987. "National Survey on Punishment for Criminal Offenses." Paper presented at the National Conference on Punishment for Criminal Offenses, Ann Arbor, Michigan, November.

Jamieson, Katherine, and Timothy Flanagan, eds. 1987. *Sourcebook of Criminal Justice Statistics—1986*. Washington, D.C.: U.S. Department of Justice, Bureau of Justice Statistics.

———. 1989. *Sourcebook of Criminal Justice Statistics—1988*. Washington, D.C.: U.S. Department of Justice, Bureau of Justice Statistics.

Jones, Sandra, and Michael Levi. 1987. "Law and Order and the Causes of Crime: Some Police and Public Perspectives." *Howard Journal of Criminal Justice* 26:1–14.

Kalven, Harry, and Hans Zeisel. 1966. *The American Jury*. Chicago: University of Chicago Press.

Kenny, David. 1975. "Cross-lagged Panel Correlation: A Test for Spuriousness." *Psychological Bulletin* 82:887–903.

Kessel, John. 1966. "Public Perceptions of the Supreme Court." *Midwest Journal of Political Science* 10:167–91.

Klecka, William R., and Alfred J. Tuchfarber. 1978. "Random Digit Dialing: A Comparison of Personal Surveys." *Public Opinion Quarterly* 105–14.

Klein, Ronald J., Isadore Newman, David M. Weis, and Ronald F. Bobner. 1983. "The Continuum of Criminal Offenses Instrument: Further Development and Modification of Sellin and Wolfgang's Original Criminal Index." *Journal of Offender Counseling, Services and Rehabilitation* 7:33–53.

Knight, Douglas W. 1965. "Punishment Selection as a Function of Biographical Information." *Journal of Criminal Law, Criminology and Police Science* 56:325–27.

Knowles, Jeffrey. 1979. *Ohio Citizen Attitudes: A Survey of Public Opinion on Crime and Criminal Justice*. Columbus, Ohio: Office of Criminal Justice Services.

———. 1980. *Ohio Citizen Attitudes concerning Criminal Justice*. 2d ed. Columbus, Ohio: Department of Economic and Community Development.

———. 1982. *Ohio Citizen Attitudes concerning Crime and Criminal Justice*. 3d ed. Columbus, Ohio: Governor's Office of Criminal Justice Services.

————. 1984. *Ohio Citizen Attitudes concerning Crime and Criminal Justice.* 4th ed. Columbus, Ohio: Governor's Office of Criminal Justice Services.

————. 1987. *Ohio Citizen Attitudes concerning Crime and Criminal Justice.* 5th ed. Columbus, Ohio: Governor's Office of Criminal Justice Services.

Krueger, Richard. 1988. *Focus Groups: A Practical Guide for Applied Research.* Beverly Hills, Calif.: Sage.

Kuklinski, James H., and John E. Stanga. 1979. "Political Participation and Government Responsiveness: The Behavior of California Superior Courts." *American Political Science Review* 4:1090–99.

Kutchinsky, Berl. 1968. "Knowledge and Attitudes regarding Legal Phenomena in Denmark." In *Scandinavian Studies in Criminology.* Vol. 2: *Aspects of Social Control in Welfare States,* edited by Nils Christie. London: Tavistock.

————. 1973. "The Legal Consciousness: A Survey of Research on Knowledge and Opinion about Law." In *Knowledge and Opinion about Law,* edited by Adam Podgorecki, Wolfgang Kaupen, J. van Houtte, P. Vincke, and Berl Kutchinsky. London: Martin Robertson.

Lenke, L. 1974. "Criminal Justice Policy and Public Opinion towards Crimes of Violence." In *Collected Studies in Criminological Research.* Vol. 11: *Violence in Society.* Strasbourg: Council of Europe.

Levin, Theodore. 1966. "Toward a More Enlightened Sentencing Procedure." *Nebraska Law Review* 45:499–525.

Lewis, Dan, and Greta Salem. 1986. *Fear of Crime: Incivility and the Production of a Social Problem.* New Brunswick, N.J.: Transaction.

Lichtenstein, S., Paul Slovic, Baruch Fischoff, M. Layman, and B. Combs. 1978. "Judged Frequency of Lethal Events." *Journal of Experimental Psychology: Human Learning and Memory* 4:551–78.

Liska, Allen, and William Baccaglini. 1990. "Feeling Safe by Comparison: Crime in the Newspapers." *Social Problems* 37:360–74.

Lord, Charles, Lee Ross, and M. Lepper. 1979. "Biased Assimilation and Attitude Polarization: The Effects of Prior Theories on Subsequently Considered Evidence." *Journal of Personality and Social Psychology* 37:2098–2109.

Lotz, Roy, and Robert M. Regoli. 1980. "Public Support for the Death Penalty." *Criminal Justice Review* 5:55–66.

Louis Harris. 1968. "The Public Looks at Crime and Corrections." Washington D.C.: Joint Commission on Correctional Manpower and Training.

McClosky, Herbert, and Alda Brill. 1983. *Dimensions of Tolerance: What Do Americans Think about Civil Liberties?* New York: Russell Sage.

McFatter, Robert M. 1978. "Sentencing Strategies and Justice: Effects of Punishment Philosophy on Sentencing Decisions." *Journal of Personality and Social Psychology* 36:1490–500.

————. 1982. "Purposes of Punishment: Effects of Utilities of Criminal Sanctions on Perceived Appropriateness." *Journal of Applied Psychology* 67:255–67.

McGarrell, Edmund, and Timothy Flanagan, eds. 1985. *Sourcebook of Criminal Justice Statistics—1984.* Washington, D.C.: U.S. Department of Justice, Bureau of Justice Statistics.

McIntyre, Jennie. 1967. "Public Attitudes toward Crime and Law Enforcement." *American Criminal Law Quarterly* 6:66–81.

Mäkelä, Klaus. 1966. "Public Sense of Justice and Judicial Practice." *Acta Sociologica* 10–11:42–67.

Mande, Mary, and Paul Butler. 1982. *Crime in Colorado: A Survey of Citizens.* Denver: Colorado Department of Public Safety, Division of Criminal Justice.

Mande, Mary, and Joan Crouch. 1984. *Crime in Colorado: 1984 Citizen Survey.* Denver: Colorado Department of Public Safety, Division of Criminal Justice.

Mande, Mary, and Kim English. 1989. *The Effect of Public Opinion on Correctional Policy: A Comparison of Opinions and Practice.* Denver: Colorado Department of Public Safety, Division of Criminal Justice.

Margarita, Mona, and Nicolette Parisi. 1979. *Public Opinion and Criminal Justice: Selected Issues and Trends.* Albany, N.Y.: Criminal Justice Research Center.

Marsh, Jeanne, Alison Geist, and Nathan Caplan. 1982. *Rape and the Limits of Law Reform.* Boston: Auburn House.

Mawby, Rob, and Judith Brown. 1984. "Newspaper Images of the Victim: A British Study." *Victimology: An International Journal* 9:82–94.

Mayhew, Pat, David Elliott, and Lizanne Dowds. 1989. *The 1988 British Crime Survey.* Home Office Research Study no. 111. London: H.M. Stationery Office.

Mellinger, Glen D., Carol L. Huffine, and Mitchell Balter. 1982. "Assuming Comprehension in a Survey of Public Reactions to Complex Issues." *Public Opinion Quarterly* 46:97–109.

Merton, Robert K. 1987. "The Focussed Interview and Focus Groups: Continuities and Discontinuities." *Public Opinion Quarterly* 51:550–66.

Michigan Law Review. 1973. "Legal Knowledge of Michigan Citizens." 71: 1463–86.

Miethe, Terance D. 1982. "Public Consensus on Crime Seriousness." *Criminology* 20:515–26.

Miller, J. L., P. H. Rossi, and J. E. Simpson. 1986. "Perceptions of Justice: Race and Gender Differences in Judgments of Appropriate Prison Sentences." *Law and Society Review* 20:313–34.

Moore, Robert J. 1985. "Reflections of Canadians on the Law and the Legal System: Legal Research Institute Survey of Respondents in Montreal, Toronto and Winnipeg." In *Law in a Cynical Society? Opinion and Law in the 1980's,* edited by Dale Gibson and Janet Baldwin. Calgary: Carswell.

Nesdale, Andrew R. 1980. "The Law and Social Attitudes: Effects of Proposed Changes in Drug Legislation on Attitudes toward Drug Use." *Canadian Journal of Criminology* 22:176–87.

Newsweek. 1981. "The Plague of Violent Crime" (March 23), p. 47.

Nisbett, Richard E., and Lee Ross. 1980. *Human Inference: Strategies and Shortcomings of Social Judgment.* Englewood Cliffs, N.J.: Prentice Hall.

Nisbett, Richard E., and Timothy D. Wilson. 1977. "Telling More than We Can Know: Verbal Reports on Mental Processes." *Psychological Review* 84:231–59.

O'Connor, Michael E. 1978. "A Community's Opinion on Crime: Some Preliminary Findings." *Australian and New Zealand Journal of Sociology* 14:61–64.

———. 1984. "The Perception of Crime and Criminality: The Violent Criminal and Swindler as Social Types." *Deviant Behavior* 5:255–74.

Ocqueteau, Frederic, and Claudine Perez-Diaz. 1990*a*. "Public Opinion, Crime and Criminal Justice Policies in France." *Penal Issues: Research in Crime and Criminal Justice in France* 1:7–10.

———. 1990*b*. "Comment les francais reprouvent-ils le crime aujourd'hui?" *Deviance et societe* 14:253–74.

Ouellet, Shirley. 1991. *Public Attitudes towards the Legitimacy of Our Institutions and the Administration of Justice.* Ottawa: Department of Justice, Canada, Research and Development Directorate.

Ouimet, Marc. 1990. "Profil d'une recherche appliquee sur le sentencing." *Canadian Journal of Criminology* 32:471–77.

Palys, Ted, and Stan Divorski. 1986. "Explaining Sentence Disparity." *Canadian Journal of Criminology* 28:347–62.

Parisi, Nicolette, Michael Gottfredson, Michael Hindelang, and Timothy Flanagan, eds. 1979. *Sourcebook of Criminal Justice Statistics—1978.* Washington: U.S. Department of Justice, Bureau of Justice Statistics.

Parker, Howard. 1970. "Juvenile Court Actions and Public Response." In *Becoming Delinquent*, edited by Peter Garabedian and Don Gibbons. Chicago: Aldine.

Parton, David, Mark Hansel, and John Stratton. 1991. "Measuring Crime Seriousness: Lessons from the National Crime Survey on Crime Severity." *British Journal of Criminology* 31:72–85.

Pasewark, Richard, Deborah Seidenzahl, and Mark Pantle. 1981. "Opinions concerning Criminality among Mental Patients." *Journal of Community Psychology* 9:367–70.

Pease, Kenneth, Judith Ireson, Stuart Billingham, and Jennifer Thorpe. 1977. "The Development of a Scale of Offence Seriousness." *International Journal of Criminology and Penology* 5:17–29.

Pease, Kenneth, Judith Ireson, and Jennifer Thorpe. 1974. "Additivity Assumptions in the Measurement of Delinquency." *British Journal of Criminology* 14:256–63.

Pepitone, Albert, and Mark DiNubile. 1976. "Contrast Effects in Judgments of Crime Severity and the Punishment of Criminal Violators." *Journal of Personality and Social Psychology* 33:448–59.

Podgorecki, Adam, Wolfgang Kaupen, J. Van Houtte, P. Vinke, and Berl Kutchinsky. 1973. *Knowledge and Opinion about Law.* London: Robertson.

Quinn, Robert, Barbara Gutek, and Jeffrey Walsh. 1980. "Telephone Interviewing: A Reappraisal and a Field Experiment." *Basic and Applied Social Psychology* 1:127–53.

Quinney, Richard. 1973. *Critique of Legal Order: Crime Control in Capitalist Society.* Boston: Little, Brown.

———. 1975. "Public Conceptions of Crime." In *Perception in Criminology*, edited by Richard L. Henshel and Robert A. Silverman. Toronto: Methuen.

Ray, John. 1982. "Prison Sentences and Public Opinion." *Australian Quarterly* 54:435–43.

Reed, John P., and Robin S. Reed. 1973. "Status, Images and Consequence: Once a Criminal Always a Criminal." *Sociology and Social Research* 57:460–72.

Research and Forecasts, Inc. 1983. *America Afraid: How Fear of Crime Changes the Way We Live (The Figgie Reports)*. New York: NAL.

Riedel, Marc. 1975. "Perceived Circumstances, Inferences of Intent and Judgments of Offense Seriousness." *Journal of Criminal Law and Criminology* 66:201–09.

Riley, Paula J., and Vicki M. Rose. 1980. "Public vs. Elite Opinion on Correctional Reform: Implications for Social Policy." *Journal of Criminal Justice* 8:345–56.

Roberts, Julian V. 1988a. "Early Release from Prison: What Do the Canadian Public Really Think?" *Canadian Journal of Criminology* 30:231–49.

———. 1988b. "Public Opinion about Sentencing: Some Popular Myths." *Justice Report* 5:7–9.

———. 1988c. *Public Opinion and Sentencing: The Surveys of the Canadian Sentencing Commission*. Research Reports of the Canadian Sentencing Commission. Ottawa: Department of Justice Canada.

———. 1988d. *Sentencing in the Media: A Content Analysis of English-Language Newspapers in Canada*. Research Reports of the Canadian Sentencing Commission. Ottawa: Department of Justice Canada.

———. 1989. *Public Opinion and Criminal Justice: A Proposal for a Computerized Data-base*. Ottawa: University of Ottawa, Department of Criminology.

———. 1990. *Sexual Assault Legislation in Canada: An Evaluation. An Analysis of National Statistics*. Ottawa: Department of Justice Canada.

Roberts, Julian V., and Anthony N. Doob. 1989. "Sentencing and Public Opinion: Taking False Shadows for True Substances." *Osgoode Hall Law Journal* 27:491–515.

———. 1990. "News Media Influences on Public Views of Sentencing." *Law and Human Behavior* 14:451–68.

Roberts, Julian V., and Don Edwards. 1989. "Contextual Effects in Judgments of Crimes, Criminals and the Purposes of Sentencing." *Journal of Applied Social Psychology* 19:902–17.

Roberts, Julian V., and Michelle G. Grossman. 1990. "Crime Prevention and Public Opinion." *Canadian Journal of Criminology* 32:75–90.

Roberts, Julian V., and Nicholas R. White. 1986. "Public Estimates of Recidivism Rates: Consequences of a Criminal Stereotype." *Canadian Journal of Criminology* 28:229–41.

Rodgers, Harrell. 1969a. "A Case Study of the Effects of Public Opinion on the Utilization of Law in Conflict Resolution: An Exemplification of Cahn's Sense of Injustice." *Duquesne Law Review* 7:558–70.

———. 1969b. *Community Conflict, Public Opinion and the Law*. Columbus, Ohio: Charles Merrill.

Rose, Arnold M., and Arthur E. Prell. 1955. "Does the Punishment Fit the Crime? A Study in Social Valuation." *American Journal of Sociology* 61:247–59.

Ross, Lee. 1977. "The Intuitive Psychologist and His Shortcomings: Distortions in the Attribution Process." In *Advances in Experimental Social Psychology*, vol. 10, edited by Leonard Berkowitz. New York: Academic Press.

Rossi, P. H., and A. B. Anderson. 1982. "The Factorial Survey Approach: An Introduction." In *Measuring Social Judgments: The Factorial Survey Approach*, edited by P. Rossi and S. Nock. Beverly Hills, Calif.: Sage.

Rossi, Peter H., and J. Patrick Henry. 1980. "Seriousness: A Measure for All Purposes?" In *Handbook of Criminal Justice Evaluation*, edited by Malcolm W. Klein and Katherine S. Teilmann. Beverly Hills, Calif.: Sage.

Rossi, Peter, and Stephen Nock, eds. 1982. *Measuring Social Judgments: The Factorial Survey Approach*. Beverly Hills, Calif.: Sage.

Rossi, Peter H., Jon E. Simpson, and JoAnn L. Miller. 1985. "Beyond Crime Seriousness: Fitting the Punishment to the Crime." *Journal of Quantitative Criminology* 1:59–90.

Ryan, Mick. 1983. *The Politics of Penal Reform*. London: Longman.

Sacco, Vincent, and Holly Johnson. 1990. *Patterns of Criminal Victimization in Canada*. Ottawa: Ministry of Supply and Services.

Saladin, Michael, Zalman Saper, and Lawrence Breen. 1988. "Perceived Attractiveness and Attributions of Criminality: What Is Beautiful Is Not Criminal." *Canadian Journal of Criminology* 30:251–59.

Samuel, William, and Elizabeth Moulds. 1986. "The Effect of Crime Severity on Perceptions of Fair Punishment: A California Case Study." *Journal of Criminal Law and Criminology* 77:931–47.

Sarat, Austin. 1975. "Support for the Legal System: An Analysis of Knowledge, Attitudes and Behavior." *American Politics Quarterly* 3:3–24.

———. 1977. "Studying American Legal Culture: An Assessment of Survey Evidence." *Law and Society Review* 11:427–88.

Sarat, Austin, and Neil Vidmar. 1976. "Public Opinion, the Death Penalty, and the Eighth Amendment: Testing the Marshall Hypothesis." *Wisconsin Law Review*, pp. 171–206.

Schroot, David G., and Jeffrey J. Knowles. 1990. *Ohio Citizens Attitudes concerning Drug and Alcohol Use and Abuse: General Findings*. Columbus, Ohio: Governor's Office of Criminal Justice.

Scott, Joseph E., and Fahad Al-Thakeb. 1977. "The Public's Perceptions of Crime: A Comparative Analysis of Scandinavia, Western Europe, the Middle East, and the United States." In *Contemporary Corrections*, edited by C. Huff. Beverly Hills, Calif.: Sage.

Sebba, Leslie. 1978. "Some Explorations in the Scaling of Penalties." *Journal of Research in Crime and Delinquency* 15:247–65.

———. 1980. "Is Mens Rea a Component of Perceived Offense Seriousness?" *Journal of Criminal Law and Criminology* 71:124–35.

———. 1983. "Attitudes of New Immigrants toward White-Collar Crime: A Cross Cultural Exploration." *Human Relations* 36:1091–110.

Sebba, Leslie, and Gad Nathan. 1984. "Further Explorations in the Scaling of Penalties." *British Journal of Criminology* 23:221–47.

Secret, Philip E., and James B. Johnson. 1989. "Racial Differences in Attitudes toward Crime Control." *Journal of Criminal Justice* 17:361–75.

Security. 1989. "Causes of Crime." 26:10.

Sellin, Thorsten, and Marvin Wolfgang. 1964. *The Measurement of Delinquency*. New York: Wiley.

Sharp, F. C., and M. C. Otto. 1909. "A Study of the Popular Attitude towards Retributive Punishment." *International Journal of Ethics* 20:341–57.

Sheley, Joseph F. 1980. "Crime Seriousness Ratings: The Impact of Survey Questionnaire Form and Item Context." *British Journal of Criminology* 20:123–33.

Sherizen, S. 1978. "Social Creation of Crime News: All the News Fitted to Print." In *Deviance and Mass Media*, edited by Charles Winick. Beverly Hills, Calif.: Sage.

Shoemaker, Donald J., and Donald R. South. 1978. "Nonverbal Images of Criminality and Deviance: Existence and Consequence." *Criminal Justice Review* 3:65–80.

Shoemaker, Donald J., Donald South, and J. Lowe. 1973. "Facial Stereotypes of Deviants and Judgments of Guilt or Innocence." *Social Forces* 51:427–33.

Silvey, Jonathan. 1961. "The Criminal Law and Public Opinion." *Criminal Law Review* 349–58.

Simmons, J. 1965. "Public Stereotypes of Deviants." *Social Problems* 13:223–32.

Skovron, Sandra E., Joseph E. Scott, and Francis T. Cullen. 1988. "Prison Crowding: Public Attitudes toward Strategies of Population Control." *Journal of Research in Crime and Delinquency* 25:150–69.

Smith, David Lewis, and C. McCurdy Lipsey. 1976. "Public Opinion and Penal Policy." *Criminology* 14:113–24.

Smith, Mary Lee, and Gene Glass. 1977. "Meta-analysis of Psychotherapy Outcome Studies." *American Psychologist* 32:752–77.

Smith, Paul, and Richard Hawkins. 1973. "Victimization, Types of Citizen-Police Contacts and Attitudes toward the Police." *Law and Society Review* 8:135–52.

Solicitor General Canada. 1980. *Attitudes regarding Courts Dealing with Criminals*. Ottawa: Ministry of the Solicitor General Canada.

———. 1981. *Solicitor General's Study of Conditional Release*. Ottawa: Solicitor General Canada.

———. 1984a. *Selected Trends in Canadian Criminal Justice*. Ottawa: Canadian Government Publishing Centre.

———. 1984b. *Canadian Urban Victimization Survey: Reported and Unreported Offences*. Ottawa: Supply and Services Canada.

Sourcebook of Criminal Justice Statistics. Various years. Washington, D.C.: U.S. Department of Justice, Bureau of Justice Statistics.

Stalans, Loretta J., and Shari Seidman Diamond. 1990. "Formation and Change in Lay Evaluations of Criminal Sentencing: Misperception and Discontent." *Law and Human Behavior* 14:199–214.

Steadman, Henry J., and Joseph J. Cocozza. 1978. "Selective Reporting and the Public's Misconceptions of the Criminally Insane." *Public Opinion Quarterly* 41:523–33.

Stephen, James Fitzjames. 1883. *A History of the Criminal Law of England*. London: Macmillan.

Stinchcombe, Arthur L., Rebecca Adams, Carol A. Heimer, Kim Scheppele,

Tom W. Smith, and D. Garth Taylor. 1980. *Crime and Punishment—Changing Attitudes in America.* San Francisco: Jossey-Bass.

Sumner, William G. 1906. *Folkways: A Study of the Sociological Importance of Usages, Manners, Customs, Mores and Morals.* Boston: Ginn.

Sunnafrank, Michael, and Norman Fontes. 1983. "General and Crime-related Racial Stereotypes and Influence on Juridic Decisions." *Cornell Journal of Social Relations* 17:1–15.

Surette, Ray. 1984. *Justice and the Media.* Springfield, Ill.: Thomas.

Taylor, Garth D., Lane Scheppele, Kim Scheppele, and Arthur L. Stinch-combe. 1979. "Salience of Crime and Support for Harsher Criminal Sanctions." *Social Problems* 26:413–24.

Thomas, Charles W, and Robin J. Cage. 1976. "Correlates of Public Attitudes toward Legal Sanctions." *International Journal of Criminology and Penology* 4:239–55.

Thomas, Charles W., Robin J. Cage, and Samuel C. Foster. 1976. "Public Opinion on Criminal Law and Legal Sanctions: An Examination of Two Conceptual Models." *Journal of Criminal Law and Criminology* 67:110–16.

Thomas, Charles W., and Samuel C. Foster. 1975. "A Sociological Perspective on Support for Capital Punishment." *American Journal of Orthopsychiatry* 45:641–57.

Thomas, Charles W., and Jeffrey M. Hyman. 1977. "Perceptions of Crime, Fear of Victimization, and Public Perceptions of Police Performance." *Journal of Police Science and Administration* 5:305–17.

Thomson, Douglas, R., and Anthony J. Ragona. 1987. "Popular Moderation versus Governmental Authoritarianism: An Interactionist View of Public Sentiments toward Criminal Sanctions." *Crime and Delinquency* 33:337–57.

Thurman, Quint C. 1989. "General Prevention of Tax Evasion: A Factorial Survey Approach." *Journal of Quantitative Criminology* 5:127–46.

Thurstone, L. L. 1927a. "Method of Paired Comparisons for Social Values." *Journal of Abnormal and Social Psychology* 21:384–400.

———. 1927b. "A Law of Comparative Judgement." *Psychological Review* 34:273–86.

Travis, Lawrence F., Francis T. Cullen, Bruce G. Link, and John F. Wozniak. 1986. "The Impact of Instructions on Seriousness Ratings." *Journal of Criminal Justice* 14:433–40.

Tremblay, Pierre. 1988. "On Penal Metrics." *Journal of Quantitative Criminology* 4:225–45.

Tremblay, Pierre, Gilbert Cordeau, and Marc Ouimet. 1991. "Underpunishing Offenders: Towards a Theory of Legal Tolerance." Working Papers in Social Behaviour. Montreal: McGill University, Department of Sociology.

Turner, S. 1978. "Introduction to the Reprint Edition." In *The Measurement of Delinquency,* by Thorsten Sellin and Marvin Wolfgang. Chicago: University of Chicago Press.

Tversky, Amos, and Daniel Kahneman. 1973. "Availability: A Heuristic for Judging Frequency and Probability" *Cognitive Psychology* 5:207–32.

Useem, Bert, Johnson Knowlton, Linda Burgess, Angela Lewis-Klein, and

Brenda Curry-White. 1990. *Public Opinions on and Perspectives of Drugs and Crime in Missouri.* Louisville, Ky.: University of Louisville, Urban Institute.

van Dijk, Jan. 1978. *The Extent of Public Information and the Nature of Public Attitudes towards Crime.* The Hague: Ministry of Justice, Research and Documentation Centre.

———. 1980. "L'influence des medias sur l'opinion publique relative a la criminalite: Un phenomene exceptionnel?" *Deviance et societe* 4:107–29.

Vidmar, Neil. 1974. "Retributive and Utilitarian Motives and Other Correlates of Canadian Attitudes toward the Death Penalty." *Canadian Psychologist* 15:337–56.

Vidmar, Neil, and Tony Dittenhoffer. 1981. "Informed Public Opinion and Death Penalty Attitudes." *Canadian Journal of Criminology* 23:43–55.

Vidmar, Neil, and Phoebe Ellsworth. 1974. "Public Opinion and the Death Penalty." *Stanford Law Review* 26:1245–70.

von Hirsch, Andrew. 1985. *Past or Future Crimes: Deservedness and Dangerousness in the Sentencing of Criminals.* New Brunswick, N.J.: Rutgers University Press.

———. 1986. *Doing Justice. The Choice of Punishments. Report of the Committee for the Study of Incarceration.* Boston: Northeastern University Press.

Walker, John, Mark Collins, and Paul Wilson. 1988. "How the Public Sees Sentencing: An Australian Survey." In *Public Attitudes to Sentencing: Surveys from Five Countries,* edited by Nigel Walker and Mike Hough. Aldershot: Gower.

Walker, Lenore. 1979. *The Battered Woman.* New York: Harper & Row.

Walker, Monica A. 1978. "Measuring the Seriousness of Crimes." *British Journal of Criminology* 18:348–64.

Walker, Nigel. 1981. "The Ultimate Justification." In *Crime, Proof and Punishment: Essays in Memory of Sir Rupert Cross,* edited by C. Tapper. London: Butterworths.

———. 1985. *Sentencing: Theory, Law and Practice.* London: Butterworths.

Walker, Nigel, and Michael Argyle. 1974. "Does the Law Affect Moral Judgements?" In *Perception in Criminology,* edited by Richard L. Henshel and Robert A. Silverman. Toronto: Methuen.

Walker, Nigel, and Catherine Marsh. 1984. "Do Sentences Affect Public Disapproval?" *British Journal of Criminology* 24:27–48.

Warr, Mark. 1980. "The Accuracy of Public Beliefs about Crime." *Social Forces* 59:456–70.

———. 1982. "The Accuracy of Public Beliefs about Crime: Further Evidence." *Criminology* 20:185–204.

———. 1989. "What Is the Perceived Seriousness of Crimes?" *Criminology* 27:795–821.

Warr, Mark, Robert F. Meier, and Maynard L. Erickson. 1983. "Norms, Theories of Punishment, and Publicly Preferred Penalties for Crimes." *Sociological Quarterly* 24:75–91.

Webb, Eugene, Don Campbell, R. Schwartz, and Lee Sechrest. 1981. *Unobtrusive Measures: Non-reactive Research in the Social Sciences.* Chicago: Rand McNally.

Weidner, Gerdi, and William Griffit. 1983. "Rape: A Sexual Stigma?" *Journal of Personality* 51:152–66.

Wellford, Charles, and Michael Wiatrowski. 1975. "On the Measurement of Delinquency." *Journal of Criminal Law and Criminology* 66:175–88.

White, Garland F. 1975. "Public Responses to Hypothetical Crimes: Effect of Offender and Victim Status and Seriousness of the Offense on Punitive Reactions." *Social Forces* 53:411–19.

Williams, Frank, Dennis Longmire, and David Gulik. 1988. "The Public and the Death Penalty: Opinion as an Artifact of Question Type." *Criminal Justice Research Bulletin* 3:8.

Williams, Kirk R., Jack P. Gibbs, and Maynard L. Erickson. 1980. "Public Knowledge of Statutory Penalties: The Extent and Basis of Accurate Perception." *Pacific Sociological Review* 23:105–28.

Williams, Martha, and Jay Hall. 1972. "Knowledge of the Law in Texas: Socioeconomic and Ethnic Differences." *Law and Society Review* 7:99–118.

Wilson, P. R., and J. W. Brown. 1973. *Crime in the Community*. Queensland: University of Queensland Press.

Wober, Mallory, and Barrie Gunter. 1982. "Television and Personal Threat: Fact or Artifact?" *British Journal of Social Psychology* 21:239–47.

Wolfgang, Marvin, Robert Figlio, Paul Tracy, and Simon Singer. 1985. *The National Survey of Crime Severity*. Washington, D.C.: U.S. Department of Justice.

Yankelovich, Daniel. 1991. *Coming to Public Judgment: Making Democracy Work in a Complex World*. Syracuse, N.Y.: Syracuse University Press.

Zamble, Edward. 1990. "Public Support for Criminal Justice Policies: Some Specific Findings." *Forum on Corrections Research* 2:14–19.

Zamble, Edward, and Phyllis Annesley. 1987. "Some Determinants of Public Attitudes toward the Police." *Journal of Police Science and Administration* 15:285–90.

Zamble, Edward, and Kerry Kalm. 1990. "General and Specific Measures of Public Attitudes toward Sentencing." *Canadian Journal of Behavioural Science* 22:327–37.

Zeisel, Hans, and Alec M. Gallup. 1989. "Death Penalty Sentiment in the United States." *Journal of Quantitative Criminology* 5:285–96.

Zimmerman, E. C., D. Jeangros, D. Hausser, and P. Zeugin. 1991. "La drogue dans l'opinion publique suisse: Perception du probleme et des mesures a prendre." *Deviance et societe* 15:157–73.

Zimmerman, Sherwood E., David J. Van Alstyne, and Christopher S. Dunn. 1988. "The National Punishment Survey and Public Policy Consequences." *Journal of Research in Crime and Delinquency* 25:120–49.

Andrew J. Ashworth

Sentencing Reform
Structures

ABSTRACT

Sentencing reforms have been implemented or considered in recent years
in Europe, North America, and Australia. Major initiatives have been
undertaken in the United States, the United Kingdom, Sweden, and
various Canadian provinces and Australian and American states. Most
have been efforts to reduce sentencing disparities, among other and
differing goals. Constitutional objections to limitation or elimination of
judicial discretion have seldom been successful. The principle of respect
for judicial independence to decide cases free from bias, partiality, or
undue influence is distinguishable from the principle that the judge's
sentencing discretion must be wholly unregulated. Reforms have
included mandatory sentencing laws; statutory "fixed point" guidelines;
presumptive, strengthened appellate sentence review; and improved
information systems. What "works best" necessarily depends on the legal
and political situation in each jurisdiction.

The last two decades have seen a wave of reforms and proposed reforms of sentencing in many jurisdictions in Europe, North America,
Australasia, and elsewhere. The concerns that have led to this widespread reappraisal of sentencing vary from country to country, as do
the reforms proposed or implemented. Much depends on the social
and political context. Yet there are some common elements that run
through the reforms, which make it worthwhile considering them together. Moreover, although one must guard against the assumption

Andrew J. Ashworth is Edmund-Davies Professor of Criminal Law and Criminal
Justice at King's College, University of London. He wishes to thank Austin Lovegrove,
Andrew von Hirsch, Michael Tonry, and the anonymous referees for their comments
on previous drafts. This essay was accepted for publication in February 1991.

that sentencing reforms are simply transferable from one criminal justice system to another, the techniques used in one jurisdiction might be suitable, albeit in a modified form, for adoption in another. The impact of several American reforms was examined in *Crime and Justice* a few years ago (Tonry 1988). This essay attempts to consider the new sentencing structures issue-by-issue rather than state-by-state and draws into the discussion other common-law jurisdictions and some other European countries (particularly Sweden) that have recent and relevant experiences.

The major goal of the enquiry is to evaluate some of the many techniques for structuring and confining the sentencing of offenders. What structural properties ought a sentencing system have? What are the advantages of guideline systems over appellate review and judicial precedent, and vice versa? If guidelines are to be the main feature of the system, what are the most fruitful methods of constructing and promulgating them? What legislative refinements, if any, may profitably be made to a system based on appellate review? These and related questions are examined in Section III below from the point of view of legal culture as well as practical efficacy. Section IV continues the enquiry by considering various consensual approaches to the initiation of changes in sentencing practice, approaches that assume particular importance where there is resistance to imposed reforms.

The goal of this enquiry cannot be attained, however, without placing the various reforms in context. First and foremost there is the broader criminal justice context. A fully satisfying discussion could not be conducted without an overlarge digression to describe elements of the criminal justice systems of Canada, Australia, England and Wales, the U.S. federal jurisdiction, several American states, Sweden, and the other countries whose experiences are drawn on in Sections III and IV. Instead, what follows in Section I of this essay is a relatively brief discussion of some recurrent preoccupations of criminal justice systems that bear on sentencing. This should help to explain the mainsprings of the sentencing reform "movement" of recent years and provide a sufficient backdrop for discussion of sentencing structures. Second, there is the constitutional context: this varies greatly among the various jurisdictions considered here, and so the focus in Section II is on general questions of constitutional responsibility for sentencing policy, the scope of the principle of judicial independence, and the constitutional status of sentencing commissions.

I. The Mainsprings of Sentencing Reform

From the many factors that have provided the stimuli to sentencing reform or reform proposals in recent years, three main issues are selected for discussion here—inconsistency in sentences imposed, inconsistency in sentences as implemented, and concerns about the use of custody—and then a few other factors are discussed briefly. There is little doubt that a central concern about sentencing has been inconsistency in the sentences handed down by courts in various countries, and it is to this that we turn first.

A. *Inconsistency in the Sentences Imposed*

It is easier to agree that inconsistency in sentencing is or has been a problem in many jurisdictions than it is to reach agreement on a definition of inconsistency or disparity. The basic precept of justice from which the notion of inconsistency derives is to "treat like cases alike and treat different cases differently." In theory, then, the concept of inconsistency is not likely to be helpful unless there are agreed ideas about the criteria for sentencing and the proper approach to different groups of cases (Jareborg 1989). Yet in many countries the concern about apparent inconsistency in sentencing has become widespread before there has been agreement on the proper approach: the inconsistency has amounted simply to deviation from the traditional pattern of sentences. Typically, a jurisdiction has only developed a proper, coherent or consistent approach after some enquiry or committee report. Thus the spur to reform has been provided by some obviously disparate sentencing practices that have given rise to concerns about the compatibility of the sentencing system with basic notions of justice. One expression of this came from Mason, J., in the High Court of Australia in *Lowe v. R.:* "Just as consistency in punishment—a reflection of the notion of equal justice—is a fundamental element in any rational and fair system of criminal justice, so inconsistency in punishment, because it is regarded as a badge of unfairness and unequal treatment under the law, is calculated to lead to an erosion of public confidence in the integrity of the administration of justice" ([1984] 58 A.J.L.R. 414, at p. 415).

The Australian Law Reform Commission used this declaration in support of their commitment to devising reforms that would conduce to consistency in sentencing, concluding that "disparity in sentencing can be justified only if there are acceptable and convincing grounds for differentiating between offenses or offenders" (Australian Law Reform Commission 1988, para. 155). They also showed awareness that excessive uniformity may also produce injustice—fixed penalty sentencing would be unacceptable for many offenses—and the danger of treating large groups of cases as if they were alike when they are not has been emphasized particularly within those European countries committed to the philosophy of "individualization" (Robert 1989, p. 22).

The idea of consistency that has formed part of the engine of reform in the United States involves a rejection of individualized approaches in favor of concentration on the seriousness of the offense and, to a lesser extent, the prior record of the offender. Too much emphasis on the personality, background, and supposed needs of the offender led to sentences that bore little relation to the crime committed, and as a matter of individual justice (see below) the primacy of the seriousness of the offense came to be reasserted. In this way, new and clearer criteria of consistency emerged, and the measurement of inconsistency became easier in principle.

1. *Evidence of Inconsistency.*   Variation in sentencing practices is not a newly discovered phenomenon, but it was not until there was a finer appreciation of the factors involved in sentencing and the application of multivariate techniques of analysis that the evidence of disparity became clear and convincing. Without surveying the research here, it may be said that most major enquiries into sentencing in recent years have found considerable evidence of inconsistency, which in turn has been a factor in precipitating reform (e.g., Blumstein et al. 1983). Disparity in federal sentencing was one of the major spurs to the passing by Congress of the Sentencing Reform Act of 1984 and the subsequent establishment of the U.S. Sentencing Commission (U.S. Sentencing Commission 1991, p. 1, citing the Sentencing Reform Act, sec. 991 [b]). In particular, "white collar" offenders who had committed similar types of offense might receive significantly different sentences in different courts (Wheeler, Mann, and Sarat 1989). The Canadian Sentencing Commission, while recognizing the difficulty of defining and identifying disparity, nonetheless assembled research findings that "strongly suggest that there is considerable unwarranted variation in sentencing" (Canadian Sentencing Commission 1987, para. 4.1.2). In their view, a major cause of this lay in the different sentencing philosophies of different judges and magistrates. In Australia, the Victorian Sentencing Committee concluded after a wide-ranging survey that "unjustified disparities occur in sentencing processes in most jurisdictions"

(Victorian Sentencing Committee 1988, para. 4.4.30). They were hampered by the paucity of systematic research in their own jurisdiction and yet received support from the unlikely source of the memorandum to the committee from the majority of Supreme Court judges, which included these strong observations:

> [The judges] regard it as vital that there be no disparity in the justice with which every offender is dealt and therefore believe that the widest discretion should remain with the sentencing judges. It is only if judges retain a wide sentencing discretion that they can respond to current community views and problems, that they can reflect changing attitudes to particular crimes and that they can do justice in all the changing circumstances of life. The judges recognize that there will be differences between judges and that some apparent disparities of sentence will be reported. Those are the inevitable consequences of a wide judicial discretion but the judges are adamant that there must be no disparity in justice from one case to another.
>
> Those who sit in the Court of Criminal Appeal in Victoria would not subscribe to the view that there is such "unjustified disparity" among judges in Victoria, though some judges tend to be more severe or more lenient in sentencing than others. [Victorian Sentencing Committee 1988, app. A, p. 6]

On the last point—which appears to evince either self-contradiction or nonchalance—the judges were confident that the appeal system would eradicate those variations; the committee took the view that they should not occur in the first place. Once again, evidence of inconsistency was a spur to reform proposals.

2. *Social Consequences of Inconsistency.*   One of the most obvious consequences of inconsistent sentencing is a loss of public faith in, and support for, the criminal justice system. Mason, J., clearly had this in mind in *Lowe v. R.* (1984), and the need to maintain public support has been an influential factor in several sentencing reforms. Another social consequence of inconsistency highlighted in some committee reports is discriminatory sentencing, in particular, discrimination against certain racial groups. Insofar as sentencers are left with wide and unstructured discretion, this allows greater scope for the prejudices of the individual judge to operate, knowingly or unknowingly. One of the purposes of the reforms in the state of Minnesota was to produce "sentencing neutrality" (i.e., factors such as race, sex, or social and

economic circumstances should have no effect on the sentence passed), but it appears that success in this has only been partial (Parent 1988, pp. 196–97; Frase 1991a, 1991b). The guidelines for federal sentencing in the United States are intended to pursue the same goal of neutrality as to the race, sex, national origin, creed, and socioeconomic status of the offender (Sentencing Reform Act, sec. 994 [d]). While clear and reliable research findings on racially discriminatory sentencing remain fairly rare—since one would have to eliminate the possibility that members of certain racial groups commit crimes more frequently than others, or are prosecuted more frequently than others—the prison statistics in many jurisdictions show members of some racial groups imprisoned at a comparatively higher rate than others. The black male incarceration rate in the United States is seven times higher than the white male incarceration rate; some, though not all, of this difference corresponds to racial differences in offending rates for kinds of crime that typically result in prison sentences (Blumstein 1988). There have been particular problems with abnormally high custody rates for aboriginal groups in Australia and in Canada, and reports in both countries have pointed out the contribution that clearer structuring of sentencing discretion could make to the reduction of such disparities (Australian Law Reform Commission 1988, para. 197; Canadian Ministry of Justice 1990a, p. 2; LaPrairie 1990).

3. *Sources of Disparity: Legislative Abstention.*   The sources of disparity vary from jurisdiction to jurisdiction and are usually to be found in a conjunction of factors rather than in a single or separate cause. The first factor to be considered here will be termed "legislative abstention"—the traditional reluctance of legislatures to go further than providing maximum penalties for offenses and a range of sentences from which the courts may select. To some extent this may have been a deliberate policy in jurisdictions committed to rehabilitation or individualization as the primary aim of sentencing, insofar as maximum discretion for the court in each case was then thought advisable. But more frequently the abstention has been rather unreflective. The Canadian Sentencing Commission made a telling comparison with income tax legislation: "if Parliament were to pass a tax bill indicating that certain kinds of income were to be taxed at a rate of 'up to 34 per cent,' to accomplish goals that were never specified . . . most citizens would not tolerate such ambiguity." And ". . . undoubtedly the government would act quickly to change the situation." Yet in the sphere of sen-

tencing "we have long tolerated this kind of ambiguity" (Canadian Sentencing Commission 1987, para. 1.2). Even where a jurisdiction has a developed system of appellate review, the result is likely to be a mixture of judge-made guidance with unstructured discretion rather than the existence of some overall strategy. Moreover in some jurisdictions the appellate courts have also abstained to some extent from providing guidance to sentencers: their role has often been reactive and limited (Ashworth 1984), resulting in patchy coverage of the problems.

Another manifestation of legislative abstention is the tendency of legislatures to provide courts with new and ever more diverse noncustodial penalties, in pursuit of a declared policy of reducing the use of imprisonment, and yet without proper legislative guidance on the offenses or offenders for which a new measure is designed or on the way in which the new penalty relates to other available penalties. This unstructured proliferation of noncustodial sentences is a veritable invitation to disparity, as has been recognized in the Supreme Court of Victoria (*R v. O'Connor* [1987]).

4. *Sources of Disparity: Legality versus Flexibility.*   A second source of disparity may be found in the practical consequences of the constant struggle between the advocates of flexibility in sentencing and the advocates of the principle of legality and "rule of law" values. The advocates of maximum flexibility in sentencing are primarily judges: while they might agree with the abstract proposition that consistency in sentencing is an important value, they would be swift to insist on the need for flexibility in individual cases. Deeply ingrained in judicial lore are such statements as "no two cases are alike" and "each case has to be decided on its own facts" (Ashworth et al. 1984, pp. 20–24). The difficulty with such statements is not that they are necessarily untrue— on the contrary, one can argue strongly that judges should give proper weight to any special features of particular cases—but that they are too frequently used to obscure the fact that there are recurrent and nonindividual factors in cases. Thus the very people who argue for flexibility in sentencing in order to give effect to individual factors will often be those who argue that sentencing is a matter of experience, an "art" rather than a "science" (Ashworth et al. 1984, pp. 60–64). The flaw in this reasoning was identified some years ago by Roger Hood: "Magistrates and judges . . . place particular value upon their experience in sentencing. Now, if this experience is to be of value, then all cases cannot be unique, they must be comparable at least in some

respects; and even if it is agreed that all cases are unique in some sense, this cannot be decisive in the practice of sentencing, for frequently decisions are reached with the aid of 'experience'" (Hood 1962, p. 16).

Despite this and other demonstrations that there are recurrent and objective factors in cases for sentencing purposes (e.g., Moxon 1988, p. 64), the "individual case" ideology has maintained a strong grip on judicial attitudes to sentencing in several jurisdictions.

In the last two decades, however, it has had to contend with mounting opposition based on the "rule of law" ideology. The argument is that wide discretion at the sentencing stage is a violation of the principle of legality, which requires the law to be administered according to clear standards openly declared and laid down in advance. The legislative tradition of setting maximum penalties and providing little further guidance fails to satisfy the requirements of legality. Paradoxically it was a judge, Marvin Frankel, in his influential critique of sentencing (Frankel 1973), who gave impetus to this challenge to the "individual case" ideology espoused by many other judges. Others have since reinforced the argument that legal systems that show respect for these "legality" or "rule of law" values up to the stage of criminal conviction often abandon them at the sentencing stage and leave a wide and little-structured discretion (Robinson 1988).

The influence of the "rule of law" ideology on sentencing reform proposals may be illustrated by the report of the Canadian Sentencing Commission, which advocated greater "clarity, certainty, and predictability" in sentencing (Canadian Sentencing Commission 1987, p. 164). But the arguments have not been all one way. Judicial resistance to sentencing reforms or reform proposals has often been based, at least in part, on arguments stemming from the "individual case" ideology (e.g., the memorandum of the Victoria judges in the Victorian Sentencing Committee [1988, app. A]). In terms of practical application the values of legality and flexibility do not necessarily stand in polar opposition since, as I discuss below, significant advances in legality are not incompatible with the retention of some flexibility. Yet a continuing tension between the competing "individual case" and "rule of law" ideologies remains a notable element in the background to recent sentencing reforms.

5. *Sources of Disparity: Coherence or Incoherence of Aims.* Another area of tension, which cannot be explored in depth here, is that of the aims of sentencing. "Just deserts," incapacitation, rehabilitation, and individual and general deterrence all have their advocates, but they are

capable of leading to very different sentences. It will be recalled that the Canadian Sentencing Commission found, from its review of research, that inconsistency in sentencing stemmed, in part at least, from the differing sentencing philosophies of judges and magistrates (Canadian Sentencing Commission 1987, para. 4.1.2). This led the commission to the view that one essential element in any sentencing reforms should be "a clear order of priority" of the aims of sentencing. The relevance of various aims of sentencing might be conceded, but "the fundamental goal of sentencing takes precedence over the content of all other sections of the Declaration" (Canadian Sentencing Commission 1987, p. 152). The Determinate Sentencing Act of 1976 in California (see von Hirsch and Mueller 1984) and the Sentencing Commission of Minnesota (see Parent 1988, chaps. 2 and 3) had adopted a similar approach some years earlier, proclaiming "just deserts" as the leading aim of sentencing in those jurisdictions. The British legislature has now trodden the same path, in a statute, the Criminal Justice Act of 1991, which installs "the seriousness of the offense" as the primary criterion of sentence in most cases (Wasik and Taylor 1991; Ashworth 1992).

Once again, the point has not gone uncontested. Subsequent reports in Canada have turned away from the Sentencing Commission's insistence on a clear order of priority for aims and have preferred a "multi-faceted approach." Thus the Daubney Committee recommended that public protection and ensuring that offenders take responsibility for the consequences of their conduct should be highlighted as aims of sentencing, in addition to proportionality (Daubney 1988, pp. 43–57). Later Ministry of Justice proposals adopt the terminology of balance, proclaiming the need for "balance among the various subsidiary aims of the system, such as denunciation, deterrence and rehabilitation." The "statement of purpose" explicitly allows courts to take account, in sentencing, of denunciation, deterrence, incapacitation, reparation, and promoting a sense of responsibility in offenders (Campbell 1990; Canadian Ministry of Justice 1990a, pp. 7–10). It therefore appears that the reduction of disparity in sentencing is giving way, in Canada at least, to rather indecisive formulae that are broad enough to cover a large number of (conflicting) aims in the hope of securing public or political acceptability. If it is correct to explain sentencing inconsistencies by reference to differing aims of sentencers, in part at least, then this source of inconsistency would be institutionalized if the latest Canadian proposals were to be enacted.

A similar development has taken place in the U.S. federal jurisdiction: the statement of the goals of sentencing in Section 3553 of the Sentencing Reform Act of 1984 proclaims four purposes, which cover almost all the possible aims of sentencing. The commission therefore felt bound, it is said, to develop guidelines that find no place for a single leading aim of sentencing or even for any prioritization of the several aims (see U.S. Sentencing Commission [1987, p. 1.4] and, criticizing the commission on this point, von Hirsch [1988]). Perhaps this assumes a position similar to the judicial approach propounded in the Australian decision of *Williscroft*, in the state of Victoria: "The purposes of punishment are manifold and each element will assume a different significance not only in different crimes but in the individual commission of each crime. . . . Ultimately every sentence imposed represents a sentencing judge's instinctive synthesis of all the various aspects involved in the punitive process" (*R v. Williscroft* [1975], pp. 299–300, reiterated in *R v. Young, Dickenson and West* [1990], discussed by Corns [1990]).

In a similar vein are the Alaska Supreme Court's decisions in *State v. Chaney* (1970) and *Nicholas v. State* (1970), listing rehabilitation, incapacitation, individual deterrence, general deterrence, and others as the relevant "standards" and stating that the trial court should "determine the priority and relationship of these objectives in any particular case" (see DiPietro 1990, pp. 271–72).

The different approaches are sometimes presented as if the only two alternatives are to have a sentencing system with a single aim and to allow sentencers a free choice among several aims. Critics of the first approach argue that it is too rigid, especially in the context of formal social responses to a wide range of human misconduct. They feel that the second approach is the only "realistic" one. Terms such as "balance" and "multifaceted" are used to convey its worldliness, as opposed to the academic, even ascetic regime of a single aim (e.g., Nagel 1990, p. 940). But there is a third alternative, already well established in practice: to declare a primary aim of sentencing, and to provide that in certain types of case one or more different aims may be accorded priority. One example of this used to be Minnesota, where "just deserts" was the primary aim in sentencing serious offenses but could be displaced by rehabilitation in certain instances, and where different aims have operated for less serious offenses (Frase [1991*b*], noting that in 1989 the primary aim was altered to "public safety"). Another example is Sweden, where a 1988 law declares a primary aim of sentencing (proportionality) and then clearly provides that other aims may be accorded priority when sentencing certain types of offense or offender (see von Hirsch and Jareborg 1989 and, more fully, von Hirsch 1987*a*). This approach is multifaceted without amounting to a free-for-all since it accepts the relevance of other aims and identifies the types of case where they might apply. It can therefore claim to produce consistency of approach without the self-denying ordinance of a single aim. Thus it is not the distinction between one aim and many that is important but the distinction between a structured choice and a free choice of aims to pursue. A structured choice is coherent because it states priorities where there are multiple aims. A free choice is incoherent because it leaves unresolved the conflicts between the different aims, and in doing so it encourages disparity. A vague primary aim, such as "the maintenance of respect for the law," is likely to offer a fairly free choice.

6. *Sources of Disparity: Practices of Other Professionals.* If the practices of police and prosecutors in different regions of a country vary, this is likely to be a source of inconsistency over which the courts have little control. Generally speaking, a court can only deal with a case on the basis of the facts presented to it. Where a defendant pleads guilty to one or more charges, the court is more or less bound to base the sentence on that plea. Since the rate of guilty pleas is high in many jurisdictions, both the police (insofar as they directly or indirectly determine charges to be brought) and the prosecutors (by offering or agreeing to reduce or drop some charges) may exert a powerful influence on the form in which the case appears to the sentencer. This has long been evident in Minnesota, where plea bargaining was a common feature of the sentencing system before the introduction of sentencing guidelines, and where prosecutorial practices have continued to have a constraining effect on sentencing practice (Knapp 1987; Parent 1988, pp. 179–86). Plea bargaining has also been common in the U.S. federal sentencing system: the attorney general has issued a directive to government attorneys to adapt their practices so as to support the new sentencing guidelines, but research shows that plea arrangements circumvent the guidelines in a substantial minority of cases (Schulhofer and Nagel 1989). The Canadian Sentencing Commission concluded that charging practices have the potential to undermine formal sentencing policy, by distorting proportionality, predictability, and uniformity (Canadian Sentencing Commission 1987, chap. 13), and concern about the priorities and practices of "nonsentencing" professionals is

repeated in the latest Canadian proposals (Canadian Ministry of Justice 1990*b*, p. 7), which proclaim "the need for greater integration" of policies. However, the division of responsibilities between the federal government and the provinces makes national consistency in pretrial practices difficult to achieve.

B. Inconsistency in Sentences as Implemented

The widespread disparities in sentences imposed have tended to be magnified by inconsistencies in the practical implementation of sentences. Even where judges' sentencing decisions do have a measure of consistency, this can be thwarted during what continental Europeans call "the execution of the sanction." If a sentence requires the offender to attend at a certain place for supervision or for community service and the offender fails to attend on one or more occasions, practices often vary. Will the absences be tolerated, or will action be taken against the offender? If a court imposes a financial penalty, are all offenders who fail to pay dealt with in the same way?

Differences at the stage of implementation are magnified when it comes to custodial sentences. Most jurisdictions have operated one or more forms of executive release, whether termed remission, "good time," parole, conditional release, or whatever. Some of the systems are or have been discretionary; all of them detract from the sentences announced in court, sometimes to a degree that empties that sentence of much significance. It may be inherently likely that a single parole authority would be effective in reducing sentencing disparities created by many judges sitting in different places (Zimring 1976), but other aims have often had priority (see von Hirsch and Hanrahan 1979; Bottomley 1990). Judicial opposition to such schemes has been widespread—not so much a rejection of the idea of supervised early release but more a rejection of the way in which some governments have manipulated its application for reasons of economics and prison capacity and have thereby devalued the sentences handed down by the courts. In Australia the Supreme Court of Victoria has referred to "administrative erosion" of judicial sentences and conjectured that an intelligent observer might regard the system as "an elaborate charade designed to conceal from the public the real punishment inflicted on an offender" (*R v. Yates* [1985], pp. 43–44; accord, Victorian Sentencing Committee 1988, para. 2.10.2; Australian Law Reform Commission 1988, para. 70).

Sentencing reform committees have recognized the problem and have largely sympathized with the judicial opposition. Indeed, their language has been strong. The U.S. Sentencing Commission charged the old federal system with "dishonesty" in allowing the pronunciation of sentences in court that bore little relation to the time served (U.S. Sentencing Commission 1987, pp. 1–2). The Australian federal report made proposals that would produce "truth in sentencing" (Australian Law Reform Commission 1988, paras. 69–93). And Delaware has recently joined the list of states that have abolished parole in favor of truth in sentencing (Gebelein 1991).

The problem here is not, however, solely one of consistency in sentencing. Enquiries have found that discretionary parole systems tend to engender a sense of unfairness among prisoners, as well as confusion among members of the public (e.g., Canadian Sentencing Commission 1987, pp. 242–43). Moreover, systems of discretionary parole conflict with the "rule of law" ideology: just as it has been argued that principles of legality that operate at the stage of criminal liability should not be discarded at the sentencing stage (Frankel 1973; Robinson 1988), so it might equally be argued that those principles of legality should be no less applicable at the stage of execution of the sanction than they ought to be in sentencing itself. Yet legality values can be protected without abolishing parole—through a system of supervised early release that is automatic, and that therefore gives prisoners (and society) the benefit of parole (cf. Hann, Harman, and Pease 1991) without the drawbacks of a selection process. Provided that the revocation procedures conform to the principle of legality, such an approach can introduce a form of "truth in sentencing" without the substantial reduction in declared prison terms that parole abolition requires. In that way, legislators can respond to concerns about the overuse of imprisonment without running the risk of political shipwreck, where local conditions make that likely. The proposals of Lord Carlisle's committee in England go some distance down this road, with their aim of restoring meaning to the sentence pronounced in court (Carlisle 1988), and the Criminal Justice Act of 1991 introduces many of the recommended changes.

C. Concerns about the Use of Imprisonment

A third major factor in the background to recent sentencing reforms is a concern about the use of imprisonment, an issue examined in *Crime and Justice* a few years ago (Blumstein 1988). The concerns, however, have not been all one way. Many of the sentencing reforms of the early 1980s were premised on the need to reduce the use of imprisonment in particular jurisdictions. From the outset the Sentencing Commission in Minnesota, taking its cue from the enabling statute, incorporated a "prison capacity" constraint into its guidelines, so as to control rises in the overall use of custody (Parent 1988, pp. 40–45). The Canadian Sentencing Commission concluded that there is "an over-reliance on imprisonment" in Canada and recommended the lowering of maximum prison sentences (Canadian Sentencing Commission 1987, pp. 76–78, 164–66). The Australian federal report proclaimed "the need to reduce emphasis on imprisonment," supporting this with arguments not just about the high costs and low benefits of imprisonment but also with an analysis of the "negative and destructive" experience that it involves (Australian Law Reform Commission 1988, paras. 41–67). England's new Criminal Justice Act of 1991 follows a government policy document that drew attention to the negative and even crime-productive effects of imprisonment and its encouragement of a dependent lifestyle and that stated that prison is overused for less serious offenses and offenders (Home Office 1990, esp. para. 2.7).

The British government's approach, however, is expressed as a "twin track" policy. While custody should be used less at the lower end of the scale, long sentences should continue to be imposed for very serious offenses (Home Office 1990, para. 2.8). The reasoning behind this appears to rely on a concept of proportionality that stretches out the differential between serious violence, sex and drug offenses, and the lesser forms of criminality. In other jurisdictions, it is the rhetoric of public protection that has gradually turned the tide. In 1987 the Canadian report argued that imprisonment provides little public protection because it applies only to a very small minority of offenders (Canadian Sentencing Commission 1987, pp. 119–20). The British government seems to have accepted this argument that sentencing in general, and custodial sentencing in particular, is not the most productive route to crime prevention and public protection (Home Office 1990, para. 1.8). But the argument has been cast aside in Canada. The Daubney Committee did not doubt its logic: they simply asserted that "public confidence in the criminal justice system demands that public protection be considered as the fundamental purpose of each of its components. In this respect, sentencing is no exception" (Daubney 1988, p. 45). Assertions about "the protection of the public" are also prominent in the latest proposals in Canada (Canadian Ministry of Justice 1990*a*, pp. 6–8). As for federal sentencing in the United States, "excessive leniency" for some offenses was identified as a major concern by the Sentencing Commission (U.S. Sentencing Commission 1991, p. i), and the guidelines were designed so as to respond to the legislature's call for higher sentences for career offenders, those who support themselves through criminal means, and those convicted of violent or drug offenses (Sentencing Reform Act 1984, sec. 994 [i]).

There can be little doubt that the approaches of the Canadian, U.S. federal, and British governments are motivated in large part by political concerns: even if longer sentences for some groups are not the surest way of increasing public protection, many members of the public and many politicians believe they are. Governments are likely to receive credit for taking that approach. Yet there are at least two paradoxes here. One is that U.S. Sentencing Commission member Ilene Nagel cites an opinion poll in support of the argument that some federal sentences have been too low (Nagel [1990, p. 884], citing U.S. Department of Justice [1988, pp. 142–43]). However, other American research findings point in a different direction, as does British research that demonstrates that victims and other members of the public usually do not favor sentences higher than current levels and would support more constructive and restitutionary measures rather than imprisonment (e.g., Maguire 1982; Hough, Moxon, and Lewis 1987; cf. also Walker and Hough 1988). The second paradox is that, while tougher sentences might be politically "safe," many governments are also under pressure to reduce their financial commitments to prisons. The tension is apparent in Minnesota's recent legislative modification of its capacity constraint (Frase 1991*a*, p. 1406) and in Oregon's decision to tackle its prison problem both by some building and by capacity-constrained sentencing guidelines (Bogan 1990). The Minnesota developments show that, important as a capacity constraint on incarcerative sentences may be in times of burgeoning American prison populations, the question of who determines the prison capacity to be provided is also crucial (Frase 1991*a*, pp. 1409–10).

D. The Background of Dissatisfaction

The paragraphs in the first portion of this essay have described some of the concerns that have led to the sentencing reform movement of recent years. The various inconsistencies in sentences and their practical effects have loomed largest, but it remains possible that the reason why they have been so influential is less a matter of their existence (disparities in sentencing have been known for many years) than the publicity given to them and the consequent effect on "public confidence" in criminal justice. Since the concern about inconsistency lies in the public and political arena, it is perhaps not surprising that the question whether sentences should be made more or less severe has often been resolved by reference to political appearances rather than criminological research. However, the research findings have had an unlikely ally in the debate over prison use, and that is public expenditure requirements. Some governments have taken the economic aspects of sentencing seriously, and this may have helped to lure them away from the political attractions of greater punitiveness when criminological considerations had proved unpersuasive.

Among the many other factors that have contributed to the mood of change, two more may be singled out for mention. First, the decline of faith in rehabilitative sentencing since the 1960s exerted a considerable effect in the United States, if only because much rehabilitative sentencing relied on large amounts of executive discretion in determining the nature and duration of sentences (Allen 1964). Such broad discretion was difficult to control, led to widely differing sentences in practice, and generated a sense of unfairness among offenders. This is not to suggest that all jurisdictions have abandoned or should abandon rehabilitative elements in sentencing (see Cullen and Gilbert 1982; Gendreau and Ross 1988), but the excesses of those states that went a long way in that direction in the 1960s have undoubtedly assisted the subsequent development of consistency and proportionality as desirable features of sentencing systems. The second factor seems quite unconnected with all that has gone before, and it is the rise of the victim movement (Maguire 1991). The 1980s saw a burgeoning of concern for victims in the criminal justice system that has manifested itself in a variety of new procedures and provisions. This movement has not greatly assisted the case for broad sentencing reforms, but it has exerted some influence on the shape of reform proposals in some jurisdictions (Australian Law Reform Commission 1988, paras. 36, 191–94; Canadian Ministry of Justice 1990a, p. 8; cf. Wright 1991).

II. Constitutional Responsibility for Sentencing

Most countries have an explicit or implicit commitment to the doctrine of separation of powers, in the sense that certain functions are allocated constitutionally to separate organs of the state (legislature, judiciary, or executive). It is relatively rare, however, for there to be an explicit constitutional allocation of functions in relation to sentencing, and it is only the events of the last two decades that have brought the issue into focus.

A. *The Extent of Legislative Competence*

There is widespread acceptance of the notion that the legislature has the function of setting the maximum penalties for offenses. In a few jurisdictions there remain some crimes for which no legislative maximum has ever been set—in English common law, manslaughter is an example—but there is no doubting that it would be constitutionally proper for the legislature to impose such a maximum.

In many jurisdictions, the legislature has gone little further than the setting of maximum penalties. The tradition has been to leave a broad discretion to the judiciary below the statutory maximum, and the persistence of this tradition over several generations may have led to the assumption that as a matter of constitutional principle discretion in sentencing *belongs to* the judiciary. On this view, the legislature has the function of setting the limits of state intervention by sentencing, and the role of the judiciary is to use their discretion to select the appropriate sentence in individual cases. A consequence of this view, however, would be that it would be unconstitutional for the legislature to cut down the sentencing discretion of the courts by means such as mandatory sentences, mandatory minimum sentences, or other statutory restrictions. In fact, as we know, mandatory minimum sentences are now to be found in many jurisdictions, and that alone suggests that there is little substance in the notion that sentencing discretion in individual cases "belongs" constitutionally to the judiciary. The matter has, however, been litigated before the High Court of Australia. In the case of *Palling v. Corfield* (1970) there was a constitutional challenge to the validity of a law that required courts to impose a certain mandatory sentence for an offense. Chief Justice Barwick, delivering the judgment of the court rejecting the challenge, stated,

> It is both unusual and in general, in my opinion, undesirable
> that the court should not have a discretion in the imposition of
> sentences, for circumstances alter cases and it is a traditional
> function of a court of justice to endeavour to make the punishment
> appropriate to the circumstances as well as to the nature of the
> crime. But whether or not such discretion shall be given to

the court in relation to a statutory offense is for the decision
of the Parliament. It cannot be denied that there are circumstances
which may warrant the imposition on the court of a duty to
impose specific punishment. If Parliament chooses to deny the
court such a discretion and to impose such a duty, as I have
mentioned the court must obey the statute in this respect
assuming its validity in other respects. It is not, in my opinion, a
breach of the Constitution not to confide any discretion to the
court as to the penalty to be imposed. [1970, p. 58]

This is an important judgment, not simply for its rejection of the
constitutional challenge, but also for its evident sympathy with the
thesis that judges should in general be left with as much discretion as
possible. Such a feeling has been evident in many of the jurisdictions
in which sentencing reforms have been proposed or enacted: perhaps
the most vigorous assertions are to be found in the memorandum of
the judges of the Supreme Court of Victoria (Victorian Sentencing
Committee 1988, app. A).

This strong sentiment is evident among the judges of many jurisdictions. It has been cultivated by long periods of legislative abstention
from detailed statutory intervention in sentencing matters. Indeed,
even in nineteenth-century England, when there were numerous mandatory or mandatory minimum sentences, influential figures such as
Lord Halsbury (a lord chancellor) stated that sentencing is exclusively
the business of the courts, and the agreement by the English judges
on a "Memorandum of Normal Punishments" in 1901 may be seen
as an attempt to reinforce the judiciary's claim to regulate their own
discretion beneath the statutory maxima (see Radzinowicz and Hood
1986, pp. 754 ff.). In most countries, the twentieth century has seen
relatively little legislative intervention in sentencing until the reemer-
gence of mandatory minimum sentences in recent years. Some mandatory minima have been successfully challenged in a few places on the
ground that they are so disproportionately high as to constitute "cruel
and unusual punishment" for the crime (*Smith v. R.* [1987], applying
the Canadian Charter of Rights and Freedoms), but that casts no doubt
on the legitimacy of removing or reducing judicial discretion.

In terms of constitutional analysis, then, it remains important to
distinguish the proposition that parliaments may legislate on sentencing matters in a way that leaves courts with little or no discretion in
individual cases, which is a correct proposition, from the view that

reductions in the sentencing discretion of the courts are generally unwise and productive of injustice in individual cases, which is a value judgment, on which there is room for debate. Perhaps the final words on this issue should be those of Justice Blackmun in the Supreme Court of the United States in *Mistretta v. U.S.*, *488 U.S. 361* (1989): although at one time "Congress delegated almost unfettered discretion to the sentencing judge to determine what the sentence should be within the customarily wide range," the true constitutional position is that "the scope of judicial discretion with respect to a sentence is subject to congressional control."

B. *The Principle of the Independence of the Judiciary*

A second argument in favor of maximum judicial discretion in sentencing derives from the principle of judicial independence. In crude terms, the argument is that when legislatures constrain the discretion of the courts in sentencing matters, they encroach on judicial independence. Since the independence of the judiciary is central to the constitutions of many states, this is a serious charge. Can it be sustained?

In answering this question, the starting point must be the definition of judicial independence. The principle is such a powerful constitutional pillar that it is hardly surprising that proponents of maximum judicial discretion should wish to rely on it, and only a careful examination of the definition will determine whether they can properly do so. The difficulties increase when it is found that many constitutions do not contain a definition of the principle. Its essence surely lies close to neutrality and impartiality as values in the administration of the law: a judge or magistrate should be in a position to administer the law without fear or favor. No pressures on the court to decide this way or that way should be countenanced. Thus freedom from bias, partiality, and undue influence—part of the essence of the rule of law, in its narrow or neutral sense—is enhanced.

Now it is a long way from this definition of judicial independence to the claim that if a legislature imposes detailed requirements on courts in respect of sentencing it is infringing the constitutional principle of judicial independence. The weakness of the claim is apparent: it is nothing more than a relabeled version of the argument that sentencing is constitutionally the preserve of the judiciary, the argument refuted in the previous section. The principle of judicial independence is a principle of impartiality and freedom from influence when administering justice, not a principle that demarcates sentencing as a sphere that is the province of the courts. The conclusion must therefore be that legislation that restricts or removes the sentencing discretion of the courts does not infringe the constitutional principle of judicial independence since unlimited sentencing discretion does not form part of that principle—as the British government has recently reasserted, after many years of ambivalence (Home Office 1990, para. 2.1).

The "Basic Principles on the Independence of the Judiciary" adopted by the Seventh United Nations Crime Congress introduce an element that may be open to a slightly different interpretation: "The judiciary shall decide matters before them with impartiality on the basis of facts, in accordance with the law, without any improper influences or pressures" (United Nations 1990, p. 74).

This affirms the narrow or neutral conception of judicial independence, but the reference to deciding issues "in accordance with the law" may prove restrictive. The constitutions of some countries (e.g., Belgium) declare the independence of the judge and have been interpreted as preventing any limitation on a judge's sentencing discretion other than restrictions created by legislation. The effect, therefore, is to exclude any structuring of discretion by an appeal court or other nonstatutory body. The significance of this approach is that it goes beyond the independence of the judiciary, from the legislature and from the executive, to assert the independence of the individual judge, from everything except legislation (see Council of Europe 1989, pp. 119–21).

C. The Constitutionality of Sentencing Commissions

Whether a sentencing commission is constitutional will obviously depend on the means by which it was established and on the constitution of the jurisdiction concerned. In focusing here on the constitutional challenge to the U.S. Sentencing Commission (USSC), this general limitation must be borne in mind. A sentencing commission or council is usually a body created by the legislature with powers to draft and promulgate, subject to legislative approval, guidelines, and other principles of sentencing designed to have binding effect on the courts. Many jurisdictions have no experience of such a body: it will therefore be a constitutional novelty, whose status has to be assessed by reference to standards originally laid down in a somewhat different context.

The USSC was created by the Sentencing Reform Act of 1984. It was directed to establish guidelines that would serve the various goals of federal sentencing. The act specified four goals and also indicated in considerable detail the factors that the guidelines should reflect. The USSC, with one dissenter, laid before Congress a set of guidelines in April 1987 that, after the statutory six-month period during which no negative resolution was passed, became law in November 1987 (see Breyer 1988). It emerged that some federal judges regarded the guidelines as unconstitutional whereas others accepted them as legally sound. The constitutional challenge eventually went to the Supreme Court in *Mistretta v. U.S., 488 U.S. 361* (1989), and the Court confirmed the constitutionality of the USSC and its guidelines by a majority of eight to one.

The first ground of challenge was that the creation of the USSC amounted to an unlawful delegation of legislative power. Article 1 of the United States Constitution states that "all legislative powers . . . shall be vested in a Congress of the United States." In the majority judgment, Justice Blackmun held that the Sentencing Reform Act of 1984 did not delegate lawmaking power unconstitutionally. Previous decisions had accepted the impracticability of requiring Congress to legislate itself on technical and detailed matters and had approved delegation so long as Congress declares an "intelligible principle" and requires conformity to it. The Sentencing Reform Act achieves this with its statement of purposes and its detailed specification of factors that the guidelines should reflect.

The second ground of challenge was that the Sentencing Commission contravenes the separation of powers. The United States Constitution vests legislative power in Congress, executive power in the president, and judicial power in the Supreme Court. Since the Sentencing Commission by statute is located within the judicial branch, the argument was that its legislative functions are inconsistent with the separation of powers. In the Supreme Court, Justice Blackmun followed previous decisions in stating that the Constitution does not require a rigid separation of powers, so long as there is no encroachment or aggrandizement of one branch at the expense of another. Statutes that mix the functions of two branches had been upheld before, and the majority of the Supreme Court were satisfied that the formulation of sentencing guidelines is sufficiently close to the judiciary's responsibilities that the judiciary may properly be regarded as the appropriate branch to deal with them. It was on this point that Justice Scalia's dissent was most vigorous: he maintained that the doctrine of separation of powers should be more strongly enforced, that the USSC is not a court and has no judicial powers, and therefore that it was a legislative body placed under the judicial branch. While one might have sympathy with his argument that the USSC should be regarded as a delegated legislative authority rather than placed under the judicial branch, it appears that he would nevertheless have rejected this delegation on the ground that the Sentencing Reform Act of 1984 does not lay down adequate standards to control the commission's rule making. In view of the detailed specifications in the act, this may be thought to take the objections one step too far.

The constitutionality of sentencing commissions in other jurisdictions will depend on the wording of the constitution, on the traditional approach to interpreting it, and on the form and contents of the statute that establishes the commission. For example, the Pennsylvania Supreme Court declared the state's sentencing guidelines invalid in *Commonwealth v. Sessoms* (1987), and corrective legislation was subsequently passed. Familiarity with this decision and *Mistretta* may avoid some pitfalls in the establishment of other commissions. It remains for argument whether such a commission is more appropriately located in the judicial or the legislative branch for constitutional purposes.

III. The Shape of Guidance on Sentencing

In the previous section it has been argued that sentencing policy is a matter for the legislature. It may decide to relinquish it to the judiciary or to some other body or it may keep control itself. When there is a decision to pursue a certain policy or to foster greater consistency, three interrelated issues then arise. What should be the *source* of guidance on sentencing—should it be a parliamentary committee, or the courts, or a specially appointed committee such as a sentencing commission? By what *authority* should the sentencing guidance be laid down—should it be embodied in primary legislation, or issued through some other medium? What should be the *style* of sentencing guidance—should it consist of numerical sentencing "grids," or narrative guidelines, or a set of general principles, or some other style? And are there any general propositions that can be advanced about the *content* of sentencing guidance? Often these issues have not been kept distinct in the reforms and reform proposals, and it is hoped that their separation here will assist in assessing the advantages and disadvantages of each approach, without obscuring the links between them.

A. *Sources of Guidance*

Most of the jurisdictions that have had sentencing reforms or reform proposals in the last two decades have appointed a special committee or commission to formulate recommendations for change. This has been done in Canada, Australia, the state of Victoria, Sweden, the U.S. federal jurisdiction, and in American states such as Minnesota, Washington, Delaware, New York, Pennsylvania, Connecticut, Maine, South Carolina, and Oregon. In almost all the American jurisdictions, the same committee or commission has also been authorized to formulate the actual guidance, but this is not the only possible approach. In Canada, Australia, and Victoria, for example, the body was more in the nature of an advisory committee reporting to the legislature: the government would decide whether to proceed, and if so, how. In England and Wales, in contrast, sentencing reform has been regarded as a matter of ordinary government policy, to be determined without any committee enquiry.

Why has resort to the appointment of a special body been so common? One way of approaching the issue is to look at the alternatives. Could the judiciary function as an adequate source of guidance and of change? Much depends, here, on the structure of the sentencing system and the legal tradition to which it belongs. Few jurisdictions have a tradition of appellate review in sentencing matters, and fewer still have a tradition whereby the court of appeal lays down guidance in its judgments: England is the prime example of this, and it is found to some extent in Canada and its provinces, in Australia and its states, and in New Zealand and Ireland. If the task of creating sentencing guidance is to be left to the judiciary, it is clearly an advantage if they have experience of the task. Is experience sufficient? Two arguments suggest that it may not be. First, the way in which appellate courts operate makes them accustomed to dealing with particular cases and particular issues and unaccustomed to looking at the structure and practice of sentencing as a whole. Since sentencing reform is likely to require an overall view of offenses and penalties, particularly in systems where proportionality is an aim, judicial experience may be relatively small in this respect. Second, judges tend to lack experience of wider aspects of criminal justice: they may have visited prisons and probation schemes, but their knowledge of the operation and perspectives of these other agencies is likely to be partial. If it is accepted that sentencing policy should be shaped so as to form part of wider criminal justice policy, then the process of policy formation ought to include people with knowledge of these other aspects, and an academic with relevant knowledge, to add to the judiciary's own experience of crime and criminals.

If these two points are accepted, the judiciary would emerge as a necessary but not a sufficient component of a body to propose sentencing reforms. Those countries that have appointed sentencing commissions seem to share this conclusion. Indeed, to rely on the judiciary to propose major reforms seems unpractical in many jurisdictions, where judges rarely meet and form views as a body. To leave it to appellate courts has the further weakness that their members are sometimes not apprised of the up-to-date realities of trial court sentencing.

Whether a government could adequately perform the task of creating sentencing guidance on its own would depend on the quality and strength of its advisers. In a system where there are good statistics and detailed research findings on sentencing practice, it may well be possible for a ministry of justice to draw together advisers with a sufficient range of experience of criminal justice to produce workable guidance. However, one possible disadvantage of this approach is that the guidance is identified politically with the government—which may occur to a significantly lesser degree with guidance emanating from the judiciary or from a sentencing commission. Whether sentencing guidance created directly by a government did prove to be a political embarrassment would depend on the aims of the sentencing reforms, and the temper of the country itself. If one element in the sentencing reforms is a reduction in the severity of sanctions (typically, a reduction in the use of custody), this might be unpopular with the electorate in many countries. A government in such a country that wishes to pursue some such policy might therefore be driven to balance its proposals with other elements designed to restore its popularity, usually through some "twin-track" policy. Thus the British government's policy of reducing the use of imprisonment for less serious offenders is twinned with a continuing encouragement of high sentences for those involved in violent, sexual, or drug crimes (Home Office 1990). In the states of Washington and Oregon, where the existence of a prison capacity constraint also entered into the calculations, lower sentences for property offenders have been balanced by higher sentences for violent offenders (Bogan 1990).

Three attractions of a sentencing commission or council emerge from this discussion of possible alternatives. First, its membership should be broad enough to provide a proper criminal justice perspective to the task of creating sentencing guidance: judicial members would bring their experience, those in prisons and community corrections would bring their experience, and other members might be able to add further expertise. Second, it should have sufficient time and the distinct task of taking an overall view of sentencing. Third, it should have sufficient detachment from the distorting effect of political pressures. This third point should not, of course, be overdone. Those sentencing commissions that are given the power not only of proposing reforms but also of formulating the guidance authoritatively may well have political constraints built into the legislative framework within which they must operate.

Even without such fetters, however, sentencing commissions are likely to be sensitive to possible political repercussions. The catalog of failures is striking: the report of the Canadian Sentencing Commission has proved politically unacceptable, largely because of its proposal to reduce prison sentences significantly and its debunking of the idea of "public protection" as an aim for sentences (Canadian Sentencing Commission 1987, pp. 119, 145–49; cf. Daubney 1988 and Canadian Ministry of Justice 1990a, 1990b). The sentencing commission in Connecticut recommended that a statutory determinate sentencing system would be preferable to commission-created guidelines, and the Connecticut legislature followed the recommendation (Tonry 1987a, p. 21). The State Committee on Sentencing Guidelines in New York produced guidelines that drew objections from various quarters, including claims that they were too harsh and claims that they were too lenient, and in such a polarized political climate they were dropped (Tonry 1987a, pp. 21–23). The Pennsylvania Commission on Sentencing produced guidelines that were rejected by the legislature on the grounds that they were too lenient and too restrictive of judicial discretion. Further guidelines were produced and have been allowed to stand, but they prescribe only minimum sentences and leave a great deal to judicial discretion (Tonry 1987a, pp. 23–24). There were also failures in the states of South Carolina and Maine.

These failures include committees of both kinds—the kind of advisory committee that is invited to study sentencing and to propose reforms (as in New York and Canada) and the kind of sentencing commission that is mandated to draft guidance with a view to its direct implementation (as in Maine, South Carolina, and Pennsylvania). Although our primary interest here is in the *source* of new sentencing guidance, we must continue to look at committees and commissions of both kinds. There are several that have been successful to the extent of producing guidance that has then been implemented. Of the sentencing commissions charged with proposing and drafting guidance, the best-known example is Minnesota, where the guidelines have been in force for more than a dozen years. One factor in the Minnesota Sentencing Commission's success, compared with those of other states, was its open decision-making process and its willingness to hear the arguments of interest groups that were not represented among commission members. By this means and, it seems, through the personality of the chair at that time, support was won for the various compromises made, and, most notably, the commission's adoption of a "prison capacity constraint" in its sentencing guidelines was allowed to stand (Parent 1988, chap. 3). Minnesota has, however, suffered a changing penal climate in recent years, and the Sentencing Commission has been directed to alter some of its policies (Frase 1991a). The early experience in Minnesota seems to have been influential in the state of Washington, where the Sentencing Commission's guidelines were also accepted by the legislature and have been in force since 1984. As Tonry has put it, "most of the Minnesota ingredients were present: a capable staff, an effective chairman, an adequate budget, achievement of a sense of joint mission among the Commission's members, a comprehensive and principled approach to policy problems, and an acknowledgement of the need to make simple political compromises during development of the guidelines" (Tonry 1987b, p. 57).

The U.S. Sentencing Commission was also successful in having its guidelines accepted by Congress (no negative resolution having been passed), and they have been in force since late 1987. The result, however, has been much less widely acclaimed than the outcomes in Minnesota and Washington (and, as we shall see below, Oregon and Delaware). In their defense, members of the USSC have argued that the federal legislation was much more detailed, leaving the commission with fewer policy decisions to make (Breyer 1988; Nagel 1990). But the comparison is unconvincing. The USSC did have a decision to make about the aims of sentencing under the guidelines: Commissioner Nagel stresses the reference to multiple goals in the Sentencing Reform Act as a reason for the Commission's decision not to make a clear statement on the aims of sentencing (Nagel 1990, pp. 914–20), but it would have been open to the commission to adopt a form of hybrid system that ranked the various aims rather than leaving judges with a relatively unstructured choice (Robinson 1987; von Hirsch 1988;

Tonry 1991). The statutory language gave the USSC ample opportunity to take account of prison capacity in setting the guidelines, but it declined to do so (von Hirsch 1988). The USSC also had choices to make about whether to adopt "real offense" sentencing and about the extent to which past sentencing practice should determine the content of the guidelines (Nagel 1990, pp. 925–32). It is therefore difficult to say that the federal guidelines, which are incoherent in theory and which appear complex and confusing in practice (e.g., Miller and Freed 1991), were dictated by the legislative provisions.

Turning to advisory committees, three that were successful in having their proposals accepted, in general, by legislatures were those in Sweden, Victoria, and Delaware. Sweden's Committee on Imprisonment reported in 1986 after six years' work on matters of sentencing and prison policy. The committee had been appointed by the Minister of Justice and thus made proposals that the Swedish government might or might not adopt. In the event, the Swedish government accepted the proposals on sentencing, and they are enshrined in two new chapters of the Swedish Penal Code that passed through the Swedish parliament and became law in January 1989 (von Hirsch 1987a; von Hirsch and Jareborg 1989). In the Australian state of Victoria, the Sentencing Committee had been appointed by the attorney-general and reported to him. Its three-volume report traversed much ground, and the main conclusions—that the legislature should articulate the general policies and principles to be followed in sentencing, whereas detailed guidelines for sentencing should be laid down by the Full Court and supplemented by voluntary guidelines devised by a Judicial Studies Board (Victorian Sentencing Committee 1988, pp. 212–30)—have been accepted in broad outline and incorporated in legislation. In Delaware the Sentencing Accountability Commission made proposals for sentencing reform that were adopted by the legislature in 1987 and proposals for "truth in sentencing" that were adopted by the legislature in 1989.

These experiences with sentencing commissions send mixed messages on many issues, and the one clear message—that political acceptability is crucial—is not greatly helpful in itself. At that level, it becomes a question of the personalities involved at the commission and in the political sphere and of the mood of the public, the judges, and politicians in the jurisdiction. Sentencing commissions have the apparent advantage of drawing into the process of policy formation professionals from different parts of the criminal justice system, but one of the reasons for failure of the State Committee on Sentencing Guidelines in New York was apparently that some members adhered doggedly to their own institutional interests as prosecutors or whatever and never developed a shared sense of mission toward the crafting of a guideline system that would command widespread acceptance (von Hirsch 1987*b*, pp. 79–83). This can only serve to emphasize the critical importance of the choice of individuals to serve as members and of the general political atmosphere in the jurisdiction (Parent 1988, pp. 211–18). Another apparent advantage of sentencing commissions is that they are somewhat insulated from direct political pressure of the kind that could be exerted on a government minister, for example. Of course, where the body is an advisory committee, as in Sweden, Canada, Delaware, and the state of Victoria, this has meant submission to ordinary political processes, with varying results—broad acceptance in Sweden, Victoria, and Delaware but in Canada a subsequent committee followed by a further set of government proposals for reform (Daubney 1988; Canadian Ministry of Justice 1990*a*). A further variation occurred in Oregon, where the state's Criminal Justice Council first made proposals for sentencing reform to the legislature and later developed guidelines that came into force in 1989 (Bogan 1990), thereby operating first as an advisory committee and later as a sentencing commission.

In those jurisdictions where there is a sentencing commission with legislative authority to develop guidelines, there is usually a provision for legislative review. Typically the guidelines have to be laid before the legislature. On one model, the guidelines become law unless they are the subject of a negative resolution within a given period of months: this was the approach in Minnesota, Oregon, Pennsylvania, and the U.S. federal jurisdiction. An alternative model is that the guidelines take effect only if subject to an affirmative resolution in the legislature: the states of Washington and New York adopted this approach. At an abstract level it seems that guidelines subject only to a negative resolution are more likely to go through than those requiring an affirmative resolution since inertia favors the former whereas the ease of nitpicking stands in the way of the latter. But the political record is not clear cut. A negative resolution did defeat the first set of guidelines in Pennsylvania, on the grounds that the guidelines were too lenient and too restrictive of judicial discretion, but the Minnesota, Oregon, and USSC guidelines were not blocked. New York's guidelines failed to muster sufficient support for approval, but in the state of Washington no difficulty was encountered in securing the necessary affirmative resolution (von Hirsch, Knapp, and Tonry 1987, pp. 18–26, 72–73).

What should be the composition of a sentencing committee or commission? To some extent this may depend on whether its role is as an advisory committee proposing reforms to the government, or as a commission charged with the task of devising guidance—in the latter case, at least, a relatively small group may be more effective. The figure of nine members has frequently been mentioned as an ideal size (Parent 1988, pp. 31–32), but the U.S. Sentencing Commission has seven members whereas others have considerably more members. The most favored composition is a mixture of judges, other criminal justice professionals (e.g., prosecutors, prison department officials, community corrections officers, and defenders), and one or more academics. This heightens the advantage of a wide spread of experience of criminal justice and should therefore prevent any narrowness of perspective in the commission's work. It is sometimes termed the "representative model" (Knapp 1987), a term that brings to mind the difficulties encountered in New York when some members of the commission functioned only as representatives and without any shared mission. It might more fruitfully be called the "criminal justice model": its aim is to draw together the various criminal justice perspectives, and in this respect it differs from a judicial model. Committees composed solely of judges have been proposed and established in some jurisdictions. Even if the arguments against a judicial model are accepted, there should be substantial judicial membership of a sentencing commission. At the very least there should be one sentencer from each level or type of court affected by the guidelines (Ashworth 1982, chap. 12). In some jurisdictions it might be thought right (on account of the considerable judicial experience of sentencing) or prudent (in deference to the power of the judicial lobby, or with a view to increasing public confidence in the commission) to build a judicial majority into the commission. The debate about which criminal justice agencies should have members on the commission (e.g., the police, a legislator, a member of the public?) descends into too much detail for the present survey, but there is certainly good reason to have at least one academic member who has studied sentencing and has a broad criminological background.

B. Authority for Issuing Guidance

Alongside the question whether the source of the guidance should be the government itself or a special committee or the judiciary, there is also the question of the authority by which the guidance should be issued. Should the guidance be incorporated into primary legislation passed by the legislature, or should the legislature establish the general framework of principles and leave it to some other body to develop the details? Both these approaches assume some legislative involvement, an assumption that is unlikely to be controversial in view of the social importance of sentencing policy. The use of primary legislation for detailed guidelines has obvious drawbacks, whereas the approach of restricting the involvement of the legislature brings other uncertainties.

1. *Guidelines in Primary Legislation.*   One of the earliest systems of sentencing guidelines, that established in California, is incorporated into primary legislation. Indiana and North Carolina are among the states that have adopted a similar approach. The California Determinate Sentencing Act of 1976 contains sections that set sentencing guidelines for various degrees of each offense, together with details of enhancements that increase the penalty. We are not concerned here with the degree of detail in the statute or the strong controls it places on judicial sentencing but with the advantages and disadvantages of using primary legislation for this purpose. One claimed advantage is the democratic process: sentencing standards that are subject to direct legislative scrutiny are likely to be much more "democratic" (in the terms of that particular jurisdiction) than those emanating from a commission or from the judiciary, whose members are not directly elected.

The corresponding disadvantages are threefold: first, there is the possibility that individual amendments in the legislature will impair the overall scheme by distorting sentences for certain offenses; second, individual politicians may propose the raising of certain sentencing standards in order to make political gains for themselves; and third, it may be more difficult to modify the guidance in the light of experience and new information, if amending legislation is needed every time. The first two disadvantages were both manifest in the history of the Californian statute (von Hirsch and Mueller 1984; Davies 1985), which may be thought to bolster the "insulation from direct political pressure" argument in favor of a sentencing commission. In fact they merely tell against placing detailed guidance in primary legislation and leave open the question whether some form of delegated legislation (probably emanating from a sentencing commission) or judicial guidelines are the better approach.

2. *Primary and Delegated Legislation.*   If it is agreed that primary legislation is unsuitable for the detailed structuring of sentencing practice, one obvious alternative is to employ primary legislation for the guiding principles of sentencing and then to leave the details to a form of delegated legislation. By that means the general lines of sentencing

policy would be subject to the direct control of the legislature (thus satisfying the democratic argument), and the details would be promulgated in delegated legislation, not subject to the cumbersome parliamentary procedure but nonetheless subject to some form of control (e.g., positive or negative resolution of the legislature, or judicial review).

The degree of guidance incorporated in the primary legislation can vary, most notably as to whether the legislature indicates the policies and aims to be followed or leaves the committee or commission to decide on those matters. The U.S. Sentencing Commission is subject in the Sentencing Reform Act of 1984 to fairly detailed guidance on some issues, with some fourteen or more stipulations relating to such matters as previous convictions for violence or drug offenses, multiple offenses, neutrality and nondiscrimination, mitigation for assisting the authorities, and so forth. However, as argued above, the USSC did have choices to make on several key issues, and the Minnesota Sentencing Commission had earlier shown the way with its decisions on a primary rationale and on other policies to be pursued. Indeed, a legislature that adopts this approach ought to require the sentencing commission to decide on a primary rationale for the sentencing system, so as to direct its mind to the importance of a coherent structure even if two or more aims of sentencing are thought relevant (e.g., Tonry 1991). However, the essence of this strategy of dividing the guidance between two forms, primary and delegated legislation, is that a committee or commission be left to develop the practical details of the guidance.

3. *Primary Legislation and Judicial Development.* A third approach is characterized by reliance on cooperation of the judiciary with the legislature, and it has recently been adopted or proposed in three jurisdictions. The clearest example of this approach is to be found in Sweden, where the new chapters of the criminal code set forth a number of principles for sentencers to take into account. Chapter 29 lays down guidance to courts on how to determine the "penal value" of an offense (i.e., its relative seriousness) and what personal factors to take into account in mitigation. Chapter 30 deals with the choice of sanctions, setting out principles to assist courts in determining whether to impose a fine, probation, imprisonment, or whatever. These provisions do not indicate ranges of sentences—indeed, they contain no numerical guidance at all—but they do give the courts the tools with which to work. The expectation is that judicial practice, assisted by appellate review, will develop detailed sentencing norms in line with the princi-

ples in the criminal code (von Hirsch 1987a; von Hirsch and Jareborg 1989).

The Victorian Sentencing Committee made proposals along similar lines. It recommended that "the function of Parliament in the sentencing process be the articulation of policies to govern the sentencing process; the delegation of power to give effect to such policies, and the allocation of resources to ensure that they are carried out; the general overseeing of the exercise of the powers delegated; and the use of resources through the usual democratic processes" (Victorian Sentencing Committee 1988, para. 4.19.6).

The committee went on to recommend how the courts should exercise their function of sentencing in individual cases and that the court of criminal appeal should review sentences in individual cases. Further, the court of criminal appeal should "give assistance to individual sentencers in the Supreme Court, County Court and Magistrates' Courts through the development of guidelines aimed at helping such sentencers to identify relevant policy considerations, identify relevant mitigating and aggravating factors, give appropriate weight to such policies and factors, and determine the right sentence to impose in any given case" (Victorian Sentencing Committee 1988, paras. 4.19.12, see also para. 4.20.12).

The provisions of the Victorian Sentencing Act of 1991 broadly follow these recommendations. The appellate court is expected to perform a function similar to that of sentencing commissions under a system of delegated legislation. There is also a major role for the newly constituted Judicial Studies Board, which will not only provide seminars for judges but will also carry out research and initiate policy developments (on a voluntary basis).

In England and Wales, the Criminal Justice Act of 1991 also establishes what the government hopes will be a partnership between legislature and judiciary (Home Office 1990, para. 2.17). The new legislation lays down criteria for sentencing decisions in respect of offenses of moderate or low seriousness, establishing proportionality as the leading principle but leaving the courts to work out its applications to the different kinds of offense. Thus the courts are left untrammeled in their approach to the most serious crimes, but Parliament has imposed a structure on sentencing for other crimes. In this way the government hopes to ensure the continuity (and perhaps traditionalism) of judicial development. The general disadvantage of this approach is that the perspective of the judiciary may be somewhat narrow in criminal justice terms, and the judiciary are not accustomed to taking the kind of overall view of proportionality among offenses that is needed if the new scheme is to succeed. In fact, the new legislation is not well drafted—thereby fortifying many judges in their view that the legislature should stay out of sentencing—and it is unclear how the English tradition of development through appellate review and guidance will be affected by the new scheme.

Success in relying on judicial development is heavily dependent on the prevailing legal culture. It would simply not be constitutionally possible in several European countries, whose legal traditions deny the possibility of binding guidance laid down by appeal courts (Council of Europe 1989, pp. 119–21). In other jurisdictions, its success would depend on the judicial tradition: would judges take seriously the legislative declarations of the aims of sentencing, or would they exploit the inevitable generality so as to weaken their thrust? Would the appellate courts conscientiously develop an interpretive jurisprudence that could guide sentencers in lower courts? The Swedish legal culture was thought to be propitious in these respects, and it remains to be seen whether the same is true of Victoria and England, where appellate review is well established but legislative declarations of principle are not. It is also important to consider the quality and coverage of appellate guidance: the court of appeal's record in England is varied, with clear and well-constructed guidance on some issues but little or nothing on some others (Ashworth 1984, 1989).

C. Styles of Guidance

The next question is the style or styles in which the guidance is best written. The range of alternative methods here is vast, and it is this wide variation that suggests that there may be a benefit in making some techniques known to those working in different jurisdictions.

1. *Mandatory or Mandatory Minimum Sentences.* The strongest device by which a legislature can determine sentencing is the mandatory sentence, requiring courts to pass a particular sentence on convicting a person of a certain crime. It is common for legislatures to prescribe a mandatory sentence for murder, or at least for first degree murder. Recent decades have, however, seen the spread of mandatory minimum sentences in many jurisdictions. The legislature sets a minimum sentence for a certain offense, and courts have the discretion to pass higher sentences but not lower ones. Most jurisdictions adopt this approach for drunk-driving offenses, and many adopt it for other types

of offense such as firearms or drug crimes—indeed, almost all the states in the United States have one or more such laws (Shane-DuBow, Brown, and Olsen 1985, table 30).

One of the reasons for enacting such laws is to create a general deterrent effect, but the evidence suggests that there is little impact on behavior (Tonry 1987*b*, chap. 3). Another and connected reason is to create consistency in sentencing, but it seems that the consistency that is achieved may be illusory. It is indeed highly likely that where there is a mandatory minimum sentence the vast majority of those convicted of the offense will receive the minimum sentence or more. But, viewing sentencing as one stage in the larger process of criminal justice, it is found that prosecutors and judges often make strenuous efforts to divert cases away from a mandatory minimum sentence that they believe to be unduly harsh in general or in particular cases. The evidence from various American states shows clearly that prosecutors charge an offense carrying a mandatory sentence less frequently, that trial delays increase, and that a whole host of legal arguments are deployed to soften the impact of the law (Tonry 1987*b*; U.S. Sentencing Commission 1991).

Mandatory minimum sentences have been roundly rejected by the Canadian Sentencing Commission (1987, p. 189 and chap. 8) and the Victorian Sentencing Committee (1988, paras. 4.9.6 ff.) and have been the subject of mounting opposition from the judges who have to operate them in the U.S. federal sentencing system (Federal Courts Study Committee 1990; Miller and Freed 1990*a*). Whatever the political claims made for their deterrent effects, and these seem to be debatable, they come into conflict with basic judicial feelings about the need to take account of individual factors in the sentencing of some cases. They are regarded as creating injustice and indeed inconsistency, in the sense that they attempt to force courts to treat unalike cases as if they were alike. Avoidance techniques by prosecutors and judges then become common, and a system in which professionals collaborate to circumvent the written law can hardly be satisfactory.

2. *Fixed-Point Sentencing.* There is some difficulty in settling the terminology for the next style of guidance to be considered. It will here be called "fixed-point sentencing," and the main example is California. The essence of the Californian system is that the law lays down a standard sentence for each offense, together with an aggravated sentence and a mitigated sentence. Where the judge decides on prison, he or she is limited to a choice of three sentences. However, only for the

most serious crimes is the judge required to give a prison sentence. For most others, the judge has an initial choice between prison, probation, or jail, and at that stage there is considerable discretion. If this is added to the ample discretion retained by Californian prosecutors in charging and in plea bargaining, it will be seen that the apparent rigidity of parts of the Determinate Sentencing Act of 1976 in California is somewhat dissolved in practice. Nonetheless, as a possible technique, fixed-point sentencing is potentially one of the most restrictive (second only to mandatory and mandatory minimum sentences) and probably therefore likely to generate judicial dissatisfaction and a degree of circumvention.

3. *Numerical Guidelines.* Under this heading three different approaches are to be considered—guidelines that establish ranges of sentences, those that indicate a base sentence and enhancements, and those that provide starting points and no formal structure beyond. What they have in common, as the name suggests, is that they attempt to guide sentencing discretion by numbers. Guideline systems usually establish presumptive sentences, not removing judicial discretion but structuring it and allowing the judge to depart from the guideline upon giving reasons. Guidelines are usually combined with a system of appellate review in order to ensure that departures from them are supported by reasons consistent with the aims of the sentencing system.

The first variety of numerical guidelines to be considered is that which indicates sentence ranges or bands for offenses. Clearly this technique may have a different impact according to the degree to which offenses are divided up (into many or few classes) and according to the breadth of the range or band (which may vary, say, from twenty-seven to thirty months' imprisonment to twenty-seven to fifty months' imprisonment for a certain offense). It is therefore manifest that such systems can embody attempts to constrain sentencers more or less firmly, and that, for example, the frequency of departures may be related to the breadth of the ranges set down. Pennsylvania, which has had numerical guidelines since 1982, has ranges of sentences that are typically about ten months wide around the level of three years' imprisonment, and which are typically wider for the longer prison terms and narrower for the shorter prison terms. The Pennsylvania Commission on Sentencing divided all felonies into ten groups, and for each grouping provided three guideline ranges (the minimum range, the aggravated minimum, and the mitigated minimum), further subdivided according to the offender's prior record score (Martin 1983). The best-known approach of this kind is that of Minnesota, introduced in 1980. There the Sentencing Commission divided all felonies into ten groups, and its sentencing grid indicates one sentence range for each offense group, according to the offender's criminal history score. The Minnesota ranges tend to be considerably narrower than those in Pennsylvania: the format is to indicate a single fixed sentence together with a durational range of around 8 percent from the fixed sentence (Parent 1988, chap. 7). Thus, if we take sentences around the three-year mark, the Minnesota format would be thirty-eight months (thirty-six to forty months). The effective range is thus around four months at that level, becoming wider for the longer sentences. However, it must be borne in mind that the Minnesota judge has, in many cases, a choice whether to impose prison or to find the defendant "amenable to probation" (Frase 1991a).

An integral part of a guideline system is a policy for departures from the guidelines. This was apparently one of the most contentious issues in devising the Minnesota guidelines, and the result is an elaborate set of three lists—mitigating factors, aggravating factors, and excluded (nonpermissible) factors (Parent 1988, chap. 8). The list of excluded factors is relatively noncontentious, as it is designed to render sentencing neutral as to race, sex, employment factors, social factors, and the exercise of constitutional rights by the defendant. The three lists of factors are stated to be "nonexclusive," but judges are not free to give weight to mitigating and aggravating factors whenever they please. The guideline sentence is presumed appropriate for all cases, and a judge may depart only on a finding of "substantial and compelling circumstances." Whenever a judge takes this course, either the defendant or the state may appeal against the sentence, and the judge is in any event required to specify in writing the reasons for departure. These are monitored by the Sentencing Commission. Departure rates have been variously calculated (Frase 1991b) and are probably around 20 percent overall.

As a technique for the structuring of sentencing discretion, the numerical range cannot be considered in isolation. Much depends on the division of offenses: many would feel that to divide all felonies into only ten groups is too crude and is likely to trample on important differences in the relative gravity of offenses. Much also depends on the breadth of the ranges: compliance with broad ranges is likely to be more frequent than compliance with narrow ranges. The question of departure policy is also of importance: a jurisprudence of sentencing decisions has developed in Minnesota to refine the broad statements in the commission's own departure criteria, and the Supreme Court limited upward departures to double the top of the guideline.

Some methods of undermining the broad aims of guidelines have surfaced in Minnesota. One of the primary aims was to use incarceration more for offenses against the person and less for offenses against property, but, after an initial swing in this direction, it appears that prosecutorial practices and condonement by the judiciary has led to a reversion to the preguideline position (Parent 1988, pp. 197–99; Frase 1991b). This suggests, once again, that the views of professionals within the criminal justice system are the key to the success of new measures and that where these professionals do not share the new values they are likely to seek and to find ways of neutralizing the intended changes.

The second variety of numerical guidelines is to provide base sentences and certain enhancements. The U.S. Sentencing Commission followed this path in devising its guidelines. The category of offense is assigned a certain base sentence. The judge then has to consider which, if any, of various specific offense characteristics apply in the case (e.g., points would be added for the use of a weapon or for stealing a large amount, and points would be deducted for acceptance of responsibility). This should lead the judge to an "offense score" on a scale from one to forty-three. The judge then turns to calculate the offender's criminal history score. The intersection of the offense score and criminal history score on a grid indicates the guideline sentencing range (see von Hirsch 1988; Nagel 1990). The court is permitted to depart from the guideline only if it finds that "an aggravating or mitigating circumstance exists that was not adequately considered" by the commission, and it is not permitted to depart on grounds of race, gender, or socioeconomic status. The early stages of a jurisprudence of departures are evident, the statute requiring that departures be "reasonable" (Miller and Freed 1990b). However, one of the emergent difficulties in judicial interpretation of the federal guidelines is that some judges are reluctant to depart from the mere policy statement (not guideline) that states that personal characteristics are "not ordinarily relevant" to guideline sentencing (Miller and Freed 1990c).

The commission's approach of setting a base sentence and then indicating additions to and subtractions from that base may be regarded as nothing more than a formalization of typical judicial reasoning. However, it is a formalization that may cramp the process of calculation: many of the factors are weighted so as to allow only two or three points to be added or subtracted, and so the calculation is inevitably fairly rough and ready. It may be true that the typical judicial reasoning on these matters is unduly impressionistic, but the opposite approach of precise numerical weightings may give a spurious appearance of objectivity when particular factors may vary in their intensity in individual cases. Moreover, the federal guidelines are so complex in their operation and so lacking in overall coherence that they seem likely to be dragged down by their own weight. Criticisms of the commission by the U.S. General Accounting Office (1990) and of the guidelines themselves by the Federal Courts Study Committee (1990) serve as authoritative reinforcement of the widely expressed doubts about the style and orientation of the federal guidelines (Tonry 1991).

The third variety of numerical guidelines is that pioneered by the English judiciary. The use of guideline judgments by the English Court of Appeal has already been mentioned; what concerns us here is their style. This is by no means uniform, but the leading characteristics are the selection of certain key distinctions of degree within a given offense category (e.g., quantity in drug importation, amount taken in thefts by persons in positions of trust, presence of certain aggravating factors in rape) and the assignment of starting points to the various degrees. In the guideline judgment on drugs, for example, the main distinctions are by weight or "street value" of drugs, ranging from fourteen years or more where the drugs are worth over $1.5 million, down to a lower threshold of four years for trafficking in any significant quantity of a class A drug (*R. v. Aramah* [1983]; cf. Ashworth 1990). The judgment also indicates factors that may or may not mitigate. The guideline judgment on rape sets out three starting points for the sentencer—five years in ordinary cases; eight years where the offense involved two or more men, or took place in the victim's home, or involved abduction, or where the offender abused a position of trust; and fifteen years where there are several offenses amounting to a "campaign of rape." This judgment then mentions eight possible aggravating factors that can take the sentence upwards from the starting point, although no attempt is made to indicate the numerical effect that they should have on the sentence. It also mentions three possible mitigating factors and warns of three factors that should not be accorded any mitigating effect (*R. v. Billam* [1986]). It therefore provides a framework for sentencing, and the function of the numbers (five, eight, and fifteen years) is merely to orient the sentencer before other factors in each case are considered. The guideline judgment implies that sentences below five, or certainly four, years will be exceptional, but there is no formal minimum, and in one unusual case involving a mentally handicapped offender a nonincarcerative sentence for rape was held proper by the Court of Appeal (*R. v. Taylor* [1983]).

One advantage of this "starting point" approach over the other two forms of numerical guidance (sentence ranges and base sentences with enhancements) is that it imposes a framework while leaving ample room for judicial discretion to give effect to the combination of factors in each case. Sentencers like this and feel able to do justice by responding to unusual factors while keeping within the parameters set by the guideline. An obvious danger is inconsistency: to the extent that more leeway is allowed for proper modifications of the sentence, so also is leeway allowed for improper modifications and for the infiltration of irrelevant or discriminatory factors. This stands somewhat in contrast to the two other forms of numerical guidance. In the English system the judiciary is confident that the Court of Appeal will eradicate significant departures, but others would be less sanguine about this. A second advantage of this form of guidance is that it is numerical in a weak rather than a strong sense, an advantage enhanced by the narrative form of the guidelines. There are many who mistrust the apparent rigidity of numerical guidelines, but who might welcome a guideline judgment in the English style, with the numbers woven into the typical narrative style of an appellate judgment. Nevertheless, it should not be thought that these two advantages lie at the heart of English sentencing guidance. In fact, only a small number of crimes are covered by these guideline judgments: for the rest, the guidance stemming from individual appellate judgments is patchy—sometimes good, sometimes nonexistent.

Appellate review is clearly the origin of the English narrative guidelines, but it does not follow that appeal courts are the best or the only vehicle for formulating starting points. There is no reason why a sentencing commission could not adopt this narrative style, preferring starting points and the enumeration of detailed factors affecting the particular crime to the more usual approach of a sentencing grid. Moreover, it is fair to point out that the English guideline judgment on drug sentencing could be reformulated in a more stark numerical style, according to the type and quantity of drug involved. Insofar as that judgment does constitute a kind of sentencing grid in disguise, this strengthens the point made earlier that, for judicial acceptance, the source and form of guidance may be more important than its style. The Victorian Sentencing Committee, which recommended guideline judgments as the principal method of structuring judicial discretion, was unclear whether its style should be to give starting points or sentence ranges. When describing the functions of a guideline judgment, the report refers to "the appropriate range" of sentences, to the criteria for determining the seriousness of a particular offense, and to "the weighting to be given to relevant criteria," but it is unclear how closely it would be possible for the appeal court to follow these and other specifications (Victorian Sentencing Committee 1988, para. 4.20.13).

An example of starting points being devised by a committee rather than by the appellate judiciary is provided by the English Magistrates' Association's *Sentencing Guide for Criminal Offences* (Magistrates' Association 1989). The Association is a voluntary body to which most magistrates belong, and it has issued a booklet with starting points for some twenty common nontraffic offenses in an attempt to bring consistency to the efforts of local benches in different parts of the country. For each offense there is a guideline fine, and there are lists of factors that may indicate that a particular offense is more or less serious than normal. For example, the guidelines deal with four separate forms of theft; for theft in general, there are four "seriousness indicators" that might take the sentence up from the guideline (large amount, planned, sophisticated, vulnerable victim) and three that might take the sentence down from the guideline (impulsive action, small amount, voluntary restitution). Once again, no precise values are put on these factors, which are not exhaustive: courts are pointed in a particular direction, and left to concretize the sentence by applying the guidance given. These are not starting points in the narrative style of appellate judgments, but they are so constructed as to encourage sentencers to weigh all the factors in each case rather than to regard the starting point as a finishing point.

The strengths and weaknesses of the "starting point" approach depend considerably on the legal and criminal justice system in which they are placed. For example, starting points are unlikely to command respect unless they form a logical scheme: the Magistrates' Association has attempted to achieve this in respect of twenty offenses, but it is now recognized that it must be extended further. All the major or frequent offenses ought ideally to be integrated into a framework of starting points that distinguish acceptably among offenses. This is a broad enterprise to which courts are unaccustomed, and so one feature of the English Court of Appeal's guidelines is that, elegant and technically accomplished as each one might be, they form merely a fragment of a system. The court sees its function as deciding cases rather than overall policy issues and has not sought to take an overall view of the relative seriousness of all major offenses. A sentencing commission would be expected to do this, but no commission has yet issued guidance in the form of starting points—either with a narrative, in the style of the few English Court of Appeal guideline judgments, or simply with seriousness indicators, in the style of the English Magistrates' Association's guidelines. One reason for this may be the large element of discretion that starting points leave to sentencers, and the need for both a sympathetic legal culture and an effective appeal system if the starting points are to generate conformity of approach rather than avoidance. In some systems, to leave such wide discretion might be regarded as inviting the very inconsistency it is sought to reduce, especially if judges and prosecutors have not internalized the spirit of the new sentencing approach. These themes will be taken further after the next section.

4. *Hierarchy of Principles and Policies.*   The next style of guidance to be considered is one that eschews numbers altogether, and prefers to set out the principles and policies that sentencers should adopt, leaving them to concretize them in individual cases. This is the approach of the two new chapters of the Swedish Criminal Code, which came into force at the beginning of 1989. The court's first task is to assess the "penal value" of the offense, taking account of its harmfulness, the defendant's culpability, and a number of other specified factors. The court's aim at this stage is to assess the proportionate seriousness of the offense. The second task is then to determine whether the case requires imprisonment or a fine, based on the scale of seriousness; a list of factors is again supplied. If the case is thought so serious as to require imprisonment, the third stage is to consider whether probation or a conditional sentence should be ordered instead of imprisonment; various principles are set out here too (special reasons required if an offender under the age of twenty-one is imprisoned; probation is indicated where there is a favorable change of personal circumstances, or need for treatment, etc.). The essence of this approach, then, is that the guidance does not set out sentence ranges or starting points, but furnishes the courts with general instructions on how to develop such ranges and starting points (von Hirsch 1987*a*). To a certain extent this is the reverse of some numerical guidelines: they provide a concretization without the reasons, whereas the Swedish approach provides the

reasons without a concretization. This degree of trust in the judiciary may be explained by reference to Swedish legal culture: not only is there a career judiciary but, unlike most continental European systems, the decisions of appeal courts stand as precedents for future cases. Moreover, the Swedish guidance also encompasses the choice of sanctions, neglected by most of the prison-oriented guidance discussed thus far. The two relatively terse chapters of the Swedish Criminal Code therefore supply a general structure for a large part of judicial sentencing, trusting the judges to put the flesh on the bones.

5. *Presumed Dispositions.*   One of the most difficult issues confronted by most sentencing systems is the decision of whether a case justifies an incarcerative sentence. This is one respect in which, for example, the Minnesota guidelines appear to fall short. Where the guidelines do not require imprisonment, the judge is left with discretion that includes local jail (a form of incarceration, of course) and probation. The Sentencing Commission in Minnesota was empowered to develop guidelines governing conditions of probation, but the issue divided the commission so deeply that it never did so (Parent 1988, p. 94). Prosecutors thought that such guidelines would weaken their position in plea bargaining and prevent them from obtaining stringent probation conditions. Other opponents pointed to the differences in correctional resources in various parts of the state. The result is a lopsided system of guidance.

Many sentencing systems have some legislative provision designed to restrict the use of prison sentences for some groups of offense and offender. New Zealand's Criminal Justice Act of 1985 states that prison should be the presumed disposal for offenses involving serious violence or serious danger to the safety of any other person and that a noncustodial sentence should be the presumed disposal for most offenses against property. The statute is fairly detailed but allows courts to depart from the policy in "special circumstances"; it is unclear whether it has led to a significant shift in sentencing practice. For many years England and Wales have had statutory provisions restricting the use of imprisonment, particularly for young offenders. These have been progressively tightened, so that the most recent legislation imposes (subject to some exceptions) two conditions on the imposition and duration of a custodial sentence. The conditions are that either the offense must be so serious that only a custodial sentence could be justified or only a custodial sentence would be adequate to protect the public from serious harm from the offender. If imprisonment is justified by reference to one of these conditions, the length of the sentence must be commensurate with the seriousness of the offense or the degree of predicted risk, as the case may be (Criminal Justice Act 1991). The effect of these criteria will be to import more legal argument and appellate review into these critical borderline decisions, with the consequent development of a jurisprudence of appellate decisions on types of offense and offender falling inside or outside the criteria. Recent years have seen a growing body of case law on the previous statute restricting custody for young offenders, and the custody rate for this age-group has certainly declined. However, the Court of Appeal has not issued any guideline judgments in this sphere, and the individual decisions do not yet provide lower courts with a coherent framework of guidance.

The Canadian Sentencing Commission also tackled this sphere of sentencing, out of concern for the overuse of imprisonment and also the disorder that appears to characterize the use of noncustodial sentences. The main plank of the commission's proposals was the development of guidance that would assign each class of offense to one of four presumptive categories: custody, qualified custody (i.e., custody unless the offense was a minor example of the type and was committed by an offender with a good prior record), qualified community sanction (i.e., a nonincarcerative measure unless the offense was a particularly serious example of its type and was committed by an offender with a bad prior record), and community sanction only (Canadian Sentencing Commission 1987, pp. 309–16).

Sentencing guidelines would then be developed for the custody cases. For community sanctions, the commission made a number of proposals of importance. One was that the presumptive community sanction should be a financial penalty in most cases; another was that noncustodial sentences should be regarded as sentences in their own right and not dependent on custodial sentences, a proposal also adopted by the Australian Law Reform Commission (1988, paras. 101–5).

This move away from the concept of "alternatives to custody" has achieved legislative recognition in England. Influenced by a scheme proposed by Wasik and von Hirsch (1988), the government proposed (Home Office 1990) and the legislature enacted (Criminal Justice Act 1991) a new scheme for noncustodial sentencing. The fine is to be the presumptive penalty for most offenses, and the principle of equality of impact is to be furthered by adopting a system of "day fines" or "unit fines." A court that wishes to impose a more severe sanction than a fine will have to justify its decision. Thus the community penalties, such as community service orders and probation with conditions, are to be treated as "graduated restrictions on liberty": both the decision to impose such an order, and the extent of the obligations imposed, must be related to the seriousness of the offense. Once that has been achieved, the court should choose the sentence, of appropriate severity, that is "most suitable for the offender": in other words, there may be two or three possible sentences of appropriate severity (e.g., probation with certain conditions, community service of a certain duration), and the choice is then made on an individualized basis.

The latest proposal from the Canadian Ministry of Justice envisages legislation that will rank all available sentences in order of severity (Canadian Ministry of Justice 1990a, pp. 15–16). It does not appear to address the problem of regarding one measure (e.g., community service, probation) as having a single severity ranking, whereas an earlier attempt by the Victorian Sentencing Committee at least ranked fines as "substantial," "moderate," and "small" (1988, para. 7.4). Some attempt to structure noncustodial penalties is essential if principled consistency is to be introduced to those sanctions that, in most jurisdictions, form a majority of sentences imposed. Such developments have sometimes been opposed on the ground that they rule out rehabilitative sentencing, even in clear cases of need for treatment, but the approach under the English Criminal Justice Act of 1991 shows that this does not follow. Another possible approach would be to regard the principles of desert and proportionality as setting the upper and lower limits and then to provide for the interchangeability of "intermediate sanctions" according to the court's view of the needs of the offender and the desirability of parsimony in punishment. The proponents of this approach, Morris and Tonry, recognize that American jurisdictions lag behind European and other systems in developing a range of noncustodial, community penalties, and one element in their scheme is the widespread adoption of new forms of sentence. Then—and this is crucial whatever approach is taken—the noncustodial sentences must be integrated into whatever form of sentencing guidelines or guidance is provided (Morris and Tonry 1990). A start has been made in this direction in Oregon, with its misdemeanor sentencing guidelines (Bogan 1991), but few other states have taken this step.

6. *Other Styles of Guidance.*   Sentencing systems have within them a vast range of other techniques for guiding courts, but it is fair to say that most of them are piecemeal provisions that do not form part of a comprehensive strategy. Mandatory minimum sentences were dis-

cussed earlier, but space constraints preclude discussion of other techniques such as the presumed disposition unless "special reasons" are given for departure, which is a hybrid between mandatory sentences and ordinary presumptive sentencing, outright restrictions on combining two forms of sentence, and restrictions on passing custodial sentences shorter than three months.

One feature often regarded as the mark of more advanced sentencing systems is a requirement that courts give reasons for their sentences, but this should not be overestimated. For one thing, a system with detailed sentencing guidance might only require reason giving in cases of departure from the guidance, although it may be important to give reasons for following the presumptive sentence and failing to depart from it in a particular case. For another, reason giving without detailed guidance may prove unhelpful: the point of requiring reasons is to justify the sentence to the defendant, to the public, and to an appellate court that might review it, and this can only be a meaningful exercise if there are some established parameters for sentencing. To justify sentences by reference to powerfully delivered but woefully vague statements that the offense is "very serious" or "damaging to the fabric of society," or whatever, fails to meet the point of the exercise. To be worthwhile, reasons must explain and justify the departure from certain norms. A weakness in this regard was identified by Zeisel and Diamond in their analysis of sentencing review in Connecticut and Massachusetts, where they found inter alia that the reasons given by the appeal courts did not assist in establishing principled guidance (Zeisel and Diamond 1977). However, in systems or areas where no norms yet exist, reason giving can generate sentencing standards if the reasons relate each sentence to sentences for similar or even different offenses or offenders.

D. The Contents of Guidance

Although the principal concern here is with formal issues of the shape of sentencing guidance, the question of the contents that guidance should have is closely related. If one of the reasons for wishing to structure sentencing is to reduce sentencing disparity, while preserving an element of judicial discretion (cf. the widespread opposition to mandatory minimum sentences), then the contents of the guidance ought surely to declare either a leading aim of sentencing or a hierarchy of aims. The importance of this was stressed in Section I above, and it is a point that has been strongly urged against the U.S. federal guidelines (von Hirsch 1988; Tonry 1991). The declaration of aims should afford guidance to sentencers when they are considering departures from any guidelines, or other exercises of discretion. This does not mean that one aim only must be adopted; what it means is that, where two or more aims are declared, it should be clear which aim has general priority and in what types of case the other aims might prevail (see Robinson 1988; von Hirsch and Jareborg 1989).

Other broad issues of policy might also be the subject of a general declaration: if there is a policy of restraint in the use of custodial sentences, similar reasoning would favor a clear legislative statement to this effect. A developed system of guidance is likely to deal mostly with classes of offense and characteristics of offenders, but a number of general sentencing problems need also to be confronted. Two related issues are the extent to which unforeseen consequences should be relevant to sentence, and a sentencing approach for inchoate offenses of attempt, conspiracy, and solicitation. The approach to sentencing multiple offenders also calls for general guidance, in line with the overall aims and policies of the scheme (e.g., Canadian Sentencing Commission 1987, pp. 217–26; Parent 1988, pp. 225–29). A further issue, closely related to the practices of other professionals and therefore to the practical impact of any sentencing system, is the unit of behavior on which sentence should be based. Whose version of the facts of the current offense should be adopted as the basis for sentence? Should any behavior apart from the current offense be relevant to sentence? The issue of the factual basis of sentences has been the subject of considerable common-law development in English law (*R. v. Newton* [1983]; Thomas 1982, sec. 2.2). The question of "relevant conduct," basing sentences on "actual offense behavior" rather than the offense of conviction, is said to be the key to the U.S. federal guidelines, but the ideas on which it is based might profit from reexamination (cf. Wilkins and Steer [1990] with Miller and Weich [1989]).

IV. Consistency without Compulsion

All the approaches discussed so far involve the use of legal authority to enforce, or at least to provide a framework for, consistent sentencing practices. Primary legislation binds the courts without a doubt. Sentencing commissions may have a form of delegated legislative authority, which takes on the authority of legislation. Appellate courts usually have the doctrine of precedent to cloak their judgments with authority, although it was noted that in some civil law jurisdictions decisions of appellate courts have authority only in the individual case. Recent years have seen the development of further methods of fostering consistency in sentencing that do not involve legal compulsion, but rather approach the problem through the provision of information, the involvement of sentencers in new initiatives, and other forms of subtle persuasion. Some of these methods are now reviewed.

A. Information Systems

One obvious barrier to the achievement of consistent sentencing practices is that individual judges may not know what the practices of other judges are—they may simply be unable to find out or, if they are told, the account they are given may be inaccurate, incomplete, or imperfectly understood (Ashworth et al. 1984). These remarks are not intended to suggest that "judges do not know what they are doing"; rather, their import is that, since sentencing is a complex task with such a variety of offenses and offender characteristics, it is difficult to convey a sufficiently clear and detailed picture. In many jurisdictions there are textbooks and collections of appellate judgments that attempt to achieve this, but their success is limited. A collection of appellate judgments is only an adequate guide to sentencing practice if those judgments cover all the major areas of sentencing in sufficient detail. In practice, appellate systems tend to operate for the most part reactively, dealing with problems as they are presented to the appellate court rather than setting out to devise a sufficiently broad set of guidance for sentencers. It follows that the utility of a collection of judgments will be limited by the activities of the appellate court. Textbooks can go further than this and sometimes do: they can, for example, draw on regular statistics or on particular research findings in order to reveal the practices that courts actually follow. Thus, for example, in a system of appellate review in which the court has given little systematic attention to crimes of moderate-to-low gravity, such as burglary, receiving stolen goods, and various forms of theft, it may be helpful to present the statistical groupings and trends in sentencing for those offenses (if the statistics are sufficiently detailed) in order to indicate the extent to which there is a common approach. Sentencing statistics may have inherent drawbacks, but in the absence of appellate guidance they may provide some pointers for the sentencer, who would otherwise be thrown back upon the anecdotal resource of word-of-mouth suggestions from other sentencers.

Would it be worthwhile to present statistics specially for the purpose of informing judges about the practices of others, rather than relying on statistics collected for some other purpose that may or may not be suitable? The Daubney report in Canada observed aptly that "currently judges have too little information in an easily usable form and too much in a form that cannot be used effectively" (Daubney 1988, p. 64). Three schemes aimed at improving the relevance and accessibility of sentencing information have been initiated in different jurisdictions, and they can be described briefly.

In the Canadian province of British Columbia, a Sentencing Data Base was devised by Hogarth and has been available in many courtrooms since 1988 (Hogarth 1987). Essentially it can provide references to relevant appellate judgments in British Columbia in the previous fifteen years, information about the relative use of different sentences for this offense in the previous four years, information about general sentencing principles and procedures, and information about local facilities. The information about sentencing practice is categorized by gender, age, marital status, and criminal record, but all those categories are relatively crude. For example, criminal record is either absent or present, with no subdivisions. Data may well need to be more detailed than this if the information is to have a significant effect on disparity, but the system is developing all the time.

A second Canadian system is that developed by Doob and Park (1987). This has the immediate advantage, within Canada, that its data base is not limited to one province, and it may therefore make some contribution to national consistency. The data are supplied by the sentencing judges themselves, who fill in a form that appears to give a slightly more detailed and sophisticated result than the Hogarth system. It is, however, limited to some thirty-four common offenses. For those it provides information on sentencing patterns in the judge's own province and other participating provinces and information on relevant appellate judgments from all the participating provinces.

A third approach is that developed by the Judicial Commission of New South Wales in Australia (Chan 1989; Potas 1990). The Sentencing Information System (SIS) has been available to some courts in New South Wales since 1988, and the aim is to make it available statewide by 1993. Four data bases are to be maintained: the "Penalty Statistics" data base, giving information on sentencing practice; the "Sentencing Law" data base, which lists the available options and any legislative restrictions on sentence; a data base containing appellate judgments; and a data base of local sentencing facilities. The overall similarity with the British Columbia system will be apparent, but only the first and second data bases are on line in New South Wales at present. The "Penalty Statistics" data base responds when a sentencer keys in certain characteristics of a case (characteristics selected by judges in a survey in New South Wales), and it is fed by data collected by the Judicial Commission on sentences passed by the courts in the previous two years. This is to ensure that the statistics are always up to date, although where the number of cases is small (as for some unusual offenses), older data are retained. On some matters the SIS has greater detail than its British Columbia counterpart: for example, prior record is indicated on a scale of four rather than a simple yes or no, and there are four age groupings. The data base will yield an overall distribution of sentences and will also furnish more detailed information about the use of a particular sanction (e.g., amounts of fines, lengths of imprisonment).

The "success" of information systems depends on their reception by the courts and on the quality of the information collected. If the system is used relatively infrequently by the judges, as appears to be the case in British Columbia, its contribution to consistency is likely to be minimal. The quality of the information depends on two elements— the extent to which it is classified and the frequency of cases within the various subclassifications. The review of guideline systems above has shown the drawback of relatively crude classifications of types of offense and the extent to which sentencing must be recognized as a multifactorial exercise. It follows that, as a way of assuring at least minimum acceptance among sentencers, an information system must adopt familiar categories. If a guideline system is in operation, then the categories must match the guidelines and their mitigating and aggravating factors, not to mention variations for prior criminal record. The three information systems above have been developed in non- guideline jurisdictions that depend on appellate review, and the categorization of data must therefore be more detailed since judges in common-law systems tend to find a wider range of factors relevant or potentially relevant to sentence. This need to subdivide the data causes problems at the next stage, which is the collection of adequate data to provide a statistically sound database. If, on the one hand, there are too few cases within certain subcategories, any unusual features among them might have a disproportionate statistical effect. If, on the other hand, subcategories with insufficient cases are left blank on the information system, it might be criticized as offering no help in the cases where judges need it most.

One way of remedying these problems is to adopt Lovegrove's proposal to incorporate a normative element into the information system (Lovegrove 1989). Rather than attempting simply to reflect practice, with the empirical difficulties outlined above, the system would endeavour to provide fuller information by offering guidance for all variations of each offense type. The factors to be taken into account would be ascertained by a thorough study of judicial decision making. Once a model had been devised so as to reflect these factors, a group of judges would then be invited to participate in a series of sentencing exercises designed to yield normative sentences for each combination of factors. It is evident that the sophistication and desire for completeness embodied in this approach would lead to extensive work for the judges, work of just the kind that a sentencing commission could be expected to perform in an equally sophisticated guideline system. The result, in Lovegrove's strategy, would be advisory rather than compulsory, and that is why his work is discussed at this juncture. He shares with the proponents of the empirical information systems a belief in the continued development of the common law of sentencing supervised and structured by appellate review. The purpose of the information system is to orient rather than to constrain and to help sentencers toward consistency rather than seeking to impose it on them. Various judicial surveys suggest that judges do wish to know more about their colleagues' sentencing practices (Ashworth et al. 1984; Canadian Sentencing Commission 1987, pp. 61–62). What remains to be seen is whether most judges would use such information, whether they would use it routinely or only rarely, and whether this would conduce to greater consistency.

B. Judicial Studies

Several jurisdictions now have a more or less systematic program for training judges. For example, in Europe there are such programs in Denmark, France, Portugal, Spain, and the United Kingdom, with occasional judicial conferences in other countries such as Austria and Cyprus (Council of Europe 1989, p. 127). Training programs have formed an important element in the introduction of the U.S. federal guidelines (Nagel 1990, pp. 937–38), and similar courses are in place elsewhere. In the United Kingdom the Judicial Studies Board has a program of seminars for newly appointed judges, with "refresher" courses at regular intervals for more experienced judges (Judicial Studies Board 1988). These seminars also serve as a conduit for suggestions by judges on matters of policy, both in relation to policies laid down by the Court of Appeal and in relation to proposals for legislative or other changes in the criminal justice system. The board has some involvement in the training of magistrates too and has occasionally taken steps designed to foster greater consistency in magistrates' sentencing.

The formation of a Judicial Studies Board was one of the main planks of the Victorian Sentencing Committee's recommendations (1988, paras. 4.13, 4.21.15). The committee wished to see a continuation and development of a common law of sentencing, with guideline judgments laid down by the Supreme Court, and it saw the need for a board to operate in support of this judiciary-based system. The board would have a majority of judges in its membership, and it would have four functions in addition to the training function of its British counterpart. It would promulgate voluntary guidelines to fill gaps left by guideline judgments, collate statistics relevant to sentencing, carry out research related to sentencing, and disseminate relevant material and information to sentencers. For these purposes, it would be furnished with a permanent staff and proper funding. The Judicial Studies Board Act of 1990 enacts most of these recommendations.

Clearly some form of training of sentencers is essential if sentencing reforms are to have their full effect. Unless the details and the guiding philosophy of reform are explained to those who must operate the system, its impact is likely to be impaired. A less obvious point is that training is unlikely to foster consistency unless there are clear principles that can be explained and then applied. Training cannot be a substitute for guidance and is therefore limited by the amount of guidance available. The Victorian Sentencing Committee seems to have taken this point when it assigned to its proposed Judicial Studies Board the additional task of drawing up and promulgating voluntary sentencing guidelines to deal with offenses for which the Supreme Court had not yet laid down authoritative guidelines (1988, para. 4.21.2). In a system that relies on appellate review, guidance is likely to remain patchy unless some such action is taken. A corresponding weakness of the English model is that there are several areas of sentencing on which there can be no effective training because there is a lack of authoritative or even "voluntary" guidance. Yet the more this function of generating guidance is given to a Judicial Studies Board, the closer it approximates to a sentencing commission. In effect, a body with a majority of judges in its membership is devising a framework for sentencing: guidance emanating from such a body is more likely to be compatible with the authoritative guidance so far laid down, but some sentencing commissions have also kept close to current practice in their guidelines.

A final point relating to the Victorian proposals is their recognition of the need for sentencing research to provide a sound basis for development. In order to ascertain what the prevailing sentencing practices are, well-conceived research is vastly superior to the individual impressions of the members of a Judicial Studies Board. Yet one of the great difficulties over the years has been the obtaining of permission to undertake sentencing research in the courts, as distinct from making use of statistics emerging from the courts. This problem was pointed out by committees of the Council of Europe (1974, 1989). In Britain it has been less of a problem in the magistrates' courts than in the Crown Court, where access has been severely limited. The Victorian approach is that the Judicial Studies Board should have a duty to undertake research and the funding to do this (Victorian Sentencing Committee 1988, para. 4.21.15). This promises both advantages and disadvantages: on the one hand, the substantial judicial membership of the board may reduce any judicial resistance to the research, but, on the other hand, judicial dominance might restrict the kind of research that is conducted.

C. Involvement of Sentencers in New Initiatives

To the extent that the variable use of certain sentencing options results from a lack of judicial understanding of their operation and potential impact on offenders, one approach might be to involve sentencers in the setting up and running of certain programs. This has been done successfully in England and Wales, where it was thought imperative to achieve a distinct shift from incarcerating juvenile offenders to dealing with them through community-based schemes. Local schemes for "Intermediate Treatment" were set up, and magistrates became involved (with social workers and others) in their administration, having an input into the content of the programs, and so forth. The policy appears to have been successful, inasmuch as the custody rate declined sharply and the use of Intermediate Treatment increased (Home Office 1988). The benefits appear to be that, not only do the sentencers acquire firsthand knowledge of what the sanction involves, but they may also become committed to its success and may spread the message among other sentencers. The importance of this should not be underestimated when it is so frequently said that some sentencers make little use of certain measures because they lack "confidence" in them. If lack of confidence derives from lack of knowledge, or from the tenacity of anecdotes about one or two unfortunate cases, it might be dispelled in this way. Even if the lack of confidence derives from opposition to the way in which such programs are organized, the infusion of a judicial element into their administration might alter this in a mutually acceptable way. In jurisdictions where ways of expanding the use of community sanctions are being sought, this approach might bear fruit if the sentencers can be persuaded to participate.

V. Conclusions

What conclusions can be drawn from this survey of different approaches to the structuring of judicial sentencing? First, it was argued above that on a constitutional level there is no justification for the view that sentencing is solely a judicial matter and that the principle of judicial independence cannot be relied on to support such a view. Sentencing policy lies within the purview of the legislature; some legislatures have, either by deliberate policy or through neglect, allowed the judiciary to develop policy, but this is a permission that can be revoked; the creation of a sentencing commission to formulate principles and guidelines by way of delegated legislation, although a constitutional novelty, may be accomplished in many jurisdictions by constitutional means.

Second, a principal reason for moving toward greater structuring of sentencing is to eliminate disparity and inconsistency of approach to the passing of sentences. This is not merely a matter of legitimate public expectation, but signifies the introduction of the principle of legality and "rule of law" values into the sphere of sentencing. The goal should, it has been submitted, be consistency of approach rather than consistency of outcome. In order to ensure consistency of approach, it is important to reach agreement on the aims of sentencing and on any further policies and principles that are to be pursued. Agreement on these issues is fundamental to the drawing up of coherent sentencing guidance and is also a necessary point of reference for sentencers when exercising their discretion. It was argued above that agreement on the aims of sentencing does not necessitate agreement on a single aim: multiple aims can also lead to consistent sentencing, but only if the relationship between those aims is clearly settled in advance. By way of contrast, "cafeteria-style" sentencing that permits judges to choose freely among alternative aims is a recipe for producing rather than reducing disparity.

Third, in constant tension with the arguments for consistency of approach are the arguments in favor of retaining an element of discretion in sentencing. It is noticeable that mandatory minimum sentences are widely opposed by the judiciary in many countries because they go against basic instincts of fairness in preventing courts from taking account of unusual features in individual cases. Mandatory minimum sentences seek consistency of outcome rather than consistency of approach, and they do so by lumping together cases that are alike and others that are unalike. Judicial discretion, moreover, recognizes that judges should be allowed to exercise judgment in the task of "individualizing and interpreting" general standards and assessing the relative importance of the various factors, principles, and policies bearing on an individual case (Galligan 1986). Much of the argument in this essay has been directed at exploring different ways of structuring judicial discretion, so as to achieve a balance between discretion for sentencers in individual cases and general standards and principles formulated by those who have the experience, perspective, and time to undertake that task. The advantages and disadvantages of various methods have been set out. What is the most suitable relationship between rule and discretion in a particular jurisdiction, and by what means this should be achieved, depends peculiarly on the legal culture and political situation within that jurisdiction.

This brings the debate back to the practical realities of sentencing reform. Resistance might come from various quarters, and experience suggests that politicians, the judiciary, and prosecutors are key groups in the success of any reform initiative. In a political sense much depends on the ends that are desired for sentencing reform: if it is simply consistency of outcome, that can be achieved through mandatory minima. But if what is desired is greater consistency of approach in sentencing, this requires a more sophisticated and sensitive program of sentencing reform. The political reality is that neither goal is likely to be sought *in abstracto*. Those who press for mandatory minima are likely to want higher sentences in the hope of greater deterrence or for pure political gain. And even where sentencing reform is desired so as to enhance fairness and consistency, the political situation might be unpropitious because of media concern about rises in the recorded crime rate, or because some politicians are arguing for a "get tough" approach, or because certain political parties play on this theme (von Hirsch 1990). Consistency of approach is neutral as between different levels of severity. Sentencing reforms can serve the punitive as well as the constructive. Usually there is an agenda of criminal justice policies that shape the sentencing reforms in a particular jurisdiction—perhaps concerned with the use of imprisonment, or with greater attention to the victims of crime, or with wider use of community-based sentences. The briefest glance at recent sentencing reforms will confirm that they do not take place in a political vacuum or a laboratory situation. Thus in Sweden there was no great political pressure for increased severity, whereas the U.S. federal reforms were affected by this, and in England and Wales the official approach rests on a "twin-track" or bifurcated ideology that insists on toughness for serious crimes but a lowering of the penal response to less serious offenses (Home Office 1990; cf. Bottoms 1977). In practice, the political debates may be further complicated by public expenditure considerations: in many countries expenditure on the penal system has soared greatly, and questions are then asked about whether high expenditure is necessary or effective. The result of such an enquiry might be to counterbalance the more punitive political tendencies.

The judicial response to greater structuring of sentencing depends to some extent on the legal culture. In jurisdictions where there is a tradition of "legalism," in terms of following faithfully the legislature's direct or indirect prescriptions, the spirit of the reforms may be swiftly embraced. However, in jurisdictions where judges have for many years enjoyed wide discretion in sentencing, it is natural that they may resent attempts to narrow it down. Minnesota provides one example of "adaptive behavior" by judges, which obviously occurred because they did not fully accept the policies underlying the new structures. Some of the methods of consistency without compulsion considered in Section IV would be possible means of preventing this outcome. Indeed, the more unpropitious the political situation, too, the more practical it might be to adopt low-profile, noncompulsory approaches. The degree of success will depend on the skill with which they are managed as well as on the culture and traditions of the local judiciary. Similar remarks may be made about the role of prosecutors in a reformed sentencing system: resistance will be less likely if attempts are made to imbue them with the spirit of the new sentencing structures. For prosecutors, also, there are more formal means of structuring their practices by the use of guidelines and guidance. So closely interwoven are the issues with those involved in sentencing that any sentencing reforms ought to take prosecutorial practice into account. The same applies to parole, as has been emphasized above.

This is not the first survey of sentencing structures to conclude that so much depends on the legal and political situation in each jurisdiction that there can be no universal recommendation of "what works best." That is not a limp conclusion, it is a realistic one. It also calls for careful interpretation. Sentencing is instrumental, its contours having penological, philosophical, and political dimensions. How these contours are drawn in a particular jurisdiction will inevitably influence the substance of any sentencing reforms. But the emphasis in this essay has been on the more technical aspects of sentencing. Of course, much here also depends on legal traditions, past practices, and the distribution of power. If there is a tradition of appellate review, it might be wiser to adapt it than to override it if it has been predominantly successful. Correspondingly, to introduce appellate review of sentences into a system for the first time might not bring the hoped-for advantages. By identifying the separate choices of technique that have to be made, even after the substantive questions of sentencing policy have been resolved, this essay has demonstrated the wide range of possible approaches. It is wrong to suppose, as some still do, that the appointment of a sentencing commission means that the style of guidance must inevitably be numerical guidelines in a "grid." It is also wrong to suppose that numerical guidelines have to be presented in the form of a "grid": narrative guidelines can be developed. It is wrong to suppose that appellate review has succeeded, even at its best, in dealing with the whole range of issues that ought to be resolved. Some of the noncompulsory methods described above could be molded into compulsory form, and likewise some of the other forms and styles of guidance could be introduced on a voluntary basis. There are key issues that the contents of guidance ought to cover, but the range of techniques is considerable. Whatever its traditions, no jurisdiction should become blinded to the possibilities that exist.

REFERENCES

Allen, Francis. 1964. "Legal Values and the Rehabilitative Ideal." In *Borderlands of Criminal Justice*, edited by Francis Allen. Chicago: University of Chicago Press.

Ashworth, Andrew. 1984. "Technique of Guidance on Sentencing." *Criminal Law Review* (U.K.), pp. 519–30.

———. 1989. *Custody Reconsidered: Clarity and Consistency in Sentencing.* Policy Study no. 104. London: Centre for Policy Studies.

———. 1990. "Sentencing for Drug Offenses in England." *Federal Sentencing Reporter* 3:67–68.

———. 1992. *Sentencing and Criminal Justice.* London: Weidenfeld & Nicolson.

Ashworth, Andrew, Elaine Genders, Graham Mansfield, Jill Peay, and Elaine Player. 1984. *Sentencing in the Crown Court.* Oxford: University of Oxford, Centre for Criminological Research.

Australian Law Reform Commission. 1988. *Sentencing.* Report no. 44. Canberra: Government Printer.

Blumstein, Alfred. 1988. "Prison Populations: A System out of Control?" In *Crime and Justice: A Review of Research,* vol. 10, edited by Michael Tonry and Norval Morris. Chicago: University of Chicago Press.

Blumstein, Alfred, Jacqueline Cohen, Susan Martin, and Michael Tonry, eds. 1983. *Research on Sentencing: The Search for Reform.* Washington, D.C.: National Academy Press.

Bogan, Kathleen M. 1990. "Constructing Felony Sentencing Guidelines in an Already Crowded State: Oregon Breaks New Ground." *Crime and Delinquency* 36(4):467–87.

———. 1991. "Sentencing Reform in Oregon." *Overcrowded Times* 2(2):5, 14–15.

Bottomley, A. Keith. 1990. "Parole in Transition: A Comparative Study of Origins, Developments, and Prospects for the 1990s." In *Crime and Justice: A Review of Research,* vol. 10, edited by Michael Tonry and Norval Morris. Chicago: University of Chicago Press.

Bottoms, Anthony E. 1977. "The Renaissance of Dangerousness." *Howard Journal* 18:77–98.

Breyer, Stephen. 1988. "The Federal Sentencing Guidelines and the Key Compromises on Which They Rest." *Hofstra Law Review* 17:1–50.

Campbell, A. Kim. 1990. "Sentencing Reform in Canada." *Canadian Journal of Criminology* 32:387–95.

Canadian Ministry of Justice. 1990a. *Sentencing: Directions for Reform.* Ottawa: Minister of Supply and Services.

———. 1990b. *A Framework for Sentencing, Corrections and Conditional Release.* Ottawa: Minister of Supply and Services.

Canadian Sentencing Commission. 1987. *Sentencing Reform: A Canadian Approach.* Ottawa: Minister of Supply and Services.

Carlisle, Lord. 1988. *The Parole System in England and Wales: Report of the Review Committee.* London: H.M. Stationery Office.

Chan, Janet. 1989. "Developing a Sentencing Information System in New South Wales." *Australia and New Zealand Journal of Criminology* 22:13–23.

Corns, C. 1990. "Destructuring Sentencing Decision-making in Victoria." *Australia and New Zealand Journal of Criminology* 23:145–57.

Council of Europe. 1974. *Sentencing.* Report by the Sub-Committee of the European Committee on Crime Problems. Strasbourg: Council of Europe.

———. 1989. *Disparities in Sentencing: Causes and Solutions.* Collected Studies in Criminological Research, vol. 26. Strasbourg: Council of Europe.

Cullen, Francis, and Karen Gilbert. 1982. *Reaffirming Rehabilitation.* Cincinnati: Anderson.

Daubney, David. 1988. *Taking Responsibility.* Report of the Standing Committee on Justice and Solicitor General on Its Review of Sentencing, Conditional Release and Related Aspects of Corrections. Ottawa: Canadian Government Publishing Center.

Davies, Malcolm. 1985. "Determinate Sentencing Reform in California and Its Impact on the Penal System." *British Journal of Criminology* 25:1–30.

DiPietro, Susanne D. 1990. "The Development of Appellate Sentencing Law in Alaska." *Alaska Law Review* 7:265–98.

Doob, Anthony, and Norman Park. 1987. "Computerized Sentencing Information for Judges: An Aid to the Sentencing Process." *Criminal Law Quarterly* 30:54–72.

Federal Courts Study Committee. 1990. *Report.* Washington, D.C.: Federal Courts Study Committee.

Frankel, Marvin. 1973. *Criminal Sentences: Law without Order.* New York: Hill & Wang.

Frase, Richard S. 1991*a.* "Sentencing Reform in Minnesota, Ten Years After: Reflections on Dale G. Parent's *Structuring Criminal Sentences: The Evolution of Minnesota's Sentencing Guidelines.*" *Minnesota Law Review* 75:1401–28.

———. 1991*b.* "Implementing Commission-based Sentencing Guidelines: The Lessons of the First Ten Years in Minnesota." Paper presented at the annual meeting of the American Society of Criminology, San Francisco, November.

Galligan, Dennis J. 1986. *Discretionary Powers.* Oxford: Oxford University Press.

Gebelein, Richard S. 1991. "Sentencing Reform in Delaware." *Overcrowded Times* 2(2):5, 12–13.

Gendreau, P., and R. Ross. 1988. "The Revivification of Rehabilitation: Evidence from the 1980s." *Justice Quarterly* 4:349–65.

Hann, R. A., W. G. Harman, and K. G. Pease. 1991. "Does Parole Reduce the Risk of Reconviction?" *Howard Journal of Criminal Justice* 30:66–75.

Hogarth, John. 1987. "Computers and the Law: Sentencing Data Base Study." Unpublished manuscript. Vancouver: University of British Columbia, Faculty of Law.

Home Office. 1988. *Punishment, Custody and the Community.* London: H.M. Stationery Office.

———. 1990. *Crime, Justice and Protecting the Public.* London: H.M. Stationery Office.

Hood, Roger. 1962. *Sentencing in Magistrates' Courts.* London: Heinemann.

Hough, Mike, David Moxon, and Helen Lewis. 1987. "Attitudes to Punishment: Findings from the British Crime Survey." In *The Psychology of Sentencing,* edited by Donald C. Pennington and Sally Lloyd-Bostock. Oxford: Wolfson College, Centre for Socio-Legal Studies.

Jareborg, Nils. 1989. *Introductory Report*. In *Disparities in Sentencing: Causes and Solutions*. Strasbourg: Council of Europe.

Judicial Studies Board. 1988. *Triennial Report, 1984–87*. London: H.M. Stationery Office.

Knapp, Kay A. 1987. "Implementation of the Minnesota Guidelines: Can the Innovative Spirit Be Preserved?" In *The Sentencing Commission and Its Guidelines*, edited by Andrew von Hirsch, Kay A. Knapp, and Michael Tonry. Boston: Northeastern University Press.

LaPrairie, C. 1990. "The Role of Sentencing in the Over-representation of Aboriginal People in Correctional Institutions." *Canadian Journal of Criminology* 32:429–40.

Lovegrove, Austin. 1989. *Judicial Decision-making, Sentencing Policy and Numerical Guidance*. New York: Springer-Verlag.

Magistrates' Association. 1989. *Sentencing Guide for Criminal Offences (Other Than Road Traffic) and Compensation Table*. London: Magistrates' Association.

Maguire, Mike. 1982. *Burglary in a Dwelling*. London: Heinemann.

———. 1991. "The Needs and Rights of Victims of Crime." In *Crime and Justice: A Review of Research*, vol. 14, edited by Michael Tonry. Chicago: University of Chicago Press.

Martin, Susan. 1983. "The Politics of Sentencing Reform: Sentencing Guidelines in Pennsylvania and Minnesota." In *Research on Sentencing: The Search for Reform*, vol. 2, edited by Alfred Blumstein, Jacqueline Cohen, Susan Martin, and Michael Tonry. Washington D.C.: National Academy Press.

Miller, Marc, and Daniel Freed. 1990a. "Handcuffing the Sentencing Judge." *Federal Sentencing Reporter* 2:189–91.

———. 1990b. "The Emerging Proportionality Law for Measuring Departures." *Federal Sentencing Reporter* 2:255–56.

———. 1990c. "Offender Characteristics and Victim Vulnerability." *Federal Sentencing Reporter* 3:3–7.

———. 1991. "Plea-bargained Sentences, Disparity and 'Guidelines Justice.' " *Federal Sentencing Reporter* 3:175–78.

Miller, Marc, and Robert Weich. 1989. "The Relevant Conduct Controversy." *Federal Sentencing Reporter* 2:150–51.

Morris, Norval, and Michael Tonry. 1990. *Between Prison and Probation*. New York: Oxford University Press.

Moxon, David. 1988. *Sentencing Practice in the Crown Court*. Home Office Research Study no. 103. London: H.M. Stationery Office.

Nagel, Ilene. 1990. "Structuring Sentencing Discretion: The New Federal Sentencing Guidelines." *Journal of Criminal Law and Criminology* 80:883–943.

Parent, Dale G. 1988. *Structuring Sentencing Discretion: The Evaluation of Minnesota's Sentencing Guidelines*. Stoneham, Mass: Butterworth.

Potas, Ivan. 1990. *The Sentencing Information Systems of New South Wales*. Paper presented to the eighth United Nations Congress on the Prevention of Crime and the Treatment of Offenders, Havana, Cuba, August.

Radzinowicz, Sir Leon, and Roger Hood. 1986. *The History of English Criminal Law*, vol. 5, *The Emergence of Penal Policy*. London: Stevens.

Robert, Marc. 1989. "Inequalities in Sentencing." In *Disparities in Sentencing: Causes and Solutions*. Strasbourg: Council of Europe.

Robinson, Paul H. 1987. "Hybrid Principles for the Distribution of Criminal Sanctions." *Northwestern University Law Review* 82:19–42.

———. 1988. "Legality and Discretion in the Distribution of Criminal Sanctions." *Harvard Journal on Legislation* 25:393–460.

Schulhofer, Steven, and Ilene Nagel. 1989. "Negotiated Pleas under the Federal Sentencing Guidelines: The First Fifteen Months." *American Criminal Law Review* 27:231–88.

Shane-Dubow, S., A. P. Brown, and E. Olsen. 1985. *Sentencing Reform in the United States: History, Content, and Effect*. Washington, D.C.: U.S. Government Printing Office.

Thomas, David A. 1982. *Current Sentencing Practice* (loose-leaf, with regular updating). London: Sweet & Maxwell.

Tonry, Michael H. 1987a. "Sentencing Guidelines and Their Effects." In *The Sentencing Commission and Its Guidelines*, edited by Andrew von Hirsch, Kay A. Knapp, and Michael Tonry. Boston: Northeastern University Press.

———. 1987b. *Sentencing Reform Impacts*. Washington, D.C.: National Institute of Justice.

———. 1988. "Structuring Sentencing." In *Crime and Justice: A Review of Research*, vol. 10, edited by Michael Tonry and Norval Morris. Chicago: University of Chicago Press.

———. 1991. "The Politics and Processes of Sentencing Commissions." *Crime and Delinquency* 37:307–29.

United Nations. 1990. *The United Nations and Crime Prevention and Criminal Justice*. New York: United Nations.

U.S. Department of Justice. 1988. *Sourcebook of Criminal Statistics*. Washington, D.C.: Bureau of Justice Statistics.

U.S. General Accounting Office. 1990. "U.S. Sentencing Commission: Changes Needed to Improve Effectiveness." Testimony of Lowell Dodge before the Subcommittee on Criminal Justice of the Committee on the Judiciary, House of Representatives, March. Washington, D.C.: U.S. General Accounting Office.

U.S. Sentencing Commission. 1987. *Sentencing Guidelines and Policy Statements (April 13, 1987)*. Washington, D.C.: U.S. Government Printing Office.

———. 1991. *Mandatory Minimum Penalties in the Federal Criminal Justice System*. Washington, D.C.: U.S. Sentencing Commission.

Victorian Sentencing Committee. 1988. *Report*. Melbourne: Victorian Attorney-General's Department.

von Hirsch, Andrew. 1987a. "Principles for Choosing Sanctions: Sweden's Proposed Sentencing Statute." *New England Journal of Criminal and Civil Confinement* 13:171–95.

———. 1987b. "The Enabling Legislation." In *The Sentencing Commission and Its Guidelines*, edited by Andrew von Hirsch, Kay A. Knapp, and Michael Tonry. Boston: Northeastern University Press.

———. 1988. "Federal Sentencing Guidelines: The United States and Canadian Schemes Compared." Occasional Papers from the Center for Research in Crime and Justice, no. 4. New York: New York University School of Law.

———. 1990. "The Politics of Just Deserts." *Canadian Journal of Criminology* 32:397–413.

von Hirsch, Andrew, and Kathleen Hanrahan. 1979. *The Question of Parole: Retention, Reform or Abolition?* Cambridge, Mass.: Ballinger.

von Hirsch, Andrew, and Nils Jareborg. 1989. "Sweden's Sentencing Statute Enacted." *Criminal Law Review*, 1989, pp. 275–81.

von Hirsch, Andrew, Kay A. Knapp, and Michael Tonry, eds. 1987. *The Sentencing Commission and Its Guidelines.* Boston, Mass.: Northeastern University Press.

von Hirsch, Andrew, and Julia M. Mueller. 1984. "California's Determinate Sentencing Law: An Analysis of Its Structure." *New England Journal of Criminal and Civil Confinement* 10:253–300.

Walker, Nigel, and Mike Hough. 1988. *Public Attitudes to Sentencing.* Aldershot, England: Gower.

Wasik, Martin, and Richard D. Taylor. 1991. *Blackstone's Guide to the Criminal Justice Act of 1991.* London: Blackstone.

Wasik, Martin, and Andrew von Hirsch. 1988. "Noncustodial Sentences and the Principles of Desert." *Criminal Law Review*, 1988, pp. 555–72.

Wheeler, Stanton, Kenneth Mann, and Austin Sarat. 1989. *Sitting in Judgment: The Sentencing of White-Collar Criminals.* New Haven, Conn.: Yale University Press.

Wilkins, William, and J. Steer. 1990. "Relevant Conduct: The Cornerstone of the Federal Sentencing Guidelines." *South Carolina Law Review* 41:495–531.

Wright, Martin. 1991. *Justice for Victims and Offenders.* Milton Keynes, England: Open University Press.

Zeisel, Hans, and Shari Diamond. 1977. "Search for Sentencing Equity: Sentence Review in Massachusetts and Connecticut." *American Bar Foundation Research Journal*, pp. 881–940.

Zimring, Franklin. 1976. "Making the Punishment Fit the Crime: A Consumer's Guide to Sentencing Reform." *Hasting Center Report* 6:13–17.

Michael Tonry

Mandatory Penalties

ABSTRACT

To many public officials, promotion and enactment of mandatory penalty laws are important symbols of their concern for public safety and citizens' fear of crime. In practice, mandatory minimum-penalty laws accomplish few of their stated objectives and produce unwanted consequences. Their deterrent effects range from nonexistent to short-lived. When they call for short mandatory prison terms for serious crimes, they are often irrelevant because longer sentences are generally imposed. When they mandate longer terms (five, ten, twenty years), they are often circumvented by lawyers and judges. They reduce defendants' incentives to plead guilty, reduce guilty plea rates, and lengthen case processing time. They sometimes result in imposition of penalties more severe than anyone immediately involved believes appropriate. A number of devices exist, ranging from repeal to reconfiguration, for avoiding the unwanted effects of mandatory penalties. Whether such devices can adequately reconcile public officials' needs to take symbolic actions with court officials' needs to be both just and efficient remains to be seen.

Mandatory penalties do not work. The record is clear from research in the 1950s, the 1970s, the 1980s, and, thanks to the U.S. Sentencing Commission, the 1990s that mandatory penalty laws shift power from judges to prosecutors, meet with widespread circumvention, produce dislocations in case processing, and too often result in imposition of penalties that everyone involved believes to be unduly harsh. From research in the 1970s and 1980s, the weight of the evidence clearly

Michael Tonry, Sonosky Professor of Law and Public Policy at the University of Minnesota, is grateful to John DiIulio, Frank Hartmann, Marc Miller, and Andrew von Hirsch for helpful comments on an earlier draft.

shows that enactment of mandatory penalties has either no demonstrable marginal deterrent effects or short-term effects that rapidly waste away.[1] Why, then, did legislatures in all fifty states enact mandatory penalty laws in the 1970s and 1980s, and why do legislatures continue to enact them?

The reason is that most elected officials who support such laws are only secondarily interested in their effects; officials' primary interests are rhetorical and symbolic. Calling and voting for mandatory penalties, as many state and federal officials repeatedly have done in recent years, is demonstration that officials are "tough on crime." If the laws "work," all the better, but that is hardly crucial. In a time of heightened public anxiety about crime and social unrest, being on the right side of the crime issue is much more important politically than making sound and sensible public policy choices.

This essay retells a story, at least three centuries old, of the political appeal and practical limits of mandatory sentencing laws. The retelling is occasioned by the publication of a U.S. Sentencing Commission report on mandatory penalties in the federal courts and by the possibility that prison crowding, budgetary crises, and a changing professional climate may make more public officials willing to be reminded of what we have long known about mandatory penalties. Officials in some states (there seems little hope at the federal level) may in coming years be more inclined than in the recent past to make policy choices based on knowledge of how mandatory penalties operate in practice. Surprisingly, few published works offer overviews of research on mandatory penalties. This essay is one effort to fill that void.

That mandatory penalties have more costs than benefits does not mean that rational social policies might not incorporate serious penalties for serious crimes. There are more effective, less costly ways than creation of mandatory penalties to achieve that end. In every era, some

---

[1] Because few studies attempt to examine the mandatory penalty laws' deterrent effects, and because the clear weight of the evidence on the deterrent effects of marginal manipulation of penalties demonstrates few or no effects (e.g., Blumstein, Cohen, and Nagin 1978), except in this note I do not explore that subject. Several studies of the Massachusetts firearms law concluded that it had a short-term deterrent effect on the use of firearms in violent crimes (e.g., Pierce and Bowers 1981). However, studies of mandatory sentencing laws for firearms offenses in Michigan (Loftin, Heumann, and McDowall 1983) and Florida (Loftin and McDowall 1984) concluded that no discernible effect on the level of crime could be attributed to the mandatory sentencing laws. The Rockefeller Drug Law evaluation also found no demonstrable impact of that law on drug use or crime in New York (Joint Committee on New York Drug Law Evaluation 1978). The proliferation of mandatory penalties for drug crimes in the 1980s did not demonstrably reduce drug trafficking or affect its most common measure, the street prices of illicit substances (Reuter and Kleiman 1986, table 5; Moore 1990, fig. 1).

kinds of crime are regarded as so serious that harsh penalties appear called for. Examples in our time include aggravated forms of stranger violence, nonfamilial sexual abuse of young children, and flagrant fraudulence in the financial markets. Assuming that legislators will want to provide for severe penalties for especially serious crime, there are ways to avoid or ameliorate the foreseeable dysfunctional effects of mandatory penalties. Here are four examples. First, in order to establish policies calling for severe penalties for serious crimes, while allowing sufficient flexibility to avoid foreseeable unintended consequences, penalties for especially serious crimes might be made presumptive rather than mandatory. Prosecutors and judges both have powerful voices in sentencing; disregard of the presumption would require that one or both decide either that the penalty would be too severe in a particular case or that the political climate has altered and public sensibilities no longer demand such harsh penalties. Second, as a matter of course, legislators might add "sunset provisions" to mandatory penalty laws. This would assure that laws passed in the passion of the moment will not endure for decades. Legislators can much more comfortably accede to the lapse of a punitive law than vote for its repeal. Third, mandatory (or presumptive) penalties might be limited to serious crimes like armed robbery, aggravated rape, and murder. The most widespread and cynical circumventions of mandatory penalty laws, and the most extreme injustices in individual cases, arise under laws requiring severe penalties for minor crimes like possession or trafficking of small amounts of controlled substances. Fourth, correctional officials might be authorized to reconsider release dates of all offenders receiving prison sentences exceeding a designated length (say three or five years). This would allow eventual release of people receiving unusually long sentences, life sentences without eligibility for parole, and sentences under "habitual offender" fixed-term laws, without requiring extraordinary political decisions like gubernatorial pardons or commutations.

This essay summarizes the available research on the implementation and operation of mandatory sentencing laws. Section I provides a brief summary of the state of knowledge concerning mandatory penalties before 1970. Section II examines the major empirical evaluations of mandatory penalties, beginning with the most ambitious, the U.S. Sentencing Commission's 1991 study of federal mandatories and the 1978 evaluation of New York's "Rockefeller Drug Laws." Section III tries to make sense of those findings and to outline their implications for elected officials who want simultaneously to respond to public anxi-

ety about serious crime and yet to enact laws that waste as few public resources, foster as few hypocrisies, and do as little injustice as
possible.

I. Mandatory Penalties before 1970

The foreseeable problems in implementing mandatory penalties have
been well known for 200 years. Most systematic empirical research
postdates 1970. This section summarizes knowledge to that date. Perhaps the best way to summarize past knowledge concerning mandatory
penalties is to quote from a U.S. House of Representatives report
that explained why the Congress in 1970 repealed almost all federal
mandatory penalties for drug offenses. "The severity of existing penalties, involving in many instances minimum mandatory sentences, has
led in many instances to reluctance on the part of prosecutors to prosecute some violations, where the penalties seem to be out of line with
the seriousness of the offenses. In addition, severe penalties, which do
not take into account individual circumstances, and which treat casual
violators as severely as they treat hardened criminals, tend to make
conviction . . . more difficult to obtain" (House of Representatives
1970, quoted in U.S. Sentencing Commission 1991, pp. 6–7). Our
knowledge in the 1990s concerning mandatory penalties is little different. More to the point, knowledge in the 1790s was much the same.

The least subtle way to avoid imposition of harsh penalties is to
nullify them by refusing to convict offenders subject to them. "Nullification," a term in common usage for more than two centuries, encap-
sulates the process by which judges and juries, but particularly juries,
willfully refuse to enforce laws or apply penalties that seem to them
unjust. Oliver Wendell Holmes, Jr., described the jury's capacity to
nullify harsh laws as its central virtue (Holmes 1889). Roscoe Pound
claimed that "jury lawlessness is the great corrective of law in its actual
administration" (1910, p. 18). John Baldwin and Michael McConville,
in a review of research on juries, observed: "The refusal of juries to
convict in cases of criminal libel, the 'pious perjury' they welcomed in
order to avoid conviction on a capital offense, the indulgence shown
toward 'mercy killings,' and the nullification of the Prohibition laws
during the 1920s are simply the most famous examples of this exercise
of discretion" (1980, p. 272). The leading criminal law casebook in use
in American law schools for twenty-five years, Michael and Wechsler's
Criminal Law and Its Administration (1940), dedicated lengthy consideration to nullification. Although the term is no longer in vogue, a sum-

mary of the evidence concerning nullification and similar processes may be useful.

A. The Death Penalty in Eighteenth-Century England

The death penalty in eighteenth- and nineteenth-century England was the subject of policy debates strikingly like late twentieth-century American debates about mandatory penalties. In July 1991, in the face of claims that newly proposed mandatory penalty laws would overburden the courts and have little practical effect, one congressman told the *New York Times*, "Congressmen and senators are afraid to vote no" on crime and punishment bills, "even if they don't think it will accomplish anything." A senate aide suggested that "it's tough to vote against tough sentences for criminals" (Ifill 1991). At the end of the eighteenth century, Edmund Burke declared "that he could obtain the consent of the House of Commons to any Bill imposing the punishment of death" (Select Committee on Capital Punishment 1930, paras. 10, 11). Samuel Romilly, England's most celebrated contemporary prison reformer, by contrast, repeatedly called for repeal of capital punishment provisions because the laws were applied erratically and unfairly and because the erratic application inevitably undermined the laws' deterrent effects (Romilly 1820).[2] During the reigns of the four British King Georges, between 1714 and 1830, the British Parliament created 156 new capital offenses. By 1819, British law recognized 220 capital offenses, most of them property crimes.

During the same period, however, the number of executions carried out not only failed to increase commensurately with the passage of new laws but declined. Executions were four times more common in the early 1600s than in the mid-1700s (Hay 1975, p. 22). According to Sir Leon Radzinowicz, executions in the late eighteenth century varied between a low of twenty-one per year during the 1780s and a high of fifty-three in the 1790s (Radzinowicz 1948–68, 1:141, 147).

Douglas Hay (1975), in a famous essay, "Property, Authority, and the Criminal Law," tries to explain the contrast between continuous extension of the reach of the death penalty and steady decline in the incidence of its use. He argues that the explanation can be found in the efforts of propertied classes in the early years of the Industrial Revolution to protect their class interests through passage of laws that

[2] To like effect, the U.S. Sentencing Commission's report on mandatory penalties argued that their inconsistent application is likely to undermine their deterrent effects (1991, p. ii, iii).

symbolically emphasized the importance of private property (by making numerous property crimes punishable by death) while operating a legal system that provided both exemplary punishments and, by frequent merciful exceptions and observing procedural rules, supported its own public legitimacy. In this period before creation of professional police departments and widespread use of prisons for punishment, the civil peace depended on general acceptance of the legitimacy of the existing social order.

More important for purposes of this essay, however, are the methods used in practice to avoid carrying out death sentences. First, and most important, juries often refused to convict offenders; an acquittal is a simple but effective way to avoid a mandatory penalty (Baldwin and McConville 1980, p. 272). A variant, which has twentieth-century echoes, was for the jury to convict of a lesser offense. According to a 1930 report of the British Select Committee on Capital Punishment describing eighteenth-century practices:

> In vast numbers of cases, the sentence of death was not passed, or if passed was not carried into effect. For one thing, juries in increasing numbers refused to convict. A jury would assess the amount taken from a shop at 4s. 10d. so as to avoid the capital penalty which fell on a theft of 5s. In the case of a dwelling, where the theft of 40s. was a capital offense, even when a woman confessed that she had stolen £5, the jury notwithstanding found that the amount was only 39s. And when . . . the legislature raised the capital indictment to £5, the juries at the same time raised their verdicts £4 19s. [1930, para. 17]

Second, as more capital offenses were created, the courts adopted increasingly narrow interpretations of procedural, pleading, and evidentiary rules. Prosecutions seemingly well-founded as a factual matter would fall because a name or a date was incorrect or a defendant's occupation was wrongly described as "farmer" rather than "yeoman" (Radzinowicz 1948–68, vol. 1:25–28, 83–91, 97–103; Hay 1980, pp. 32–34).

Third, increasing numbers of offenders were accorded protection from death under the doctrine of "benefit of clergy." A doctrine that initially protected clergymen from execution following convictions at civil (as opposed to religious) courts, benefit of clergy was extended to literate laymen in the medieval period and to all accused in 1706. Its effect was to exempt first offenders convicted of lesser felonies from execution (Baker 1977, p. 41).

Fourth, even among those who were not acquitted, convicted of lesser charges, discharged on procedural technicalities, or protected by benefit of clergy, the proportion sentenced to death declined steadily throughout the late eighteenth century.

According to the Select Committee on Capital Punishment, "the Prerogative of the Crown [pardon] was increasingly exercised. Down to 1756 about two thirds of those condemned were actually brought to the scaffold; from 1756 to 1772 the proportion sank to one-half. Between 1802 and 1808 it was no more than one eighth" (1930, para. 21). Most of those pardoned received substituted punishments of a term of imprisonment or transportation (Stephen 1883, vol. 1, chap. 13).

Briefly to summarize, experience with "mandatory" capital punishment in eighteenth-century England instructed all who would pay attention that mandatory penalties, especially for crimes other than homicide, elicited a variety of adaptive responses from those charged to enforce the law, including juries' refusals to convict "guilty" offenders and decisions to bring in convictions for less serious charges not subject to the penalty, development of technical procedural devices used by judges to discharge cases, and extensive use of pardons and other post-conviction devices to avoid carrying out executions.

B. American Mandatory Penalties in the 1950s

Our best source of information on criminal court processes in the 1950s, the various reports emanating from the American Bar Foundation's Survey of the Administration of Criminal Justice in the United States, confirms the lessons from eighteenth-century England. Frank Remington, director of the eighteen-year project, in the foreword to the sentencing volume, noted, "Legislative prescription of a high mandatory sentence for certain offenders is likely to result in a reduction in charges at the prosecution stage, or if this is not done, by a refusal of the judge to convict at the adjudication stage. The issue . . . thus is not solely whether certain offenders should be dealt with severely, but also how the criminal justice system will accommodate to the legislative charge" (Dawson 1969, p. xvii).

The American Bar Association survey was conceived as an empirical investigation and description of the administration of criminal justice in the United States. "Pilot studies" were undertaken in several states in the mid-1950s. As the enormity of the project became apparent, the pilot studies became the survey and led to the publication of five volumes based on extensive reviews of files, interviews, and participant observation (including *Conviction* [Newman 1966], *Prosecution* [Miller 1969], and *Sentencing* [Dawson 1969]). Several volumes deal with charging, case processing, and sentencing aspects of mandatory penalties. The survey's findings on mandatories are exemplified by three processes the reports describe. First, Newman describes how Michigan judges dealt with a lengthy mandatory minimum for drug sales:

> Mandatory minimums are almost universally disliked by trial judges. . . . The clearest illustration of routine reductions is provided by reduction of sale of narcotics to possession or addiction . . . Judges . . . actively participated in the charge reduction process to the extent of refusing to accept guilty pleas to sale and liberally assigning counsel to work out reduced charges. . . . To demonstrate its infrequent application, from the effective date of the revised law (May 8, 1952) to the date of tabulation four years later (June 30, 1956), only twelve sale-of-narcotics convictions were recorded in Detroit out of 476 defendants originally charged with sale. The remainder (except a handful acquitted altogether) pleaded guilty to reduced charges. [1966, p. 179]

Second, on a related subject (avoidance of long statutory maximum sentences), Newman (1966, p. 182) describes efforts to avoid fifteen-year mandatory maximum sentences for breaking-and-entering and armed robbery:

> In Michigan conviction of armed robbery or breaking and entering in the nighttime (fifteen-year maximum compared to five years for daytime breaking) is rare. The pattern of downgrading is such that it becomes virtually routine, and the bargaining session becomes a ritual. The real issue in such negotiations is not whether the charge will be reduced but how far, that is, to what lesser offense. As has been pointed out, armed robbery is so often downgraded that the Michigan parole board tends to treat a conviction for unarmed robbery as prima facie proof that the defendant had a weapon. And the frequency of altering nighttime burglary to breaking and entering in the daytime led one

prosecutor to remark: "You'd think all our burglaries occur at high noon."

Third, Dawson (1969, p. 201) describes "very strong" judicial resistance to a twenty-year mandatory minimum for sale of narcotics: "All of the judges of Recorder's Court, in registering their dislike for the provision, cited the hypothetical case of a young man having no criminal record being given a twenty-year minimum sentence for selling a single marijuana cigarette. Charge reductions to possession or use are routine. Indeed, in some cases, judges have refused to accept guilty pleas to sale of narcotics, but have continued the case and appointed counsel with instructions to negotiate a charge reduction." These findings from the American Bar Foundation differ in detail from those of eighteenth-century England, but only in detail. When the U.S. Congress repealed most mandatory penalties for drug offenses in 1970, it was merely acknowledging enforcement problems that had been recognized for centuries.

II. Mandatory Penalties in the 1970s, 1980s, and 1990s

Despite earlier generations' understanding of why mandatory penalties are unsound as a matter of policy, mandatory sentencing laws since 1975 have been America's most popular sentencing innovation. By 1983, forty-nine of the fifty states had adopted mandatory sentencing laws for offenses other than murder or drunk driving (Shane-DuBow, Brown, and Olsen 1985, table 30). Most mandatories apply to murder or aggravated rape, drug offenses, felonies involving firearms, or felonies committed by persons who have previous felony convictions.[3] Between 1985 and mid-1991, the U.S. Congress enacted at least twenty new mandatory penalty provisions; by 1991, more than sixty federal statutes defined more than one hundred crimes subject to mandatories (U.S. Sentencing Commission 1991, pp. 8–10). The experience in most states in the late 1980s was similar. In Florida, for example, seven new mandatory sentencing bills were enacted between 1988 and 1990 (Austin 1991, p. 4). In Arizona, for another example, mandatory sentencing laws are so common that 57 percent of felony offenders in fiscal year 1990 were subject to mandatory sentencing enhancements (Knapp 1991, p. 10).

[3] Legislation in the 1980s in many states established forty-eight-hour and other brief mandatory minimum terms for many drunk driving offenses (Jacobs 1988).

The political attractiveness of mandatory sentencing laws is not difficult to understand. During the 1980s many political figures of both parties campaigned on "tough on crime" platforms and few elected officials dared risk being seen as "soft." A recent *New York Times* story captures the climate in its title: "Senate's Rule for Its Anti-crime Bill: The Tougher the Provision, the Better" (Ifill 1991). Mandatories are often targeted on especially disturbing behaviors, such as large-scale drug sales, murder, or rape, or especially unattractive characters, such as repeat violent offenders or people who use guns in violent crimes. In the case of firearms offenses, mandatory laws allow the state, like Janus, to frown on law-defying villains who use firearms for criminal purposes and to smile on law-abiding citizens who use firearms for legitimate purposes. In a nation in which most approaches to control of gun use are politically impracticable, mandatory sentencing laws are a mechanism for attempting to deter illegal gun use and encourage offenders to use less lethal weapons.

Although the uninitiated citizen might reasonably believe that, under a mandatory sentencing law, anyone who commits the target offense will receive the mandated sentence, the reality is more complicated. Sentencing policy is only as mandatory as police, prosecutors, and judges choose to make it. The people who operate the criminal justice system generally find mandatory sentencing laws too inflexible for their taste and take steps to avoid what they consider unduly harsh, and therefore unjust, sentences in individual cases. And, frequently, the mandatory sentencing law is simply ignored. For example, in Minnesota in 1981, of persons convicted of weapons offenses to which a mandatory minimum applied, only 76.5 percent actually received prison sentences (Knapp 1984, p. 28).[4]

Research on mandatory sentencing laws during the 1970s and 1980s reveals a number of avoidance strategies. Boston police avoided application of a 1975 Massachusetts law calling for mandatory one-year sentences for persons convicted of carrying a gun by decreasing the number of arrests made for that offense and increasing (by 120 percent between 1974 and 1976) the number of weapons seizures without arrest (Carlson 1982). Prosecutors often avoid application of mandatory sen-

---

[4] One striking form of plea bargaining around mandatory penalties occurs in Arizona, where Knapp (1991, pp. 10–11) found that 3,739 (24 percent) of 15,720 felony convictions in 1990 were for the inchoate offenses of attempt and conspiracy. Inchoate offenses are not subject to mandatory penalties. Defendants charged with completed felonies subject to mandatories are routinely allowed to bargain down to inchoate offenses.

tencing laws simply by filing charges for different, but roughly comparable, offenses that are not subject to mandatory sentences. Judges too can circumvent such laws. Detroit judges sidestepped a 1977 law requiring a two-year sentence for persons convicted of possession of a firearm in the commission of a felony by acquitting defendants of the gun charge (even though the evidence would support a conviction) or by decreasing the sentence they would otherwise impose by two years to offset the mandatory two-year term (Heumann and Loftin 1979).

There has been considerable recent research and, taken together, like the work of earlier generations, it supports the following generalizations:

1. lawyers and judges will take steps to avoid application of laws they consider unduly harsh;

2. dismissal rates typically increase at early stages of the criminal justice process after effectuation of a mandatory penalty as practitioners attempt to shield some defendants from the law's reach;

3. defendants whose cases are not dismissed or diverted make more vigorous efforts to avoid conviction and to delay sentencing with the results that trial rates and case processing times increase;

4. defendants who are convicted of the target offense are often sentenced more severely than they would have been in the absence of the mandatory penalty provision; and

5. because declines in conviction rates for those arrested tend to offset increases in imprisonment rates for those convicted, the overall probability that defendants will be incarcerated remains about the same after enactment of a mandatory sentencing law.[5]

The empirical evidence concerning the operation of mandatory sentencing laws comes primarily from five major studies. One is the U.S. Sentencing Commission's recent study of mandatory penalties in the U.S. federal courts (U.S. Sentencing Commission 1991). The second concerns the "Rockefeller Drug Laws," which required mandatory prison sentences for persons convicted of a variety of drug felonies (Joint Committee on New York Drug Law Evaluation 1978). One concerns the operation of a 1977 Michigan law requiring imposition of a two-year mandatory prison sentence on persons convicted of possession of a gun during commission of a felony (Loftin and McDowall

---

[5] This finding recurs in research on mandatories in the 1970s. Whether it will be found in the 1990s is unknown. The U.S. Sentencing Commission study of mandatory penalties, like earlier research, revealed longer case processing times and lower guilty plea rates than for non-mandatory-penalty crimes but does not consider whether incarceration probabilities, given an arrest, have changed.

1981; Loftin, Heumann, and McDowall 1983). Two concern a Massachusetts law requiring a one-year prison sentence for persons convicted of carrying a firearm unlawfully (Beha 1977; Rossman et al. 1979).

A. U.S. Sentencing Commission Report

Were federal officials more interested in rational policy-making than in political posturing, the U.S. Sentencing Commission report, "Mandatory Minimum Penalties in the Federal Criminal Justice System," would result in withdrawal of all mandatory sentencing proposals and repeal of those now in effect.

The commission's report demonstrates that mandatory minimum sentencing laws unwarrantedly shift discretion from judges to prosecutors, result in higher trial rates and lengthened case processing times, arbitrarily fail to acknowledge salient differences between cases, and often punish minor offenders much more harshly than anyone involved believes is warranted. Interviews with judges, lawyers, and probation officers at twelve sites showed that heavy majorities of judges, defense counsel, and probation officers dislike mandatory penalties; prosecutors are about evenly divided. Finally, and perhaps not surprisingly given the other findings, the report shows that judges and lawyers not uncommonly circumvent mandatories.

The commission's study was prompted by a congressional mandate.[6] The congressional charge had eight parts, including an assessment of the effects of mandatories on sentencing disparities, a description of the interaction between mandatories and plea bargaining, and "a detailed empirical research study of the effect of mandatory minimum penalties in the Federal system."

The commission's research design effectively combined methods and data sources for investigating charging, bargaining, and sentencing patterns. The combination of quantitative analyses of 1984–90 sentencing patterns, a detailed quantitative analysis of case processing in 1990, and various interviews and surveys aimed at capturing officials' opinions provide complementary sources of information. In presenting and discussing findings, the report carefully notes the limits of the claims it can make and describes alternative interpretations of findings.

The commission analyzed three data sets describing federal sentencing and two sources of data concerning the opinions of judges, assistant U.S. attorneys, and others. The three sentencing data sets were

[6] Pub. L. No. 101-647, sec. 1703 [104 Stat. 4846].

FPSSIS,[7] sentencing commission monitoring data for fiscal year 1990, and a 12.5 percent random sample from the sentencing commission's file of defendants sentenced in fiscal year 1990.[8] Data for the random sample were augmented by examining computerized and paper case files to identify cases (there proved to be 1,165 defendants) that met statutory criteria for receipt of a mandatory minimum drug or weapon sentence.

The two sources of data on practitioners' opinions were structured interviews in twelve sites of 234 practitioners (forty-eight judges, seventy-two assistant U.S. attorneys, forty-eight defense attorneys, sixty-six probation officers), and a May 1991 mail survey of 2,998 practitioners (the same groups as were interviewed; 1,261 had responded by the time the report was written).

1. *Results of the Sentencing Analyses.* The sentencing data revealed a number of patterns that the commission found disturbing. First, there were clear indications that prosecutors often do not file charges that carry mandatory minimums when the evidence would have supported such charges. For one example, prosecutors failed to file charges for mandatory weapons enhancements against 45 percent of drug defendants for whom they would have been appropriate. For another, prosecutors failed to seek mandatory sentencing enhancements for prior felony convictions in 63 percent of cases in which they could have been sought. For a third, defendants were charged with the offense carrying the highest applicable mandatory minimum in only 74 percent of cases.

Second, there were clear indications that prosecutors used mandatory provisions tactically to induce guilty pleas. For one example, among defendants who were fully charged with applicable mandatory sentence charges and who were convicted at trial, 96 percent received the full mandatory minimum sentence; by contrast, 27 percent of those who pled guilty pled to charges bearing no mandatory minimum or a lower one. For another example, of all defendants who pled guilty (whether or not initially charged with all the applicable mandatory-bearing charges), 32 percent had no mandatory minimum at conviction

---

[7] FPSSIS, pronounced "fipsiss," is an acronym for "Federal Probation Sentencing and Supervision Information System," the Administrative Office of the U.S. Courts' automated information system for federal sentencing.

[8] The FPSSIS and monitoring data are insufficiently detailed to permit the fine-grained factual analyses of actual offense behavior that are required to determine whether facts alleged in specific cases might warrant filing of mandatory-bearing charges. As a result, those data sources are used to provide more general portraits of sentencing patterns over time and in 1990.

and 53 percent were sentenced below the minimum that the evidence would have justified. For a third example, among those defendants against whom mandatory weapons enhancements were filed, the weapons charges were later dismissed in 26 percent of cases.

Third, mandatories increased trial rates and presumably also increased workloads and case processing times. Nearly 30 percent of those convicted of offenses bearing mandatory minimums were convicted at trial, a rate two-and-one-half times the overall trial rate for federal criminal defendants.

Fourth, there were indications that judges (often presumably with the assent of prosecutors) imposed sentences less severe than applicable mandatory provisions would appear to require. Before examples are given, it bears mention that the sentencing commission's "modified real offense" policies direct judges, especially in drug cases, to sentence on the basis of actual offense behavior and not simply the offense of conviction.

Here are a couple of the commission's findings that suggest judicial willingness to work around, and under, the mandatories. Forty percent of all defendants whose cases the commission believed warranted specific mandatory minimums received shorter sentences than the applicable statutes would have specified. Another example: mandatory minimum defendants received downward departures 22 percent of the time. The commission observes that "the increased departure rate may reflect a greater tendency to exercise prosecutorial or judicial discretion as the severity of the penalties increases" (U.S. Sentencing Commission 1991, p. 53). To like effect, "The prosecutors' reasons for reducing or dismissing mandatory charges . . . may be attributable to . . . satisfaction with the punishment received" (U.S. Sentencing Commission 1991, p. 58).

Taken together, these findings suggested to the commission that mandatory minimums are not working. They were shifting too much discretion to the prosecutor. They were provoking judges and prosecutors willfully to circumvent their application (U.S. Sentencing Commission 1991, pp. ii, 76). They were producing high trial rates and unacceptable sentencing disparities.

2. *Results of the Opinion Surveys.*   No category of federal court practitioners, including prosecutors, much likes mandatory minimum sentencing laws (U.S. Sentencing Commission 1991, chap. 6). In one-hour structured interviews, thirty-eight of forty-eight federal district court judges offered unfavorable comments. The most common were that the mandatory sentences are too harsh and that they eliminate judicial

discretion. Among forty-eight defense counsel, only one had anything positive to say about guidelines, and he also had negative comments. The most common complaints were that the mandatories are too harsh, that they result in too many trials, and that they eliminate judicial discretion. Probation officers were also overwhelmingly hostile to the mandatories; their most common complaints were that the mandatories are too harsh, result in prison overcrowding, and eliminate judicial discretion. Only among prosecutors was sentiment more favorable to mandatories, and even then thirty-four of sixty-one interviewed who expressed a view were wholly (twenty-three) or partly (eleven) negative.

Consistent with the interview data, the mail survey showed that 62 percent of judges, 52 percent of private counsel, and 89 percent of federal defenders want mandatories for drug crimes eliminated, compared to only 10 percent of prosecutors and 22 percent of probation officers.

B. The Rockefeller Drug Laws in New York

Perhaps the most exhaustive examination of mandatory sentencing laws before the commission's work was an evaluation of the later repealed Rockefeller Drug Laws in New York. The "Rockefeller Drug Laws" took effect in New York on September 1, 1973. They prescribed severe mandatory prison sentences for narcotics offenses and included selective statutory limits on plea bargaining. A major evaluation (Joint Committee on New York Drug Law Evaluation 1978) focused primarily on the effects of the drug laws on drug use and drug related crime and only to a lesser extent on case processing. The study was based primarily on analyses of official record data routinely collected by public agencies. The key findings were these:

1. drug felony arrests, indictment rates, and conviction rates all declined after the law took effect;

2. for those who were convicted, however, the likelihood of being imprisoned and the average length of prison term increased;

3. the two preceding patterns cancelled each other out and the likelihood that a person arrested for a drug felony would be imprisoned was the same—11 percent—after the law took effect as before;

4. because defendants struggled to avoid the mandatory sentences, the proportion of drug felony dispositions resulting from trials tripled between 1973 and 1976 and the average time required for processing of a single case doubled.

Table 1 shows case processing patterns for drug felony cases in New

TABLE 1

Drug Felony Processing in New York State

	1972	1973*	1974	1975	1976 (January–June)
Arrests	19,269	15,594	17,670	15,941	8,166
Indictments:					
N	7,528	5,969	5,791	4,283	2,073
Percent of arrests	39.1	38.3	32.8	26.9	25.4
Indictments disposed	6,911	5,580	3,939	3,989	2,173
Convictions:					
N	6,033	4,739	3,085	3,147	1,724
Percent of dispositions	87.3	84.9	78.3	78.9	79.3
Prison and jail sentences:					
N	2,039	1,555	1,074	1,369	945
Percent of convictions	33.8	32.8	34.8	43.5	54.8
Percent of arrests	10.6	10.0	6.1	8.6	11.6

SOURCE.—Joint Committee (1978), tables 19, 24, 27, 29.

* The drug law went into effect September 1, 1973.

York during the period 1972–76. The percentage of drug felony arrests resulting in indictments declined steadily from 39.1 percent in 1972, before the law took effect, to 25.4 percent in the first half of 1976. Similarly, the likelihood of conviction, given indictment, declined from 87.3 percent in 1972 to 79.3 percent in the first half of 1976. Of those defendants, however, who were not winnowed out earlier, the likelihood that a person convicted of a drug felony would be incarcerated increased from 33.8 percent in 1972 to 54.8 percent in 1976.

The interpretation conventionally put on the preceding findings is that defense lawyers, prosecutors, and judges made vigorous efforts to avoid application of the mandatory sentences in cases in which they viewed those sentences as being too harsh and that the remaining cases were dealt with harshly as the law dictated (Blumstein et al. 1983, pp. 188–89). Thus, the percentage of drug felonies in New York City disposed of after a trial rose from 6 percent in 1972 to 17 percent in the first six months of 1976 (Joint Committee on New York Drug Law Evaluation 1978, p. 104). In other words, many fewer defendants pled guilty, and the trial rate tripled. No doubt as a consequence of the increased trial rates, it "took between ten and fifteen times as much court time to dispose of a case by trial as by plea," and the average case processing time for disposed cases increased from 172 days in the last four months of 1973 to 351 days in the first six months of 1976. Backlogs rose commensurately notwithstanding the creation of thirty-one additional criminal courts in New York City for handling of drug prosecutions (Joint Committee on New York Drug Law Evaluation 1978, tables 33–35 and p. 105).

Sentencing severity increased substantially for defendants who were eventually convicted. Only 3 percent of sentenced drug felons received minimum sentences of more than three years between 1972 and 1974 under the old law. Under the new law, the percentage of convicted drug felons receiving sentences of three years or longer increased to 22 percent. The likelihood that a person convicted of a drug felony would receive an incarcerative sentence increased in New York State from 33.8 percent in 1972, before the new law took effect, to 54.8 percent in the first six months of 1976 (Joint Committee on New York Drug Law Evaluation 1978, pp. 99–103).

The broad pattern of findings in the New York study, while more stark in New York than in other mandatory sentencing jurisdictions that have been evaluated, recurs throughout the impact evaluations. The combination of the Rockefeller Drug Laws' effects was more than the system could absorb, and many key features were repealed in mid-1976.

C. Massachusetts's Bartley-Fox Amendment

Massachusetts's Bartley-Fox Amendment required imposition of a one-year mandatory minimum prison sentence, without suspension, furlough, or parole, for anyone convicted of unlawful carrying of an unlicensed firearm. An offender need not have committed any other crime; the Massachusetts law thus was different from many mandatory sentencing firearms laws that require imposition of a minimum prison sentence for the use or possession of a firearm in the commission of a felony.

Two major evaluations of the Massachusetts gun law were conducted (Beha 1977; Rossman et al. 1979). Some background on the Boston courts may make the following discussion of their findings more intelligible. The Boston Municipal Court is both a trial court and a preliminary hearing court. If a defendant is dissatisfied with either his conviction or his sentence, he may appeal to the Suffolk County Superior Court where he is entitled to a trial de novo.

The Beha (1977) analysis is based primarily on comparisons of police and court records for the periods six months before and six months after the effective date of the mandatory sentencing law. The Rossman et al. (1979) study dealt with official records from 1974, 1975, and 1976 supplemented by interviews with police, lawyers, and court personnel. The primary findings:

1. police altered their behavior in a variety of ways aimed at limiting the law's reach; they became more selective about whom to frisk; the absolute number of reports of gun incidents taking place out-of-doors decreased, which meant a concomitant decrease in arrests, and the number of weapons seized without arrest increased by 120 percent from 1974 to 1976 (Carlson 1982, p. 6, relying on Rossman et al. 1979);

2. the number of persons "absconding" increased substantially between the period before the law took effect and the period after (both studies);

3. outcomes favorable to defendants, including both dismissals and acquittals, increased significantly between the before and after periods (both studies);

4. of persons convicted of firearms carrying charges in Boston Municipal Court, appeal rates increased radically (Beha 1977, table 2); in 1974, 21 percent of municipal court convictions were appealed to the Superior Court, and by 1976 that rate had increased to 94 percent (Rossman et al. 1979);

5. the percentage of defendants who entirely avoided a conviction rose from 53.5 percent in 1974 to 80 percent in 1976 (Carlson 1982, p. 10, relying on Rossman et al. 1979);

6. of that residuum of offenders who were finally convicted, the probability of receiving an incarcerative sentence increased from 23 percent to 100 percent (Carlson 1982, p. 8, relying on Rossman et al. 1979).

Thus the broad patterns of findings for the U.S. Sentencing Commission and Rockefeller Drug Law evaluations carries over to Massachusetts—more early dismissals, more protracted proceedings, increased sentencing severity for those finally convicted.

D. The Michigan Felony Firearms Statute

The Michigan Felony Firearms Statute created a new offense of possessing a firearm while engaging in a felony and specified a two-year mandatory prison sentence that could not be suspended or shortened by release on parole and that must be served consecutively to a sentence imposed for the underlying felony. The law took effect on January 1,

1977. The Wayne County prosecutor banned charge bargaining in firearms cases and took measures to enforce the ban, suggesting that the likelihood of circumvention should have been less than was experienced in New York and Massachusetts.

There has been one major evaluation of the Michigan law that gave rise to a number of related publications (Heumann and Loftin 1979; Loftin and McDowall 1981; Loftin, Heumann, and McDowall 1983). Several other articles concerning the Michigan gun law have been published, and one of these (Bynum 1982) also discusses empirical data.

The Bynum study (1982) demonstrates how prosecutors control the use of mandatory sentencing laws. Drawing on a sample of cases from a statewide data set collected during the course of a sentencing guidelines project, Bynum identified 426 cases that, from records, involved robberies with firearms that were committed after January 1, 1977, and were therefore eligible for prosecution under the felony firearms statute. In only 65 percent of the eligible cases was the firearms charge filed.[9] More indicative, however, of prosecutorial manipulation of mandatory sentencing laws was the finding that in some courts firearms charges were filed in 100 percent of the eligible cases and in other courts firearms charges were filed in none of the eligible cases (Bynum 1982, table 4.1).

Heumann and Loftin observed a strong tendency in Wayne County toward early dismissal of charges other than on the merits, which they interpret as evidence of efforts to avoid applying the mandatory penalties. Their inquiry focused on three offenses that were relatively common—felonious assault, "other assault," and armed robbery. Armed robbery means in Wayne County what it means most places. "Felonious assaults" tend to arise from "disputes among acquaintances or relatives and are, by conventional standards, less predatory than armed robbery." "Other assaults" is an intermediate category of "assault with intent to . . ." offenses. These three categories offered a severity continuum. Most armed robberies would generally be perceived as serious crimes. Many felonious assaults would commonly be regarded as impulsive and expressive and less serious then armed robbery. Other assaults are more heterogeneous.

Felonious assault disposition patterns did not change after the mandatory penalty provision took effect. There was some increase in early

[9] Heumann and Loftin in their examination of case records to determine the existence and extent of undercharging found that the gun law charge had been made in 96 percent of the eligible cases in Wayne County (1979, p. 407).

dismissal of armed robbery charges and a substantial increase in the rate of early dismissals of "other assault" charges. These findings are consistent with the hypothesis that efforts will be made to avoid application of harsh sentencing laws to defendants for whom lawyers and judges feel that they are inappropriately severe: "other assault" was the offense category in which the greatest ambiguities about culpability were likely to exist.

The probabilities of conviction differed after implementation depending on the offense at issue. Consistent with the Massachusetts findings that mandatory sentences reduce the probability of convictions, Loftin and his colleagues concluded that conviction probabilities declined for "other assaults" and armed robbery (Loftin, Heumann, and McDowall 1983, p. 295).

Loftin and his colleagues assessed the impacts of the Felony Firearm Statute on sentencing severity in two ways. Using quantitative methods, they concluded that the statute did not generally increase the probability that prison sentences would be imposed but that, for those receiving prison sentences, it did increase the expected lengths of sentences for some offenses (Loftin, Heumann, and McDowall 1983, pp. 297–98). Using simpler tabular analyses in an earlier article, they concluded that, overall, the percentage of defendants vulnerable to the firearms law who were incarcerated did not change markedly in Wayne County after implementation of the new law (Heumann and Loftin 1979). As table 2 indicates, the probability of receiving a prison sentence, given filing of the charge, increased slightly for felonious assault and other assault and decreased slightly for armed robbery. The probability of incarceration given conviction also did not change markedly for felonious assault or armed robbery but did change for "other assault" and increased from 57 percent of convictions prior to implementation of the firearm law to 82 percent afterward. This resulted in part from the substantial shift toward early dismissal of "other assault" charges reducing the residuum of cases to be sentenced from 65 percent of all cases to 50 percent.

Finally, trial rates remained roughly comparable before and after implementation except for the least serious category of offenses, "felonious assaults," for which the percentage of cases resolved at trial increased from 16 percent of cases to 41 percent of cases (Heumann and Loftin 1979, table 4). This is explained by Heumann and Loftin in terms of an innovative adaptive response, the "waiver trial." Either by agreement or by expectation, the judge would convict the defendant

TABLE 2

Disposition of Original Charges in Wayne County, Michigan, by
Offense Type and Time Period

	N	Dismissed at/before Pretrial (Percent)	Dismissed or Acquitted after Pretrial (Percent)	Convicted/ No Prison (Percent)	Some Prison (Percent)	Total (Percent)
Felonious assault:						
Before*	145	24	31	31	14	100
After†	39	26	26	31	18	101
Other assault:						
Before	240	12	24	28	37	101
After	53	26	24	9	41	100
Armed robbery:						
Before	471	13	19	4	64	100
After	136	22	17	2	60	101

Source.—Cohen and Tonry (1983), tables 7–10; adapted from Heumann and Loftin (1979), table 3.

Note.—The totals do not always sum to 100 percent because of rounding.

* Offense committed before January 1, 1977, and case disposed between July 1, 1976, and June 30, 1977.

† Offense committed and case disposed between January 1, 1977, and June 30, 1977.

of a misdemeanor rather than the charged felony (which made the firearm law inapplicable because it specified a two-year add-on following conviction of a felony) or would simply, with the prosecutor's acquiescence, acquit the defendant on the firearms charge. Either approach eliminated the mandatory sentence threat and both are consistent with processes described in the American Bar Foundation Survey twenty years earlier to avoid imposition of twenty-year minimum sentences for drug sales (Dawson 1969, p. 201). A third mechanism for nullifying the mandatory sentencing law in cases in which imprisonment would be ordered in any case was to decrease the sentence that otherwise would have been imposed in respect of the underlying felony by two years and then add the two years back on the basis of the firearms law (Heumann and Loftin 1979, pp. 416–24).

E. Observations on New York, Massachusetts, and Michigan Studies

For a variety of reasons, the Massachusetts, Michigan, and New York laws ought to be especially good illustrations of the operation of mandatory sentencing laws. Many such laws are on the books but exist simply as part of a larger statutory backdrop before which the drama of crime and punishment takes place.[10] In these three instances, however, for differing reasons, vigorous and highly publicized efforts were made to make the mandatory sentencing laws stick. In New York, amidst enormous publicity and massive media attention, the legislature established thirty-one new courts, including creation of additional judges, construction of new courtrooms, and provision of supporting personnel and resources, and expressly forbade some kinds of plea bargaining in an effort to assure that the mandatory sentences were imposed. In Massachusetts, while the statute did not address plea bargaining, it expressly forbade "diversion in the form of continuance without a finding or filing of cases," both devices used in the Boston Municipal Court for disposition of cases other than on the merits. (Filing is a practice in which cases are left open with no expectation that they will ever be closed; continuance without finding leaves the case open in anticipation of eventual dismissal if the defendant avoids further trouble.) In Michigan, while the statute did not address plea bargaining, the Wayne County prosecutor established and enforced a ban on plea bargaining in cases coming within the operation of the mandatory sentencing law. He also launched a major publicity campaign, promising on billboards and bumper stickers that "One with a Gun Gets You Two."

Thus, in all three states, the new laws were accompanied by evidence of seriousness of purpose. If mandatory sentencing laws are to operate as their supporters hope they will, the experience in these three states should provide a good test of the realism of those hopes.

Those hopes are unrealistic. Findings from all three states suggest that mandatory sentencing laws are not an especially effective way to achieve certainty and predictability in sentencing. To the extent that they prescribe sanctions more severe than lawyers and judges believe appropriate, they can be, and are, circumvented. For serious criminal charges, the mandatory sentencing laws are often redundant in that offenders are, in any case, likely to receive prison sentences longer than those mandated by statute. For less serious cases, mandatory sentencing laws tend to be arbitrary; they result in either increased rates of dismissal or diversion of some defendants to avoid application of the statute or occasionally result in sentencing of "marginal" offenders in ways that most parties involved consider unduly harsh.

---

[10] For example, the U.S. Sentencing Commission (1991, p. 10) concluded that four of the approximately one hundred federal mandatory penalty provisions then in effect accounted for 94 percent of mandatory penalties imposed.

III. Mandatory Penalties as Instruments and Symbols

George Santayana's admonition that "those who do not remember the past are condemned to relive it" does not capture the policy dilemma posed by mandatory penalties. Officials who support such laws often do not much care about problems of implementation, foreseeable patterns of circumvention, or the certainty of excessively and unjustly severe penalties for some offenders. Their interests are different, as recent policy debates demonstrate. According to a recent *New York Times* article about mandatory proposals offered by New York Senator Alfonse D'Amato: "Mr. D'Amato conceded that his two successful amendments, which Justice Department officials say would have little practical effect on prosecution of crimes, might not solve the problem. 'But,' he said, 'it does bring about a sense that we are serious'" (Ifill 1991).

Supporters of mandatory penalties in anxious times are concerned with political and symbolic goals. Put positively, elected officials want to reassure the public generally that their fears have been noted and that the causes of their fears have been acted on. Put negatively, officials want to curry public favor and electoral support by pandering, by making promises that the law can at best imperfectly and incompletely deliver.

However their motives are portrayed, for many legislators, their primary purpose has been achieved when their vote is cast. They have been seen to be tough on crime. Calls for enactment of mandatory penalties, or introductions of bills, or castings of votes are symbolic statements. Instrumental arguments about effectiveness or normative arguments about injustice to offenders, whether by Sir Samuel Romilly in eighteenth-century England or by Senator Edward Kennedy in our own place and time, fall on deaf ears.[11]

The dilemma is that the public officials who enact mandatory sentencing laws support them for symbolic and political reasons while the public officials who administer mandatory sentencing laws oppose them for instrumental and normative reasons.

The instrumental argument against mandatory penalties is clear. First, they increase public expense by increasing trial rates and case processing times. The U.S. Sentencing Commission study found that

[11] Nearly every major modern American organization that has considered the merits of mandatory penalties has opposed them, including the American Bar Association (1968, standard 2.3, pp. 63–66), the American Law Institute (1962), and, most recently, the Federal Courts Study Committee (1991).

trial rates were two and one half times greater (30 percent of dispositions) for offenses bearing mandatory penalties than for other offenses (12 percent of dispositions); disposition by trial tripled under the Rockefeller Drug Laws (17 percent of dispositions after taking effect vs. 6 percent before); in Michigan, dispositions by trial for felonious assaults involving firearms increased from 16 percent to 41 percent after mandatory penalties became applicable.

Second, in every published evaluation, judges and prosecutors were shown to have devised ways to circumvent application of the mandatories. Sometimes prosecutors simply refused to file mandatory-bearing charges; sometimes plea bargaining was used; sometimes judges refused to convict; sometimes judges ignored the statute and imposed sentences inconsistent with it.

The normative arguments against mandatories are also straightforward. First, simple justice: because of their inflexibility, such laws sometimes result in imposition of penalties in individual cases that everyone involved believes to be unjustly severe. Second, perhaps more important, mandatory penalties encourage hypocrisy on the part of prosecutors and judges. To avoid injustices in individual cases, officials engage in the adaptive responses and circumventions described throughout this essay.

The hypocrisies that mandatory penalties engender are what most troubles prosecutors and judges with whom I speak. Plea bargaining may be a necessary evil, an essential lubricant without which the machinery of justice would break down, but it is typically routinized. Armed robbery is pled down to robbery, aggravated assault to assault, theft 1 to theft 2. Prosecutors, defense counsel, judges, probation officers—all involved—know what is happening, understand why, and acknowledge the legitimacy of the reasons.

Mandatory penalties elicit more devious forms of adaptation. When Michigan judges in the 1950s or the 1970s acquit factually guilty defendants, or when Arizona prosecutors in the 1980s permit people who have committed serious crimes to plead guilty to attempt or conspiracy, or when prosecutors and judges fashion new patterns of plea bargaining solely to sidestep mandatories, important values are being sacrificed. Many practitioners find these processes dishonest and tawdry.

Legislators, whatever their purposes for supporting mandatory sentencing laws, once the vote is cast move on to other issues. For judges, prosecutors, and defense counsel, it is another story. They must live with their own consciences and with their shared views of the bounds of fair treatment of offenders. They must also keep the courts functioning. That they sometimes devise ways to avoid application of laws they believe to be uncommonly harsh should come as no surprise.

If the findings of empirical evaluations of mandatory sentencing laws were heeded, there would be no mandatory penalties. Given the American political climate of the early 1990s, wholesale repeals are unlikely. A more modest hope is that elected officials will become slightly more responsible about crime control policy and balance their felt need to make symbolic and rhetorical statements through passage of legislation with our well-established knowledge of how mandatories operate in practice. Four suggestions for how that might be done follow.

A. Making Mandatory Penalties Presumptive

Much of what legislators hope to accomplish with mandatory sentencing laws could be achieved by making such laws presumptive. In a few states, Minnesota is an example, judges are given authority to disregard mandatory penalties and impose some other sentence if reasons are given. Converting all mandatory penalties to presumptive penalties would sacrifice few of the values sought to be achieved by such laws but would avoid many of the undesirable side effects.

By enacting a mandatory (presumptive) penalty law, the legislature would be expressing its policy judgment that, say, people who commit robberies with firearms deserve at least a three-year minimum prison term. Most prosecutors and judges would accept that such policy decisions are the legislature's to make and that that one is not patently unreasonable. The law's facial legitimacy would presumably cause many prosecutors and judges to deal in good faith with it. The law's presumptive character, however, would let judges take account of mitigating circumstances (the defendant was an underage, bullied, unarmed participant who remained in the car) without resort to subterfuge. That the judge possessed authority to decide that special circumstances rebutted the presumption would signal that prosecutors also could legitimately take special circumstances into account in plea bargaining.

If official circumvention of mandatory penalties in cases where they seem unduly harsh is foreseeable, and it is, conversion to mandatory (presumptive) penalties is likely to result in no less systematic enforcement but to avoid hypocritical efforts at avoidance.

B. Mandatory Penalties and "Sunset" Clauses

Our understandings of the politics and empirical experience of mandatories could be married by including sunset clauses in all future mandatory penalty laws and adding them to existing ones. "Sunset clauses" provide for automatic repeal of a statute at a fixed time unless a new vote is taken to extend its life. This proposal, first made to my knowledge by Alfred Blumstein of Carnegie-Mellon University at a "presidential crime summit" in 1991, would both acknowledge felt political imperatives and limit the damage mandatory penalties do.

Any honest politician will concede two points—that it is often difficult to resist political pressures to vote for tough penalties, and that it is always difficult to vote to make penalties more "lenient." Blumstein's proposal addresses both propositions. If a charged political climate or campaign, or a series of notorious crimes, makes it difficult to resist "tough-on-crime" proposals, such laws will continue to be enacted. Statute books are cluttered with provisions passed on the passions of moments. Often, however, passions subside with time and competing values and calmer consideration make the wisdom of such laws less clear. Sunset clauses would permit laws to lapse without the need for legislators to vote for repeal and thereby expose themselves to "soft-on-crime" attacks.

C. Narrowing Mandatories' Scope

From this point my suggestions for reform of mandatory penalties became less politically realistic. If the bases for passing sentencing laws were concerns for justice and institutional effectiveness, most mandatories would be repealed and few others would be enacted to take their places. That is unlikely. Horrible, senseless crimes do occur, public fears and anxieties are heightened, and elected officials want to respond. There being in practice little that officials can do about crime, the attractions of mandatory penalties as a rhetorical demonstration of concern are great.

If a call for repeal of all mandatories is likely to pass unheard, conceivably a call for a narrowing of their scope might be credible. The most extreme versions of nullification and circumvention involve laws that mandate severe penalties for minor crimes. In eighteenth-century England, juries often refused to convict of capital offenses that were property crimes. In Michigan in the fifties, judges refused to impose mandatory minimum twenty-year sentences for drug sales.

Similar instances of imbalance between the gravities of crimes and the severity of penalties occur in our time. In Alabama, for example, any sale of narcotics within three miles of a school provokes a mandatory minimum. While the goal of protecting children from drugs has obvious appeal, the three-mile radius encompasses all of the area of most cities and towns.

One way, therefore, to bring the symbolic goals of legislators and the instrumental and normative concerns of criminal justice practitioners into better balance would be to confine the scope of mandatory penalties to patently serious crimes like homicide and aggravated rape and to maintain an empirically realistic balance between gravity of crimes and severity of punishments.

D. Reconsideration of Mandatory Penalties

Little public harm would accrue, and considerable private benefit obtain, if correctional or parole authorities were accorded routine discretion to release prisoners serving mandatory terms after some decent interval. Increasing numbers of prisoners are now being held under ten- or twenty-year mandatory minimum terms or under sentences of life without parole. In many states, the steady accumulation of such prisoners promises sizeable long-term increases in prison populations and budgets. More important, many such long-term prisoners continue to be held long after they present any threat to anyone, and long after any clamor for their continuing incarceration has subsided. Under present laws of most states, such prisoners can be released only by pardon or commutation. In our era, these powers are seldom exercised, in part because they make public officials vulnerable to "soft-on-crime" attacks.

The argument for administrative reconsideration of lengthy mandatory sentences parallels the argument for sunset clauses in mandatory penalty statutes—some decisions present such excruciating political problems for elected officials that it is better to eliminate the need to make them. Almost despite the desirability of repealing a mandatory penalty, or releasing from prison an old and harmless prisoner, political vulnerability prevents decisions that on their merits ought to be made. Permitting corrections or parole officials to decide when a prisoner under mandatory sentence has served long enough would remove those decisions from the public eye.

IV. Conclusion

Perhaps unusually for an essay that mostly reviews research, this one does not end with a research agenda. The issues are primarily political and prudential. Basic new insights concerning application of mandatory penalties are unlikely to emerge. Research designs can however be devised that would provide narrower instruction about mandatories. For example, the effects of my proposal for replacing mandatories now in effect might be measured by substituting "mandatory/presumptive" laws for a representative half (or other fraction) of existing mandatory penalties. Thus there would be one-year, two-year, five-year, and ten-year mandatory (presumptive) crimes and one-year, two-year, five-year, and ten-year conventional mandatory-penalty crimes. By use of quantitative time-series analyses of cases disposed before and after the law change and through use of qualitative and quantitative methods to examine case disposition before and afterward, we would learn both how processing of cases changed after mandatories became presumptive and, by comparing case dispositions of mandatories and presumptives afterward, we could learn what differences in case processing the change to presumptive sentences produces.

This is not a realm, however, where research counts for much. Policy debates are likely neither to wait for nor much depend on research results. We now know what we are likely to know, and what our predecessors knew, about mandatory penalties. As instruments of public policy, they do little good and much harm. If America does sometime become a "kinder, gentler place," there will be little need for mandatory penalties and academics will have no need to propose "reforms" premised on the inability of elected officials to make decisions that take account of existing knowledge. As yet, however, America is neither completely kind nor universally gentle, and proposals such as those offered here might provide mechanisms for reconciling the symbolic and rhetorical needs of elected officials with the legal system's needs for integrity in process and justice in punishment.

REFERENCES

American Bar Association Project on Standards for Criminal Justice. 1968. *Sentencing Alternatives and Procedures.* Chicago: American Bar Association.

American Law Institute. 1962. *Model Penal Code (Proposed Official Draft)*. Philadelphia: American Law Institute.

Austin, James. 1991. *The Consequences of Escalating the Use of Imprisonment: The Case Study of Florida*. San Francisco: National Council on Crime and Delinquency.

Baker, J. H. 1977. "Criminal Courts and Procedure at Common Law, 1550–1800." In *Crime in England, 1550–1800*, edited by J. S. Cockburn. Princeton, N.J.: Princeton University Press.

Baldwin, John, and Michael McConville. 1980. "Criminal Juries." In *Crime and Justice: An Annual Review of Research*, vol. 2, edited by Norval Morris and Michael Tonry. Chicago: University of Chicago Press.

Beha, James A. II. 1977. " 'And Nobody Can Get You Out': The Impact of a Mandatory Prison Sentence for the Illegal Carrying of a Firearm on the Use of Firearms and on the Administration of Criminal Justice in Boston." *Boston University Law Review* 57:96–146 (pt. 1), 289–333 (pt. 2).

Blumstein, Alfred, Jacqueline Cohen, Susan E. Martin, and Michael Tonry, eds. 1983. *Research on Sentencing: The Search for Reform*. Vol. 1. Washington, D.C.: National Academy of Sciences.

Blumstein, Alfred, Jacqueline Cohen, and Daniel Nagin. 1978. *Deterrence and Incapacitation: Estimating the Effects of Criminal Sanctions on Crime Rates*. Washington, D.C.: National Academy of Sciences.

Bynum, Timothy S. 1982. "Prosecutorial Discretion and the Implementation of a Legislative Mandate." In *Implementing Criminal Justice Policies*, edited by Merry Morash. Beverly Hills, Calif.: Sage.

Carlson, Kenneth. 1982. *Mandatory Sentencing: The Experience of Two States*. National Institute of Justice, U.S. Department of Justice. Washington, D.C.: U.S. Government Printing Office.

Cohen, Jacqueline, and Michael Tonry. 1983. "Sentencing Reforms and Their Impacts." In *Research on Sentencing: The Search for Reform*, vol. 2, edited by Alfred Blumstein, Jacqueline Cohen, Susan E. Martin, and Michael Tonry. Washington, D.C.: National Academy Press.

Dawson, Robert O. 1969. *Sentencing*. Boston: Little, Brown.

Federal Courts Study Committee. 1991. *Report*. Washington, D.C.: Federal Courts Study Committee.

Hay, Douglas. 1975. "Property, Authority, and the Criminal Law." In *Albion's Fatal Tree: Crime and Society in Eighteenth Century England*, edited by Douglas Hay, Peter Linebaugh, and E. P. Thompson. New York: Pantheon.

———. 1980. "Crime and Justice in Eighteenth and Nineteenth Century England." In *Crime and Justice: An Annual Review of Research*, vol. 2, edited by Norval Morris and Michael Tonry. Chicago: University of Chicago Press.

Heumann, Milton, and Colin Loftin. 1979. "Mandatory Sentencing and the Abolition of Plea Bargaining: The Michigan Felony Firearms Statute." *Law and Society Review* 13:393–430.

Holmes, Oliver Wendell. 1889. "Law in Science and Science in Law." *Harvard Law Review* 12:443–63.

Ifill, Gwen. 1991. "Senate's Rule for Its Anti-crime Bill: The Tougher the Provision, the Better." *New York Times* (July 8, national ed.), p. A6.

Jacobs, James B. 1988. "The Law and Criminology of Drunk Driving." In *Crime and Justice: A Review of Research*, vol. 10, edited by Michael Tonry and Norval Morris. Chicago: University of Chicago Press.

Joint Committee on New York Drug Law Evaluation. 1978. *The Nation's Toughest Drug Law: Evaluating the New York Experience.* A project of the Association of the Bar of the City of New York and the Drug Abuse Council, Inc. Washington, D.C.: U.S. Government Printing Office.

Knapp, Kay A. 1984. *The Impact of the Minnesota Sentencing Guidelines—Three Year Evaluation.* St. Paul, Minn.: Minnesota Sentencing Guidelines Commission.

———. 1991. "Arizona: Unprincipled Sentencing, Mandatory Minimums, and Prison Crowding." *Overcrowded Times* 2(5):10–12.

Loftin, Colin, Milton Heumann, and David McDowall. 1983. "Mandatory Sentencing and Firearms Violence: Evaluating an Alternative to Gun Control." *Law and Society Review* 17:287–318.

Loftin, Colin, and David McDowall. 1981. " 'One with a Gun Gets You Two': Mandatory Sentencing and Firearms Violence in Detroit." *Annals of the American Academy of Political and Social Science* 455:150.

———. 1984. "The Deterrent Effects of the Florida Felony Firearm Law." *Journal of Criminal Law and Criminology* 75:250–59.

Michael, Jerome, and Herbert Wechsler. 1940. *Criminal Law and Its Administration.* Chicago: Foundation.

Miller, Frank W. 1969. *Prosecution.* Boston: Little, Brown.

Moore, Mark H. 1990. "Supply Reduction and Drug Law Enforcement." In *Drugs and Crime*, edited by Michael Tonry and James Q. Wilson. Vol. 13 of *Crime and Justice: A Review of Research*, edited by Michael Tonry and Norval Morris. Chicago: University of Chicago Press.

Newman, Donald. 1966. *Conviction.* Boston: Little, Brown.

Pierce, Glen L., and William J. Bowers. 1981. "The Bartley-Fox Gun Law's Short-Term Impact on Crime in Boston." *Annals of the American Academy of Political and Social Science* 455:120–32.

Pound, Roscoe. 1910. "Law in Books and Law in Action." *American Law Review* 44:12–36.

Radzinowicz, Leon. 1948–68. *A History of English Criminal Law and Its Administration from 1750.* 4 vols. London: Stevens.

Reuter, Peter, and Mark A. R. Kleiman. 1986. "Risks and Prices: An Economic Analysis of Drug Prices." In *Crime and Justice: A Review of Research*, vol. 7, edited by Michael Tonry and Norval Morris. Chicago: University of Chicago Press.

Romilly, Samuel. 1820. *Speeches.* Excerpts reprinted in Jerome Michael and Herbert Wechsler, *Criminal Law and Its Administration.* 1940. Chicago: Foundation.

Rossman, David, Paul Froyd, Glen L. Pierce, John McDevitt, and William J. Bowers. 1979. *The Impact of the Mandatory Gun Law in Massachusetts.* Report to the National Institute of Law Enforcement and Criminal Justice, Law Enforcement Assistance Administration, U.S. Department of Justice, Washington, D.C.

Select Committee on Capital Punishment. 1930. *Report*. London: H.M. Stationery Office.

Shane-DuBow, Sandra, Alice P. Brown, and Erik Olsen. 1985. *Sentencing Reform in the United States: History, Content, and Effect*. Washington, D.C.: U.S. Government Printing Office.

Stephen, James Fitzjames. 1883. *A History of the Criminal Law of England*. (Reprinted 1977. New York: B. Franklin.)

U.S. Sentencing Commission. 1991. *Special Report to the Congress: Mandatory Minimum Penalties in the Federal Criminal Justice System*. Washington, D.C.: U.S. Sentencing Commission.

Kenneth Adams

Adjusting to Prison Life

ABSTRACT

While most inmates, including long-term prisoners, adjust successfully
to prison life, many do not cope well with the pains of imprisonment.
Maladaptive responses such as emotional disorders, self-mutilation, suicide
attempts, and prison misbehavior are most common during the early
phases of incarceration. Most studies show that white inmates more often
exhibit psychological distress than do blacks or Hispanics. Black inmates,
young inmates, and recently arrived inmates are more likely to violate
prison rules than their inmate counterparts. Offenders who have the
greatest difficulty adapting to prison tend to have difficulty functioning
in other environments. Attributes of individuals and of environments
combine to influence inmate adjustment.

Although incarceration is a punishment, and punishment is meant to
be unpleasant, the fact that prisons will always be unattractive places
does not mean that all inmate difficulties can be ignored. While society
no longer demands that inmates leave prisons changed for the better,
it is both counterproductive and inhumane for inmates to leave prisons
in much worse shape than when they entered. Indeed, this principle
has been acknowledged by the courts, which have declared that inmates have a constitutional right to treatment for serious emotional
disorders, including disorders that are instigated or aggravated by
prison experiences. Inmate adjustment problems are important on several counts to people who believe that prisons should perform correctional or rehabilitative functions. When inmates experience continued

Kenneth Adams is associate professor and assistant dean for graduate studies, College
of Criminal Justice, Sam Houston State University.

states of emotional crisis, it is difficult to work toward long-range behavioral change. Less dramatic reactions to confinement provide opportunities for inmates and therapists to focus on current experiences,
emotions, and behavior, with an eye toward personal growth and development.

Issues of prison adjustment are linked to the inmate classification
process, including administrative concerns for security (Toch 1981).
Classification procedures evaluate an inmate's need for various types
of correctional programming and assess the degree of risk that an inmate poses to security, with the goal of matching inmates to institutional settings. These classification concerns are affected by how inmates adjust to prison. Inmates with serious adjustment problems are
poorly situated to participate in correctional programs and can drain
institutional resources by consuming an inordinate amount of staff
attention. When an inmate's difficulties are manifested as disruptive
behavior, adjustment problems necessarily implicate security concerns.

Very often, different institutions have had to deal with the same
offender at different times. Inmates typically arrive at prison with a
long history of institutional experiences, which means that they are
likely to have been in settings where their adjustment was at issue.
Nearly all prison inmates have been in school, many have been incarcerated previously in either juvenile or adult facilities, and some have
been in specialized therapeutic settings such as psychiatric hospitals.
By tracing an individual's behavior across settings and across time, we
can discern individual patterns and sequences of adjustment that are
relevant to both theory and policy. Some individuals show chronic
adjustment difficulties, others adjust poorly to one setting but not to
another, while still others encounter difficulties at a particular point
in life. By studying such continuities and discontinuities, it becomes
possible to identify critical features of individuals, environments, and
stages of development that influence behavior.

This essay examines research on inmate adaptation to prison life.
Section I provides a backdrop for what follows by introducing sociological research on inmate subcultures, including the importation and
adaptation models of inmate behavior, and introduces contemporary
perspectives that derive from stress-coping research and from environmental psychology. Observational and descriptive studies of the
stresses of prison life and coping strategies are examined, as are the
major research strategies and important methodological issues. Sections II–IV, the major part of the essay, review the research on prison

noncoping and maladaptation, chiefly as demonstrated by disruptive behaviors, including disciplinary violations, and by emotional disorders, including suicide and self-injury. The assessment of research findings is organized into three sections that center on the influences of individual characteristics, environmental characteristics, and sentence characteristics.

In Section II, which deals with inmate attributes, the relation of race, gender, age, criminal history, and mental health history to inmate adjustment problems is evaluated. The research confirms that sociocultural factors are at work in the adjustment process and that specific historical continuities in antisocial behaviors and in emotional problems are observed from community to prison. Multiproblem inmates, or offenders with complex adjustment difficulties that combine different types of problem behaviors, constitute a significant segment of the inmate population.

Section III covers aspects of prison settings that contribute to adjustment difficulties. The discussion begins with studies that use administrative schemes, such as security levels, to classify prisons. Next, studies using survey-based measures of prison environments, such as Moos's Correctional Institution Environment Scale and Toch's Prison Preference Inventory, are reviewed. Subsequently, issues of prison overcrowding as well as inmate programming and contact with the outside world are considered. Finally, attention is given to environmental aspects of prison violence. This research confirms that inmate behavior is influenced by contextual or situational factors and highlights the importance of congruence between individual needs and environmental settings in facilitating adjustment.

Section IV discusses research on relations between characteristics of an inmate's sentence and adjustment. In particular, attention is given to how the length and type of prison sentence influence adjustment. The findings of this research are especially timely given the growing number of long-term inmates and the popularity of fixed or determinate sentencing schemes. This section also reviews studies that bear on issues of how adjustment varies over the course of the incarceration experience and that report on patterns and trends in adjustment. Finally, research that relates inmate adjustment to the offender's subsequent behavior in the community is discussed. The early portion of incarceration is a critical period in that adjustment difficulties are most likely to surface at this time, and the evidence suggests that patterns of institutional adjustment are related to postrelease behavior. However, little support is found for the notion that long-term imprisonment is harmful psychologically.

Lastly, in Section V, the implications of research in terms of a theoretical understanding of prison adjustment are discussed and an agenda for future work is outlined. In this section, the problems of inmate adjustment are viewed from a perspective that emphasizes changes over the prison experience and across the life span. Prison adjustment cannot be viewed as an isolated phenomenon. In order to understand fully the reactions of inmates to confinement, it is necessary to place inmate adjustment problems in the larger context of multiple-problem behaviors across time. Adjustment is not a static event. Important changes in inmate attitudes and behavior occur throughout incarceration. Prison adjustment not only is influenced by antecedent life experiences but also has an effect on the offender's subsequent adjustment in other settings. Thus, an inmate's ability to deal with incarceration is contingent on the history of experiences that inmate brings to prison and holds significance for how successful the inmate will be in facing impending extramural challenges.

I. Perspectives on Prison Adjustment

Early researchers were fascinated with the social organization and culture of the inmate community and with the unique and salient features of prisons as organizations. Many of these scholars emphasized the prison's status as a "total institution," meaning an isolated, artificially created, social enclave in which people are subjected to a depersonalizing and totalitarian regimen. Researchers also were concerned with how the organizational characteristics of prisons shaped the social organization of inmates and with how the inmate society in turn influenced the adaptation and functioning of individuals. Early theoretical perspectives emphasized that inmates find solidarity in the inmate code that holds among its central tenets norms of noncooperation and hostility toward staff. The oppositional inmate code, which governs inmate-staff interactions, was seen as a functional response to confinement, allowing inmates to "reject their rejectors" (McCorkle and Korn 1954) and to salvage a sense of self-worth in the face of intense pressures to the contrary. The process of assimilation into the inmate community was termed "prisonization" (Clemmer 1958), an adjustment process in which inmates adopt the normative proscriptions of the prison culture. In addition, there was an interest in studying the social roles of the inmate community (Garabedian 1963, 1964). In many of the early studies of inmate adjustment, the central focus was on the attitudes and values of the prison culture, particularly with regard to the ways in which antiauthoritarian values might impede rehabilitation.

An implicit assumption of most early research is that the institutional features of prisons are so influential and pervasive that they operate as the primary determinant of inmate adjustment. Within this framework, there was, of course, some latitude for accommodating other types of influences. An interest in the variety of inmate roles shows recognition that inmate behavior is not uniform, and attention also was given to the ways in which transitions between prison and community life influence prisoners. However, most of the scholarly emphasis was placed on organizational goals and structures, both formal and informal, that forced the hand of inmates in terms of how they might respond to prison life.

Several developments helped to bring about a shift in perspective. One was that as scholars began to scrutinize the concepts and processes that were postulated to explain inmate adjustment, they found the theories to be lacking in substance as well as in scientific rigor. The "prisonization" hypothesis has been criticized for not paying sufficient attention to key individual attributes, such as race, and to salient forms of inmate social organization, such as gangs (Jacobs 1977). Others have criticized the concept of prisonization as excessively vague and imprecise and have found fault with the ways in which the concept has been measured (Zamble and Porporino 1988; Goodstein and Wright 1989).

The "importation" model of adjustment challenged previously well-established theoretical views. Proponents of the importation model argued that characteristics of individuals that predate confinement (thus, attributes that are "imported" into prison settings), such as criminal history and ethnic culture, are critical factors in determining modes of inmate adjustment. This contrasts with earlier perspectives, subsumed under the heading of the "deprivation" model, which emphasized the restrictive nature of prisons as the dominant factor in inmate adjustment. Initially, the two models were cast as competing explanations of inmate behavior, and an extensive line of research followed in an effort to assess the relative validity of the two perspectives. After many studies reported evidence in support of both perspectives, researchers concluded that attributes of both the inmate and the prison setting were at work in the adjustment process (Wellford 1967; Thomas 1977). The state of knowledge produced by this line of investigation is perhaps best captured by a review of research that concluded that "each individual who experiences prolonged confinement reacts to this situation in an idiosyncratic manner: Some individuals show deterioration in response to confinement, others show improved functioning, whereas others show no appreciable change" (Bukstel and Kilmann 1980, p. 487). Scholars came to recognize that inmates react to prison in a variety of ways, individual variations that could only be described as "idiosyncratic" by the then-prevailing theories. Thus, a stalemate in theory development had been reached, and this led researchers to search for more expansive and integrative models of inmate adjustment.

Two perspectives currently dominate the research on inmate adjustment. The first is the stress-coping paradigm, while the second stems from environmental psychology and emphasizes the transactional nature of behavior, or the processes by which attributes of persons and of settings combine to determine adjustment outcomes. Although these two perspectives are complementary, and in many respects each can accommodate the other, they differ in the emphases they place on various factors.

A. The Stress-coping Paradigm

Stress research originated with the study of physiological reactions to potentially threatening situations. The stress reaction was seen as a psychological trigger for the body's defense mechanisms, and attempts were made to identify stressful conditions that could be linked to changes in blood pressure, galvanic skin response, and heart rate. Recently, the perspective has broadened to include a cognitive dimension, and the current thinking is that inmate adjustment is best conceptualized as a process in which cognition, behaviors, and environments interact to ameliorate or to exacerbate stressful situations (Porporino and Zamble 1984). In this regard, the stress-coping paradigm includes a focus on transactional relations between persons and environments that is compatible with the view of environmental psychologists who advocate an interactionist perspective on behavior.

The stress-coping paradigm (Lazarus 1966; McGrath 1970; Lazarus and Folkman 1983) describes a multistage process that can be used to understand adaptive and maladaptive responses to difficult situations. The coping process is theoretically complex, in that it allows for iterations and feedback between hypothesized stages. The following summary represents a simplified version of the theory. In the first stage, demands are made on the individual in the form of stressors, which can be defined as threats to a person's physical or psychological well-being. The second stage involves an appraisal process with two elements. To begin with, the stressors are recognized and then evaluated in terms of the nature and degree of threat being posed. Subsequently, appropriate reactions to the situation are inventoried and reviewed. Given the same external stimulus, persons may vary in their perceptions and assessments of the situation, and they may vary in their preferred responses. These differences are important for explaining an individual's reaction to stress. The final stage involves the carrying out of the individual's response to his or her situation. Within this framework, unsuccessful coping can result from overwhelming levels of stress, from skewed or counterproductive appraisals of situations, or from deficits in coping skills.

The stress-coping paradigm focuses on a number of considerations in the prison adjustment process: first, the external features of the environment that act as stressors; second, the individual's perception of the situation, particularly with regard to the degree of threat that the stressors pose; third, the influence of a variety of developmental factors such as culture, education, and experience on the coping process; and, last, the repertoire of coping strategies and behavioral responses acquired by the individual over time. Research interests might extend to the range of different coping responses, tendencies for dominant or primary adjustment patterns, deficits in coping repertoires, abilities to acquire new coping strategies, and the effectiveness of coping strategies in terms of whether they diminish initial stress or engender new difficulties for the individual.

B. The Interactionist Perspective

The second perspective on inmate adjustment derives from research in environmental psychology and is grounded in an "interactionist" view in which aspects of the environment influence behavior by making demands that are either congruent or incongruent with an individual's psychological orientation (Murray 1938). Although physical aspects of a setting can be important, the environmental characteristics that most often concern researchers who operate in this tradition involve social-psychological dimensions of the milieu. Some environments are orderly and predictable, other environments feature safety and support, while still other environments highlight freedom, autonomy, and expressiveness. These dimensions of settings, which are sometimes subsumed under the heading of "climate," stand apart from characteristics of individuals, although attributes of groups, such as the mix of persons with whom one must associate, can be critical features of the environment. From this perspective, the probability of adjustment problems is greater when there is a mismatch between persons and environments, and, likewise, adjustment problems can be avoided or remedied by paying attention to issues of congruency (Wright and Goodstein 1989).

These contemporary views of prison adjustment can be seen as building on the findings of prior studies and extending the insights of earlier researchers in new directions. There still exists a concern for identifying the difficulties or "pains" of incarceration that challenge the coping skills of inmates. Similarly, attention is given to organizational and institutional aspects of prisons that influence inmate behavior. Also, there remains an interest in studying patterns of inmate change throughout the incarceration experience. However, contemporary approaches diverge from earlier views by emphasizing at the outset that characteristics both of the individual and of the setting are important determinants of behavior. As corollaries of this view, individual differences in perceptions, needs, skills, and abilities are seen as critical factors in adjustment, and prisons are viewed not as uniform environments, but as organizations that vary along critical dimensions with important differences in settings both across and within prisons. In addition, emphasis is given to the study of behaviors, as opposed to values and attitudes, and there is interest in a broad variety of adjustment problems. As part of this focus, there is an interest in studying multiproblem inmates and the relationships among problem behaviors. Finally, in keeping with the view that adjustment varies across individuals and settings, it is assumed that adjustment varies for the same individual across time. Although many recent investigations highlight the early stage of confinement as a stressful transition period during which a wide variety of adjustment problems are most likely to surface, contemporary researchers join with their predecessors in emphasizing the importance of studying individual patterns of change using longitudinal designs.

C. Stresses of Prison Confinement

Dictionaries define stress as "a mentally or emotionally disruptive or disquieting influence," and students of penology have identified many attributes of prison life fitting this definition. In his classic study of a maximum-security prison, Sykes (1958) identified five categories of stresses experienced by inmates. The "pains of imprisonment," as Sykes characterized them, refer to the deprivations that inmates routinely experience with regard to goods and services, liberty, heterosexual relationships, autonomy, and security. In Sykes's view, these deprivations, which stand at the core of the prison experience, are critical elements for understanding inmate reactions to confinement. The reality of institutional violence threatens an inmate's basic concerns for safety, and the resulting fear-induced stress may trigger fight-flight responses in specific situations or, more generally, may lead to adaptive role behaviors (e.g., "gorilla," "weakling," "punk") organized around themes of dominance and submission in relationships. Similarly, a severe loss of autonomy, as brought about by institutional rules that limit choice in nearly every aspect of an inmate's life, including the most trivial matters, can generate feelings of helplessness and dependency that are inconsistent with the inmate's status of adult. At the extremes, this tension between being treated like a child while trying to be seen as an adult may be resolved in two very different ways. The "center man" (Sykes 1958) undergoes a process of conversion (Goffman 1961) in which the inmate adopts the official view and aspires to become the model inmate. In contrast, the "ball buster" (Sykes 1958) cultivates a posture of intransigence (Goffman 1961) toward staff, taking advantage of every opportunity to demonstrate an attitude of rebellious defiance.

Subsequent investigators have highlighted a variety of other attributes of prisons that can act as stressors for inmates. Environmental overstimulation or understimulation, which occurs when the pace of activities approaches extremes, can tax individual tolerance levels, thereby influencing modes of adjustment (Toch 1977). In prisons, problems of understimulation are likely to be more serious in overcrowded facilities where many inmates are idle. A boring, monotonous, prison routine not only deprives inmates of activities that can distract from personal concerns and difficulties but also often creates additional stress by reinforcing negative feelings such as emptiness, despondency, and despair. Some scholars have pointed to sentencing disparity, which inmates generally view as unfair, and discretionary parole release decisions, which create uncertainty and which inmates often perceive as arbitrary, as stressors (Parisi 1982). A classic study by Mathiesen showed that Norwegian inmates at a progressive, treatment-oriented prison were very uncomfortable with the high degree of uncertainty surrounding staff decisions, such as parole release and the granting of furloughs, that were seen as particularly consequential by inmates (Mathiesen 1965). Finally, Waller (1974) points out that in making the transition from prison to community, inmates face challenges, such as finding employment and reestablishing family relationships, that can be stressful.

Over the years, researchers have both corroborated Sykes's observations and provided information on the relative salience of inmate adjustment difficulties. Zamble and Porporino (1988), in a study of 133 inmates entering Canadian prisons, confirmed that the problems inmates experience in prison differ significantly from those on the outside. The problems of preprison civilian life most often mentioned by inmates are conflicts with a wife or girlfriend (59 percent of inmates), financial difficulties (49 percent), and conflicts with friends (39 percent). At the time of prison entry, the difficulty most frequently cited by inmates is that of being separated from family members and friends (82 percent). Other reported problems include lack of freedom (44 percent), missing specific activities (35 percent), conflicts with other inmates (32 percent), regrets about the past (31 percent), concerns about challenges they will face on release (31 percent), boredom (25 percent), cell conditions (18 percent), medical services (15 percent), lack of staff support (14 percent), personal safety (12 percent), and lack of desired programs or facilities (11 percent). When the same inmates were reinterviewed at four months and again at sixteen months in their sentence, the ranking of problems was relatively unchanged, the most notable exceptions being that concerns about life while on parole (44 percent) were greater in the second interview, as were complaints about cell conditions (31 percent) in the third interview. Roughly half of the difficulties mentioned by inmates in later interviews represented the continuation of an earlier problem. At both the group and individual levels, the researchers found substantial consistency in the types of problems inmates experience during incarceration.

In a study of the difficulties of extended incarceration, Richards (1978) asked two groups of British inmates, serving long and short sentences, to rate the severity of twenty different problems. The results showed considerable agreement in ratings across the two inmate groups, and a lack of contact with family and friends was rated as the most severe problem. Other problems considered serious by inmates, such as missing social life, worrying about how to deal with release, and feeling that life is being wasted, likewise centered on the inmate's relationship to the outside world. A subsequent study comparing the concerns of American and British long-term inmates showed their rankings of problem seriousness to be nearly identical (Flanagan 1980*a*).

Although research suggests that inmates experience many of the same difficulties regardless of sentence length, the element of time can exacerbate common inmate problems into issues of psychological survival for those serving long prison terms. Long-term inmates often fear that relationships will be lost irrevocably, a concern that is not shared to the same degree by short-termers. In addition, long-term inmates typically are older than other inmates, which makes it harder for them to find companions with similar interests, and the fact that most other inmates are serving shorter terms means that many friendships end prematurely (Flanagan 1982). Also, long-term inmates tend to view casual relationships with other inmates along with involvement in the prison social network as increasing the chances of disciplinary problems (Zamble 1992). These observations help to explain why older inmates are less likely to seek out friends in prison (Glaser 1964). Finally, long-term inmates become increasingly concerned over the course of incarceration with difficulties in their relationships with staff and with problems of negotiating the prison bureaucracy (Zamble 1992).

Separation from family and friends is one of the more burdensome problems for inmates, and prisoners sometimes respond to the experience in extreme ways. Inmates who attempt suicide often do so in reaction to the perceived threats that incarceration poses to significant relationships (Rieger 1971; Wool and Dooley 1987). However, the saliency of concern for being separated from family members varies across racial groups, and Hispanic inmates stand out in this regard, a fact that largely is attributable to the importance that Hispanic cultures place on family relationships. Thus, Johnson (1976) reports that psychological breakdowns among Hispanic inmates occur more frequently in reaction to separation from their family. In addition, female inmates tend to suffer more than males from the disruption of important and meaningful familial relationships (Toch 1986), mostly in connection with their roles as mother and wife. Inmates who give birth while incarcerated or who are separated from young children are especially likely to experience feelings of anxiety and guilt (Fox 1982).

Jail inmates likewise demonstrate a strong concern for maintaining relationships with persons on the outside. A comparison of self-injuries between jails and prisons finds that emotional breakdowns among jail inmates more often reflect a need for support from significant others, whereas breakdowns in prison typically reflect a concern for personal safety (Gibbs 1978). Jails present a somewhat different set of adjustment challenges than do prisons. In particular, jail inmates must find ways to occupy large amounts of idle time and must learn to deal with considerable unpredictability and instability in their environment, especially with regard to legal issues (Gibbs 1982a, 1982b). Finally, inmates on death row confront a special set of concerns. When a group of inmates facing execution, many of whom had been on death row for years, were surveyed about their difficulties, feelings of powerlessness were universally expressed, as were feelings of emotional emptiness (Johnson 1981, 1982).

In general, research confirms that separation from and loss of contact with family, relatives, and friends is one of the more difficult features of prison life to endure. In addition, challenges of adjusting to more immediate features of confinement, such as living conditions and administrative procedures, stand out in the scheme of perceived inmate difficulties. The major stresses of prison life are widely experienced, although long-term inmates and jail inmates bring unique concerns to incarceration experiences. Finally, while longitudinal follow-up studies reveal a degree of consistency in the types of stresses experienced over the prison term, the concerns of inmates shift with time, being most notably different toward the beginning and end of incarceration.

D. Coping Styles and Strategies among Inmates

When confronted with stressful and challenging situations, inmates can respond in a variety of ways. In addition to charting this diversity of inmate responses, the task of research also includes studying the efficacy of coping strategies, identifying ways of mitigating adjustment difficulties, showing how preferences for coping strategies are shaped by individual characteristics and experiences, and placing the coping strategies of incarcerated offenders who are in prison in the larger context of the person's behavioral repertoire across different settings and across time. Many studies indicate that prison inmates hold a strong preference for coping strategies that emphasize self-reliance and personal strength. When inmates are asked how they would handle various difficulties, the preferred strategy for nearly every type of problem situation is to deal with the problem by oneself (Flanagan 1980a). This finding has been documented in both American and British prisons, and it is consistent with the "real man" image that many researchers have found the inmate society to hold in high esteem. Although coping strategies of self-reliance may be rooted in the inmate culture, several inmate groups have developed other strategies to deal with distinctive attributes of their situation or with their distinctive psychological needs. Long-term inmates often cultivate a posture of minimum expectation, which involves not hoping for too much in the future, in order to deal with extended confinement (Unkovic and Albini 1969). A related strategy of long-term inmates is to restrict their future time perspective by concentrating on the immediate present and by not planning too far ahead (Sapsford 1978).

Female inmates are especially upset by their separation from family members and have evolved a distinct way of dealing with this stress. Whereas the preference for males is to be tough, self-reliant, and independent, the "real woman" inmate places a strong emphasis on the expression of emotions (Fox 1975). Female inmates are more inclined to look to their fellow inmates for support, and efforts at creating and sustaining personal relationships have a positive influence on adjustment for female inmates but not for males (Zingraff 1980). Female offenders sometimes organize play families with relationships patterned after conventional family roles (Giallombardo 1966). These relationships typically offer emotional and economic support to counterbalance the deprivations of prison life, and sexual relations may be involved if conjugal roles are established (Heffernan 1972). One study finds that newly arrived female inmates are more inclined to join play families, suggesting that these relationships operate as a mechanism for dealing with the transition from community to prison (MacKenzie, Robinson, and Campbell 1989). However, Morris (1987, p. 126) reports that several British studies of penal institutions for females have failed to observe the existence of play families, a finding that may be attributable to shorter prison terms in England discouraging the development of an inmate culture. Finally, Hispanic inmates, who also are disproportionately affected by a loss of contact with family members, sometimes become members of prison gangs, which can serve as family surrogates (Carroll 1974, 1982).

Sexual harassment and assault represent extremely threatening situations that pose difficult adjustment challenges, and inmates often cultivate a violent or excessively masculine posture as a way of dealing with these situations. At least one study has observed that fight responses, including violence, are common reactions to sexual harassment (Lock-

wood 1982a). As a less outwardly aggressive coping strategy, inmates
may strengthen their position by forging an association with a clique
or gang. Inmates who are sexually assaulted or harassed also may attempt to withdraw from threatening situations, such as by spending
more time in their cell, by asking to be transferred to another cell block
or prison, or by enlisting in protective custody. The selection of specific coping strategies is influenced by a variety of factors including
race, subcultural norms and values, aspects of prison confinement, and
personality traits (Lockwood 1982a). Race, in particular, appears to be
an especially significant factor in that white inmates are most inclined
to seek protective custody. In the young adult institution studied by
Lockwood (1982a), nearly all the inmates (90 percent) in protective
custody were whites seeking protection from sexual harassment, even
though white inmates comprised a minority (25 percent) of the prison
population.

Adjustment problems that lead to acts of self-injury have also been
studied in relation to coping strategies. In interviews with several hundred inmates who had injured themselves, Toch (1975) vividly portrayed the attempts of inmates to alleviate themselves of severe emotional distress. He noted that in order to deal with feelings of
helplessness and resentment, inmates might search for a quiet setting
in which they can escape from their preoccupations. Inmates might
also classify themselves as victims and make clear to staff their inability
to deal with this status. When faced with social isolation, some inmates
will panic and make forceful demands to be released from their situation. Inmates also may enlist the assistance of staff in trying to deal
with their difficulties. One strategy, described as self-classification,
involves attempts by the inmate to convince staff that he or she must
be placed in a specific prison environment or setting. As a more direct
approach, inmates will make demands on staff for services, often for
physical problems, which the inmate feels can not be ignored.

Zamble and Porporino (1988), building directly on the work of Lazarus (Lazarus 1966; Lazarus and Folkman 1983), have investigated the
coping strategies of inmates in considerable detail. They found that
the most common inmate coping strategy, one that is used almost
universally, is a reactive approach to problem solving. The distinctive
attributes of this strategy include a failure to show persistence, organization, planning, or anticipation of future results. Over the course
of three interviews, 98–99 percent of the inmates reported that they
approached difficult prison situations in this manner. Other ways in

which inmates frequently tried to deal with problems included efforts at physical escape from problem situations (54–60 percent of inmates across three interviews) and avoiding problem situations (47–53 percent). Consistent with observations that inmates are inclined to cultivate a "real man" image, searching out others for social support was not among the preferred coping strategies (25–29 percent of inmates).

Among the significant findings of this research is that inmate preferences for specific coping strategies are consistent across the prison term. Changes in the proportion of inmates reporting that they used a given coping strategy were not dramatic, the most substantial shift being an increase in the use of palliative strategies, or strategies involving a search for contrasting pleasurable experiences (62–84 percent). Less substantial changes also were noted in the use of strategies that involve reinterpretative appraisals of situations that reduce perceptions of threat (22–35 percent), and the use of self-control techniques to manage emotional responses (19–31 percent). Additionally, the authors observed a striking continuity from community to prison in demonstrated preferences for coping strategies. In both settings, offenders tended to approach problem situations in the same ways. The only significant difference was in the use of alcohol and drugs, a coping response unavailable in prisons but adopted by nearly two-thirds of the inmates while in the community. There was no indication that the choice of coping strategies was affected by prior incarceration experiences, although the rated efficacy of coping strategies for inmates with prior prison terms was lower than that of other inmates (Zamble and Porporino 1988).

Another significant finding relates to the coping strategies that inmates used only rarely. In very few instances did inmates report that they approach difficult situations in prisons in a way that reflects systematic planning or organization (8–14 percent of inmates). The researchers evaluated the majority of inmate coping strategies as entirely ineffective, observing that in many instances the reactions of inmates often made situations worse. Surprisingly, the rated efficacy of coping strategies was greater in prison than in the community, and Zamble and Porporino speculate that this finding can be traced to the fact that prisons structure and constrain behavior in ways that make it more difficult for inmates to create problems for themselves.

Inmates who demonstrated the worst coping skills on the streets prior to incarceration tended to be single, have an unstable residence, show a lack of planning, have histories of alcohol and drug abuse and of psychological problems, and have more extensive criminal records. Given that types of coping strategies and levels of coping effectiveness were found to be consistent from community to prison, we can infer that the same characteristics are typical of inmates who show poor coping abilities in prison.

There remain several important issues to be addressed in future research. In particular, the available research provides little insight into the generalizibility of inmate coping strategies beyond prison settings, across groups of inmates, offenders, and nonoffenders, and in response to a variety of situational problems. The "real man" theme, which is prominently featured in descriptions of the inmate society, may largely be a product of lower-social-class subcultures insofar as it reflects a focal concern for "toughness" (Miller 1958). The "real man" theme also may be a function of settings that are managed along authoritarian lines and that bring together males exclusively. In support of this argument, several investigations suggest that inmate norms and social relationships are influenced by the administrative and management practices of the institution (Grusky 1959; Berk 1966; Street, Vinter, and Perrow 1966). We also know that long-term inmates have developed specialized coping strategies, but we do not know much about how the coping strategies of this group compare with those of shorter-term inmates or with older inmates. We also know something about the coping strategies of inmates who engage in self-destructive behavior, but how do these strategies compare to those used by inmates whose adjustment difficulties are manifested in other ways?

Zamble and Porporino (1988) categorized individual coping strategies in a way that allowed for comparisons between the community and prison. The findings suggest that offenders show consistent patterns of maladaptive behavior across settings and over time. However, this research leaves important questions unanswered. We need to know more about how specific coping strategies are tied to specific problem situations. We also need to know more about how demonstrated preferences for coping strategies vary by important inmate characteristics such as race, gender, and criminal history. Given that 88 percent of Zamble and Porporino's sample was comprised of white males, a situation reflecting the lack of racial diversity in the Canadian prison system, it was impossible for the investigators to study this issue.

E. Researching Inmate Adjustment Problems

In studying issues of prison adjustment, there is a tendency to focus on the problems of inmates. There are several reasons for this emphasis. Problem behaviors capture attention and can be hard to ignore, especially when they represent dramatic instances of coping failure. In prisons, where concerns for security are paramount, serious inmate adjustment problems threaten to undermine the stability of the organization. Consequently, prison administrators keep detailed records on inmate problem behaviors, a situation that facilitates research on the topic. However, an absence of adjustment problems does not imply positive adjustment; we cannot assume that personal growth and development has taken place because adjustment difficulties are not evident. From the standpoint of studying the reactions of offenders to confinement, one of the most significant limitations of current research is the lack of attention to issues of successful adjustment. This shortcoming is especially critical in view of recent metaevaluations of the effectiveness of correctional programs (Gendreau and Ross 1987; Andrews et al. 1990). These evaluations indicate that therapy, education, and work programs can foster prosocial behaviors and attitudes in inmates, and these positive changes may facilitate inmate adjustment within the correctional environment. Issues of successful coping and of positive change represent an important direction for future research if we are to develop a full and complete picture of the ways in which inmates respond to incarceration experiences.

Given that various methodologies have been used in quantitative studies of inmate adjustment, it may be useful to review the approaches taken by several researchers, the first by Zamble and Porporino (1988), and the second by Toch and Adams (1989a). Both studies represent large-scale research efforts that generated significant findings discussed throughout this essay. The former study used structured interviews and survey instruments to measure adjustment, while the latter relied heavily on prison records to study patterns of maladaptive behaviors.

The study by Zamble and Porporino (1988) involved a sample of 133 inmates entering the Canadian prison system randomly selected from categories of short (two to five years), medium (five to ten years), and long (ten years to life) sentences in roughly equal numbers across categories. In addition to collecting background information and psychological test data, the researchers interviewed the inmates on three occasions—at entry and at points about four and sixteen months into the prison sentence. At each interview, inmates were asked to list the problems they experienced in prison. From each inmate's list, three problems were chosen, usually the highest ranked, and inmates then were asked about how they handled the problem situation. The investigators also asked inmates about difficulties they experienced prior to incarceration. The answers to these inquiries were classified in terms of the nature and effectiveness of the inmate's coping responses.

Toch and Adams (1989a) studied inmate adjustment problems in terms of mental disorder and disciplinary violations. They had a special interest in "disturbed-disruptive" inmates or prisoners who showed conjoint patterns of symptomatic and antisocial behaviors. The study involved a release cohort of over 10,000 inmates on whom information regarding disciplinary and mental health status was collected from prison files. More detailed analyses were carried out on a stratified subsample of about 2,500 inmates that overrepresented offenders with chronic discipline and serious mental health problems. For this smaller group, the investigators documented the date and description of behaviors for all instances of symptomatology and prison rules violations recorded in the inmate's files. These data allowed specific behavior to be located in time and patterns of behavior change to be studied over the prison term. Finally, 239 inmates were selected, representing the most extreme instances of maladaptation, and a set of case studies were produced using clinical and administrative records to describe inmates' prison experiences.

Zamble and Porporino (1988) relied heavily on interviews and survey instruments for their data collection, and this strategy has a number of advantages. Most important, it provides for an independent assessment of an inmate's adjustment uncontaminated by the views of prison staff. The strategy also allows for the use of standardized measures of known reliability and validity, some of which may be useful in comparisons with research on nonincarcerated populations. Also, since the data are collected with the researcher's goals specifically in mind, the substantive fit between the types of data collected and the theory or question being investigated can be maximized.

Among the disadvantages, however, is the amount of effort and resources required by this strategy. Research staff need to be trained in interview and survey techniques, and the process of data collection is labor intensive and time consuming. As a consequence, sample sizes tend to be modest. Small samples can be problematic not only because they may affect the results of statistical analyses but also because they make it difficult to disaggregate results and to study important subpopulations such as inmates who engage in extreme or chronic behaviors. Furthermore, when survey and interview methods are used prospectively in a longitudinal design, data collection efforts typically span a long period and lead to practical difficulties, such as obstacles in tracking subjects and sustaining their cooperation, problems of maintaining funding, and liabilities of having to defer data analysis well into the future. Finally, concerns can be raised over the validity of inmate responses to interview and survey questions. Inmates may respond in ways that mirror the perceived expectations of the researcher, that reflect the norms of the inmate society, or that inappropriately capitalize on the presence of a sympathetic listener.

Compared to interview and survey techniques, the use of official records provides for relatively quick, convenient, and economical data collection. Researchers who use official records often are in a position to assemble more observations on a greater number of subjects covering a longer period of time. Larger samples combined with more expansive data sets allow for more statistically reliable and more finely detailed analyses. Expeditious data collection means that the analysis stage is reached more quickly, and, consequently, the findings of the research tend to be more pertinent to contemporary issues and situations. Also, since the information contained in official records often documents the operation of the agency, the data are conducive to the study of policy-relevant issues. Finally, by using some types of prison records, researchers may capitalize on the fact that inmates are under continuous surveillance while in custody.

The use of official records in prison research, however, is not without disadvantages. The front-line staff of the prison system exercise great control over which events and what types of information get put on record. These gatekeeping activities, if not carried out with reference to a known, common set of criteria, can introduce unknown biases into the data that can jeopardize the validity of research findings. Also, since the researcher who uses official records has relatively little control over the data collection process, he or she simply must accommodate situations where information is missing or is not logged in the most desirable format. For these reasons, it is important to use reliable record-keeping systems in which missing data and reporting biases are kept to a minimum. Such systems are typically well-established and reflect circumstances in which staff are motivated to provide accurate information.

F. Issues Surrounding the Use of Disciplinary Records

Given that the overwhelming majority of studies on inmate antisocial behavior rely on official misconduct reports as a source of data, issues surrounding this research strategy transcend the use of disciplinary records in any one study. Prison disciplinary files can be an attractive data source for several reasons. Inmate disciplinary records constitute one of the oldest record-keeping systems in prisons. All inmates are issued a copy of the prison rule book, which means that ignorance of the rules is not a complicating factor, and the identification and reporting of serious inmate misconduct is accorded high priority by the institution. Also, the quasi-legal nature of the disciplinary process helps to insure that records are maintained in a complete and uniform manner. However, prison disciplinary records clearly are imperfect measures of inmate behavior, being subject to detection and reporting biases. The staff component of official data becomes especially important when considering issues such as race and gender differences in misbehavior since it can be argued that these inmate characteristics are implicated in the differential handling of disciplinary incidents by staff.

The few studies that have been carried out on detection and reporting biases in the prison disciplinary system have yielded inconclusive results. Some researchers find evidence of significant underreporting in official records when comparisons are made with self-reported infractions (Poole and Regoli 1980). They also find evidence of racial bias in that blacks are more often referred to the prison disciplinary system, even though levels of self-reported rules violations are comparable across racial groups (Poole and Regoli 1980). However, the conclusion of racial bias is complicated by the findings that an inmate's record of past misbehavior is a major determinant of disciplinary referral decisions and that blacks have more extensive infraction histories than whites. Thus, to the extent that more extensive prior disciplinary histories are not themselves a product of racial bias and instead reflect a greater propensity for antisocial behavior, the conclusion that corrections officers discriminate against black inmates is not supported.

Other researchers also report mixed findings with regard to issues of racial bias. Carroll (1974) notes that black inmates have lower rates of minor infractions but higher rates of major infractions as compared to white inmates. In explaining these divergent tendencies, he observed that black inmates can intimidate white prison staff into overlooking minor infractions, resulting in greater leniency for black inmates, and that the use of confrontational tactics by black inmates can escalate minor violations into major incidents that can not be ignored, leading to more serious disciplinary records centered around refusals to follow orders (Carroll 1974). In this study, issues of racial bias are complicated by the finding that black inmates behave differently toward corrections officers than do white inmates.

Davies (1982), using a particularly inventive strategy, compared official disciplinary reports for assaults with hospital injury records for a prison in Great Britain. The comparison indicates that many violent incidents among inmates are not reflected in disciplinary records, with the rate of underreporting being greater for long-term inmates and young inmates. The author explains these findings by arguing that the attitudes that corrections officers have toward different inmate groups influence the reporting threshold for disciplinary incidents. He speculates that corrections officers afford greater latitude to long-term inmates because they are seen as being under stress and to young inmates because they are seen as naturally rambunctious and troublesome. However, no empirical evidence is presented to support these speculations.

In trying to resolve issues surrounding the research uses of prison disciplinary records, we could examine the considerable body of research on biases in other types of criminal justice records, but many of these studies also have produced conflicting findings and divergent interpretations of results. Furthermore, the conclusions of this research may have limited applicability to prisons because the considerations that enter into the decisions of criminal justice officials may differ by setting. Although it can be argued convincingly that the degree of seriousness or harmfulness of behavior constrains discretionary decisionmaking (Gottfredson and Gottfredson 1980), the specific factors that enter into assessments of seriousness may differ for prison guards as compared to police, prosecutors, and judges. Additionally, prison guards depend to a large extent on the cooperative attitudes of inmates for carrying out their work, and officers have an interest in being perceived as fair and impartial by inmates (Sykes 1958). Otherwise, inmates may become resentful and hostile, making the officer's job more difficult. Furthermore, overzealous recourse to the formal disciplinary process may be interpreted by supervisors as a sign that an officer lacks the skills and abilities to handle problem situations effectively.

These observations suggest that in attempting to understand the operation of the prison disciplinary system in a broader context, we might look beyond obvious similarities between the work of prison guards and police officers and instead look toward the prosecutor's role as a point for comparison. Both prosecutors and corrections officers depend heavily on the cooperation of offenders for carrying out daily work tasks. A prosecutor's decision to press forward with a case nearly always results in a conviction, and almost all disciplinary write-ups by corrections officers lead to the finding that the inmate is guilty. We know that in making charging and dismissal decisions the prosecutor often encroaches on the fact-finding and guilt-adjudging functions of the judiciary. Do corrections officers also selectively process disciplinary cases where the evidence is strong and the probability of conviction is high? Or do members of disciplinary committees take the correction's officers report at face value, failing to act as independent arbitrators of facts, and dismiss an inmate's contradictory report of an incident as self-serving? Or do disciplinary committees fear that the deterrent effects of the punishment system will be compromised unduly if inmates are found innocent and cases are dismissed?

In sum, research confirms that disciplinary records fail to capture all inmate transgressions against prison rules. However, issues of whether differences in rates of disciplinary violations across inmate groups represent the detection and reporting biases of correctional officers or true differences in rates of misbehavior have yet to be resolved. Further research directed at this issue would be very useful in interpreting the findings of a large number of studies on the characteristics of inmates who violate prison rules.

Notwithstanding their limitations, records of inmate misbehavior are an attractive source of data for researchers studying inmate coping and adjustment (Wolf, Freinek, and Shaffer 1966). While an occasional misbehavior report cannot be accorded much significance as an adjustment problem, frequent or systematic violations of prison rules are much less ambiguous signs of adjustment difficulties, especially when the focus is on extreme or chronic offenders. In many situations, use of the prison disciplinary system indicates that informal mechanisms for dealing with the inmate's difficulties either have failed or have been preempted by the gravity of the inmate's acts. An official record of chronic misbehavior suggests coping difficulties in the sense that the inmate cannot establish workable relationships with staff at some minimal level or that the inmate has a conspicuous disregard for the norms that govern prison life and for the safety and security of others. The interpretation of frequent violations of prison rules as a sign of coping difficulty is reinforced further by the implausibility of describing inmate misbehavior as constructive problem-solving efforts to deal with one's situation given that the formal disciplinary process carries serious adverse consequences for the inmate. Finally, by concentrating on patterns of misbehavior and, in particular, on chronic misbehavior, the researcher insures that disciplinary records reflect the judgments of many staff who have observed the inmate in a variety of settings, thereby reducing the chances of significant reporting biases.

II. Empirical Research Findings on Inmate Adjustment

The review of research is organized into three sections: individual correlates, environmental factors, and sentence characteristics. In discussing the relation of these three sets of factors to inmate adjustment, we will separately consider two broad categories of adjustment problems—emotional disorders and disruptive behavior. Under the heading of emotional disorders, a range of mental illnesses—such as psychoses, anxiety, and depression—along with self-injury and suicide attempts is included. These disorders and behaviors, which often are the focus of mental health treatment, are the types of problems that most readily come to mind when thinking of inmate adjustment difficulties. The category of disruptive behavior covers a variety of antisocial acts, many of which represent violations of prison rules, including violence and sexual assault.

A. The Effects of Individual Characteristics on Inmate Adjustment

The individual-level correlates of various adjustment problems are reviewed in this section, starting with a discussion of sociodemographic items, such as age, race, gender, marital status, and employment history, variables that are included in most inmate studies. The focus then shifts to relations between inmate adjustment and criminal and mental health history. These life history variables are important because they illuminate issues of behavioral continuity and discontinuity.

1. *Demographic Correlates—Emotional Disorder.*   A number of studies have found that black inmates are less susceptible to emotional disorder and breakdown than white inmates. Although the number of studies is modest, the findings are very consistent. White inmates are repeatedly found to be more likely to engage in self-injury, both in prisons and in jails (Johnson 1976; Gibbs 1982c). In some instances, the observed differences in rates of self-injury between races are dramatic. In a study of the Tennessee prison system, one-third of white inmates considered committing suicide during confinement compared to only three percent of black inmates (Jones 1976). White inmates demonstrate symptoms of psychological distress, such as confusion, anxiety, depression, and

other mood disturbances, more frequently than do inmates of other races (Jones 1976; Fagan and Lira 1978). The differing propensities between races even extends to death row, where it has been observed that white inmates experience more death anxiety than black inmates (Johnson 1981, 1982).

Exceptions to the pattern that white inmates show more psychological distress than black inmates are few. Goodstein and MacKenzie (1984) found that blacks and whites had the same score on an anxiety scale and that blacks scored higher on a depression scale. The picture also shows some inconsistency when the use of prison mental health services is considered. One study finds no racial difference in the proportion of prison inmates who are hospitalized (Toch and Adams 1989a), while jail studies report conflicting findings as to which racial groups of inmates are more likely to be referred for mental health services (Petrich 1976; Swank and Winer 1976). The extent to which inmate use of mental health services is influenced by processes of self-selection or staff selection is unknown.

Few studies have looked at the psychological problems of Hispanic inmates, perhaps because they do not figure prominently as a group in many prison systems. The available research indicates that Hispanics show a greater concern for being separated from their families, a concern that is especially likely to surface in crisis situations. Johnson (1976) finds that "self-linking," or protests against being separated from loved ones, is a common theme among Hispanic inmates who injure themselves. In contrast, self-injuries for white inmates more commonly reflect neurotic features suggesting that anger and resentment over confinement is being directed inward.

Several hypotheses have been advanced to explain the finding that blacks experience less psychological distress during confinement than do whites. It has been observed that white inmates often are in the minority, a situation that can generate anxiety over personal safety and security (Fagan and Lira 1978). Explanations, however, more commonly focus on differences in culture and socialization between races. In particular, it has been argued that because black inmates show less cultural diversity as a group, they experience a sense of ethnic solidarity that helps buffer the hardships of prison life. Observational studies support this argument insofar as they describe how prison gangs, which are often organized along racial lines, create and sustain personal identities and provide social support, economic benefits, and physical protection to inmates who are gang members. However, quantitative studies of the ways in which gang membership, as well as other inmate group affiliations and social networks, facilitate prison adjustment are lacking.

Other scholars have pointed out that black inmates also disproportionately come from urban ghettos, where life experiences train people in street survival skills that can be used to advantage in prison (Johnson 1976). A variation of this argument applies to "state-raised" youth, or persons who have spent the better part of their childhood and adolescence in institutions (Irwin and Cressey 1962; Irwin 1970, 1980; Bartollas 1982). Presumably, these experiences of prior institutionalization help prepare individuals for prison by familiarizing them with institutional life. However, most of the evidence for this argument derives from observational studies.

It has been found that women prisoners are more likely to have histories of psychiatric treatment (Panton 1974) and are more disposed to self-injury than men (Fox 1975). Also, female inmates are more inclined to use mental health services in prisons, a difference that can be seen most clearly for outpatient services given the small number of female inmates in prison systems and the low rates of hospitalization for inmate populations (Toch and Adams 1989a, p. 13). Similar observations come from British prisons where it is reported that problems of self-injury and psychiatric disturbance are greater in female prisons (Heidensohn 1985) and that many women inmates who injure themselves have a history of self-mutilation and previously have spent time in psychiatric institutions (Cookson 1977). Several factors are involved in explaining the more extensive mental health involvements of female inmates. It has been observed that women feel the pains of separation from family and children more sharply than men and that women often use self-injury as a form of emotional catharsis (Fox 1975, 1982). Also, the majority of women report being physically and sexually abused as children (Chesney-Lind and Rodriquez 1983), and research confirms that abusive childhood experiences are associated with violent behavior and emotional difficulties in adulthood (Widom 1989).

With regard to other individual characteristics, older inmates (over forty-five years of age) have been described as disproportionately involved in reports of psychological problems (Jones 1976). Similarly, inmates who are committed to psychiatric hospitals from prison tend to be older (Toch and Adams 1989a), as are jail inmates referred for mental health services (Petrich 1976). Inmates who require mental health assistance are more likely to be unmarried (Petrich 1976; Swank and Winer 1976; Toch and Adams 1989*a*) and to be living alone around the time of the offense for which they were incarcerated (Toch and Adams 1989*a*).

2. *Demographic Characteristics—Suicide and Self-Injury.* Inmate suicides and self-injuries are a major problem in correctional institutions. Davies (1982) reports that 12 percent of inmate injuries are self-inflicted. Acts of self-mutilation and self-injury among institutionalized populations appear to be motivated by a variety of concerns including rage, frustration, retaliation, contagion, conformity, and secondary gain (Feldman 1988). There have been two comprehensive reviews of the research on inmate suicide, one of which has been carried out very recently by the British Home Office (Burtch and Ericson 1979; Lloyd 1990). The rate of suicide among inmates is greater than that among demographically comparable groups in the community, suggesting that typical incarceration experiences not only trigger preexisting tendencies but enhance the attractiveness of self-destructive solutions to one's problems. In general, young offenders, males, unmarried offenders, and offenders who abuse alcohol and drugs are more predisposed to suicide. In this regard, suicidal inmates tend to resemble inmates who are most unruly. In many instances, suicidal inmates have a history of psychiatric disorder, although it is unclear if the rate of mental illness for suicidal inmates is higher than for the general inmate population. In addition, many studies find that prison inmates who attempt suicide have been convicted of a violent offense, suggesting a relation between self-directed and other-directed violence. In jails, however, where the range of offense behavior among the inmate population is greater, many suicidal inmates are charged with minor offenses. Also, suicides are more likely to occur in the early stages of incarceration, especially in jails where the first few days of confinement represent the highest risk period.

3. *Demographic Characteristics—Prison Misbehavior.* The research on inmate misbehavior reveals many similarities with more general studies of criminality. Many investigators find racial differences in disciplinary involvement, with black inmates being more unruly and white inmates being more prone to victimization. In addition, young inmates reliably surface as most disruptive. Although the interpretation of these findings is controversial, most explanations of racial differences focus on subcultural differences while explanations of age differences focus on processes of learning and maturation. The profile of inmates who experience disciplinary problems in prison indicates that these persons have

led relatively marginal lives in the community, having unimpressive records of accomplishment in domestic, educational, and occupational spheres of life. Although it is unclear how the infraction rates of females compare to that of males, the attributes that distinguish female infractors tend to be similar to those that distinguish male infractors.

A large variety of individual characteristics have been studied in relation to prison misbehavior, and among the best-researched correlates are age and race. Many studies find substantial racial differences in rates of disruptive behavior, although the picture that emerges from the research is not entirely consistent. A number of studies report that blacks are more likely to be charged with institutional rules violations (Poole and Regoli 1980; Flanagan 1983; Ramirez 1983; Goetting and Howsen 1986; Toch and Adams 1989a; Wright 1989) and are disproportionately represented among chronic disciplinary violators (Myers and Levy 1978). When prison staff are asked to identify well-adjusted inmates, they more frequently point to white inmates (Coe 1961). On occasion, however, researchers find that whites have higher prison infraction rates than blacks (Johnson 1966), although the more common finding is of no racial differences in infraction rates (Wolfgang 1961; Ellis, Grasmick, and Gilman 1974). A study of the disciplinary involvement of inmates across three state prison systems captured the range of mixed results: in California white inmates had higher infraction rates than black inmates, in Texas black inmates had higher rates, while in Michigan infraction rates were indistinguishable across racial groups (Petersilia and Honig 1980).

Studies on the characteristics of inmate aggressors and their victims more reliably find racial differences. In general, the research indicates that black inmates are more likely to be aggressors and white inmates to be victims (Fuller and Orsagh 1977; Toch 1977). Similar racial differences in aggressor and victim roles have been observed for sexual assaults (Davis 1968; Carroll 1974; Jones 1976; Lockwood 1980). In general, as compared to studies of general prison misbehavior, the research on aggressive and violent behavior shows more consistent racial differences. No study has yet to report that black inmates are less aggressive than white inmates. While it is possible that the appearance of consistency in research findings is a function of the modest number of studies on prison victimization and sexual violence, scholars have advanced several explanations to account for the findings. The most common explanations argue that a greater degree of aggressive behavior among black inmates can be traced to the cultivation of subcultural values that promote violence. Along these lines, scholars have suggested that racial differences in prison misbehavior are largely a function of differences in prior criminal history or in urban-rural experiences, and these arguments find some support in the research. In several instances, it has been shown that the disciplinary rates of black and white inmates are nearly identical when inmates with equivalent criminal histories (Wright 1989) or with similar backgrounds (Goodstein and MacKenzie 1984) are compared. However, more direct tests of subcultural explanations, for example, studies that directly measure subcultural values or that identify violence as a specific coping style among racial groups, have yet to be carried out among prison inmates.

Age has proven to be the strongest, most robust correlate of prison misconduct (Hanks 1940; Schnur 1949; Zink 1958; Wolfgang 1961; Johnson 1966; Jensen 1977; Myers and Levy 1978; Mabli et al. 1979; Petersilia and Honig 1980; Flanagan 1983; Goetting and Howsen 1986; Toch and Adams 1989a). Younger inmates have been shown to have consistently higher infraction rates than older inmates, a finding that has been replicated across several countries, including the United States, Canada, and England. Also, the propensity for younger inmates to be disruptive extends throughout incarceration. Younger inmates have higher infraction rates across all points of the prison term (Toch and Adams 1989a).

There are many views on why youth is associated with antisocial behavior, delinquency, and crime (Hirschi and Gottfredson 1983; Greenberg 1985; Farrington 1986); the research on prison misbehavior offers several clues. Fox (1958) characterizes disciplinary offenders, who tend to be young, as less mature and less well adjusted. Toch and Adams (1989a) report that for young inmates of the same age, those at the end of their prison term have lower infraction rates than those at the beginning. This finding, that younger, more rambunctious inmates tend to settle down independent of the effects of chronological aging, can be interpreted as evidence of learning and maturation. MacKenzie (1987) finds that even though they are more frequently cited by staff for misconduct, younger inmates do not report having more conflicts with inmates and guards. She also finds that young inmates with high infraction rates tend to be more assertive than other inmates. These findings suggest that a major source of the difficulties that younger inmates have with the prison disciplinary system is their preference for resolving conflicts in ways that are demonstrably visible and that advertise toughness and strength.

Particularly noteworthy in this context are the findings reported by Zamble and Porporino (1988). They find that the correlations of infraction rates with age ($r = -.27$) and with ratings of coping efficacy ($r = -.28$) are virtually identical. Furthermore, they find that age ranks fourth in terms of strength of relationship with infraction rates, behind drug use, negative perceptions of prison, and number of friends, when using a stepwise regression procedure. These findings are interesting on a number of counts. First, when psychological variables are measured directly (e.g., coping efficacy), the strength of the relation with infraction rates is the same as that of chronological age, suggesting that attempts to identify intervening processes that might explain the relation of age to antisocial behavior should prove fruitful. Second, a history of maladaptive coping strategies in the community (e.g., drug use) is a strong predictor of prison misbehavior. Third, the findings highlight the importance of contextual influences on prison misbehavior; inmates who keep to themselves and have few friends are less inclined to get into trouble, while gregarious inmates more often run afoul of institutional rules. Finally, inmates with disciplinary problems more generally view their situation in prison as bothersome, suggesting that negative cognitive perceptions are implicated in unsuccessful coping and adaptation.

A variety of other inmate characteristics have been studied in relation to prison misbehavior, including sex, marital status, drug use, emotional disorder, mental retardation, criminal history, prior incarceration experiences, employment history, and educational achievement. Discussion of the relation of mental illness and mental retardation to disciplinary involvement is reserved for a later section on multiproblem inmates. Regarding sex differences in prison misbehavior, there is mixed evidence on the question of whether the infraction rates of female inmates differ from those of males. A national survey of inmates in state prisons (Goetting and Howsen 1986) found that women have lower rates of self-reported rules violations. In addition, Toch and Adams (1989a, p. 13) observed that female inmates had lower disciplinary infraction rates than their male counterparts. However, other studies find that female inmates have higher infraction rates (Lindquist 1980). It also has been reported that female prisons in Great Britain have higher infraction rates than male prisons, although the difference is mostly accounted for by minor offenses (Morris 1987). Studies of female infractors indicate that those who are more likely to violate prison rules are young, black, unmarried, without children, and have been convicted of a violent or drug-related offense (Faily and Roundtree 1979; Roundtree, Mohan, and Mahaffey 1980). Thus, female infractors share many of the characteristics of their male counterparts.

Results regarding other characteristics of individuals are generally mixed. For the most part, the inconsistency in research findings can be attributed to studies that fail to show relationships. However, putting these studies aside, those studies in which significant relationships do emerge often reveal very similar findings. That is, by focusing on the nature of relations when they are observed, a substantial degree of consistency can be observed in research results.[1] In general, the research shows that inmates with higher infraction rates are more likely to be unmarried (Jaman 1972; Myers and Levy 1978; Toch and Adams 1989a), high school dropouts (Zamble and Porporino 1988; Wright 1991a) who are unemployed prior to incarceration (Goetting and Howsen 1986; Toch and Adams 1989a), who use drugs (Flanagan 1983; Zamble and Porporino 1988), and who have a history of mental health treatment (Adams 1983; Toch and Adams 1989a). Thus, offenders with the most marginal lifestyles in the community, who are least successful at negotiating conventional social interactions, and who repeatedly demonstrate deviant and maladaptive patterns of behavior are the inmates who are most likely to have trouble adjusting to prison life.

B. Criminal History

Research on the relation of criminal history variables to inmate adjustment shows mixed findings, and it is unclear how histories of offense behavior and prior institutional experiences influence inmate behavior. However, the research underscores the significance of past violence for incarcerated offenders. Inmates with a history of violent criminal offenses are more likely to require mental health services and to injure themselves. They also have higher disciplinary infraction rates. These findings indicate that propensities for violence are implicated in a variety of prison adjustment problems.

[1] There are a variety of statistical reasons why studies might not find a relation between two variables, and therefore to interpret all negative findings as having substantive significance can be misleading. Some reasons include multicollinearity among variables, differences in measurement levels between variables, and differences in the distribution of observed values across samples. This is not to argue that negative findings can be dismissed summarily as unimportant. However, given the limited information we have about some issues of prison adjustment, alternative ways of viewing the evidence may be useful.

Aspects of criminal history distinguish inmates who show signs of serious emotional problems in both prisons and jails. Compared to other inmates, those who require psychiatric hospitalization are more likely to stand convicted of rape, murder, and assault; to have a history of violence; and to have served a previous prison sentence (Toch and Adams 1989a). Among jail inmates, those requiring mental health assistance are disproportionately felony offenders (Petrich 1976; Swank and Winer 1976) with a prior arrest history (Petrich 1976). When comparisons are made between jail inmates who injure themselves and the general inmate population, it is found that inmates who engage in self-injury are more likely to have been incarcerated previously and to have charges pending for a violent crime (Gibbs 1978, 1982c).

In contrast, criminal history items show inconsistent associations with prison infraction rates. Brown and Spevacek (1971) find that high-rate infractors have fewer juvenile offenses and prior felonies, while other researchers report that a history of juvenile offending is related to higher rates of prison misbehavior (Zamble and Porporino 1988). With regard to institutional experiences, a similar mixed pattern emerges. Some studies find that chronic infractors are more likely to be first-time inmates (Toch and Adams 1989a) or that prior prison experience facilitates adjustment (Wolfgang 1961), while others indicate that prior incarceration has a positive relation to infraction rates (Goetting and Howsen 1986). The picture, however, becomes more consistent when types of conviction offenses are considered. Research generally indicates that violent offenders tend to have higher prison infraction rates than nonviolent offenders (Flanagan 1983; Ruback, Carr, and Hopper 1986; Toch and Adams 1989a), although inmates convicted of murder are a reliable exception to the rule (Wolfgang 1961; Jaman 1971; Flanagan 1983; Toch and Adams 1989a). Nonfelony murderers, or murderers lacking substantial premeditation, show better adjustment to prison (Wolfgang 1961), arguably because the offense is situationally influenced and because the offender fails to see violence as a legitimate solution to problem situations. One study found that inmate custody classifications, which were mostly determined by past disciplinary record, predicted future adjustment, as measured largely by disciplinary infractions (Hanson et al. 1983). Thus, past antisocial behavior within prisons predicts similar future behavior, a relation that has been well documented in community settings.

Some research suggests that offenders who by virtue of their past behavior demonstrate an obstinate commitment to antisocial acts are more likely to become troublemakers while in prison. The inconsistency of research findings, however, suggests that criminal history and offense variables operate as less than perfect proxies for individual dispositions that hold more direct associations with prison antisocial behavior. This conclusion suggests that the study of these intervening variables, as they relate both to criminal careers and to prison misbehavior, is an important direction for future research.

C. Mental Health History

Inmates who are most vulnerable to psychological breakdown are those who have shown evidence of emotional difficulties in the past. Prison inmates, for example, who are hospitalized for emotional problems often have received psychiatric treatment prior to incarceration. Offenders with histories of mental health involvement also tend to be more disruptive and violent in mainline correctional settings. However, personality studies of chronically disruptive inmates have failed to identify factors that can account for these propensities.

A substantial number of prison and jail inmates have been clients of mental health systems, although it is debatable whether rates of emotional disorder are higher for offender populations than for demographically comparable groups in the free world (Monahan and Steadman 1983). These findings, however, have become more significant with deinstitutionalization and the community mental health movement because some scholars suspect that these developments have led to an increasing number of mentally ill offenders being handled by the criminal justice system (Abramson 1972; Teplin 1983).

For a combination of reasons that pertain to the etiology of emotional disorders, the efficacy of treatment interventions, and the stressful nature of prison environments, we might suspect that a history of psychological treatment is a major risk factor for serious emotional difficulties in prison. One study reports that six out of ten psychiatrically hospitalized inmates had been hospitalized previously (Toch and Adams 1989a), while overall fewer than one in ten inmates had a pre-prison history of psychiatric commitment. Also, inmates with a pre-prison history of psychiatric hospitalization are committed earlier in the sentence than inmates who lack a comparable history (Toch and Adams 1989a). The timing of prior hospitalizations is an important aspect of risk in that inmates with recent psychiatric histories in the community are most likely to be hospitalized while in prison (Toch and Adams 1989a).

Similar evidence on the continuity of emotional disorders across community and institutional settings has been reported for jail inmates. Among jail inmates referred for mental health services, one study found that almost three-fifths had a history of prior psychiatric treatment and two-fifths had a prior psychiatric hospitalization (Swank and Winer 1976). Another study found that about one-third of jail inmates referred for mental health services had previously attempted suicide (Petrich 1976). Other researchers have observed that jail inmates with histories of psychological problems or of substance abuse are most likely to experience emotional difficulties during incarceration (Gibbs 1978, 1987). It should be noted, however, that the appearance of symptomatology is not limited to inmates with histories of psychological problems, suggesting that aspects of the jail environment contribute to inmate adjustment problems.

The psychological attributes of inmates who are chronic disciplinary violators have been researched extensively; the instrument most often used in clinical assessments of disruptive inmates is the Minnesota Multiphasic Personality Inventory (MMPI). The popularity of the MMPI in inmate research results not only from its widespread use in many other institutional and community settings but also from the work of Megargee in the federal prison system. In a highly significant project, Megargee and associates (Megargee and Bohn 1979) studied a group of federal inmates and by means of pattern analytic statistical techniques developed a typological classification system based on MMPI test scores. The typology includes ten categories or types of inmates, with each type representing a different modal pattern of test scores. Although the description of the typology is complex, given that each type summarizes a set of patterned relationships among scores on the eight MMPI subscales, the types can be ranked from least to most deviant.

Some researchers have successfully used clinical data to identify disruptive inmates (Myers and Levy 1978), and Megargee reports that his typology of personality profiles can distinguish antisocial inmates when properly classified (Edinger 1979; Megargee and Bohn 1979). However, a substantial number of studies have failed to distinguish high-rate or violent disciplinary infractors by means of MMPI personality test scores (Jaman et al. 1966; Watman 1966; White 1980). One study found the Megargee typology to have little relation to prison adjustment, which was defined primarily in terms of prison misbehavior (Hanson et al. 1983). Another study found that the typology lacked predictive validity in terms of differentiating aggressive or violent inmates from other inmates and failed to discriminate between inmates with violent and nonviolent conviction offenses (Louscher, Hosford, and Moss 1983). Other studies found that the typology is unstable in that individual classifications change with repeated measurement over a short period of time (Johnson, Simmons, and Gordon 1983).

A serious problem with much of the research using the Megargee typology is that investigators rely exclusively on computers for test scoring and inmate classification, even though the accurate classification of inmates requires substantially more effort. Very often, a significant proportion of inmates can not be uniquely classified by computer, and Megargee himself had to reclassify over 30 percent of the original sample by means of clinical resolution techniques. In general, however, studies of the relationship between MMPI test scores and prison misbehavior have yielded disappointing results.

Although personality tests have yet to offer a neat and efficient way of categorizing disruptive inmates, some of the results of this research are informative. Some researchers report that the Megargee inmate type with the most violent background is the most disruptive in prison (Louscher, Hosford, and Moss 1983). Similarly, another study found that inmates with deviant personality types were overrepresented among assaulters and aggressors (Wright 1991a). These results suggest that some dimensions of personality tap into chronicity of antisocial behavior and that deviant personality profiles tend to be associated with violence.

D. Multiproblem Inmates

Inmates who have the greatest difficulty negotiating prison experiences demonstrate a variety of problems throughout their lives. Offenders with psychiatric histories tend to be disciplinary and management problems in prison (Adams 1983, 1986; Toch and Adams 1986, 1989a). Severely disturbed inmates tend to have extensive histories of alcohol and drug abuse and often show clinically significant patterns of early, chronic antisocial behavior (Collins, Schlenger, and Jordan 1988; Abram and Teplin 1991). Mentally retarded inmates, a group that is disproportionately victimized in prison settings and that has higher-than-average disciplinary infraction rates, also may have emotional disorders. In many instances, the combination of limited intellectual abilities and mental illness exacerbates inmate adjustment difficulties (Finn 1989).

The problems of inmates can extend to many different areas including intellectual functioning, educational achievements, interpersonal relationships, mental health, family life, work experiences, and use of alcohol and drugs. We can predict that inmates who can be characterized as multiproblem individuals will experience more serious challenges in adjusting to prison life by virtue of their having a greater number of social and psychological deficits. While many types of problems may combine to produce compound adjustment difficulties, most of the prison research has focused on constellations of disruptive behavior, serious emotional disorders, mental retardation, and victimization. Questions of how learning disorders, physical disabilities and other health problems, and specific deficits in cognitive, intellectual, and emotional functioning relate to compound problems of adjustment remain to be investigated in the future.

Several studies find that inmates with a record of psychiatric treatment, either before or during incarceration, have substantially higher levels of disciplinary involvement than other inmates, and the difference holds for violent as well as nonviolent infractions (Adams 1983, 1986; Toch and Adams 1986, 1989a). Most recently, it has been shown that seriously depressed inmates are more violent toward themselves, that highly confused or disoriented inmates are more violent toward others, and that inmates who are both depressed and confused are more destructive of property (Baskin, Sommers, and Steadman 1991). A plausible interpretation of these findings is that serious emotional and psychological deficits are implicated in higher rates of antisocial behavior for some inmates. This argument receives additional support from a study showing that black inmates who suffer from serious mental illness are among the most disruptive inmates (Toch, Adams, and Greene 1987), a finding that may be produced by a pathological process whereby culturally acquired attitudes of suspiciousness frequently observed among black inmates are exaggerated into paranoia.

Emotional disorders and antisocial behavior are often related. Toch and Adams (1989a) have confirmed that a small group of seriously mentally ill inmates account for a disproportionate number of disciplinary infractions. They also found that the symptomatic and disruptive behaviors of severely disturbed inmates frequently cluster together in time. Behavioral clusters reflecting both symptomatology and disruptiveness were found to be more common than clusters with only one type of behavior for multiproblem inmates. Williams and Longley (1987) similarly found psychiatric history to be a key factor in their empirically derived classification of highly disruptive prisoners.

Further evidence for a link between emotional disorder and antisocial behavior can be seen in the types of infractions committed by mentally ill inmates. Disturbed inmates are less often involved in contraband and escape, findings that may reflect the marginal social status of mentally ill prisoners, and they are more likely to engage in acts suggesting peculiar or extreme emotional states, such as self-injury, throwing feces, and arson (Toch and Adams 1989a). In his study of prison assaults, Davies (1982) found that "odd behavior," or behavior peculiar enough to result in hospital observation, was a significant cause of violence between inmates. Although these findings indicate that emotionally disturbed inmates engage in violent behaviors, we must be careful not to exaggerate the link between mental illness and violence. Toch and Adams (1989a) found that nearly half (47 percent) of all disturbed-disruptive behavior episodes could be characterized as nonviolent-nonpsychotic, while only a very small minority (4 percent) of episodes were classified as violent-psychotic. These findings indicate that stereotypical views of disturbed offenders as irrationally violent characterize only a very small portion of the offender spectrum.

Inmates with limited intellectual abilities constitute another group of offenders who often show multifaceted adjustment problems. In a survey of administrators of state correctional systems, Brown and Courtless (1971) received reports that mentally retarded inmates were more often subject to disciplinary action than were other inmates. The administrators cited an inability to comprehend rules, scapegoating, and limited competence in concealing prison rules violations as reasons for the disproportionate involvement of mentally retarded inmates in rules violations. In addition, a majority of those surveyed indicated that mentally retarded inmates tend to be manipulated and victimized by other inmates. The forms of abuse include extortion, exploitation, ridicule, and incitement to violation of prison rules (Brown and Courtless 1971). These findings recently have been confirmed by Finn (1989), who reports that mentally retarded inmates have higher disciplinary infraction rates, especially for incidents that involve violence and self-injury. The research also showed that inmates who are both mentally retarded and mentally ill have higher symptom rates than other diagnosed inmates as well as the highest rates of violent and nonviolent infractions across all categories of intelligence level and patient status. In addition, Finn (1989) observed that a larger-than-expected proportion of mentally retarded inmates could be described as "late reformers," meaning that they persisted in having relatively high infraction rates until the last phase of incarceration. She interprets this pattern to be one of delayed adjustment resulting from a slower learning process.

There have been several descriptive studies of inmates who are prone to be victimized. The topic is a difficult one to study, however, since many victimizations go unobserved and unreported, and inmates can be reluctant to discuss victimization experiences with researchers. In general, predatory inmates tend to select as victims inmates who are perceived to be weak and easy targets, either because they are physically unimpressive or because they are intellectually or emotionally limited. The potential rape victim has been described as a small, young, white, middle-class inmate convicted of a crime against a child or of a minor property crime. Sex offenders, especially child molesters, as well as homosexuals are frequently seen as attractive victims either because their offense is viewed as reprehensible by the inmate culture or because they show signs of physical and emotional weakness. Victim-prone inmates also tend to be socially isolated, cooperative with the prison administration, and lacking mental toughness and street survival skills (Bowker 1980, 1982). Several empirical studies support these observations. Lockwood (1980) finds that white inmates are often perceived as weak because they lack significant group affiliations and consequently are more likely to be targeted for sexual assault. Brown and Courtless (1971) and Denkowski and Denkowski (1985) report that mentally retarded inmates are disproportionately victimized, Toch (1977) observes that victimized inmates often have a history of emotional disorder, and Wright (1991a) finds that offenders with the most disturbed personality profiles are overrepresented among victimized inmates. Lastly, one study finds that victimization rates parallel assault rates in that both rates decline with age (Fuller and Orsagh 1977). The downward trend in victimization rates with age can be misleading, however, since propensities to be victimized and to be assaultive go hand-in-hand. When adjustments are made for differences in assault rates, research indicates that the oldest inmates are more likely to be victimized.

The general pattern of chronicity in adjustment difficulties observed among multiproblem inmates argues for a more extended perspective tying together various coping deficits and related manifestations of adjustment problems. Multiproblem individuals raise questions that pertain to interrelationships among problem behaviors, and these questions are directly relevant to how we explain multifaceted adjustment difficulties. For example, should criminal offenses in the community and prison misconduct be viewed as related indications of an underlying tendency for antisocial behavior? Does self-inflicted violence share features with violence directed at others suggesting a common motivation? Is substance abuse a cause or a consequence of antisocial tendencies? Of emotional problems? How do limited intellectual abilities aggravate other propensities for problem behavior? Answers to questions such as these, which involve patterns of problem behaviors over time and across environments, may help to illuminate the stability of personal coping styles. They may also lead to a better understanding of the interrelationships between types of adjustment difficulties. How different types of problems relate to each other also is important because it challenges a tendency for compartmentalized thinking about behavior, a tendency that is all too often reflected in turf wars among different helping professions and among types of intervention programs.

III. Environmental Factors

The experience of imprisonment varies considerably both between and within institutions. Aspects of a prison's architecture, regime, inmate population, staff, living arrangements, and program activities all combine to create a distinctive "atmosphere" that can be identified by inmates and staff alike. The research on inmate adjustment confirms that variations in prison environments are important and that inmates respond to and thus are influenced by their environment. Among the features of prison environments that emerge as important determinants of inmate behavior are those that implicate concerns for freedom, autonomy, structure, and safety. In addition, the degree of congruence between an individual's self-perceived needs and the environment's ability to meet those needs is a critical factor in determining modes of inmate adjustment. Inmates act differently in different correctional settings, and this finding holds significant implications for correctional policy given that administrators control how prisons are managed and run. In particular, administrators can develop programs and policies for influencing inmate behavior that combine "situational" strategies with other more traditional strategies (Bottoms, Hay, and Sparks 1990).

Two general strategies have been taken in studying the relationship of prison environments to inmate adjustment. The first is to describe prison settings in terms of physical or operational characteristics. A

related approach is to concentrate on formal prison environments created for a specific purpose, such as protective custody units or specialized treatment milieus. The second strategy is to use survey methods
to ask inmates and prison staff to describe or rate the environment
along salient dimensions. The survey instruments that have been most
widely used in studying inmate adjustment are the Correctional Institution Environment Scale (Moos 1970, 1975), the Prison Preference
Inventory (Toch 1977), and the Prison Environment Inventory (Wright
1985).

A. Physical Characteristics and Security Levels

There is a long-standing tradition of concern with prison architecture particularly as related to security issues. Most often, the concerns
focus on aspects of prison design that provide for the surveillance of
inmates and that restrict inmate movement. Other concerns focus on
strategies of "target hardening" and "target removal" (Bottoms, Hay,
and Sparks 1990). The overall thrust of these efforts is to control inmates by minimizing opportunities for disruptive behavior. Although
the logic underlying such strategies is hard to dispute, there are few
empirical studies that use rigorous scientific methodology to document
the influence of prison design on inmate behavior (Canter 1987).

A variety of studies have investigated physical characteristics of prisons, such as noise levels, temperature, and aesthetics, in relation to
inmate behavior. These studies generally show mixed results (Wright
and Goodstein 1989). However, studies of inmate living arrangements,
such as those that compare cell and dormitory accommodations, highlight the importance of privacy and control over the environment to
inmates (Wright and Goodstein 1989). This conclusion is supported
by Canter's (1987) observations that in high-security settings inmate
satisfaction overall is tied to satisfaction with one's cell. In particular,
he notes that inmates have safety interests that lead them to be concerned that staff have immediate access to their cells and that other
inmates have restricted access. He also notes that having control over
aspects of the immediate cell environment such as lighting, heating,
and ventilation is important to inmates.

Other researchers have been interested in the influence of different
prison regimes, meaning the package of policies, rules, and procedures
that regulate inmate and staff activities, on inmate behavior. For example, DiIulio (1987) compared the operation of the prison systems in
Texas, California, and Michigan. He concludes that prisons that are

managed with exacting attention to issues of order, security, and safety experience less violence, have better participation in programs, and offer more humane and attractive living conditions. Other researchers, who emphasize the people-changing goals of corrections, find that inmates respond in more positive ways to treatment-oriented institutions (Street, Vinter, and Perrow 1966). The debate over "tight" and "loose" prisons reaches a high point when it comes to issues of how to deal with extremely violent and disruptive inmates. The strategy in the Federal Bureau of Prisons is to concentrate troublemakers into a single facility and to subject them to a "super-tight management regime" (DiIulio 1989, p. 83). The strategy is effective in the limited sense that a "super-maximum"-security environment removes nearly all opportunities for violence. Many penologists, however, voice serious concerns over the dehumanizing effects of "maxi-maxi" prison environments on staff and inmates (Toch 1989; Bronstein 1991). They also contend that the same goals can be achieved in more positive ways, challenging arguments that the ends, safety and order, justify the means, authoritarian control.

In contrast, the approach in the United Kingdom is to disperse highly disruptive inmates across a number of facilities. Within this system, an experimental regime at Barlinnie prison in Scotland, organized along the lines of a therapeutic community, shows promise as an effective way of dealing with violent prisoners (Cooke 1989). Rates of violent behavior are dramatically lower while inmates are in the unit, and rates continue to be low after discharge to another facility. The findings must be viewed cautiously given the small sample size and the possibility of regression effects when studying extreme groups. It is worth noting, however, that several British researchers have observed that quick access to fair grievance procedures, a key feature of the Barlinnie program, can help to neutralize aggressive and hostile feelings among inmates (Davies 1982).

A problem with comparative studies of prison regimes is that descriptions of prison administration often reflect the biases of the observer or are presented in vague, unproductive language (Ditchfield 1990). Also, it is difficult to evaluate the degree to which key features of a regime are transferable to other prisons or prison systems. Thus, when it comes to prescriptions for addressing inmate adjustment problems, portraits of effective and ineffective institutional regimes tend to be limited in their usefulness. For example, DiIulio has been criticized for slanting his descriptions of prison systems, and the type of regime he advocates has been described as "incongruently eclectic" comprising "a mix of pre-bureaucratic organization at the top and bureaucratic organization at the bottom" (Toch 1989, p. 86). The special unit for violent offenders in Scotland comprises a number of distinct features, and without further research it is difficult to know how each of these features relate to inmate behavior. The unit is extremely small, and inmates, who are mostly involved in subcultural violence, must want to be admitted and must be motivated to change (Cooke 1989). In the unit, inmates enjoy a variety of special privileges and must participate in a variety of therapeutic activities.

Considerably more research is needed in order to understand how institutional regimes affect inmate behavior. One conclusion, however, is clear. Inmates behave differently in different prison settings. To this conclusion, it can be added that inmate behavior is situationally determined in the fullest sense of the concept, stemming from a complex of interactions between persons and environments at a given time. These remarks echo the conclusions of a British researcher who was commissioned to survey and evaluate the research on prison management in relation to issues of inmate control. He writes, "Even a brief survey of the available literature indicates that there is no one regime, or type of regime, which is ideal for all inmates—or even for the same inmate at different stages of his career. . . . Instead, the analysis suggests that it is more the 'fit' or the appropriateness of the regime to the structure of the inmate population—and to the aims and objectives being pursued by staff and management—which is the important variable" (Ditchfield 1990, p. 61). As is shown in the next section, researchers operating in a very different tradition have reached the same conclusion.

With regard to mental health issues, many psychiatrists and other mental health professionals have emphasized the pathogenic qualities of prisons, especially maximum-security prisons. They describe how institutional conditions that deprive individuals of personal autonomy and that constantly send negative messages of self-worth have dehumanizing effects that can engender emotional difficulties (Halleck 1967). Although these observations are relevant to issues of inmate adjustment, particularly with regard to inmates who are psychologically vulnerable, it is difficult to assess the role of maximum-security prison settings in creating or fostering inmate emotional disorders.

If correctional systems across the states were surveyed, it would not be surprising to find that inmates who have been identified as emotionally disordered are disproportionately located at maximum-security prisons. The concentration occurs in part because mental health services tend to be located at these prisons. For instance, the New York state prison system has a network of eight mental health "satellite" units, or clinics, that provide both inpatient and outpatient treatment in conjunction with a centralized psychiatric hospital. Seven of these units are located at maximum-security prisons. Another confounding factor is that histories of violence or of chronic offending, which in many inmate classification schemes dictate placement in maximum-security prisons, overlap with the presence of mental disorders (Toch and Adams 1989*a*, 1989*b*). To the extent that offenders with serious emotional disorders also have serious criminal records, they will be concentrated at maximum-security prisons.

Owing perhaps to the formidable methodological difficulties, few large-scale empirical studies have attempted to link levels of prison security to inmate emotional disorders. Even basic descriptive data on the incidence and prevalence of mental illness across prisons rarely are available. Most epidemiological studies ignore variations by types of prison and instead focus on comparisons between prison and the community. In a study that did search for differences among prisons, the investigators concluded that levels of inmate anxiety, depression, or medical problems are unrelated to facility security levels (Zamble and Porporino 1988). This finding runs contrary to the hypothesis that a greater emphasis on security leads to a greater incidence of inmate emotional disorders within the context of ordinary institutional arrangements.

B. Survey-based Measures of Prison Environments

Researchers have employed survey methods to measure attributes of prison environments directly. However, empirical studies using these methods to study inmate adjustment are relatively sparse, having been initiated only recently. Two major survey instruments have been used——the Correctional Institution Environment Scale and the Prison Preference Inventory. Much of the adjustment research using the Correctional Institution Environment Scale has been disappointing in that many studies fail to generate significant findings. Part of the difficulty may be traced to the nature of the instrument, which stands as one of a series of instruments designed to measure a wide variety of organizational environments. Research using the Prison Preference Inventory, especially in conjunction with derivative instruments such as the Prison

Environment Inventory, has proven to be much more successful at illuminating issues of inmate adjustment. This research confirms that the degree of congruence between individual needs and environmental resources is a critical factor in the inmate adjustment process. Person-environment disjunctures are implicated in a variety of maladaptive behaviors, including emotional difficulties and antisocial behavior, and environmental dimensions of safety, freedom, and structure emerge as critical attributes of prison settings for inmates. This line of research, however, is in the early stages of development, and much remains to be done by way of replicating findings, identifying psychological processes, and specifying important combinations of individual and contextual attributes in relation to inmate adjustment difficulties.

1. *Correctional Institution Environment Scale.* The Correctional Institution Environment Scale (CIES) derives from the work of Rudolph Moos (Moos 1970, 1975; Wenk and Moos 1972). This research represents the specific application to correctional settings of a more general instrument for measuring organizational climates. The CIES has been used extensively in studying issues of correctional administration and organization (Jones, Cornes, and Stackford 1977; Duffee 1980) and in assessing the effectiveness of rehabilitation programs (Moos 1975). In some studies, the CIES also has been used to study issues of institutional adjustment. The instrument consists of nine scales: three dimensions of personal relationships (involvement, support, and expressiveness), three dimensions of institutional programming (autonomy, practical orientation, personal problem orientation), and three dimensions of institutional functioning (order and organization, clarity, staff control).

In an early study, Moos (1970) did not find any relation between CIES dimensions and levels of general satisfaction or feelings of nervousness or tenseness among inmates. However, inmates in prison units emphasizing spontaneity, insight, and autonomy reported greater levels of self-confidence. In a later book, Moos (1975) observed that inmates and staff in more treatment-oriented settings held more positive attitudes. He also reported that, within the context of intensive treatment programs, dimensions of social climate are related to parole success. However, both the reported effects of social climate and the evidence for them are weak. Finally, in evaluating the findings of a variety of studies in relation to the CIES dimensions, Moos concluded that treatment settings that emphasize relationships and that deemphasize staff control facilitate positive changes in personality and behavior.

Again, however, the evidence supporting a relation between the CIES social climate dimensions and inmate adjustment is weak and inconsistent.

In sum, the CIES has been shown to be a capable tool for differentiating correctional settings, and, as the first systematic attempt to measure salient attributes of prison environments, the CIES has earned the status of a landmark development. However, the significance of the distinctions that are made by the CIES is highly questionable, especially with regard to inmate adjustment issues. The shortcomings of the CIES partly derive from an emphasis on capturing dimensions that are shared by very different social environments, as reflected in the assumption that prisons are described best in terms of attributes that also characterize psychiatric treatment programs, military training units, university dormitories, high school classrooms, industrial work settings, and families (Moos 1975). Another limitation of research based on the CIES is that the relation between social climate dimensions and inmate behavior often is left unspecified, or, when relations are specified, the assumption is made that inmates respond to their environment as a homogeneous group. The lack of empirical evidence linking dimensions of the CIES to inmate adjustment difficulties also is unsurprising in view of the methodological reservations scholars have expressed about the instrument. More specifically, the statistical properties of the CIES have been found lacking in that factor analyses have failed to replicate the instrument's internal structure of nine dimensions (Wright and Boudouris 1982).

2. *Prison Preference Inventory.* The Prison Preference Inventory (PPI), which was developed by Hans Toch (1977), is grounded in an analysis of interviews with 900 inmates centering on their experiences in prison. The inmate group included both random and stratified samples at five New York State maximum-security prisons. The interviews included a modified version of Cantril's Self-Anchoring Striving Scale (Cantril 1965) that asked inmates to describe the best and the worst possible prison setting for themselves. A content analysis of the interviews yielded eight dimensions—privacy, safety, structure, support, emotional feedback, social stimulation, activity, and freedom—representing the common concerns of inmates about life in prison. Subsequently, a questionnaire was developed to tap these environmental concerns, and reliability was assessed with internal consistency measures. The PPI has been used in a variety of correctional settings. The instrument has been modified for use in jail settings by Smith

(1984), and, more recently, Gibbs (1991) constructed the Jail Preference Inventory (JPI), which is based in large part on the PPI. The PPI gauges an inmate's preferences for environments having different attributes (i.e., stronger or weaker preferences for settings that offer safety, privacy, etc.), and these expressed concerns often are used to study disjunctures between personal needs and environmental settings or demands.

In a related development, Wright (1985) constructed the Prison Environment Inventory (PEI) to gauge institutional climates. In contrast to the PPI, which taps an individual's preferences, needs, or concerns, the PEI measures perceptions of the environment. The instrument was constructed around the eight dimensions of the PPI and pretested at two medium security prisons. The final construction sample involved five medium security prisons and five maximum-security prisons randomly selected within the New York state correctional system. From the ten institutions, 942 inmates were selected using a probability-proportional-to-size sampling technique. The underlying theoretical structure of the PEI has been subject to statistical confirmation using factor analytic techniques and psychometric scaling techniques such as item-to-scale correlations and internal consistency measures (Wright 1985).

Although a variety of statistical analyses informed the construction of the Prison Preference Inventory, several methodological features of the instrument deserve mention. The PPI involves a series of forced-choice comparisons between items representing different scale dimensions. For example, a subject is asked to choose between a freedom item and an emotional support item. The results of this measurement yield ipsative scores gauging an individual's preference for a given dimension in relation to all other dimensions. By design, high scores must be counterbalanced by low scores (Brodsky and Smitherman 1983). This measurement technique contrasts with normative measures that allow the individual's score on each dimension to be compared with an absolute criterion (Gibbs 1991). The Prison Environment Inventory, for example, which is a normative measure, asks inmates to rate items along an ordinal scale (i.e., never, seldom, often, always) where the endpoints represent the total absence or presence of the dimensional item.

Several rationales were advanced for using the ipsative method in the PPI. Toch (1977) notes that forced-choice paired comparisons are more sensitive to small differences in measurement and are easier to administer since relative judgments provide a frame of reference for the subject. Gibbs (1991) points out that inmates probably view all the environmental dimensions in the instrument as highly desirable. Consequently, absolute ratings probably will not generate sufficient score variance to establish reliability and validity. Although these arguments are very plausible, the assumed strengths of ipsative measurement and weaknesses of normative measurement have yet to be demonstrated empirically in the context of the PPI dimensions.

This type of measurement is worth mentioning because ipsative measures limit the study of between-individual differences (Brodsky and Smitherman 1983). Researchers primarily interested in making comparisons between inmates, groups of inmates, or prison settings will find the absence of an absolute standard against which findings can be compared to be problematic in the interpretation of results. Also, correlational analyses of relations between ipsative scales and more commonly used normative scales, including the PEI, are difficult. These lines of research are important for a complete understanding of inmate adjustment processes. However, the PPI was conceived partly as a classification tool to help match inmates to environments and to identify special-needs inmates. In this context, a method that optimizes the identification of an inmate's most salient concerns makes sense. Environmental commodities are a scarce resource in prisons, and it is often the case that some inmate concerns can only be addressed at the expense of others (Toch 1977). Furthermore, the PPI and other ipsative measures facilitate the study of within-individual differences, and criminologists recently have argued that studies of within-individual change are needed to advance our understanding of causal processes (Tonry, Ohlin, and Farrington 1991). Finally, it should be mentioned that both the PPI and the PEI were constructed and validated with New York state inmates housed in higher-security prisons. The applicability of these instruments to other inmate populations, especially inmates in lower-security levels, remains to be demonstrated empirically.

In his seminal research project, Toch (1977) documented how inmates vary in their environmental preferences. He showed that older inmates value structure and place less emphasis on freedom, that black inmates accentuate freedom and support and deemphasize emotional feedback, and that inmates who have been incarcerated previously seek privacy and are less concerned with safety.

This research also developed the concept of niches, or settings within the institution that are attractive to inmates because they highlight environmental attributes. Many inmates, it was found, will search out a niche that meets their personal needs as a way of facilitating adjustment to institutional life. A distinction can be made between formal niches, which are settings created and maintained by the institution, and informal niches, which represent naturally occurring subenvironments within the prison. Protective custody units, which exist in nearly every prison, are the most familiar example of a formal niche. However, prisons may support a number of units to meet the special needs of different groups of inmates such as emotionally disturbed or intellectually limited inmates, elderly inmates, or inmates with physical disabilities. Informal niches are harder to identify, since they lack official designation, but are more numerous. Inmates may find an informal niche when they locate a job assignment that allows for more than the usual degree of freedom and autonomy, a cell block where officers and fellow inmates are concerned about respecting one's privacy, or a classroom where the teacher is particularly encouraging and supportive. Studies indicate that formal niches are most often created for inmates who are especially vulnerable and who have highly skewed safety concerns, while informal niches accommodating freedom, privacy, and safety concerns are most common (Toch 1977; Hagel-Seymour 1982).

Building on this research, Wright (1986, 1989, 1991a, 1991b; Wright and Jones 1989) has examined the relationship between environmental aspects of prisons and inmate coping problems in a series of studies. The studies were carried out on the 942 inmates involved in the construction of the PEI. The inmates were administered three instruments, and additional data were collected from prison records. First, they received the twenty-item Prison Adjustment Questionnaire (PAQ) tapping internal, external, and physical dimensions of adjustment problems. In a previous effort, Wright (1985) analyzed the psychometric properties of this instrument. Second, the inmates received the MMPI, which was used to classify inmates in terms of the Megargee typology. Third, the inmates were administered the PPI.

Wright tells us that inmates were oversampled to allow for attrition, although the size of the original sample is not mentioned. While attrition is reported to have occurred because some subjects had other commitments (e.g., disciplinary hearing, sick call, court appearance) and because some subjects refused to cooperate, the nature and extent of the attrition problem is largely unknown. In particular, it is not known if inmate adjustment problems were related to sample attrition and whether this possible selection bias influenced the results of the study. Furthermore, Wright indicates that only 55 percent of the sample completed the MMPI and that 60 percent of inmates completing the MMPI were dropped from parts of the analysis because they could not be classified into one of the Megargee types. Clearly, these attrition problems raise questions as to the reliability and validity of the reported findings.

An important feature of the PAQ is that the instrument measures only problems that an inmate reports are worse in prison than in the free world. Wright used this comparison technique to control for an individual's history of coping difficulties because his interest was in studying the adverse effects of incarceration. The instrument identifies only those inmate coping problems that have an environmental component, failing to capture the full range of adjustment difficulties. For this reason, the research cannot address questions of the relative importance of environmental attributes and individual factors, and significant issues of chronicity in coping problems across settings get overlooked. The strategy, however, does facilitate the investigation of environmental effects and of interactions between environmental and individual attributes, issues that were of primary concern to Wright.

Among Wright's findings is that negative perceptions of support and safety in the environment are most strongly linked to "internal" problems, which refer to difficulties that are symptomatic of anxiety and depression (Wright 1991b). Inmates who have been victimized are more concerned with locating safer and less active settings than are other inmates (Wright 1991a).

With regard to inmate disruptiveness, Wright (1988, 1991b) finds that expressed needs for freedom and perceptions of the environment as structured are related positively to "external" adjustment problems, which include acting-out behaviors. Similarly, he observes that assaultive and aggressive inmates express a lower need for structure and a greater need for freedom than do nonviolent inmates (Wright 1991a). These findings suggest that violent and disruptive inmates experience the restrictions of prison life as an acute source of frustration and irritation and that these feelings may be at the base of their acting-out behaviors. In addition, assaultive and aggressive inmates perceive the prison environment differently than do other inmates, differences that include perceptions of less activity and less social support (Wright 1991a). These findings are consistent with theories that attribute a propensity for antisocial behavior to sensation seeking and reduced sensitivity to external stimuli. Wright also finds evidence to support the general hypothesis that interactions between the psychological characteristics of individuals and attributes of the environment play a critical role in inmate adjustment. In one analysis, he finds that inmates with the least deviant personality profiles, defined in terms of the Megargee typology, were less assaultive when placed in less structured settings (Wright 1986). In another analysis, he concludes that the most important predictor of "external" difficulties, which include disruptive and antisocial behaviors, is the congruence between personality profiles and structure in the environment, where congruence means that the most deviant personality types are placed in the most structured settings (Wright 1991b). These findings, however, can only be considered as suggestive and are in need of replication owing to the substantial attrition problems discussed previously.

A recent study by Gibbs (1991) provides strong empirical support for the argument that disjunctures between self-assessed environmental needs and perceived environmental resources lead to psychological distress. In this study, the Jail Preference Inventory and the Environmental Quality Scale were used to classify inmates along a general scale of environmental congruence. Psychological difficulties were measured by a ninety-item symptom checklist (SCL-90). The analysis revealed that discordant-negative congruence, which occurs when personal needs are strong and environmental supply is low, was associated with higher levels of psychopathology, while concordant-positive congruence, which occurs when needs are strong and supply is high, was associated with lower levels of psychopathology. Although all symptom dimensions increased with person-environment disjunctures, levels of psychoticism, depression, and paranoid ideation were affected most greatly. The analysis, however, which defined congruence in general terms, did not focus on specific environmental dimensions, leaving the task to future research.

Wright's findings highlight the roles of safety, freedom, and structure in the adjustment problems of inmates. The findings are particularly interesting because prison administrators are likely to view the institutional arrangements that best address freedom and safety concerns as conflicting. Protective custody settings are a good example of this conflict. The typical candidate for protection is an inmate who is fearful and afraid, and in response to the situation the inmate is segregated into a special housing unit where he or she is locked up most of the day, allowing only an hour or so outside the cell for exercise. The protective custody strategy is to maximize safety by limiting movement and minimizing contact with other inmates, an approach that also brings severe restrictions on freedom. Research findings indicating that both freedom and safety are implicated in the emotional and behavioral difficulties of inmates suggest that in solving one problem protective custody settings may be creating another. That is, by requiring inmates to trade freedom for safety, prison administrators may be creating an iatrogenic situation in which the cure leads to further illness. Admittedly, the evidence on this issue is far from definitive. Researchers have just begun to focus on transactional processes of inmate adjustment, such as the one just suggested in which changes in the environment create a reordering in the inmate's hierarchy of needs and cause new concerns to surface. However, tracing patterns of concerns as inmates move about a prison system is an important area for future research.

Another interesting aspect of the environmental research findings pertains to the role of structure in the management of inmates. Structure, as operationalized in the PPI, relates to concerns about "stability and predictability" and a "preference for consistency, clear-cut rules, orderly and scheduled events and impingements" (Toch 1977, p. 16). The research indicates that structured prison environments are associated with higher rates of disruptive behavior. Although it is not clear whether selective placement effects are at work, a possible interpretation of this finding is that many inmates react negatively to authoritarian environments. Conversely, structure emerges as an important element in reducing the antisocial behavior of inmates with highly deviant personalities. Thus, the regimental aspects of prison life, which are viewed as undesirable by many offenders, may be seen as an asset for some psychologically deviant inmates. It is possible that structure in the external environment compensates for internal personality disorganization and related inabilities to control behavior, although this hypothesis requires further investigation.

C. Prison Overcrowding

Serious overcrowding has emerged in most prison systems across the nation, threatening to turn prisons into human "warehouses" and thereby undoing the reforms and advances of earlier decades.[2] There

---

[2] Prison overcrowding has become so widespread and serious that several newsletters and journals are devoted to keeping track of the problem. The National Prison Project

have been many studies of the negative effects of prison overcrowding on inmates, many of which attempt to link crowding with elevated blood pressure levels and high rates of illness (D'Atri 1975; McCain, Cox, and Paulus 1976). While the studies report mixed results overall, some researchers find that inmates who live in single rooms perceive that they have more control over their environment and experience less stress (Ruback, Carr, and Hopper 1986). Research on disruptive behavior shows inconsistent results, with some investigators finding no relation between levels of overcrowding and disciplinary infraction rate (Bonta and Nanckivell 1980) and others finding a positive relationship (Megargee 1976). A study of thirty-seven federal facilities (Nacci, Teitelbaum, and Prather 1977) found that the relation between over-crowding and assault varied by facility, suggesting that institutional characteristics are important factors that mediate the effects of prison crowding.

Several extensive reviews of the research on prison crowding have been conducted. These detailed reviews invariably observe that studies of prison crowding suffer from a number of conceptual and method-ological limitations. Many studies fail to recognize a distinction be-tween spatial density, or the number of square feet of space per person, and social density, or perceptions that the number of persons in the environment interferes with or impedes one's capacity to carry out important activities and goals. Many studies do not take into account selection effects, which result from the tendency for certain types of inmates to be placed in certain types of settings. Perhaps the state of this research can be characterized best by tracing the different conclu-sions reached over the years by an expert who has followed the prison crowding literature closely. After thoroughly reviewing the research, Gaes (1985) concluded that only a few of the claimed effects of prison crowding withstand critical scrutiny. Specifically, he found that open dormitory settings are associated with higher clinic use and with ele-vated blood pressure levels and that excessively crowded prisons have higher assault rates. More recently, Gaes (1990) has reversed position and now concludes that the methodological limitations of the research are more serious than previously thought and that none of the effects of prison crowding advanced in the literature are supported by research.

---

indicates that in 1990 forty-one states were under court order or were involved in consent decrees for overcrowding in the entire prison system or at major facilities (Bronstein 1991, p. 5). A recent addition to the field of newsletters is *Overcrowded Times*, which is supported by the Edna McConnell Clark Foundation.

Several developments in prison crowding research are relevant to a research agenda on inmate adjustment problems. It is now recognized that the demands of prison crowding are mediated by an inmate's perceptions of a situation. These perceptions are influenced by personal factors, such as age, and by features of the institutional environment (Bonta and Gendreau 1990). Among the perceptions that are most critical are those relating to an ability to satisfy needs or to accomplish goals. When inmates have available many options by which to achieve important goals, the negative effects of prison crowding are mitigated (Smith 1982). Crowding restricts an inmate's options in undesirable ways by straining program resources and by constraining prison officials in terms of how they respond to impending crisis situations (Toch 1985). These observations highlight the importance of cognitive appraisals in the stress-coping process and the influence of individual and environmental factors on such appraisals. The research also underscores the desirability of empowering prison administrators to manipulate correctional environments in ways that reduce inmate stress.

D. Environmental Correlates of Self-Injury

Suicides and self-injuries are more prevalent among jail inmates than among prison inmates (Lloyd 1990); this finding can be explained in several ways. The transition to confinement is more abrupt in jails, occurring oftentimes immediately after arrest. Also, many prison inmates spend the early, high-risk period of incarceration in jail awaiting adjudication and sentencing. However, variations in self-injury rates also can be traced to differences in the characteristics of inmate populations. Suicides in local police lockups occur more often in the United States than in Great Britain, a difference that can be attributed to the varying ways in which alcoholic offenders are handled in the two countries (Lloyd 1990). Inmate self-injuries and suicides disproportionately occur in mental health observation settings. Although this finding arguably represents a selection effect, given that inmates who are most at risk for self-injury are placed in observation, some scholars have argued that emotional problems can be exacerbated to the breaking point by the low levels of activity and social contact characteristic of most isolation settings (Toch 1975). A British Home Office study concluded that research favors the latter argument, observing that interpersonal contact with staff is the best countermeasure for inmate suicidal tendencies (Lloyd 1990).

E. Institutional Programming and Contact with the Outside World

Incarceration removes people from the general society, segregating them in institutions where they are separated from family and friends. Inmates view this aspect of confinement as a major source of stress, and some studies have attempted to link this stress to prison misbehavior. In particular, some researchers have hypothesized that more frequent contact with persons in the community reduces inmate stress thereby resulting in lower rates of misbehavior. Thus far, the evidence on this hypothesis is inconclusive. Some studies do not find any relation between frequency of outside contacts and disciplinary infraction rates (Lembo 1969; Goetting and Howsen 1986), although other studies report a significant inverse association (Ellis, Grasmick, and Gilman 1974). A possible explanation for the negative findings is that inmate contacts with the outside world are so generally infrequent that the threshold for influencing behavior is seldom reached. It is also possible that the association varies by the security level of the institution, as some researchers have found (Brown and Spevacek 1971). Nevertheless, research clearly indicates that contacts with family and friends do not exacerbate inmate disciplinary problems, as might occur if inmates were continually being informed of domestic difficulties and felt frustrated by their situation of relative powerlessness.

Another line of research has examined levels of inmate activity within prison in relation to misbehavior, the hypothesis being that meaningful participation in programs and other activities produces lower infraction rates by reducing stress. One study found the amount of time spent outside the cell to be unrelated to misbehavior, although no information was available on the nature of inmate activities (Goetting and Howsen 1986). In contrast, Petersilia and Honig (1980) observed that white prison inmates in California who lacked work or other program assignments had the highest level of misbehavior, with an infraction rate about 80 percent greater than that of other inmates. Unfortunately, the study could not determine if the lack of program involvement predated the high rates of misbehavior, leaving open the possibility that inmates first become disruptive and then withdraw from program assignments. Such issues are best addressed through longitudinal designs that allow for sequences of events to be studied.

F. Some Environmental Aspects of Prison Violence

A handful of studies on prison violence suggests interesting directions for future research, although the findings of these studies are not definitive. Some scholars have emphasized how aspects of the physical environment can facilitate crime, and in one prison study it was observed that dormitories and cottages, which allow for freer intermingling of prisoners and which often have unsupervised areas, are settings that increase the chances of prison rape (Lockwood 1982b). At present, we know very little about prison "hot spots," or the geographic locations in which prison incidents of a given type concentrate (Toch 1978). We also do not know much about the physical characteristics of prison environments that facilitate or discourage different types of inmate misbehavior. An experiment carried out by the Federal Bureau of Prisons suggests that the incidence of violence can be reduced by broadening the mix of inmates of different ages (Mabli et al. 1979). This demonstrates that characteristics of the inmate population are an important aspect of the prison environment and that these characteristics can be manipulated by correctional administrators to achieve desirable ends. Again, however, we have limited knowledge as to how changes in the composition of inmate populations alter the institutional environment and influence inmate behavior.

IV. Sentence Characteristics: Stage, Length, and Type

From the outset, students of inmate adjustment have been interested in changes in attitudes and behaviors during the prison term. Some of the earliest researchers argued that the length of stay in prisons is related directly to the development of criminal attitudes (Clemmer 1958). More recently, scholars concerned with the situation of long-term inmates have argued that prolonged exposure to prison damages inmates psychologically. Others have pointed to the middle stage of incarceration, or the point at which inmates are most removed from community influences, as a critical period during which socialization into the inmate normative code is greatest and expressions of antiauthoritarian attitudes are most likely to surface (Wheeler 1961). Still other scholars highlight the end of the prison term and the accompanying transition to civilian life as a critical period (Waller 1974).

Contemporary researchers follow in the tradition of past research by emphasizing the study of patterns of change. However, they have broadened the research focus to include a variety of adjustment problems, and many of the conclusions that derive from these research efforts diverge from those of earlier studies. In particular, research indicates that the initial stage of confinement is the greatest risk period for emotional disorder, suicide, self-injury, and violent and disruptive behavior. Rates of maladaptive behavior decline over time, suggesting that many inmates learn to adjust to the prison environment. Although there is evidence to suggest that anxiety levels increase just prior to release, the experience is quickly overcome. Finally, there is very little evidence to suggest that long-term confinement inflicts psychological harm on inmates. On one matter, however, prison researchers consistently agree. Patterns of adjustment that reflect an inmate's confinement experiences have important consequences for subsequent behavior in the community. Unfortunately, the amount of empirical evidence on this issue is limited.

A. Overall Patterns and Trends

A number of studies find that inmate emotional problems are more inclined to surface in the early stages of incarceration. The findings are very consistent and have been replicated for psychiatric hospitalization, self-injury, symptom rates, and stress levels. Roughly half of all commitments among a cohort of prison inmates occurred within the first six months of incarceration (Toch and Adams 1989a). A study of Swiss prisoners found a significant drop in symptomatology and in cognitive stress levels over the first two months of incarceration (Harding and Zimmermann 1989). Likewise, Gunn, Robertson, and Dell (1978) report that rates of anxiety and depression among British prisoners are highest during the beginning phase of imprisonment, declining significantly within six months of prison entry. Similar patterns have been observed in studies of jail settings. Gibbs (1987), after interviewing 339 newly arrived jail inmates, found higher rates of psychopathology during the first three days of confinement when compared to retrospective accounts of symptoms on the street. He also found that symptom rates declined over the next five days, although the drop was less substantial for inmates with a history of psychiatric hospitalization. In contrast, one study found that anxiety levels among jail inmates, although elevated, remain constant during the first month of incarceration, although changes beyond this point in time were not investigated (Bonta and Nanckivell 1980).

While depression is a widespread problem among offenders, longitudinal cohort analyses show that the incidence of depression declines over the course of the prison term. Zamble and Porporino (1988) found that 37 percent of the inmates they studied showed signs of serious depression around the time of prison entry, with 29 percent classified as moderately depressed and 8 percent as severely depressed.[3] Additionally, one-third of the inmates had high scores on a helplessness scale. Within four months, however, the number of inmates with moderate or severe depression dropped by more than 40 percent. Consistent with these findings are many studies reporting that acts of self-injury, which often reflect feelings of depression and hopelessness, occur more frequently in the beginning stages of incarceration (Biegel and Russell 1973; Danto 1973; Esparza 1973; Fawcett and Mars 1973; Helig 1973; as reviewed in Gibbs 1982c). Finally, the rate of self-injury is higher among jail inmates awaiting trial, a group more likely to be comprised of new arrivals, than among inmates serving sentences (Esparza 1973; Helig 1973; as reviewed in Gibbs 1982c).

In their study of prison adjustment, Toch and Adams (1989a) charted rates of mental health symptoms and disciplinary infractions for an inmate population across prison terms. The findings indicate that disciplinary infraction rates are relatively high at the start of the prison sentence and peak within the first six to nine months of incarceration; thereafter, infraction rates show a steady downward trend. This pattern was most characteristic of young inmates, who showed the highest infraction rates and who also showed the greatest improvement in behavior. Infraction rates for young inmates (under twenty-two years of age) serving long prison terms (over four years) peaked at an annualized rate of approximately 9.5 infractions at a point about nine months into the sentence, declining by more than four-fifths at the end of the prison term to an annualized rate of about 1.6 infractions. In contrast, the infraction rates of older inmates were low and showed little variation over time. For the most part, the annualized infraction rates of older inmates (over thirty years of age) ranged from between one and two infractions for all categories of sentence length. Similarly, rates of symptomatic behavior were relatively high at the beginning of the prison terms and declined over time, although the pattern was less consistent than that for disciplinary rates.

The temporal patterns of both symptomatic behaviors and misconduct follow a similar course over the prison term, with the incidence of maladaptive behaviors being highest early in the prison experience.

---

[3] Zamble and Porporino (1988, p. 83) note that the rates of moderate and severe depression they observed among inmates are respectively five and eight times greater than the rates in the general population.

This trend indicates that entry into prison is a stressful event, marking the start of a critical period in which inmates may experience difficulties of transition shock as they try to adjust to a new environment. It is perhaps unsurprising to find that incarceration is a tumultuous event given the dramatic changes in lifestyles that accompany the experience. The Social Readjustment Rating Scale ranks incarceration as the fourth most stressful event in the lives of people, following death of a spouse, divorce, and marital separation (Holmes and Rahe 1967). Also, the stress-coping literature indicates that adjustment difficulties can occur when people find themselves in situations that limit their control over the environment, as occurs in prisons, hospitals, and nursing homes (MacKenzie and Goodstein 1986). However, the overall trend for inmates is one of improvement in behavior over time, indicating that the majority learn to adapt successfully to the prison setting.

In comparison with earlier research on prison adjustment, more recent studies concentrate on behavior, rather than on attitudes, and direct our attention to the early segments of the prison term, rather than to the middle. The findings indicate that prison entry marks a critical period of adjustment, and this information allows us to channel resources into periods when inmate problems are greatest. Also, it is encouraging to find that for a majority of inmates their adjustment difficulties are relatively short-lived and that many turbulent situations eventually pass into quiescence.

B. Long-Term Inmates

Over much of the past decade, changes in laws and sentencing practices have led to increasingly longer prison terms for convicted offenders. Along with this development, researchers have been paying greater attention to the situation of long-term inmates. Some researchers have asked whether long-term confinement is harmful psychologically; studies on this issue have failed to produce evidence of serious harmful effects. Other researchers have been interested in patterns of adjustment unique to long-term prisoners. Although long-term inmates appear to cultivate distinctive coping strategies, it is not clear if patterns of adjustment characteristic of long-termers can be attributed solely to sentence length. When differences across inmate groups in terms of factors such as age are taken into account, the adjustment patterns of long-term inmates become similar to those of other inmates. Also, the composition of the long-term inmate population is rapidly changing in terms of attributes such as age, race, criminal history, conviction offense, and drug use (Flanagan et al. 1990). Much of the research on long-term inmates, although only a decade or two old, may be out of date in the sense that the studies were conducted on inmates with very different sociodemographic and criminal history characteristics. With an eye toward replicating the findings of earlier studies, there is a need to investigate how compositional changes in the long-term inmate population have affected the institutional experiences of this inmate group.

Much of the research on long-term offenders has been motivated by concerns for the possibly deleterious effects of extended incarceration. These concerns have been stimulated by several ethnographic studies, most notably that by Cohen and Taylor (1972) in England, which suggest that long-term exposure to prison environments has harmful psychological consequences. In particular, ethnographic observers of prison life suggest that a lack of productive, stimulating activity over a lengthy period leads to mental, emotional, and physical deterioration.

Partly in response to the observations made by ethnographers, more quantitatively oriented researchers have set out to verify the harmful effects of long-term imprisonment. By and large, this research has failed to uncover any adverse effects of long-term confinement (Bonta and Gendreau 1990). A particularly noteworthy research project involved a series of investigations carried out by a group of British psychologists. The study involved 175 subjects, made up of four groups of inmates categorized by time served and matched by age. The findings of this research are covered in four reports, three focusing separately on cognitive (Banister et al. 1973), personality (Heskin et al. 1973), and attitudinal (Heskin et al. 1974) variables, and another involving longitudinal analyses (Bolton et al. 1976). This project failed to uncover much support for the hypothesis that long-term incarceration is psychologically harmful. The intellectual functioning of inmates did not decline, and among personality variables only self-directed hostility increased significantly with time served in the cross-sectional analyses. The only attitudinal change observed was a decline in self-concept. The longitudinal analyses confirmed a lack of change in intelligence. However, contrary to the cross-sectional findings, longitudinal analyses indicated a reduction in hostility scores that was associated with an increase in emotional maturity. The authors speculate that the conflicting longitudinal findings may be attributable to sample attrition or to favorable changes in the prison conditions over the course of the study.

The finding that long-term inmates do not suffer more serious psychological problems as a result of incarceration also has been confirmed for female inmates (MacKenzie, Robinson, and Campbell 1989). Although the long-term female inmates experienced more situational problems (e.g., boredom, lack of privacy), these differences were not reflected in unsuccessful coping outcomes.

Not all of the research on long-term inmates, however, fails to confirm the ethnographic reports. In an earlier section it was noted that long-term confinement poses a different set of challenges and can amplify common inmate concerns into more serious adjustment problems. Many ethnographic researchers have observed that long-term inmates gradually lose interest in the outside world, and a British study of homicide offenders serving life terms confirms these reports (Richards 1978). The study found that the degree of introversion among long-term inmates increased with time and that long-term inmates became increasingly dependent on prison staff and prison routines. These developments were seen in changes in involvement with the outside world as represented by fewer letters and visits. Also, inmates serving life sentences, as well as murderers, a group likely to be serving long prison terms, tend to be overrepresented among inmate suicides (Lloyd 1990). At this point, however, the possibility that these differences are the product of selection or environment effects or are a function of the amount of time at risk cannot be ruled out.

In other research, Flanagan (1980b) reports that long-term inmates experience greater psychological stress in the early stages of incarceration, a finding that has been replicated by others. In a study of habitual offenders and lifers, it was observed that long-term inmates experienced adjustment problems during an initial transition period, followed by a period of successful coping and adjustment (MacKenzie and Goodstein 1985). More recently, it has been found that long-term inmates show higher levels of stress and emotional problems than other inmates shortly after prison entry, although the difference later disappears (Zamble and Porporino 1988). In discussing these findings, however, the researchers caution that the evidence is weak and that long-term inmates are more likely to be sent to a maximum-security facility with generally harsher confinement conditions. To these observations, it can be added that since differences are observed only in the early stages of incarceration, it is implausible to argue that they are the product of extended incarceration. Furthermore, the temporal pattern of adjustment difficulties for long-term inmates, with adjustment problems concentrated in the early stages of incarceration, is consistent with the general pattern described for other inmates in the previous section.

The adjustment experiences of long-term inmates are not entirely negative, and some studies report that long-termers demonstrate more effective and productive coping strategies than other inmates (Zamble and Porporino 1988). Flanagan (1981) notes that long-term inmates tend to be older and consequently more mature. They actively avoid trouble and try to use their time in prison fruitfully. These desires often get reflected in a greater degree of program participation and in the more serious cultivation of hobbies and other types of informal activities directed at learning and self-improvement. These findings have been confirmed recently for Canadian long-term inmates (Zamble 1992). While it is very possible that long-term inmates continue to exhibit similar strengths relative to other inmates after being released to the community, that remains to be demonstrated empirically.

Another focus of research has been on differences in rates of prison misbehavior between short-term and long-term inmates. The issue is complicated by the fact that long-term inmates tend to be distinctive in a variety of ways. Most notably, long-term inmates tend to be older, have more extensive criminal histories, and have more serious conviction offenses than other inmates. Flanagan (1980*b*) was among the first to investigate how patterns of misbehavior vary by sentence length, and he found that the infraction rate of short-term inmates is about twice that of long-term inmates. Similarly, inmates who are chronic disciplinary offenders, meaning those inmates who demonstrate high rates of misbehavior over most of the prison term, are more likely to be serving shorter prison terms (Toch and Adams 1989*a*).

Regarding changes in disciplinary involvement over the prison term, Flanagan (1980*b*) observed that when prison terms are divided into four equal periods the infraction rate of short-term inmates is greatest around midsentence, while the rate for long-term inmates is relatively invariant. From this evidence, he concluded that sentence length is a critical factor in determining career patterns of inmate misbehavior. In this particular analysis, differences in the age distribution between the short-term and long-term inmates were not taken into account. In contrast, Toch and Adams (1989*a*) controlled for age in a comparison of temporal changes in infraction rates across prison careers by sentence length. They found that rates of disciplinary involvement for young inmates increased shortly after admission and then steadily declined until discharge regardless of sentence length. Rates for older inmates were relatively constant, again, irrespective of sentence length. They therefore concluded that patterns of adjustment difficulties as reflected in prison misbehavior are more a function of age than of sentence length. Part of the explanation for the conflicting results may be that Toch and Adams were able to locate disciplinary incidents more precisely in time than could Flanagan, given that they divided the sentences of long-term inmates into twenty-four equal periods rather than four.

Other attempts at disentangling the effects of age, criminal history, and sentence length on inmate adjustment difficulties have produced inconsistent results. One study finds that younger, recidivistic, long-term inmates do not show more signs of stress, greater commitment to prison subcultural norms, or a decrease in self-esteem compared to other inmates (MacKenzie and Goodstein 1985). On the basis of these findings, the authors question the notion that young habitual offenders serving long prison terms pose greater institutional management problems. This conclusion contrasts with that of another study reporting that young long-term offenders have the highest infraction rates across all combinations of age and sentence length categories (Toch and Adams 1989*a*). The difference in findings may be attributable to different focuses on antisocial attitudes and behavior between the studies. Nonetheless, conflicting findings such as these suggest that future research might concentrate on the ways in which changes in the age, criminal history, and other characteristics of long-term inmate populations as caused by changes in sentencing practices influence observed patterns of long-term adjustment.

C. Indeterminate Sentences

Indeterminate sentencing schemes create uncertainty for an inmate regarding the date that he or she will be released to the community, and it has been hypothesized that for some inmates this uncertainty leads to anxiety. Goodstein (1982) investigated this hypothesis by comparing the adjustment of inmates with determinate and indeterminate sentences. She was able to make this comparison within the same prison system because in South Carolina split sentences bring a fixed release date while other types of sentences do not. For the most part, the type of sentence had little effect on an inmate's adjustment to prison. Both groups of inmates, those with indeterminate and those with determinate sentences, made similar informal accommodations to prison routines, held comparable attitudes toward rehabilitation programs, had similar degrees of contact with friends and relatives in the community, and had similar levels of disciplinary involvement. Inmates with determinate sentences did show less anxiety than other inmates, suggesting that they experienced less stress. The difference, however, was slight and did not appear to influence attitudes or behavior.

D. Inmate Adjustment and Return to the Community

Prison admission is characterized by high rates of maladaptive behavior, suggesting that the transition to life in prison is a stressful experience. A number of studies indicate that the transition at the other end, the release from prison to the community, is also stressful. Inmates turned parolees move from a situation of dependency in which all of their basic needs are attended to by staff into a situation of much greater autonomy that carries sink-or-swim connotations. What released inmates gain by way of freedom can be lost by way of uncertainty and challenge. Social roles and skills that have long been dormant must quickly be resuscitated if offenders are to survive as parolees in the community. When asked about specific challenges they face, inmates most often voice concerns over their ability to find a job, to reestablish family ties, and to manage finances (Waller 1974). Psychiatrists have observed that in response to these concerns some inmates exhibit "gate fever," a syndrome marked by anxiety, irritability, and other symptoms that surface around the time of release (Cormier, Kennedy, and Sendbuehler 1967).

Although the existence of the "gate fever" syndrome is widely accepted in correctional circles, few studies have attempted to investigate this phenomenon using rigorous methodology. One such project is that carried out by Renzema (1982) with a sample of fifty-three inmates who were interviewed three times—just prior to release and at three and six months after release. This study supports the hypothesis that being returned to the community is a stressful event for inmates, although the experience is not debilitating. The research confirmed that stress levels were elevated just prior to release and that a significant number of inmates expressed doubts over their ability to negotiate a return to community life. However, there was little evidence that inmates were experiencing acute stress, and stress levels quickly subsided on release. Waller (1974) similarly found that Canadian inmates showed signs of stress on release and that these symptoms diminished fairly rapidly as inmates became accustomed to their new situation.

In a related finding, Toch and Adams (1989a) report that among inmates who had received mental health services symptom rates appeared to increase several months before release. The pattern was most obvious and dramatic for short-term inmates, although similar increases could be observed for inmates serving longer prison terms. These findings should be considered only as suggestive, given that they are based on graphical displays of symptom rates over time, and the possibility that the data reflect random statistical fluctuations cannot be ruled out. The results are consistent with an hypothesized "anticipatory release" or "gate fever" effect, although the data suggest that this problem is most acute among inmates who are psychologically vulnerable.

There is a substantial body of research evaluating the effects of prison treatment programs on criminal recidivism. Early reviews of this research concluded that correctional programs did not have a substantial impact on an inmate's subsequent criminal behavior in the community (Bailey 1966; Martinson 1974). Additionally, most actuarial prediction studies found that the items that best predict recidivism among inmates are those that are more generally predictive of future criminal involvement—age and criminal history. On the basis of these findings, some commentators have suggested that information on an inmate's behavior in prison can be discounted or ignored (Morris 1974). The argument as advanced is a narrow one in that it relates to the efficiency of statistical predictions and to the allocation of decision-making authority between sentencing judges and parole boards. The argument, however, can be misleading if interpreted, as it sometimes is, to mean that nothing of consequence occurs over the course of prison terms in relation to postincarceration behavior.

Putting aside studies of treatment effectiveness and the development of prediction instruments for recidivism, there is surprisingly little research on the effects of prison experiences on subsequent behavior. The research that does exist, however, indicates that the ways in which inmates adapt to prison life hold important consequences for future adjustment in the community. Inmates cite their involvement in educational and vocational programs as well as their relationships with corrections officers and other prison staff as positive influences in later civilian life (Glaser 1964). In contrast, a minority of inmates credit their prison experience with making them more hostile and more skilled in the ways of crime (Waller 1974). While the notion that prisons are schools of crime is a pervasive one, research bearing directly on this issue is scant.

Regarding the relationship of prison misconduct to postrelease behavior, there are two schools of thought. Some scholars argue that inmates who are "prisonized," or those who adopt the norms of the inmate culture and refuse to cooperate with the institution, are better positioned to deal with the transition to community life because they demonstrate independence and autonomy (Goodstein 1979). Conversely, inmates who become "institutionalized" through passive acquiescence to prison routines will lack a capacity for autonomous decision making and independent action necessary for successful adjustment to the community. As a corollary of these arguments, inmates who show patterns of nonconformity to prison rules should demonstrate better postrelease adjustment. In support of this hypothesis, several studies report more favorable parole outcomes for rebellious or prisonized inmates (Kassebaum, Ward, and Wilner 1971; Miller and Dinitz 1973; Goodstein 1979). However, it appears that any relative disadvantage that accrues to institutionalized inmates in terms of difficulties in finding employment or in adjusting to parole supervision is short-lived, surfacing most clearly in the first month of release and disappearing by the third month (Goodstein 1979). In evaluating these results, it is important to keep in mind that the studies focus on antisocial attitudes, rather than on incidents of prison misbehavior, and that definitions of unsuccessful postrelease outcomes include a variety of adjustment difficulties, not just criminal activity.

In contrast, it can be argued that inmates who violate prison rules are more likely to recidivate or to fail on parole. The argument can be seen as an extension of the well-documented association between past and future behavior in predicting criminality. Transgressions of prison rules suggest that an inmate has difficulty conforming to restrictions on behavior, and therefore these events may constitute part of a chronic pattern. From this point of view, inmate infractors are more likely than other inmates to violate the law or disobey parole regulations on release. A follow-up study of inmates released from federal prisons supports this argument. In this project, the investigators found that prison misbehavior carried an increased probability of unsuccessful adjustment in the community, defined as rearrest or parole revocation, controlling for other individual risk factors (Gottfredson and Adams 1982).

This result is consistent with other research showing a continuity in maladaptive adjustment among offenders.

At this point, however, there is far too little research on prison misconduct and antisocial behavior in the community to make a definitive assessment of the relation. In addition to replicating the findings of the federal study, other issues to be addressed include the relations of different types of prison rules violations to subsequent criminal activity. For example, is inmate violence more predictive of recidivism than a refusal to obey an order or being out of place? Another important issue pertains to the relation of patterns of misconduct to recidivism. Given that the general pattern for infraction rates is to start high and steadily decline, are inmates who show different patterns, such as consistently high infraction rates or misbehavior rates that increase toward the end of the sentence, at greater risk for recidivism? Such relations need to be documented, if they exist, in order to verify the claim that "the path of adjustment over time is at least partly predictive of recidivism and may be determinative" (Zamble and Porporino 1990, p. 65).

Finally, there is evidence showing a continuity in mental health problems from prison to community settings. In a follow-up of a cohort of released inmates, Feder (1989) finds that inmates who had been hospitalized while in prison are very likely to require psychiatric hospitalization while on parole. In addition, parolees who had been hospitalized as inmates show greater residential instability, more sporadic employment experiences, and are more frequently evaluated by parole officers as adjusting poorly to supervision. These findings not only represent a continuity of mental health problems but highlight the need for coordinating mental health service delivery between prisons and community agencies.

V. Discussion and Conclusion

The current state of knowledge concerning inmate adjustment to prison cannot be conveniently summarized in terms of a fully articulated theory of prison adjustment. The existing research does point to conclusions, however, that hold implications for theory and policy. Issues warranting future research can be identified.

Loss of contact with the outside world, especially with regard to family members and with other persons with whom significant relationships have been established, is a burdensome experience for a majority of inmates. This finding tells us that our system of punishment works as intended. Offenders experience incarceration and the concomitant loss of liberty and separation from the community as an unpleasant consequence of their criminal involvement. However, the finding also tells us that, if we are interested in mitigating the adjustment problems of inmates, we need to make prisons more open to the outside world. Community-based prison programs, such as work release, furlough, and other forms of temporary release, are a step in this direction, as is the more general move toward use of intermediate sanctions that punish offenders through means other than incarceration (Morris and Tonry 1990). Although there are many arguments to support the broader use of community corrections programs, one consequence of initiatives that make prisons more accessible to the outside world is that the challenges of adjusting to life behind bars become easier.

The research on coping strategies, in particular the study by Zamble and Porporino (1988), reveals a striking continuity and stability in inmate styles. Between the community and prison and across the prison term, the ways in which inmates deal with problem situations are remarkably consistent. Another striking finding of this study relates to the propensity that inmates show for using relatively ineffective and counterproductive coping strategies. Taken together, these two findings suggest that a common process underlies most inmate coping problems, raising the possibility that the variety of life difficulties that offenders experience, including criminal involvements and institutional adjustment problems, are products of the same etiological process. Against this framework of continuity, however, two diverging facts can be juxtaposed. The first is that criminal history shows mixed relations with prison misbehavior, and this inconsistency suggests that issues of chronicity do not neatly translate across settings. The second is that inmate conformity to prison rules generally improves over time, a trend that not only emphasizes that changes in inmate behavior do occur but also conveys an optimistic note regarding efforts at increasing prosocial behavior among offenders. These issues of continuities across time and across settings are important, especially in relation to theory development, because they help to define the boundaries of what needs to be explained. Issues of behavioral continuity also draw our attention to parallels across types of problem behaviors that may hold implications for strategies and techniques of remediation.

The research also indicates that inmates who show adjustment difficulties in the community have trouble adjusting to prison and that those who have trouble adjusting to prison are likely to experience problems on return to the community. Attributes of a marginal lifestyle, such as unemployment, low educational achievement, and unstable family life, are predictive of a variety of inmate problem behaviors. These findings suggest a chronicity of life difficulties of a more general nature than that typically emphasized in research on crime. In this regard, the research findings on prison adjustment hold implications for the current policy emphasis being placed on career criminals. At present, it appears that the problem of chronic misbehavior is too narrowly conceived and policy initiatives are too narrowly focused if the objective is to understand and change offenders who demonstrate long-term patterns of antisocial behavior.

Early sociologists were quick to observe that some groups of people experience all manner of problems and difficulties in life. The prison research confirms this observation and shows that inmates for whom the challenges of prison adjustment are greatest are also a group for whom the range of coping difficulties is most diverse. Although the research effectively documents a confluence of problem behaviors for many individuals, much remains to be done by way of generating comprehensive explanations. With regard to theoretical explanations, at least two issues surface as important. The first relates to the generality of explanations, or the degree to which different problem behaviors can be interpreted as the result of the same process. In the case of inmate adjustment, it becomes important to ask whether prison coping problems are similar to or different from difficulties that the inmate has experienced previously with the legal system, school, work, friends, and family. The second issue pertains to the ways in which behaviors relate to each other over the developmental course of problem lives. Multiple problems might be traced to a common origin, or one problem may cause another or help determine its expression, or problems may interact with each other to exacerbate difficulties and to shape the overall course of development. A pattern in which emotional difficulties reliably coincide with disruptive behavior holds different theoretical and policy implications than a pattern in which different types of problems are far separated in time. In the first situation we might suspect that the two problems are in some ways related, in which case we can look for causal links or seek to develop hybrid interventions that address multifaceted difficulties. In fact, it has been argued that aspects of emotional disorders are intimately linked to antisocial behavior, including violence, for some mentally ill offenders, and suggestions have been made for developing residential treatment programs that combine attributes of criminal justice and mental health settings (Toch 1982; Toch and Adams 1989a, 1989b).

Resolving issues of continuity and discontinuity across multiple-problem behaviors will not be simple, and existing research highlights the inherent complexity of the task. Although some inmates show a variety of coping difficulties, such as mental illness and chronic misbehavior, there are features that differentiate those inmates with one problem from those with another and from those with both. Inmates who experience serious emotional disorders in prisons are likely to have had psychiatric difficulties in the past, revealing continuity of a fairly specific nature. Youth is associated with prison misbehavior, as it is more generally with crime, suggesting continuity on a broader plane. Disturbed-disruptive inmates combine diverging portraits of psychiatric patients as older, vulnerable, and not always mentally competent and of recidivistic offenders as young, predatory, and volitional. The process of sorting out the shared and unique features of adjustment problems and of locating inmates with multiple problems within that framework requires that we abandon preconceived notions derived from compartmentalized portraits of specific types of problems.

In reviewing the characteristics of inmates with adjustment difficulties, two variables, race and sex, stand out, the latter because it has been heavily researched and the former because it is frequently ignored in prison studies. Regarding race issues, studies indicating that black inmates demonstrate lower rates of emotional disorders suggest that this group is more psychologically resilient to the stresses of prison life. By the same token, black inmates are sometimes shown to have a higher rate of disruptive behavior, a difference that surfaces more reliably with regard to violent incidents. One of the difficulties with interpreting these associations is that race is a composite variable that captures many different influences. Although racial differences are most commonly interpreted in the context of subcultural, socialization, and criminal history effects, in most studies only the last of these influences is measured directly. One interpretation for the mixed findings on inmate misbehavior is that the significance of race varies across prison systems and even across individual prisons because racial experiences differ across the country. To illustrate the point, a substantial amount of research has been conducted in New York state prisons, and the findings consistently indicate that black inmates have higher infraction rates (Flanagan 1983; Toch and Adams 1989a; Wright 1989). While this observation does not explain the racial difference, it is an interesting one, since it points to a consistency of research findings within a specific prison context. Little consideration is generally given to individual developmental differences that might vary within racial groups in terms of personal history and experience. Similarly, little consideration is given to contextual or situational factors that might vary across prisons and prison systems. When prison gangs exist and are organized along racial lines, it can be difficult for inmates to remain unallied (Jacobs 1974, 1976, 1977). In some ways, gang membership might facilitate adjustment by creating a social support network that offers friendship, identity, protection, and access to an underground economy, or gangs may be a source of adjustment problems when pressure is put on inmates to join or when racial frictions are aggravated by gangs. Gangs can also be seen as another dimension of continuity from community to prison when leadership and membership statuses transfer from one setting to the other.

Issues relating to female inmates are not often studied, in part because of the relatively small number of women who are sent to prison. While a limited pool of potential subjects can make research unattractive and create logistical difficulties, the study of female inmates affords researchers opportunities to test hypotheses that address the universal or particular nature of inmate adjustment. Patterns of adjustment that transcend the sexes can serve as the foundation for generalized propositions about inmate reactions to confinement. By the same token, findings that are specific to a given sex can help us to isolate critical differences between groups of individuals and between types of prison environments. Many of the issues that have been studied in male prisons, such as those regarding long-term inmates, chronic offenders, self-injury, and emotional disorder, have not been investigated in female prisons. If we assume that environments differ between male and female prisons and that differences in background and socialization experiences lead to different coping strategies for men and women, then the study of female prisons becomes critical to the development of a fully articulated perspective on inmate adjustment.

The research also confirms the usefulness of studying patterns of inmate adjustment problems over the prison term. The early period of incarceration is a critical time during which problems of adjustment are most likely to surface. Studies indicate that both emotional disorder and prison misbehavior peak early in the incarceration experience. The research also shows that inmate behavior, on average, improves over time, indicating that most inmates cope successfully with the prison experience. A plausible explanation for these findings, one that is compatible with the stress-coping perspective, is that the process of transition from community to institution poses stressful challenges that inmates must surmount if they are to adapt successfully. Furthermore, we have seen that, when an inmate's coping repertoire is sufficiently limited and inflexible, the likelihood of adjustment difficulties becomes greater. These findings hold several implications for policy. If we are interested in mitigating adjustment difficulties, we should concentrate resources on newly arrived inmates. Also, by knowing the typical course of adjustment difficulties over prison careers, it becomes easier to identify atypical behavior patterns and to target these inmates for scrutiny. That rates of problem behaviors peak early in the sentence and decline thereafter offers some reassurance that many inmate adjustment difficulties will work themselves out over time. Finally, tumultuous experiences can unfreeze a person psychologically and leave him or her receptive to learning new strategies for dealing with life's difficulties. It may be possible to capitalize on this by securing early on an inmate's commitment to and involvement in programs geared toward productive behavior change.

Some scholars have characterized the early stages of imprisonment as a "window of opportunity," in the sense that many inmates who experience adjustment difficulties during this period will be especially receptive to programmatic interventions (Zamble and Porporino 1988, 1990). At the same time, however, they describe the vast portion of the prison experience as a "deep freeze," meaning that little positive change occurs in the coping behaviors and strategies of inmates. The latter characterization communicates a rather dour message about prisons in general and about the situation we face if narrowly time-bound opportunities for initiating positive changes in inmates are missed. Although prisons clearly can stand improvement, the notion of a behavioral deep freeze appears to be overly pessimistic in view of studies that report steadily decreasing rates of inmate misbehavior over the course of prison terms. The lack of change observed by Zamble and Porporino perhaps can be attributed to several distinctive features of their research. The most pressing inmate problems they studied, such as missing family and friends and missing freedom, are highly pervasive concerns largely outside an inmate's realm of direct influence. Also, an emphasis on describing how inmates cope with problems given that a problem has occurred may create a tendency to overlook changes in attitudes and behaviors that lead to fewer problems arising. In fact, when these factors are taken into account, the data run contrary to the deep-freeze hypothesis. The percentage of inmates who report having conflicts with other inmates, events that are under a person's immediate control, steadily declines with time, and long-term inmates are observed to develop a number of strategies for avoiding trouble while in prison (Zamble and Porporino 1988, pp. 91, 107; Zamble 1992).

Questions of what changes can or do occur among inmates lead to issues of how prisons can best facilitate positive change. The research on prison adjustment clearly indicates a need for programs that help inmates to develop their coping abilities early in the prison sentence. These programs could use a variety of behavioral, cognitive, and social skills techniques to teach inmates to respond more effectively to difficult situations through the use of planned, systematic approaches to problem solving. When directed at problems of adjusting to prison life, such programs are likely to be effective and can bring immediate payoff in terms of making prisons more humane. In addition, there is now substantial evidence to indicate that under the right conditions these and other types of therapeutic programs can have an effect on criminal recidivism (Gendreau and Ross 1987; Andrews et al. 1990). This development highlights possible areas of compatibility between programs designed to minimize prison adjustment difficulties and those intended to curb criminal recidivism. As Zamble and Porporino (1990) point out, common deficits in inmate coping skills, as reflected in unplanned, impulsive, habitual behaviors, are outwardly linked to criminality. Likewise, research indicates that inmates who have difficulty adjusting to prison also have difficulty meeting life's challenges in other contexts and situations. There is good reason to suggest that maladaptive behavior in prison has much in common with maladaptive behavior in the community, and to the extent that problem behaviors in prison cannot be viewed as a category sui generis, programs that bring positive change in the institutional context should have spillover effects to community settings.

Inmates who have the most serious difficulties adjusting to prison tend to have the most chronic and complex histories of life problems. In such cases, the successful integration of mental health and correctional goals is more difficult and requires that we forsake much of our fragmented thinking about problem behaviors and therapeutic interventions. Chronic problems are discouraging because they suggest an intractability of behavior and the limited efficacy of therapeutic interventions. However, chronicity also suggests a continuity of etiological processes that may make it easier to identify the sources of an offender's difficulties. If these processes can be interrupted or neutralized during the time that the offender is in prison, they might possibly be derailed for the long term. Complex behavior problems are difficult to address because their multifaceted nature often presents an ever-changing picture to observers. In such cases, the typical treatment approach that combines a variety of therapeutic packages each separately dealing with a different problem is likely to be ineffective. Complicated problems require sophisticated treatment strategies that integrate and coordinate service delivery across multiple domains, which means that disciplinary boundaries must be breached and new alliances formed among treatment professionals.

The research on inmate adjustment also highlights the influence of environmental factors on behavior. Although much of the concern has been with disjunctures between persons and settings, the other side of the coin, which points to the person-environment congruences, has implications for enhancing the effectiveness of correctional programming. Interventions can be directed at people and at environments, and if we expand and coordinate efforts along these two lines, we are likely to find that treatment programs become more effective. All prison treatment programs take place within an organizational and situational context, and it is clearly preferable to deliver services in environments that complement and enhance treatment efforts at the individual level. An integration of person-centered and environment-centered concerns will move us toward a more sophisticated view of correctional programming that attempts to deal with diverse inmate problem behaviors.

Early research on prison adjustment focused attention on attitudes during the middle stage of the prison term, or the point at which it was hypothesized that the influence of the prison culture is greatest and the influence of the community weakest. We now see that the beginning and ending points of the prison term are critical transition periods when dealing with issues of stress and maladaptive behavior. Although we are beginning to understand these transition processes, we need more information on the links that bridge community and prison experiences. This does not mean that the middle stages of incarceration can be ignored. Inmate crises can be unpredictable, and the middle period comprises the bulk of the prison term, providing staff with valuable time and opportunities to work with inmates toward positive change. Also, it is important for understanding to place inmate behavior within the full context of the prison experience, studying how inmates change throughout the entire course of the prison experience. The criminal career perspective (Blumstein et al. 1986) has drawn attention to developmental patterns of antisocial behavior, but the ways in which incarceration, which represents a significant event in the lives of offenders, might influence these developmental paths often goes unconsidered. Thus, there is a need to view prison from a larger context, one that integrates behavior and experience across settings and across time into developmental patterns that capture key attributes of offender careers. These issues are best addressed through longitudinal studies that track offenders before, during, and after prison experiences and that collect information relevant to a diverse array of developmental questions (e.g., Tonry, Ohlin, and Farrington 1991).

With regard to the study of prisons as environments, reliable instruments are now available to tap salient concerns of inmates and salient dimensions of prison settings. The research in this area is still in its early days, although useful and important findings have already emerged. We have seen that freedom and safety, and to a lesser extent structure, are critical aspects of prison environments in terms of inmate adjustment. Attempts to address issues of freedom and safety in prison typically point in different directions in the sense that arrangements that maximize safety often bring less freedom and vice versa. Although safety implicates survival and therefore must be given the highest priority, freedom can be linked to issues of responsibility, growth, and development and therefore cannot be ignored totally if prisons are to be more than warehouses for offenders. Such tensions indicate that part of the challenge for prison administrators is to develop settings that minimize the trade-offs inmates must make if their multifaceted concerns are to be addressed constructively. Interactions between individuals and their environments are important considerations in studying inmate adjustment problems. The research issues go beyond those of simply searching for interaction terms in a statistical sense, given that substantive questions of congruency and incongruency between individual attributes and counterpart environmental attributes must take precedence. Thus, research should continue to identify substantively important person-environment congruences and disjunctures and to investigate whether the benefits and adversities that are predicted to accrue to these situations are observed. Once sufficient knowledge is accumulated, it becomes possible for administrators to incorporate a contextual view of inmate behavior into prison operations. In order for administrators to take fullest advantage of this strategy, the range of environmental options in prisons will have to be broadened, inmate needs will have to play a larger role in decisions about program assignments and resource allocation, and record systems will have to be expanded to track positive changes in a more systematic fashion.

DiIulio (1987) has focused attention on the importance of prison administration and organization. These are underresearched areas that merit greater attention, particularly with regard to inmate adjustment issues. We know very little about how the structural aspects of prison organizations, such as the number and types of staff, programs, and inmates, relate to inmate adjustment. We also know very little about how variations in administrative policies and procedures facilitate or hinder inmate coping. It has been shown that specific policies and procedures for delivering mental health services and the overall priority that the institution accords to this task have important consequences for inmate adjustment (Adams 1984). Similarly, we might suspect that policies and procedures regarding inmate interactions with service and security staff, as well as regarding interactions among inmates, can have an influence on disruptive and violent behavior.

Many inmate difficulties can be traced to inherent characteristics of prisons as institutions that isolate individuals from society and deprive them of liberty. Although it is unlikely that the problems of inmate adjustment can be eradicated unless our systems of punishment are radically transformed, the picture is not so bleak at least with regard to inmate coping and adjustment issues. Most inmates are able to work through their adjustment problems, and for some inmates the experience may be regenerative. There exists a range of reactions to experiences of confinement, and what for some individuals are mildly annoying inconveniences can for other individuals be issues of psychological survival. The challenge for future research, then, is to continue organizing this individual diversity into a coherent framework of behavioral development.

REFERENCES

Abram, K., and L. Teplin. 1991. "Co-occurring Disorders among Mentally Ill Jail Detainees: Implications for Public Policy." *American Psychologist* 46:1036–45.

Abramson, M. 1972. "The Criminalization of Mentally Disordered Behavior: Possible Side Effects of a New Mental Health Law." *Hospital and Community Psychiatry* 23:101–7.

Adams, K. 1983. "Former Mental Patients in a Prison and Parole System: A Study of Socially Disruptive Behavior." *Criminal Justice and Behavior* 10:358–84.

———. 1984. "Prison Mental Health Services: An Empirical Study of the Service Delivery Process in Two New York State Prisons." Ph.D. dissertation, State University of New York at Albany, School of Criminal Justice.

———. 1986. "The Disciplinary Experiences of Mentally Disordered Inmates." *Criminal Justice and Behavior* 13:297–316.

Andrews, D., I. Zinger, R. Hoge, J. Bonta, P. Gendreau, and F. Cullen. 1990. "Does Correctional Treatment Work? A Clinically Relevant and Psychologically Informed Meta-analysis." *Criminology* 28:369–404.

Bailey, W. 1966. "Correctional Outcome: An Evaluation of 100 Reports." *Journal of Criminal Law, Criminology, and Police Science* 57:153–60.

Banister, P., F. Smith, K. Heskin, and N. Bolton. 1973. "Psychological Correlates of Long-Term Imprisonment: I. Cognitive Variables." *British Journal of Criminology* 13:312–23.

Bartollas, C. 1982. "Survival Problems of Adolescent Prisoners." In *The Pains of Imprisonment*, edited by R. Johnson and H. Toch. Beverly Hills, Calif.: Sage.

Baskin, D., I. Sommers, and H. Steadman. 1991. "Assessing the Impact of Psychiatric Impairment on Prison Violence." *Journal of Criminal Justice* 19:271–80.

Berk, Bernard. 1966. "Organizational Goals and Inmate Organization." *American Journal of Sociology* 71:522–34.

Biegel, A., and H. Russell. 1973. "Suicidal Behavior in Jails: Prognostic Consideration." In *Jail House Blues*, edited by B. Danto. Orchard Lake, Mich.: Epic.

Blumstein, A., J. Cohen, J. Roth, and C. Visher. 1986. *Criminal Careers and "Career Criminals."* Washington, D.C.: National Academy Press.

Bolton, N., F. Smith, K. Heskin, and P. Banister. 1976. "Psychological Correlates of Long-Term Imprisonment: IV. A Longitudinal Analysis." *British Journal of Criminology* 16:38–47.

Bonta, J., and P. Gendreau. 1990. "Reexamining the Cruel and Unusual Punishment of Prison Life." *Law and Human Behavior* 14:347–72.

Bonta, J., and G. Nanckivell. 1980. "Institutional Misconduct and Anxiety Levels among Jailed Inmates." *Criminal Justice and Behavior* 7:203–14.

Bottoms, A., W. Hay, and J. Sparks. 1990. "Situational and Social Approaches to the Prevention of Disorder in Long-Term Prisons." *Prison Journal* 80:83–95.

Bowker, L. H. 1980. *Prison Victimization.* New York: Elsevier.

———. 1982. "Victimizers and Victims in American Correctional Institutions." In *The Pains of Imprisonment*, edited by R. Johnson and H. Toch. Beverly Hills, Calif.: Sage.

Brodsky, S., and H. Smitherman. 1983. *Handbook of Scales for Research in Crime and Delinquency.* New York: Plenum.

Bronstein, A. 1991. "U.S. Policies Create Prison Human Rights Violations." *National Prison Project Journal* 6(Summer):4–5, 13–14.

Brown, B., and T. Courtless. 1971. *Mentally Retarded Offender*. Washington, D.C.: National Institute of Mental Health, Center for the Study of Crime and Delinquency.

Brown, B., and S. Spevacek. 1971. "Disciplinary Offenders at Two Differing Correctional Institutions." *Correctional Psychiatry Journal of Social Therapy* 17:48–56.

Bukstel, L., and P. Kilmann. 1980. "Psychological Effects of Imprisonment on Confined Individuals." *Psychological Bulletin* 88:469–93.

Burtch, B., and R. Ericson. 1979. *The Silent System: An Inquiry into Prisoners Who Suicide and Annotated Bibliography*. Toronto: University of Toronto.

Canter, D. 1987. "Implications for 'New Generation' Prisons of Existing Psychological Research into Prison Design and Use." In *Problems of Long-Term Imprisonment*, edited by A. Bottoms and R. Light. Aldershot: Gower.

Cantril, H. 1965. *The Pattern of Human Concerns*. New Brunswick, N.J.: Rutgers University Press.

Carroll, L. 1974. *Hacks, Blacks and Cons: Race Relations in a Maximum Security Prison*. Lexington, Mass.: Heath.

———. 1982. "Race, Ethnicity, and the Social Order of the Prison." In *The Pains of Imprisonment*, edited by R. Johnson and H. Toch. Beverly Hills, Calif.: Sage.

Chesney-Lind, M., and N. Rodriquez. 1983. "Women under Lock and Key: A View from the Inside." *Prison Journal* 63:47–65.

Clemmer, D. 1958. *The Prison Community*. New York: Holt, Rinehart & Winston.

Coe, R. 1961. "Characteristics of Well Adjusted and Poorly Adjusted Inmates." *Journal of Criminal Law, Criminology and Police Science* 52:178–84.

Cohen, S., and L. Taylor. 1972. *Psychological Survival: The Experience of Long-Term Imprisonment*. New York: Pantheon.

Collins, J., W. Schlenger, and B. Jordan. 1988. "Antisocial Personality and Substance Abuse Disorders." *Bulletin of the American Academy of Psychiatry and Law* 16:187–98.

Cooke, D. 1989. "Containing Violent Prisoners: An Analysis of the Barlinnie Special Unit." *British Journal of Criminology* 29:129–43.

Cookson, H. 1977. "Survey of Self-Injury in a Closed Prison for Women." *British Journal of Criminology* 11:73–79.

Cormier, B., M. Kennedy, and M. Sendbuehler. 1967. "Cell Breakage and Gate Fever." *British Journal of Criminology* 7:317–24.

Danto, B. 1973. "Suicide at the Wayne County Jail: 1967–70." In *Jail House Blues*, edited by B. Danto. Orchard Lake, Mich.: Epic.

D'Atri, D. 1975. "Psychophysiological Responses to Crowding." *Environment and Behavior* 7:237–52.

Davies, W. 1982. "Violence in Prisons." In *Developments in the Study of Criminal Behavior*, vol. 2, edited by P. Feldman. Chinchester: Wiley.

Davis, A. 1968. "Report on Sexual Assaults in the Philadelphia Prison System and Sheriff's Vans." *Trans-Action* 6:8–16.

Denkowski, G., and K. Denkowski. 1985. "The Mentally Retarded Offender in the State Prison System: Identification, Prevalence, Adjustment, and Rehabilitation." *Criminal Justice and Behavior* 12:55–70.

DiIulio, J., Jr. 1987. *Governing Prisons: A Comparative Study of Correctional Management.* New York: Free Press.

———. 1989. "Managing Constitutionally." *Society* (July/August), pp. 81–83.

Ditchfield, J. 1990. *Control in Prisons: A Review of the Literature.* Home Office Research Study no. 118. London: H.M. Stationery Office.

Duffee, D. 1980. *Correctional Management: Change and Control in Correctional Organizations.* Englewood Cliffs, N.J.: Prentice Hall.

Edinger, J. 1979. "Cross Validation of the Megargee MMPI Typology for Prisoners." *Journal of Consulting and Clinical Psychology* 47:234–42.

Ellis, D., H. Grasmick, and B. Gilman. 1974. "Violence in Prison: A Sociological Analysis." *American Journal of Sociology* 80:16–43.

Esparza, R. 1973. "Attempted and Committed Suicide in County Jails." In *Jail House Blues,* edited by B. Danto. Orchard Lake, Mich.: Epic.

Fagan, T., and F. Lira. 1978. "Profile of Mood States: Racial Differences in a Delinquent Population." *Psychological Reports* 43:348–50.

Faily, A., and G. Roundtree. 1979. "Study of the Aggressions and Rule Violations in a Female Prison Population." *Journal of Offender Counseling, Services, and Rehabilitation* 4:81–87.

Farrington, D. 1986. "Age and Crime." In *Crime and Justice: An Annual Review of Research,* vol. 7, edited by M. Tonry and N. Morris. Chicago: University of Chicago Press.

Fawcett, J., and B. Mars. 1973. "Suicide at the County Jail." In *Jail House Blues,* edited by B. Danto. Orchard Lake, Mich.: Epic.

Feder, L. 1989. "The Community Adjustment of Mentally Disordered Offenders." Ph.D. dissertation, State University of New York at Albany, School of Criminal Justice.

Feldman, M. 1988. "The Challenge of Self-Mutilation: A Review." *Comprehensive Psychiatry* 29:252–69.

Finn, M. 1989. "The Disciplinary Adjustment of Mentally Retarded Inmates." Ph.D. dissertation, State University of New York at Albany, School of Criminal Justice.

Flanagan, T. 1980*a.* "The Pains of Long-Term Imprisonment: A Comparison of British and American Perspectives." *British Journal of Criminology* 20:148–56.

———. 1980*b.* "Time-Served and Institutional Misconduct: Patterns of Involvement in Disciplinary Infractions among Long-Term and Short-Term Inmates." *Journal of Criminal Justice* 8:357–67.

———. 1981. "Dealing with Long-Term Confinement: Adaptive Strategies and Perspectives among Long-Term Prisoners." *Criminal Justice Behavior* 8:201–22.

———. 1982. "Lifers and Long-Termers: Doing Big Time." In *The Pains of Imprisonment,* edited by R. Johnson and H. Toch. Beverly Hills, Calif.: Sage.

———. 1983. "Correlates of Institutional Misconduct among State Prisoners." *Criminology* 21:29–39.

Flanagan, T., D. Clark, D. Aziz, and B. Szelest. 1990. "Compositional Changes in a Long-Term Prisoner Population: 1956–89." *Prison Journal* 80:15–34.

Fox, J. 1975. "Women in Crisis." In *Men in Crisis: Human Breakdowns in Prison*, by Hans Toch. Chicago: Aldine.

———. 1982. "Women in Prison: A Case Study in the Social Reality of Stress." In *The Pains of Imprisonment*, edited by R. Johnson and H. Toch. Beverly Hills, Calif.: Sage.

Fox, V. 1958. "Analysis of Prison Disciplinary Problems." *Journal of Criminal Law, Criminology, and Police Science* 49:321–26.

Fuller, D., and T. Orsagh. 1977. "Violence and Victimization within a State Prison System." *Criminal Justice Review* 2:35–55.

Gaes, G. 1985. "The Effects of Overcrowding in Prison." In *Crime and Justice: An Annual Review of Research*, vol. 6, edited by M. Tonry and N. Morris. Chicago: University of Chicago Press.

———. 1990. "Prison Crowding Research Reexamined." Unpublished manuscript. Washington, D.C.: U.S. Department of Justice, Federal Bureau of Prisons.

Garabedian, P. 1963. "Social Roles and Processes of Socialization in the Prison Community." *Social Problems* 11:139–52.

———. 1964. "Social Roles in a Correctional Community." *Journal of Criminal Law, Criminology, and Police Science* 55:235–47.

Gendreau P., and P. Ross. 1987. "Revivification of Rehabilitation: Evidence from the 1980's." *Justice Quarterly* 4:349–408.

Giallombardo, R. 1966. *Society of Women: A Study of a Woman's Prison*. New York: Wiley.

Gibbs, J. 1978. "Stress and Self-Injury in Jail." Ph.D. dissertation, State University of New York at Albany, School of Criminal Justice.

———. 1982a. "Disruption and Distress: Going from the Street to Jail." In *Coping with Imprisonment*, edited by N. Parisi. Beverly Hills, Calif.: Sage.

———. 1982b. "The First Cut Is the Deepest: Psychological Breakdown and Survival in the Detention Setting." In *The Pains of Imprisonment*, edited by R. Johnson and H. Toch. Beverly Hills, Calif.: Sage.

———. 1982c. "On 'Demons' and 'Gaols': A Summary and Review of Investigations Concerning the Psychological Problems of Jail Prisoners." In *Mental Health Services in Local Jails: Report of a Special National Workshop*, edited by C. S. Dunn and H. J. Steadman. U.S. Department of Health and Human Services Publication no. ADM 82-1181. Rockville, Md.: National Institute of Mental Health.

———. 1987. "Symptoms of Psychopathology among Jail Prisoners: The Effects of Exposure to the Jail Environment." *Criminal Justice and Behavior* 14:288–310.

———. 1991. "Environmental Congruence and Symptoms of Psychopathology: A Further Exploration of the Effects of Exposure to the Jail Environment." *Criminal Justice and Behavior* 18:351–374.

Glaser, D. 1964. *The Effectiveness of a Prison and Parole System*. Indianapolis: Bobbs-Merrill.

Goetting, A., and R. Howsen. 1986. "Correlates of Prisoner Misconduct." *Journal of Quantitative Criminology* 2:49–67.

Goffman, E. 1961. *Asylums: Essays on the Social Situation of Mental Patients and Other Inmates*. Garden City, N.Y.: Doubleday.

Goodstein, L. 1979. "Inmate Adjustment to Prison and the Transition to Community Life." *Journal of Research in Crime and Delinquency* 16:246–72.

———. 1982. "A Quasi-experimental Test of Prisoner Reactions to Determinate and Indeterminate Sentencing." In *Coping with Imprisonment*, edited by N. Parisi. Beverly Hills, Calif.: Sage.

Goodstein, L., and D. MacKenzie. 1984. "Racial Differences in Adjustment Patterns of Prison Inmates: Prisonization, Conflict, Stress, and Control." In *The Criminal Justice System and Blacks*, edited by D. Georges-Abeyie. New York: Clark Boardman Co.

Goodstein, L., and K. Wright. 1989. "Inmate Adjustment to Prison." In *The American Prison System: Issues in Research and Policy*, edited by L. Goodstein and D. MacKenzie. New York: Plenum.

Gottfredson, M., and K. Adams. 1982. "Prison Behavior and Post Release Performance: Empirical Reality and Public Policy." *Law and Policy Quarterly* 4:373–91.

Gottfredson, M., and D. Gottfredson. 1980. *Decisionmaking and Criminal Justice*. Cambridge, Mass.: Ballinger.

Greenberg, D. 1985. "Age, Crime and Social Explanation." *American Journal of Sociology* 91:1–21.

Grusky, O. 1959. "Organizational Goals and the Behavior of Informal Leaders." *American Journal of Sociology* 65:452–72.

Gunn, J., G. Robertson, and S. Dell. 1978. *Psychiatric Aspects of Imprisonment*. London: Academic Press.

Hagel-Seymour, J. 1982. "Environment Sanctuaries for Susceptible Prisoners." In *The Pains of Imprisonment*, edited by R. Johnson and H. Toch. Beverly Hills, Calif.: Sage.

Halleck, S. 1967. *Psychiatry and the Dilemma of Crime*. New York: Harper & Row.

Hanks, L. 1940. "Preliminary for a Study of Problems of Discipline in Prisons." *Journal of Criminal Law, Criminology, and Police Science* 30:879–97.

Hanson, R., C. Moss, R. Hosford, and M. Johnson. 1983. "Predicting Inmate Penitentiary Adjustment: An Assessment of Four Classificatory Methods." *Criminal Justice and Behavior* 10:293–309.

Harding, T., and E. Zimmermann. 1989. "Psychiatric Symptoms, Cognitive Stress and Vulnerability Factors: A Study in a Remand Prison." *British Journal of Psychiatry* 155:36–43.

Heffernan, E. 1972. *Making It in Prison: The Square, the Cool, and the Life*. New York: Wiley.

Heidensohn, F. 1985. *Women and Crime*. London: MacMillan.

Helig, S. 1973. "Suicide in Jails." In *Jail House Blues*, edited by B. Danto. Orchard Lake, Mich.: Epic.

Heskin, K., N. Bolton, F. Smith, and P. Banister. 1974. "Psychological Correlates of Long-Term Imprisonment: III. Attitudinal Variables." *British Journal of Criminology* 14:150–57.

Heskin, K., F. Smith, P. Banister, and N. Bolton. 1973. "Psychological Correlates of Long-Term Imprisonment: II. Personality Variables." *British Journal of Criminology* 13:323–30.

Hirschi, T., and M. Gottfredson. 1983. "Age and the Explanation of Crime." *American Journal of Sociology* 89:552–84.

Holmes, T., and R. Rahe. 1967. "The Social Readjustment Rating Scale." *Journal of Psychosomatic Research* 11:213–18.

Irwin, J. 1970. *The Felon*. Englewood Cliffs, N.J.: Prentice Hall.

———. 1980. *Prisons in Turmoil*. Boston, Mass.: Little Brown.

Irwin, J., and D. Cressey. 1962. "Thieves, Convicts, and the Inmate Subculture." *Social Problems* 10:142–155.

Jacobs, J. 1974. "Street Gangs Behind Bars." *Social Problems* 21:395–409.

———. 1976. "Stratification and Conflict among Prison Inmates." *Journal of Criminal Law and Criminology* 66:476–82.

———. 1977. *Statesville: The Penitentiary in Mass Society*. Chicago: University of Chicago Press.

Jaman, D. 1971. *Behavior during the First Year in Prison—Report IV as Related to Parole Outcome*. Research Report no. 44. Sacramento: California Department of Corrections, Research Division.

———. 1972. "A Synopsis of Research Report no. 43: 'Behavior During the First Year in Prison Report III—Background Characteristics as Predictors of Behavior and Misbehavior.'" Administrative abstract. Sacramento: California Department of Corrections, Research Division.

Jaman, D., P. Coburn, J. Goddard, and P. Mueller. 1966. "Characteristics of Violent Prisoners." Research Report no. 22. Sacramento: California Department of Corrections.

Jensen, G. 1977. "Age and Rule-Breaking in Prison." *Criminology* 14:555–68.

Johnson, D., J. Simmons, and B. Gordon. 1983. "Temporal Consistency of the Meyer-Megargee Inmate Typology." *Criminal Justice and Behavior* 10:263–68.

Johnson, E. 1966. "Pilot Study: Age, Race and Recidivism as Factors in Prisoner Infractions." *Canadian Journal of Corrections* 8:268–83.

Johnson, R. 1976. *Culture and Crisis in Confinement*. Lexington, Mass.: Lexington.

———. 1981. *Condemned to Die: Life under Sentence of Death*. New York: Elsevier.

———. 1982. "Life under Sentence of Death." In *The Pains of Imprisonment*, edited by R. Johnson and H. Toch. Beverly Hills, Calif.: Sage.

Jones, D. 1976. *The Health Risks of Imprisonment*. Lexington, Mass.: Lexington.

Jones, H., P. Cornes, and R. Stackford. 1977. *Open Prisons*. London: Routledge & Kegan Paul.

Kassebaum, G., D. Ward, and D. Wilner. 1971. *Prison Treatment and Parole Survival*. New York: Wiley.

Lazarus, R. S. 1966. *Psychological Stress and the Coping Process*. New York: McGraw Hill.

Lazarus, R. S., and S. Folkman. 1983. *Stress Appraisal and Coping*. New York: Springer-Verlag.

Lembo, J. J. 1969. "Research Notes: The Relationship of Institutional Disciplinary Infractions and the Inmate's Personal Contact with the Outside Community." *Criminologica* 7:50–54.

Lindquist, C. 1980. "Prison Discipline and the Female Offender." *Journal of Offender Counseling, Services, and Rehabilitation* 4:305–19.

Lloyd, C. 1990. *Suicide and Self-Inquiry in Prison: A Literature Review*. Home Office Research Study no. 115. London: H.M. Stationery Office.

Lockwood, D. 1980. *Prison Sexual Violence*. New York: Elsevier.

———. 1982a. "The Contribution of Sexual Harassment to Stress and Coping in Confinement." In *Coping with Imprisonment*, edited by N. Parisi. Beverly Hills, Calif.: Sage.

———. 1982b. "Reducing Prison Sexual Violence." In *The Pains of Imprisonment*, edited by R. Johnson and H. Toch. Beverly Hills, Calif.: Sage.

Louscher, P., R. Hosford, and C. Moss. 1983. "Predicting Dangerous Behavior in a Penitentiary Using the Megargee Typology." *Criminal Justice and Behavior* 10:269–84.

Mabli, J., C. Holley, J. Patrick, and J. Walls. 1979. "Age and Prison Violence." *Criminal Justice and Behavior* 6:175–86.

McCain, G., V. Cox, and P. Paulus. 1976. "The Relationship between Illness Complaints and Degree of Crowding in a Prison Environment." *Environment and Behavior* 8:283–90.

McCorkle, L., and R. Korn. 1954. "Resocialization within Walls." *Annals of the American Academy of Political and Social Science* 293:88–98.

McGrath, J. 1970. "A Conceptual Formulation for Research on Stress." In *Social and Psychological Factors in Stress*, edited by J. E. McGrath. New York: Holt, Rinehart, & Winston.

MacKenzie, D. 1987. "Age and Adjustment to Prison: Interactions with Attitudes and Anxiety." *Criminal Justice and Behavior* 14:427–47.

MacKenzie, D., and L. Goodstein. 1985. "Long-Term Incarceration Impacts and Characteristics of Long-Term Offenders: An Empirical Analysis." *Criminal Justice and Behavior* 12:395–414.

———. 1986. "Stress and the Control Beliefs of Prisoners: A Test of Three Models of Control-limited Environments." *Journal of Applied Social Psychology* 16:209–28.

MacKenzie, D., J. Robinson, and C. Campbell. 1989. "Long-Term Incarceration of Female Offenders: Prison Adjustment and Coping." *Criminal Justice and Behavior* 16:223–38.

Martinson, R. 1974. "What Works? Questions and Answers about Prison Reform." *Public Interest* 35:22–54.

Mathiesen, T. 1965. *Defences of the Weak: A Study of a Norwegian Correctional Institution*. London: Tavistock.

Megargee, E. 1976. "Population Density and Disruptive Behavior in a Prison Setting." In *Prison Violence*, edited by A. Cohen, G. Cole, and R. Bailey. New York: Heath.

Megargee, E., and M. Bohn. 1979. *Classifying Criminal Offenders: A New System Based on the MMPI*. Beverly Hills, Calif.: Sage.

Miller, S., and S. Dinitz. 1973. "Measuring Institutional Impact: A Follow-up." *Criminology* 11:417–26.

Miller, W. 1958. "Lower Class Culture as a Generating Milieu of Gang Delinquency." *Journal of Social Issues* 14:5–19.

Monahan, J., and H. Steadman. 1983. "Crime and Mental Disorder: An Epidemiological Approach." In *Crime and Justice: An Annual Review of Research*, vol. 4, edited by M. Tonry and N. Morris. Chicago: University of Chicago Press.

Moos, R. 1970. "Differential Effects of the Social Climates of Correctional Institutions." *Journal of Research in Crime and Delinquency* 7:71–82.

———. 1975. *Evaluating Correctional and Community Settings*. New York: Wiley.

Morris, A. 1987. *Women, Crime and Criminal Justice*. Oxford: Basil Blackwell.

Morris, N. 1974. *The Future of Imprisonment*. Chicago: University of Chicago Press.

Morris, N., and M. Tonry. 1990. *Between Prison and Probation: Intermediate Punishments in a Rational Sentencing System*. New York: Oxford University Press.

Murray, H. 1938. *Explorations in Personality*. New York: Oxford University Press.

Myers, L., and G. Levy. 1978. "Description and Prediction of the Intractable Inmate." *Journal of Research in Crime and Delinquency* 15:214–28.

Nacci, P., H. Teitelbaum, and J. Prather. 1977. "Population Density and Inmate Misconduct Rates in the Federal Prison System." *Federal Probation* 41:26–31.

Panton, J. 1974. "Personality Differences between Male and Female Prison Inmates as Measured by the MMPI." *Criminal Justice and Behavior* 1:332–39.

Parisi, N. 1982. "The Prisoner's Pressures and Responses." In *Coping with Imprisonment*, edited by N. Parisi. Beverly Hills, Calif.: Sage.

Petersilia, J., and P. Honig. 1980. "The Prison Experience of Career Criminals." RAND Report no. R-2511-DOJ. Santa Monica, Calif.: RAND.

Petrich, J. 1976. "Rate of Psychiatric Morbidity in a Metropolitan County Jail Population." *American Journal of Psychiatry* 133:1439–44.

Poole, E., and R. Regoli. 1980. "Race, Institutional Rule-Breaking, and Institutional Response: A Study of Discretionary Decisionmaking in Prison." *Law and Society Review* 14:931–46.

Porporino, F., and E. Zamble. 1984. "Coping with Imprisonment." *Canadian Journal of Criminology* 26:403–21.

Ramirez, J. 1983. "Race and the Apprehension of Inmate Misconduct." *Journal of Criminal Justice* 11:413–27.

Renzema, M. 1982. "The Stress Comes Later." In *The Pains of Imprisonment*, edited by R. Johnson and H. Toch. Beverly Hills, Calif.: Sage.

Richards, B. 1978. "The Experience of Long-Term Imprisonment: An Exploratory Investigation." *British Journal of Criminology* 18:162–69.

Rieger, W. 1971. "Suicide Attempts in a Federal Prison." *Archives of General Psychiatry* 24:532–35.

Roundtree, G., B. Mohan, and L. Mahaffey. 1980. "Determinants of Female Aggression: A Study of a Prison Population." *International Journal of Offender Therapy and Comparative Criminology* 24:260–69.

Ruback, R., T. Carr, and C. Hopper. 1986. "Perceived Control in Prison: Its Relation to Reported Crowding, Stress, and Symptoms." *Journal of Applied Social Psychology* 16:375–86.

Sapsford, R. 1978. "Life-Sentence Prisoners: Psychological Changes during Sentence." *British Journal of Criminology* 18:128–45.

Schnur, A. 1949. "Prison Conduct and Recidivism." *Journal of Criminal Law, Criminology, and Police Science* 40:36–42.

Smith, D. 1982. "Crowding and Confinement." In *The Pains of Imprisonment*, edited by R. Johnson and H. Toch. Beverly Hills, Calif.: Sage.

———. 1984. "Local Corrections: A Profile of Inmate Concerns." *Criminal Justice and Behavior* 11:75–99.

Street, D., R. Vinter, and C. Perrow. 1966. *Organization for Treatment*. New York: Free Press.

Swank, G., and D. Winer. 1976. "Occurrence of Psychiatric Disorder in a County Jail Population." *American Journal of Psychiatry* 133:1331–33.

Sykes, G. 1958. *The Society of Captives*. Princeton, N.J.: Princeton University Press.

Teplin, L. 1983. "The Criminalization of the Mentally Ill: Speculation in Search of Data." *Psychological Bulletin* 94:54–67.

Thomas, C. 1977. "Theoretical Perspectives on Prisonization: A Comparison of the Importation and Deprivation Models." *Journal of Criminal Law and Criminology* 68:135–45.

Toch, H. 1975. *Men in Crisis: Human Breakdowns in Prison*. Chicago: Aldine.

———. 1977. *Living in Prison: The Ecology of Survival*. New York: Free Press.

———. 1978. "Social Climate and Prison Violence." *Federal Probation* 42:21–25.

———. 1981. "Classification for Programming and Survival." In *Confinement in Maximum Custody*, edited by D. A. Ward and K. F. Schoen. Lexington, Mass.: Lexington.

———. 1982. "The Disturbed Disruptive Inmate: Where Does the Bus Stop?" *Journal of Psychiatry and Law* 10:327–49.

———. 1985. "Warehouses for People." *Annals of the American Academy of Political and Social Science* 478:58–72.

———. 1986. "The Psychology of Imprisonment." In *Psychology of Crime and Criminal Justice*, edited by H. Toch. Prospect Heights, Ill.: Waveland.

———. 1989. "Books in Review: Governing Prisons: A Comparative Study of Correctional Management." *Society* (March/April), pp. 86–88.

Toch, H., and K. Adams. 1986. "Pathology and Disruptiveness among Prison Inmates." *Journal of Research in Crime and Delinquency* 23:7–21.

———. 1989a. *Coping: Maladaptation in Prisons*. New Brunswick, N.J.: Transaction.

———. 1989*b*. *The Disturbed Violent Offender*. New Haven, Conn.: Yale University Press.

Toch, H., K. Adams, and R. Greene. 1987. "Ethnicity, Disruptiveness, and Emotional Disorder among Prison Inmates." *Criminal Justice and Behavior* 14:93–109.

Tonry, M., L. Ohlin, and D. Farrington. 1991. *Human Development and Criminal Behavior: New Ways for Advancing Knowledge*. New York: Springer-Verlag.

Unkovic, C., and J. Albini. 1969. "The Lifer Speaks for Himself: An Analysis of the Assumed Homogeneity of Life-Termers." *Crime and Delinquency* 15:156–61.

Waller, I. 1974. *Men Released from Prison*. Toronto: University of Toronto Press.

Watman, W. 1966. "The Relationship between Acting Out Behavior and Some Psychological Test Indices in a Prison Population." *Journal of Clinical Psychology* 22:279–80.

Wellford, C. 1967. "Factors Associated with Adoption of the Inmate Code: A Study of Normative Socialization." *Journal of Criminal Law, Criminology, and Police Science* 58:197–203.

Wenk, E., and R. Moos. 1972. "Social Climates in Prison: An Attempt to Conceptualize and Measure Environmental Factors in Total Institutions." *Journal of Research in Crime and Delinquency* 9:134–48.

Wheeler, S. 1961. "Socialization in Correctional Communities." *American Sociological Review* 26:697–712.

White, R. 1980. "Prediction of Adjustment to Prison in a Federal Correctional Population." *Journal of Clinical Psychology* 36:1031–34.

Widom, C. 1989. "The Cycle of Violence." *Science* 244:160–66.

Williams, M., and D. Longley. 1987. "Identifying Control Problem Prisoners in Dispersal Prisons." In *Problems of Long-Term Imprisonment*, edited by A. Bottoms and R. Light. Aldershot: Gower.

Wolf, S., W. Freinek, and J. Shaffer. 1966. "Frequency and Severity of Rule Infractions as Criteria of Prison Maladjustment." *Journal of Clinical Psychology* 21:244–47.

Wolfgang, M. 1961. "Quantitative Analysis of Adjustment to the Prison Community." *Journal of Criminal Law, Criminology, and Police Science* 51:587–618.

Wool, R., and E. Dooley. 1987. "A Study of Attempted Suicides in Prison." *Medical Science and the Law* 27:297–301.

Wright, K. 1985. "Developing the Prison Environment Inventory." *Journal of Research in Crime and Delinquency* 22:257–77.

———. 1986. "An Exploratory Study of Transactional Classification." *Journal of Research in Crime and Delinquency* 23:326–48.

———. 1988. "The Relationship of Risk, Needs, and Personality Classification Systems and Prison Adjustment." *Criminal Justice and Behavior* 15:454–71.

———. 1989. "Race and Economic Marginality in Explaining Prison Adjustment." *Journal of Research in Crime and Delinquency* 26:67–89.

———. 1991*a*. "The Violent and Victimized in the Male Prison." *Journal of Offender Rehabilitation* 16:1–25.

————. 1991*b*. "A Study of Individual, Environmental, and Interactive Effects in Explaining Prison Adjustment." *Justice Quarterly* 8:217–42.

Wright, K., and J. Boudouris. 1982. "An Assessment of the Moos Correctional Institution Environment Scale." *Journal of Research in Crime and Delinquency* 19:255–76.

Wright, K., and L. Goodstein. 1989. "Correctional Environments." In *The American Prison System: Issues in Research and Policy*, edited by L. Goodstein and D. MacKenzie. New York: Plenum.

Wright, K., and D. Jones. 1989. "The Relationship of Prison Environment and Behavioral Outcomes." Unpublished manuscript. Binghamton: State University of New York at Binghamton, Center for Education and Social Research.

Zamble, E. 1992. "Behavior and Adaptation in Long-Term Prison Inmates: Descriptive Longitudinal Results." Unpublished manuscript. Kingston, Ontario: Queens University, Department of Psychology.

Zamble, E., and F. Porporino. 1988. *Coping, Behavior, and Adaptation in Prison Inmates*. New York: Springer-Verlag.

————. 1990. "Coping, Imprisonment, and Rehabilitation: Some Data and Their Implications." *Criminal Justice and Behavior* 17:53–70.

Zingraff, M. 1980. "Inmate Assimilation: A Comparison of Male and Female Delinquents." *Criminal Justice and Behavior* 7:275–92.

Zink, T. 1958. "Are Prison Troublemakers Different?" *Journal of Criminal Law, Criminology, and Police Science* 48:433–34.

Douglas C. McDonald

Private Penal Institutions

ABSTRACT

Some argue that operation and ownership of correctional facilities is a
core responsibility of government. The historical record indicates
otherwise. Private parties long played a central role in the administration
of penal sanctions in Great Britain and the United States. By the
twentieth century, government assumed operational responsibility for
most adult correctional facilities. Privately owned or operated juvenile
facilities in the United States have been more common and in 1989 held
about 40 percent of all juveniles confined. Proliferation of private juvenile
facilities did not reduce reliance on large public correctional institutions;
confinement in public facilities rose over the past several decades.
Privately operated correctional facilities for adults emerged with much
fanfare in the mid-1980s, touching off a debate about the proper and
constitutional roles of private and public agencies. Both research and
experience are likely to show that private facilities can exploit specific
conditions in specific jurisdictions and can deliver more cost-effective
service in these places, but that claims of the private sector's inherent
superiority over public correctional management will not be borne out.

In the mid-1980s, the question of whether to "privatize" prisons and
jails emerged as a much-contested issue among correctional policymakers and professionals. Prior to that, private firms had been contracting
without much controversy with federal and state governments to provide a variety of discrete services to correctional facilities, such as
health care, prison industry programs, counseling, vocational training,
education, maintenance, and food services (Camp and Camp 1984;

Douglas C. McDonald is a sociologist at Abt Associates Inc., in Cambridge, Massachusetts, where he conducts research on criminal justice and drug abuse.

Mullen, Chabotar, and Carrow 1984; Criminal Justice Associates 1985; Logan and Rausch 1985; Mullen 1985). Having private firms provide such specific services went unremarked because the practice did not seem to pose fundamental questions about the state's authority over prisoners. Even where private firms administered entire facilities, little controversy was provoked because these facilities were typically found at the "soft" end of the correctional continuum: halfway houses, residential treatment programs, detention centers for illegal immigrants, work release facilities, group homes for juveniles, and penal farms. But when private corporations, and especially for-profit ones, began assuming control of county jails and state prisons, and made such audacious proposals as the offer by the Corrections Corporation of America (CCA) in 1985 to assume control of the entire Tennessee state prison system (Corrections Corporation of America 1985; Tolchin 1985a), correctional professionals and policymakers began to see the matter in a different light (Immarigeon 1987). What appeared to be at stake was the state's dominant and even exclusive power to administer the criminal law, as well as the assumptions that legitimated this authority (e.g., American Bar Association, Section on Criminal Justice 1986, 1989; U.S. House of Representatives 1986; Robbins 1988; Press 1990).

Such heated controversy has not surrounded the private sector's involvement in services to other types of institutionalized populations in this country, even though the private role may be dominant in them. For example, approximately 60 percent of all psychiatric hospitals in the United States in 1989 were private, two-thirds of which were investor-owned profit-seeking enterprises (American Hospital Association 1990, p. 222). An even higher proportion—two-thirds—of all juvenile correctional facilities in this country are privately operated (U.S. Bureau of the Census 1989). Approximately 75 percent of all clients in residential drug treatment programs are in private facilities (Batten 1991). Of about 15,000 nursing homes in existence at the time of a 1985 survey, only 8 percent were government owned, 70 percent were private for-profits, and the remainder were private not-for-profits (Institute of Medicine 1986, p. 10).

The prospect of private prisons and jails has raised much controversy and even hostility, while privately operated facilities in other areas have not, partly because a large private role in these other domains has long been a feature of the institutional landscape, especially in the

health care services. In contrast, public authorities have been the dominant, though not always the exclusive, party in the operation of prisons
and jails in this country. To propose a significant change in this order
threatens to shake up now-traditional arrangements and to challenge
organized groups (e.g., public employee unions) that have interests in
maintaining the status quo.

Another reason, however, is ideological. Nursing homes, psychiatric
hospitals, drug treatment centers, and even juvenile correctional facilities all exist for the ostensible purpose of serving their patients or
clients. To be sure, persons are sometimes legally coerced into entering
them, but the formal justification of such orders is that government
agents are acting in the best interests of the child, the mentally ill, or
the addict. In prisons and jails, there is no such fiction. Prisoners have
either been convicted of criminal offenses against society or are being
held to determine their guilt. The dominant interests being served are
society's interests in protecting itself and in sanctioning lawbreakers.
It is not surprising that many see this coercive power as properly
belonging to the state and resist the prospect of delegating it to private,
self-interested parties.

The debate that developed in the latter half of the 1980s and continues today involves both normative and empirical issues. The resolution
of normative questions, posed either as legal or policy issues, turns on
choosing values and principles that are to govern practice. For example,
is it constitutional for government to delegate authority for administering imprisonment to private corporations? If delegation is deemed to
be constitutional, should governments be allowed to shield themselves
against prisoners' claims of mistreatment by private jailers by delegating liabilities as well?

Apart from these normative questions (although often intertwined
with them) are a variety of empirical questions—questions of fact—
that can be resolved by observation and, if necessary, systematic research. What, for example, are the consequences of delegating correctional authority to private agents? Are privately operated correctional
facilities more efficient and thereby less costly? If they are, to what is
this due? Is market provision of services inherently more efficient than
government provision, at least with respect to these types of services?
Or is superior efficiency dependent on special conditions found in some
jurisdictions but not in others? What are the consequences of delegation for inmates? Are prisoners held in private facilities cared for and

treated any differently than in government facilities? Will, for example, policy decisions regarding sentencing and detention be affected by private industry interests?

The boundary of this essay is determined somewhat by the character of the current debate over the proper division of public and private responsibilities in penal administration. Fifteen or twenty years ago this topic might have been addressed under the rubric of "public and private partnerships" in providing government services, and one could have surveyed the various forms of private involvement in public services. The concept of "privatization" suggests a different angle of vision. Rather than elaborating different methods of integrating private involvement in government services, the debate during the past decade has been over whether to roll back the state and its domain and to redraw the line between what is properly governmental and what is properly private (Savas 1982; Butler 1985; Hanke 1987; President's Commission on Privatization 1988). In most institutional spheres, and in many countries, this means the transfer of ownership and operation of state-owned enterprises or assets, such as nationalized airlines, steel plants, health care systems, and public housing (Butler 1985; MacAvoy et al. 1989). In corrections, the debate is generally not over transfer of ownership of facilities but rather over the authority to operate them. Because states and localities have been expanding their prison and jail systems at a fast pace since the mid-1970s, there has been enormous opportunity for privately owned or operated facilities to come into existence without any transfer of public property required.

These preliminary remarks suggest a fundamental distinction between ownership and operating authority. Different combinations of public and private ownership and operating authority yield four basic arrangements that characterize public and private involvement in correctional administration. Three of these are commonly considered "private." These are represented in figure 1.

The upper left cell of figure 1 represents the constellation of ownership and operating authority characteristic of the conventional public facility, which dominates the adult correctional system, but which is less dominant in the juvenile correctional system. The polar opposite of this is the fully private facility, owned and operated by a private entity. (In the industry argot, these are sometimes called "cocos"— contractor-owned, contractor-operated facilities.) Governments pay these private entities for their services, generally on a hotel-like per diem basis for each prisoner held. Because they are private, a single

Ownership

	Public	Private
Public	Conventional public facility (fully public)	Lease or lease-purchase arrangements
Private	Contracted management and operations	Fully Private

Operating Authority

Fig. 1.—Four basic forms of public and private involvement in correctional administration.

facility may receive "clients" from a variety of different government agencies. Some are built "on spec" by private entrepreneurs (Harrington 1987), who hope that they will find a market, while others are built only after a contract has been signed with a government agency that agrees to provide a specified minimum number of inmates at an agreed-on rate.

An example of a fully private prison is the U.S. Corrections Corporations' Marion Adjustment Center at Marion, Kentucky, a 300-bed minimum-security prison (Press 1990). Others include centers for detaining illegal immigrants being held for deportation. These centers began to appear in the late 1970s and are owned and operated in several cities by a variety of private firms. Among them are CCA, incorporated in 1983 with its headquarters in Nashville; the Wackenhut Corporation, a large private security firm based in Coral Gables, Florida, which set up a separate division to seek business in the private corrections market; Eclectic Communications, Inc., a California-based firm; and Behavioral Systems Southwest, a small venture begun in California in the late 1970s (McDonald 1990b; Press 1990).

In a second form of privatization, the governing unit retains facility ownership and contracts with a private firm to operate it. Again, payment is typically made to the private entities on a per diem/per prisoner basis, usually with guarantees to the contractor specifying a minimum level of payment. A variety of different private correctional firms compete with one another for such contracts, and a number of local governments have contracted for the operation of their jails (Logan 1989; Press 1990). Examples include CCA's taking over the operation of the Bay County (Florida) jail in 1985 and the Santa Fe (New Mexico) jail in 1986 and Pricor's contract in 1986 to operate a 144-bed minimum-security jail in Tuscaloosa, Alabama (Press 1990). (Pricor is a Nashville-based firm that was founded in 1985 by a former CCA executive.)

Many of the private prisons in existence have also been contractor operated but state owned. These include four 500-bed medium-security prisons in Texas built by the Texas Department of Correction in the late 1980s and operated by CCA and Wackenhut; a 425-bed preparole facility in Houston, operated by Pricor; a 350-bed minimum-security penal farm in Hamilton County, Tennessee (first contracted in 1984); and a 200-bed minimum-through-maximum security women's prison in New Mexico (Logan 1989, 1991a; McDonald 1990a; Press 1990).

The third form of privatization is the privately owned facility that is operated by a public correctional authority. Typically, a private entity finances and constructs the facility and then leases it to a governmental entity, sometimes with a provision that permits the government to purchase the facility after leasing it for a specified number of years (Chabotar 1985; Chaiken and Mennemeyer 1987; National Criminal Justice Statistics Association 1987; McDonald 1990c). The first such privatization was a lease-purchase arrangement structured by E. F. Hutton in 1982 to finance construction of the Jefferson County (Colorado) jail (a $30 million project). Since then, similarly structured projects were undertaken to create maximum-security prisons in Missouri (Rich 1987), prisons and jails in Ohio (DeWitt 1986), and many others. A review published in 1987 counted twenty-eight such financing projects in twenty different jurisdictions (Chaiken and Mennemeyer 1987).

In addition to private correctional facilities, there is a much more varied mix of public and private involvements in correctional service delivery. Private agencies have long provided various social services to the courts, parole boards, and probation departments. For example, privately run organizations provide programs administering unpaid community service sentences (Pease 1985; McDonald 1986); treatment alternatives to street crimes (TASC) programs (Lazar Institute 1976; System Science, Inc. 1978; Bureau of Justice Assistance 1988); and, more recently, firms providing what are essentially private probation services, administering home detention with electronic monitoring technologies (Friel, Vaughn, and del Carmen 1987). Pretrial diversion programs that supervise and service defendants are also operated by private organizations in many jurisdictions and constitute a quasi-correctional service ("quasi" because these defendants are not yet convicted) (Hillsman 1982). These various developments are not discussed in this essay because the focus here is primarily on prisons, jails, detention centers, and other types of correctional facilities.

The remainder of this essay is structured as follows. Section I focuses on the juvenile system and explores the extent of private involvement, the historical evolution of this involvement, and its consequences. I then turn to the adult system in Section II and examine how the boundaries between public and private responsibilities and involvements in correctional administration have changed in recent centuries. Attention is then paid to the development in the 1970s and 1980s of privately operated facilities and facilities owned by private entities but operated by public authorities and the reasons why these forms have emerged. Section III is a review of the small body of research addressing one of the central empirical questions: Is contracting with private firms more cost effective than direct public administration of corrections? The essay closes, in Section IV, with a discussion of the various arguments pro and con on whether privatization is constitutional, legal, and appropriate.

I. Deinstitutionalization and the Discovery of the Private Sector in Juvenile Corrections

The first large-scale privatization of public correctional facilities in the contemporary era occurred in the early 1970s in the juvenile field, in Massachusetts. Although it was not thought of then as "privatization" (because that terminology did not become common until the Reagan/Thatcher administrations in the 1980s), it was the first large reconfiguration of a system that was dominated by public institutions into one that was predominantly comprised of private agencies. In another sense, however, it was not quite what people have in mind these days when they speak of privatization. Operating authority for the existing institutions was not simply taken away from the public sector and handed to private parties. Instead, the whole structure of the state's system was changed. Privatization was merely a way to accomplish the "deinstitutionalization" of the state's juvenile corrections department. Moreover, as radical and as controversial as that appeared at the time, the move away from a largely public role was really a continuation of a much longer trend. Private involvement in organized juvenile justice and juvenile correctional services had long been characteristic of juvenile corrections. The scale of that involvement escaped notice, however, until the 1970s, and partly for that reason, there was little controversy about it. More recently, some have expressed concerns about how the juvenile corrections system appears to be evolving into a two-track system—a public track with large-scale institutions and a private one with smaller and less "institutional" facilities. Concern has also been voiced about discriminatory tracking of children in one or another of the two tiers.

A. *Public and Private Roles*

In 1972, after a period of trying to reform Massachusetts's juvenile correctional system, the commissioner of the state youth services department, Jerome Miller, began to empty and officially to close the juvenile institutions. "The first state-operated training school for boys in the United States," among other institutions, "was going out of business," wrote Coates, Miller, and Ohlin (1978, p. 26). Miller's purpose was not to privatize the existing system but instead to do away with it because the department's leadership was unable to make the institution-level staff improve their performance (Bakal 1973; Miller, Ohlin, and Coates 1977; Scull 1984). After the system was destroyed, places had to be found for the delinquents who were taken out of the state's facilities. Private entrepreneurs stepped forward to take advantage of the new market that the state was creating (Scull 1984). What gradually resulted was a "deinstitutionalized" system comprised of a network of smaller private facilities. A small number of children deemed too dangerous to release were placed under the authority of a private agency that had assumed control of an old detention building that the state had vacated (Bakal 1973).

In 1980, the state of Utah followed suit, closing its large state-run training school and contracting with a variety of private agencies to provide nonsecure services, following the model pioneered in Massachusetts. The number of youths in secure beds dropped, as a consequence, from 360 to 60 (Matheson 1986; Krisberg 1987).

Writing in 1984 of the movement away from institutional placement and toward community-based alternatives in juvenile corrections, Lerman noted that "[t]he emergence of proprietary organizations, as an unanticipated consequence of the deinstitutionalization movement, has not attracted much attention" (p. 23). Although the important role of the private sector had been long recognized in the child welfare system, the scale and scope of private involvement in the juvenile corrections systems was not recognized until a census of juvenile correctional facilities sponsored by the Law Enforcement Assistance Administration (LEAA) was conducted in 1974. This census found that 31,749 youths, or 41 percent of all held, were in more than 1,300 private facilities, including 9,919 in private halfway houses or group homes, and 4,078 in privately operated training schools (Law Enforcement Assistance Administration 1977).

Earlier surveys had not detected this pattern. Surveys by the Census Bureau and the National Center for Health Statistics reported finding only 120 private facilities in 1969, and then 87 two years later (National Center for Health Statistics 1972, 1974). However, what appeared to be an explosion of private facilities between 1971 and 1974 was largely an artifact of the changed census methods. The earlier surveys relied on lists maintained by the U.S. Children's Bureau, whereas the 1974 census asked judges to name facilities to which they referred juveniles. This resulted in the discovery of a large number of facilities that could be classified as "correctional" but had been considered by state and local governments to be parts of the child welfare system for dependent and neglected children because the majority of all juveniles in them were referred by the child welfare authorities rather than by the courts. But, because the courts used them for holding status offenders and delinquents, they were properly considered part of the correctional system as well (Lerman 1982, 1984).

Similar surveys have been carried out since 1974, and they show substantial growth in the private sector since then. As table 1 shows, the number of private facilities increased 70 percent, from 1,277 to 2,167, between 1975 and 1989. (Because of an improvement in survey methods between the 1974 and 1975 censuses, trends are more reliably identified using data from 1975 and later.) During the same 1975–89 period, the number of public facilities increased only 26 percent, from 874 to 1,107. The number of children held in private facilities increased 39 percent, from 27,290 in 1975 to 37,889 in 1989, while the number in public facilities increased only 16 percent, from 46,980 to 54,351 (see table 2). By 1989, 67 percent of all juvenile correctional facilities

TABLE 1

Number of Public and Private Juvenile Correctional Facilities in the United States, 1969–1989

	Public	Private	Total
1969:			
Number	620	120	740
Percent	84	16	
1971:			
Number	659	87	746
Percent	88	12	
1974:			
Number	829	1,337	2,166
Percent	38	62	
1975:			
Number	874	1,277	2,151
Percent	41	59	
1977:			
Number	992	1,600	2,592
Percent	38	62	
1979:			
Number	1,015	1,561	2,576
Percent	39	61	
1983:			
Number	1,023	1,877	2,900
Percent	35	65	
1985:			
Number	1,040	1,996	3,036
Percent	34	66	
1987:			
Number	1,107	2,195	3,302
Percent	33	67	
1989:			
Number	1,100	2,167	3,267
Percent	33	67	

SOURCES.—For 1969, see National Center for Health Statistics (1972), p. 43; for 1971, see National Center for Health Statistics (1974), p. 49; for 1974, see Law Enforcement Assistance Administration (1977), pp. 12, 62; for the years 1975, 1977, 1979, 1983, and 1985, see Bureau of Justice Statistics (1989); for 1987 and 1989, public facilities, see Allen-Hagen (1991), p. 2; for 1987, private facilities, see U.S. Bureau of the Census (1987). For 1989, private facilities, see U.S. Bureau of the Census (1989), figures computed from unpublished data.

TABLE 2

Number of Juveniles in Public and Private Juvenile Correctional Facilities in the United States, 1950–1989

	Public	Private	Total
1950:			
Number	32,936	7,934	40,870
Percent	80	20	
1970:			
Number	67,963	8,766	74,729
Percent	89	11	
1974:			
Number	44,922	31,749	76,671
Percent	59	41	
1975:			
Number	46,980	27,290	74,270
Percent	63	27	
1977:			
Number	44,096	29,070	73,166
Percent	60	40	
1979:			
Number	43,234	28,688	71,922
Percent	60	40	
1983:			
Number	48,701	31,390	80,091
Percent	61	39	
1985:			
Number	49,322	34,080	83,402
Percent	59	41	
1987:			
Number	53,503	38,040	91,543
Percent	58	42	
1989:			
Number	54,351	37,889	92,240
Percent	58	42	

SOURCES.—For 1950, see U.S. Bureau of the Census (1950), vol. 4, pt. 2, chap. C; for 1970, see U.S. Bureau of the Census (1970c), vol. 4E, Pc(2); for 1974, see Law Enforcement Assistance Administration (1977), pp. 12, 62; for the years 1975, 1977, 1979, 1983, and 1985, see Bureau of Justice Statistics (1989); for 1987 and 1989, public facilities, see Allen-Hagen (1991), p. 2; for 1987, private facilities, see U. S. Bureau of the Census (1987). For 1989, private facilities, see U.S. Bureau of the Census (1989), figures computed from unpublished data.

were privately operated, and they held 42 percent of all children in custody that year.

Ownership of these private facilities is not reported in the censuses. Private facilities are categorized as either profit-making or nonprofit organizations "under the direct administrative and operational control of private enterprise" (Bureau of Justice Statistics 1989). It is likely that most of these facilities were also privately owned.

Privately contracted facilities for juveniles have a long history in the United States. Perhaps the first was the house of refuge established in 1825 in barracks on New York City's Madison Square that were leased by the Society for the Reformation of Juvenile Delinquents. By the mid-1800s, private cottages were established in several states (Taft 1982). This parallels the British experience; charitable nonprofit organizations have long operated facilities for juvenile offenders there as well (Rutherford 1990).

It was not until the 1960s, however, that the number of private facilities began to grow rapidly. Of the private juvenile facilities that were still in existence in 1987 and reported information to the census takers, 11 percent of them first began to be used by public authorities for detention, corrections, or shelter before 1960. The number doubled in the 1960s. Forty-four percent of all private facilities in existence in 1987 were either created in or first began accepting juvenile placements during the 1970s. Thirty-three percent came into service between 1980 and 1987 (U.S. Bureau of the Census 1987). This does not count the private facilities that were created but went out of business before the 1987 census.

These private facilities differ from public ones in a variety of ways (Bureau of Justice Statistics 1989; Allen-Hagen 1991). In 1989, most (89.5 percent) had "open" rather than "institutional" environments, compared with 41 percent of the public ones. Eighty-five percent were nonsecure, compared to 37 percent of the public facilities. Most (87 percent) were for long-term care, compared with 55 percent of the public facilities. The average length of stay of children discharged from private facilities during 1989 was 266 days, from public facilities it was 108 days. Public facilities were also larger, on average. During 1989, 87 percent of all private facilities held fewer than thirty children, whereas 35 percent of all public facilities were that small. Twenty percent of all juveniles held privately were in facilities having more than 100 children; public facilities of that size held 60 percent of all children in public custody. Moreover, public facilities were more likely

TABLE 3

Types of Juvenile Correctional Facilities in the Private and Public
Sectors in the United States, 1989

	Private		Public	
Facility Type	Number	Percent	Number	Percent
Detention centers	35	2	422	38
Shelters	324	15	63	6
Reception/diagnostic centers	24	1	19	2
Training schools	93	4	201	18
Ranches, forestry camps, or farms	104	5	87	8
Halfway houses or group homes	1,587	73	308	28
Total	2,167	100	1,100	100

SOURCE.—Computed from unpublished data in U.S. Bureau of the Census (1989).

to be crowded. In 1989, 44 percent of all juveniles held by the public
sector were in facilities that had populations in excess of their design
capacities. Only 1.7 percent of all juveniles held by the private sector
were in such "overcrowded" conditions.

The different types of private and public facilities that were identified in the 1989 census are shown in table 3 (U.S. Bureau of the Census
1989). Seventy-three percent of the private facilities operating in 1989
were halfway houses or group homes, compared with 28 percent of
the public facilities. These types of private facilities held 22,137 juveniles on the day the census was taken or 58 percent of all children in
the private sector. In contrast, a smaller number (308) of publicly
operated halfway houses and group homes held only 3,532 children in
that same year. Ninety-three private training schools held 7,142 juveniles (19 percent of all privately held children), compared with 27,292
juveniles held in 201 public training schools. One hundred and four
private ranches, forestry camps, or farms held 4,852 juveniles, while
a smaller number (4,431) were held that year in eighty-seven such
publicly owned facilities.

One well-known example of a privately operated juvenile correctional program is VisionQuest, established in Arizona in 1973. By
1982, this profit-making firm had an annual budget of $7 million, with
a staff of 250, and an average enrollment of 250 juveniles from ten

states. During that year, the firm charged about sixty different agencies at the rate of $27,000 per year for each juvenile enrolled. The program included a treatment regimen that blended several elements: wilderness training, borrowing ideas from the Outward Bound program; a wagon train, in which youngsters traveled hundreds of miles across the country in mule and horse teams in primitive conditions and were required to work hard as a team; Synanon-style confrontation therapy (also called "attack therapy"); as well as schools and group homes (Sweeney 1982).

According to Logan (1990), perhaps the longest running for-profit secure facility for long-term juvenile care is the Weaversville Intensive Treatment Unit, in Northampton, Pennsylvania. Operated by RCA Services, a division of the Radio Corporation of America, the unit began operations in 1975 and contracts with the state to confine and treat up to twenty-two serious juvenile offenders. The state owns the physical plant and every three years issues competitive contracts that RCA has repeatedly won.

One of the earliest efforts to transfer an entire public training school to a private agency was the contract given in 1982 to the Eckerd Foundation, a nonprofit arm of a major drugstore chain and drug manufacturer, to operate the Florida School for Boys at Okeechobee. This facility, one of the three largest institutional training schools in the state, housed 400–450 boys. The state retained ownership but contracted with the foundation to take Jack Eckerd up on his boast that he could run it better and for less money than the state. An evaluation team examined the training school two years after the transfer took place and reported, "it is an interesting demonstration project which is still struggling to find itself." The evaluators found no evidence that Eckerd's operations had achieved significant cost savings and found that the overall level of services and quality of care was no different there than at a comparable state-run training school (Brown et al. 1985). (But see Section III for a discussion of this evaluation.) Since then, however, the State of Florida has continued to renew its contract with Eckerd for the school, which is now called the Eckerd Youth Development Center. Representatives of the school argue that, since the mid-1980s, Eckerd's firm has developed a richer variety of programs and services than is found in the other state-run training schools, and that while the school may not cost less to operate it delivers better services for the dollar (Timko 1991).

In the mid-1980s, other private for-profit firms entered the juvenile corrections business. In 1986, CCA contracted with Shelby County (Tennessee) to operate the Shelby County Training Center in Memphis, a 150-bed secure facility for delinquent boys, most of whom are property offenders (Logan 1990). In 1985, Pricor entered into a contract to operate a secure juvenile detention facility in Johnson City, Tennessee. In 1987, it signed a five-year contract with the Los Angeles Board of Supervisors to operate an eighty-four-bed residential treatment center (Pricor 1988).

B. The Function of Privatization in Juvenile Corrections

Lerman (1982, 1984) and others (e.g., Krisberg et al. 1986) argue that private facilities have been used to create a two-tier system in juvenile corrections. Lerman argues that judges have increasingly used private facilities that are considered to be part of the child welfare system for placing status offenders and minor delinquents, while the public correctional facilities are reserved for more serious delinquents. This Lerman attributes to a de facto policy of separating "children in trouble" into three types of juveniles: status offenders, minor offenders, and serious offenders. This distinction owes its origins partly to the movement that emerged in the first half of the nineteenth century, when reformers began to separate both "wayward" and dependent children from adults in jails and almshouses. During the antebellum period, government-operated houses of refuge, juvenile reformatories, and training schools were created for the care and custody of delinquents apart from adult offenders (Rothman 1971; Leiby 1978; Mennel 1983). Dependent and neglected children, who were not categorized as delinquents, became the primary responsibility of private organizations, which were often subsidized by public funds.

In the early twentieth century, reformers further distinguished between minor and serious delinquents by seeing "garden variety" delinquents (Carstens 1938) as different from more serious offenders in need of a larger measure of "compulsion and control" (Carstens 1915). Lerman argues that this ideology reinforced a de facto policy of favoring private facilities for status offenders and minor, "garden variety" delinquents after efforts of diversion, probation, and nonresidential services failed (Lerman 1984). According to Krisberg and his colleagues (1986, p. 33), this two-tier system is not color-blind: white youths are more likely to be sent to the private facilities, while minority youths have higher odds of being placed in public correctional facilities.

Data from the 1985 facilities census reveal significant differences among juvenile populations in private and public facilities. Private facilities (which, as discussed above, are more likely to be nonsecure facilities rather than "open" secure institutional ones) had a larger proportion of nondelinquents in their custody: 66 percent compared to 6 percent in the public facilities.[1] Indeed, 80 percent of all delinquents that year were held in the public facilities, while 88 percent of all nondelinquents were in private facilities. Eighty-seven percent of all delinquents charged with violent offenses and 79 percent of those charged with property offenses were held in public facilities (Bureau of Justice Statistics 1989, p. 50). Fifty-three percent of those in the public facilities that year were members of racial or ethnic minorities, compared with 37 in the private facilities. Moreover, girls were found more frequently among the privately held populations than among those in public facilities: 30 percent, as opposed to 14 percent (Bureau of Justice Statistics 1989, p. 39).

Despite these differences among populations in public and private facilities, one cannot conclude from these data alone that the differences result from discriminatory placement practices, or that the juvenile courts "track" youths on one of two correctional tiers according to their skin color, as Krisberg et al. (1986) suggest. The tendency to confine delinquents more often in public institutions may explain the disproportionate number of black youths in them, if these youths are also more likely than whites to have committed delinquent acts. Moreover, the large difference in the proportion of nondelinquents in the public and private facilities (6 and 66 percent, respectively) is explained partly by the private facilities receiving substantial numbers of youths who were referred to private facilities by nonjudicial sources. During 1985, for example, 20 percent of all private facility residents were "voluntary" admissions, which included referrals by agents other than judges (Bureau of Justice Statistics 1989, p. 50). Understanding of the precise nature of the placement process is best afforded by studies of placement decisions themselves rather than the resulting distribution of youths in different types of facilities, examined in aggregate at the national level.

[1] The category of "nondelinquent" includes status offenders, "nonoffenders," and "voluntary admissions." Status offenders are youths who are charged with acts that would not be criminal if they were adults, such as running away, truancy, and incorrigibility. Nonoffenders are persons held for dependency, neglect, abuse, emotional disturbance, or mental retardation. "Voluntary admissions" are youths confined not because of a court adjudication but because they were referred by parents, courts, schools, or social agencies (Bureau of Justice Statistics 1989, p. 5).

One study by Shichor and Bartollas (1990) of placement decisions by a large Southern California probation department during 1987 found no evidence of discriminatory tracking. "What is unexpected about juvenile placement policies in this Southern California county is that there were relatively few differences between juveniles sent to private and public placements," they concluded. "Although juveniles placed in private facilities had more personal problems and those in public institutions tended to be somewhat more delinquent, the two populations did not vary markedly" (1990, p. 295).

It is hard to know what to conclude from the apparent discrepancy between Shichor and Bartollas's findings and the pattern evident in the 1985 census at the national level of aggregation. The authors did not report the proportions of public and private placements who were officially labeled delinquent and nondelinquent, so it is difficult to tell if this department's placements resembled the national pattern in this respect. However, Bartollas and Shichor's finding of no difference in the distribution of black and white youths among public and private placements suggests that the pattern in this department did *not* reflect the pattern found at the aggregate level. It is possible, therefore, that the differences in the types of youths sent to public and private facilities result from jurisdictional differences in reliance on public or private facilities (so that, for example, states having higher populations of blacks also have fewer private facilities for placement), rather than from differential and perhaps discriminatory "tracking" by individual juvenile courts and probation departments. Evaluating placement decisions requires analysis of client-level data, which the annual census of children in custody does not provide.

As noted above, Lerman (1984) wrote that the prevalence of the private sector was "discovered" as an unanticipated consequence of the deinstitutionalization movement. But has the growth of privately operated juvenile facilities actually resulted from the deinstitutionalization of juveniles? In a later work, he argued that the growth of the private facility has *not* been accompanied by a substantial decrease in the use of public juvenile correctional facilities. He demonstrated this by reporting that the proportion of all juvenile residents of the United States under the age of eighteen who were in publicly operated juvenile correctional facilities was the same in 1977 as in 1950, while the confinement rate in private facilities increased about threefold (Lerman 1982).

Table 4 shows the rate of juvenile confinement in public and private

TABLE 4

Number of Juveniles in Public and Private Juvenile Correctional
Facilities, per 100,000 Juveniles in the U.S. Population, 1950–1989

	Public	Private	Total
1950	188	45	233
1970	209	27	236
1974	137	97	234
1975	153	89	241
1977	149	98	247
1979	151	100	251
1983	176	114	290
1985	185	128	313
1987	208	154	362
1989	221	154	375

SOURCES.—For 1950, figures computed from correctional data in U.S. Bureau of the
Census (1950), vol. 5, pt. 2, chap. C, and in U.S. Bureau of the Census (1970a). For
1970, figures computed from correctional data in U.S. Bureau of the Census (1970c),
vol. 4E, Pc(2), and in U.S. Bureau of the Census (1970b), vol. 1, pt. 1, table 50. For 1974,
figures computed from correctional data in Law Enforcement Assistance Administration
(1977) and in U.S. Bureau of the Census (1970b), vol. 1, pt, 1, table 50. For 1975, 1977,
1979, 1983, and 1985, see Bureau of Justice Statistics (1989); for 1987 and 1989, public
facilities, see Allen-Hagen (1991), p. 2. For 1987 and 1989, private facilities, figures
computed from correctional data in U.S. Bureau of the Census (1987, 1989).

facilities, measured as the number of juveniles per 100,000 juvenile
residents of the United States aged ten through seventeen, for selected
years between 1950 and 1989. These data differ from Lerman's by
including post-1977 figures and by restricting the base population to
those between the ages of ten and seventeen rather than all persons
under eighteen years of age, as Lerman did. The undercounting of
juveniles in the private facilities prior to 1974 was such that it would
be misleading to compute rates of private confinement for those periods; counts in the public facilities during this period were more likely
to be reliable, however.

The overall pattern of incarceration rates between 1950 and 1989
does not indicate the deinstitutionalization of juveniles from public
facilities—a finding consistent with Lerman's (1982). The incarceration
rate in public facilities was higher in 1989 than in 1950: 221 juveniles
incarcerated per 100,000 juveniles in the population, compared with
188 in 1950. The incarceration rate reached a high-water mark in the
1970 census and then declined slightly in the following years, although

it rose steadily from 1975 onwards (the period during which the census methods were most consistent). Throughout the period, the incarceration rates in private facilities also increased—from 89 per 100,000 in 1975 (the most reliable of these early census estimates) to 154 per 100,000 in 1987 and 1989. Overall incarceration rates consequently rose as well, from 233 per 100,000 in 1950, to 241 in 1975, to 375 in 1989—an increase of 56 percent between 1975 and 1989 alone. The emergence of private facilities consequently afforded a greater reliance on incarceration throughout this period, without a concomitant reduction of juveniles placed in the public facilities.

II. The Shifting Boundary between Public and Private Responsibilities in Adult Corrections

By the early twentieth century, the imprisonment of adults was mainly a public responsibility in European nations, Great Britain, and the United States. In the 1980s, however, private prisons and jails emerged again with some fanfare, and with claims to legitimacy. This section begins with a brief discussion of the private prison's antecedents and then examines more recent developments in somewhat more detail. The two principal forms of private correctional facilities are described as prisons or jails operated by private firms and the privately owned but publicly operated ones. The section ends with an exploration of the reasons why the private prison and jail industry appeared during the past decade.

A. Private Involvement before the Twentieth Century

The earliest jails and prisons for adults in this country were created as public institutions (Rothman 1971; Wayson et al. 1977). This represented a break with practice in England and Europe. Until the nineteenth century, imprisonment in the Old World was commonly a commercial enterprise in which private individuals earned fees for holding prisoners (Holdsworth 1922–24, p. 397; Crew 1933, p. 50). In England owners of alehouses sometimes held in their cellars defendants awaiting trial and convicted offenders awaiting transportation (Feeley 1991). Transportation to the American colonies, which was one of the main criminal sanctions between 1600 and the late eighteenth century, was also a largely private affair, with contractors responsible for shipping convicts to the colonies and selling them at auctions there (Hughes 1987).

The American preference for state control of imprisonment of adults did not indicate a more general predilection for publicly administering all aspects of the criminal law. Prior to the development of public police forces in the mid-1800s, private slave patrols and volunteer militias were relied on to hunt down fugitives and suspects (Williams and Murphy 1990). Victims were responsible for prosecuting their cases in court prior to the establishment of publicly employed prosecutors in the latter half of the nineteenth century (Steinberg 1983). Services to and surveillance of offenders serving time in the community began to be provided in the mid-1800s by private individuals and charitable organizations, and it was not until the late 1890s that government probation agencies were created (Klein 1918). And, as we have seen, private administration was common in the early correctional institutions for juveniles.

In the middle of the nineteenth century, the role of the state began to shift, and private parties began to play a larger role in adult correctional administration, principally in the form of convict leasing arrangements. This began in 1825, when an energetic merchant by the name of Joel Scott offered to pay the state of Kentucky $1,000 to lease him all prisoners in the Frankfort prison, which had been inefficiently run and was costly to the state. In return for the right to work these convicts at hard labor, Scott would feed, clothe, and house them, as well as pay the state one-half of the net profit he might make from the use of the convict labor. The state agreed, and Scott and his successor, T. S. Theobold, carried on a profitable enterprise. No allegations of ill-treatment were recorded (Lewis 1922, pp. 257–58; McKelvey 1977, pp. 44–45). This arrangement, which lasted until the 1880s, created an influential pattern for many of the prisons of the West and South. Convicts in many states were leased to contractors who put them to work in coal mines, in small-scale manufacturing, and in road and railroad construction (McKelvey 1977; Feeley 1991).

Convict leasing was an attractive solution because it helped offset the high cost to the public purse of imprisonment. Prisons that were built during the early 1800s were the most expensive construction projects in the nation's short history (Wayson et al. 1977). In the two decades following the Civil War, the battle-ravaged states in the South were unable or unwilling to support their prisons, which held large numbers of freed slaves. By 1880, all the states of the Confederacy, plus Kentucky, had surrendered large proportions of their criminal populations to lessees (McKelvey 1969, p. 207). Accounts of the camps in which they were held make it clear that conditions of confinement

Texas:

Facility	City	Agency	Capacity	Security	Operator	Date
Angelina County Detention Facility	Diboll	Deep East Texas Probation	470	Minimum	Pricor, Inc.	February 1991
City of Big Spring Correction Center	Big Spring	City of Big Spring[a]	360	Minimum	Mid-Tex Corrections, Inc.	August 1989
Bridgeport Pre-release Center	Bridgeport	Texas DOC	500	Minimum	Wackenhut Corrections Corporation	August 1989
Cleveland Pre-release Center	Cleveland	Texas DOC	500	Minimum	Corrections Corporation of America	September 1989
Eden Detention Center	Eden	City of Eden[b]	565	Minimum/medium	Eden Detention Center, Inc.	October 1985
Kyle Pre-release Center	Kyle	Texas DOC	500	Minimum	Wackenhut Corrections Corporation	June 1989
Laredo Processing Center	Laredo	U.S. Department of Justice	300	Minimum	Corrections Corporation of America	March 1985
Lockhart Correctional Center	Lockhart	City of Lockhart	500	Minimum	Wackenhut Corrections Corporation	Fall 1991
Mineral Wells Pre-parole Transfer Facility	Mineral Wells	Texas Board of Pardons and Paroles	800	Minimum	Concepts, Inc.	Unknown
Central Texas Parole Violator Facility	San Antonio	Texas Board of Pardons and Paroles	632	Minimum/medium	Wackenhut Corrections Corporation	January 1989
Sweetwater Pre-parole Center	Sweetwater	Texas Board of Pardons and Paroles	210	Minimum	Pricor, Inc.	July 1989
Venus Pre-release Center	Venus	Texas DOC	500	Minimum	Corrections Corporation of America	August 1989
Houston Processing Center	Houston	INS	350	Minimum	Corrections Corporation of America	April 1984
Bridgeport Pre-parole Transfer Facility	Bridgeport	Texas Board of Pardons and Paroles	100	Minimum	Concepts, Inc.	November 1987

TABLE 5 (*Continued*)

Facility	Location	Contracting Agency	Rated Capacity	Security Level	Private Contractor	Date Opened
Brownfield Residential Facility	Brownfield	Texas Board of Pardons and Paroles	200	Medium	Concepts, Inc.	Unknown
North Texas Intermediate Sanctions Facility	Fort Worth	State of Texas	400	Minimum	Wackenhut Corrections Corporation	August 1991
Tarrant County Detention Center	Tarrant	Tarrant County	320	Minimum	Esmore, Inc.	January 1991
City of Big Spring Correctional Center (Airport)	Big Spring	Federal Bureau of Prisons	376	Minimum	Mid-Tex Corrections, Inc.	February 1991
Washington:						
Seattle Detention Center	Seattle	INS	103	Minimum/ medium	Esmore, Inc.	July 1989

SOURCE.—Adapted from Thomas and Foard (1991).

[a] The Federal Bureau of Prisons contracts with the City of Big Spring. The City of Big Spring contracts with the Corrections Corporation of America.

[b] The Federal Bureau of Prisons contracts with the City of Eden. The City of Eden contracts with Detention Systems, Inc.

that sold "certificates of participation" to private investors. The revenue from these sales was used to build the jail, which was then leased by the private entity to the county. Funds generated by these lease payments were used to pay dividends to certificate holders, thereby paying them back, with interest.

Other state and local governments adopted these financing techniques to build prisons and jails elsewhere. In some, the deals were structured as "lease-purchase" arrangements, in which the government actually bought the facility from the private entity on what amounted to an installment plan, each lease payment being one installment (Chaiken and Mennemeyer 1987; Leonard 1990). In other jurisdictions, where state constitutions or statutes forbade lease-purchase arrangements, correctional facilities were made available to governments on a straight leasing basis.

Such "creative financing" techniques have not been restricted to prison and jail construction, for bond underwriters and municipal finance officers across the country have been using these and similar methods of financing a wide variety of needed capital projects—including, among others, fire trucks, computers, and telecommunications systems (Leonard 1986). These arrangements were made more attractive to investors by the liberalized treatments of depreciation in the Economic Recovery Tax Act of 1981 and were spurred by the growing hindrances on conventional public financing methods that relied on issuance of general obligation bonds. To circumvent these restrictions, a debt instrument was created that looked like a bond but was not one, at least according to legal definitions. According to one investment banker, "they sell like bonds, they look like bonds, they bear interest just like bonds, the payment schedule is just like bonds, the commissions to the broker are just like bonds, the default is just like the bonds, they're tax-exempt like bonds, but we make more money on them—unlike bonds" (Haas 1986).

The appeal of this form of privatization is limited to the United States because it is specifically designed to take advantage of tax law provisions and overcome constraints that are peculiar to this country. In nations where citizen approval of debt for capital projects is not required (e.g., Great Britain), private ownership is less attractive, especially because the cost of raising capital is higher when the debt instruments are not backed by the full faith and credit of the government, as general obligation bonds are. That is, investors must be promised a somewhat higher return for bearing more risk than a general obligation government bond carries.

D. Why Did Private Prisons and Jails Emerge in the 1980s?

Renewed interest in privately operated or owned facilities in the adult correctional system resulted from a confluence of several trends: demand for prison and jail cells was rising at a fast rate, public authorities were not able to construct facilities quickly enough and private entrepreneurs moved in to provide the needed space, and citizen movements to limit taxation and public indebtedness sharply narrowed public administrators' latitude to build and spend. In addition, there emerged a broader movement to limit government's reach by "privatizing" services that were once publicly provided (Savas 1982; Butler 1985; Hanke 1987; President's Commission on Privatization 1988).

Beginning in 1973, the U.S. state and federal prison population began to grow, and by 1990 it was 293 percent above its 1972 level (Bureau of Justice Statistics 1986; Bureau of Justice Statistics 1991a). To accommodate the 58,700 increase from 1989 to 1990 alone, eleven new medium-sized (500-bed) prisons were needed *each month*. The demand for cells in local jails also rose substantially during this period. Reliable surveys of jail populations in the early 1970s are not available, but two surveys in 1978 and 1990 found that the average daily population in these approximately 3,500 jails increased 117 percent (Bureau of Justice Statistics 1991b). Crowding became endemic in prisons and jails as governments were unable to add cell space quickly enough. During 1990, prison systems were operating in excess of reported capacity in all but nine states, and all jails taken together were 4 percent above capacity, on average (Bureau of Justice Statistics 1991a; Bureau of Justice Statistics 1991b). This crowding has had deleterious effects on both the ability to manage prisons and the conditions in them. One indication of this is that forty states, the District of Columbia, Puerto Rico, and the U.S. Virgin Islands were operating prisons and jails in mid-1991 that had been found by the federal courts to be in violation of constitutional standards (Bernat 1991). Courts were also finding conditions in local jails deficient, but, lacking ongoing surveys, it is difficult to know how many jails were under court order. One survey conducted in mid-1986 found that a third of the jails polled were operating under court orders, usually because of crowding and substandard conditions of confinement, but it is not known how representative this sample was of all 3,500 jails in the country (*Corrections Compendium* 1986).

Demands for additional correctional resources came at a time when state and local governments could ill afford them. Within a few years of the passage of Proposition Thirteen in California in 1978, fifty-one new expenditure controls or revenue restrictions were placed on state and local governments' spending powers. Income taxes were cut in thirty-five states and sales taxes in nineteen (Swartz 1987). Beginning in 1980, federal aid to state and local governments also began to shrink, and by 1986 the federal government's general revenue sharing program was dead, leaving many state and local governments without direct federal assistance for the first time since the early 1970s (Herbers 1987). This affected county and municipal governments' ability to finance jail operations and to construct or renovate facilities because both operations and capital construction at this level of government were paid for by locally raised tax revenues.

Most state governments raise money needed for prison construction by issuing bonds and then paying bondholders back over many years, thereby spreading the construction costs over the facility's useful life. But state constitutions establish limits on public indebtedness and require citizen approval before bonds are issued and debt is incurred. Not only do governments have to wait until the next election before they can hold a referendum on prison construction bonds, but they also face the prospect that these referenda will be voted down. During the 1980s, a high proportion of prison construction bond proposals—more than half, according to one source—were turned down at the ballot box (Peterson 1988). Correctional and budget officers in many states were consequently faced with a difficult problem: demand for prison cells was rising, federal courts were requiring that the conditions of confinement not be dropped below constitutional minima, and funds available for construction and operations were severely restricted.

Private entrepreneurs offered governments different types of financing and operations arrangements that were appealing in several ways. At the federal level, the speed of acquiring new facilities was an important incentive for going private. Rather than having to construct new facilities by a complicated procurement process that takes years, the federal Bureau of Prisons and the INS could sign a contract with a private firm that would build or acquire its own facility quickly and be ready to receive prisoners within a matter of months. For example, a private detention center for illegal aliens was built near Denver in three months (Schmidt 1987).

The ability to bypass voter approval of prison construction bonds held special attraction for state governments. Private firms could pay for the construction of correctional facilities and then charge governments a per diem "rental" price that would include not only operating costs and profit but also a portion of the capital expenditure. Because payments for such per diem fees for cell space or even leases of entire facilities were (and still are) not legally considered capital expenditures, governments could obtain the needed service and charge the entire amount against their operating budgets, even though a part of that amount actually goes to pay off the debts to private investors.

Even where there was no need to convert capital expenditures into operating expenses, governments were also attracted to contracting for management and operations of publicly owned facilities for still another reason: these firms argued that they could provide the same level of service, or better, at a lower cost to the taxpayer. As one spokesman for a private correctional firm put it, "We believe that the private sector can achieve economic efficiencies impossible to achieve working through the government bureaucracies" (Tolchin 1985b). The prospects of lower operating costs were reportedly significant motivators in a number of different instances where public officials turned to private contractors or, at least, seriously considered it. These included Santa Fe County (Press 1990), Great Britain (Rutherford 1990), Bay County, Florida (McDonald 1990c; Press 1990), Massachusetts (Legislative Research Council, Commonwealth of Massachusetts 1986), Tennessee (Tolchin 1985a, 1985b; Logan and McGriff 1989), Kentucky (Press 1990), Federal Bureau of Prisons, U.S. Immigration Service (McDonald 1990b), and New Mexico. Correctional administrators were not blazing new territory here because administrators throughout government had been turning to contracting in order to provide various types of services to the public and were motivated to do so in part because contracting was thought to be more cost effective (Poole and Fixler 1987; Touche Ross 1987).

III. Is Private Contracting More Cost Effective?

Whether private contracting for prison and jail operations is actually more cost effective than direct public administration has not been established. Claims and counterclaims abound, along with theories about why private contracting must (or cannot) be more cost effective, but few studies have been undertaken to evaluate their validity. This section first identifies some of the principal lines of argument for and against the superior cost-effectiveness of private operations and then discusses a small number of studies that have attempted to compare costs.

Unfortunately, developing an accurate assessment requires having more complete and comparable cost data than are easily available, and differences in accounting principles used by the private and public sectors must be recognized and overcome. Moreover, for cost studies to be informative, systematic attention needs to be given to the relative benefits as well as the costs, something that is nearly absent in the few cost studies published to date.

Given the paucity of data and analysis, it is premature to claim that any general proposition about the relative cost or effectiveness of private imprisonment is supported by sound empirical research. Having said that, here is my prediction: the hunt for a universally prevalent, or inherent, cost advantage of either public or private provision is not likely to find its quarry. If private contractors are found to have an advantage in one or another circumstance, it will probably be found to rest on identifiable and specific conditions rather than on universal characteristics of private-sector firms or markets. Because of various constraints on public agencies that may exist at certain times and in certain places (e.g., labor availability, restrictions on employee salary levels, regulatory requirements, government procurement procedures), private firms may be able to exploit opportunities in specific niches and find ways to deliver services at lower costs. Where such constraints and conditions do not exist, opportunities for cost savings will be fewer.

A. *Arguments For and Against Cost-Effectiveness of Private Contracting*

Proponents of contracting for correctional services assert that private firms enjoy a number of significant advantages. They can be more productive because they are not entangled in the "red tape" that encumbers public agencies, especially in their procurement decisions and labor relations. Managers' hiring and firing authority in public agencies is much constrained because of civil service rules and restrictions on creating budget lines for new employees. In contrast, managers in private firms can allocate labor and discipline it with far greater ease, especially if employees are not unionized. In states where public construction projects must be given to unionized firms, private firms are not so obliged and thereby enjoy an additional advantage if they have to expand their facilities.

A second advantage, it is claimed, is that relying on private firms creates a competitive market, and that the incentives that prevail in such markets encourage greater productivity and cost cutting than is found in government. According to this line of argument, public agencies have few incentives to discover and implement ways of improving productivity. Government positions and agency budgets, once established, are difficult to reduce because constituencies are created inside and outside government that press legislatures for continued funding. In contrast, competition in the private marketplace, and the threat of losing money or going out of business, stimulates the search for increased efficiency in service delivery. Shielded from these demands, public managers are seen to strive not for greater productivity but for maintaining their positions by avoiding risks (Savas 1982; Butler 1985; Stewart 1986; President's Commission on Privatization 1988).

Proponents also argue that private firms are able to obtain supplies at lower costs because large regional or national firms are able to buy in larger quantities at discounts and from a wider range of possible suppliers. Private firms are also thought to be freer of the pressure to "buy local" in order to shore up political support, a need felt especially by county sheriffs (Thomas 1989).

These claims of inherent private-sector superiority have not gone unchallenged. Donahue (1990) argues that the labor-intensive nature of prison and jail operations leaves little room for technological innovations that lead to increased productivity. Thus the "magic" that one seeks in the marketplace will be given little opportunity to work. If overall operating costs are indeed reduced, this is likely to be the result not of combining "inputs" more effectively (i.e., by increasing productivity), but of reducing the costs of those inputs—chiefly, labor costs. This can be done by reducing the salaries and benefits paid to employees. Whether a reliable, trained, and efficient labor force can indeed be attracted and retained with wages that are substantially below current market levels (even if that market is established primarily by public agencies) is an open question. Moreover, the advantage that the private sector may hold in this regard may diminish if employees in the private sector unionize.

Whether public correctional managers are as likely as private managers to seek cost-controlling opportunities is a matter of speculation rather than established fact, critics argue. State and local governments especially are straining to meet rising correctional demand with limited resources, and these conditions create incentives for public administrators to seek cost-efficient solutions.

Critics have also attempted to rebut claims of the private sector's superiority by pointing to what they see as nearly inherent defects of contracting (American Federation of State, County, and Municipal Employees, AFL–CIO 1984). Whereas the stimulus of seeking profits may have its advantages, the incentive to minimize costs may also encourage reductions in service quality. "Cost-cutting measures will run rampant," argued an American Bar Association committee. "Conditions of confinement will be kept to the minimum that the law requires . . . . In short, the private sector is more interested in doing well than doing good" (American Bar Association 1986, p. 4). Those who make this argument have no dearth of examples to point to in other institutional domains, such as the extreme overcharging by defense contractors or by contractors to state governments (American Federation of State, County, and Municipal Employees 1984). Indeed, for a parade of horrible examples of correctional contractors putting private profit ahead of prisoners' welfare, one need not look further than the previous experience of "privatizing" penal administration in the nineteenth century, in the convict leasing arrangements that pervaded the South during the decades following the Civil War. As McKelvey (1977, p. 208) observes in his history of American prisons, "There were no standard living arrangements in the southern prison camps. Yet one strong factor, the demand for economy, brought them all practically to a common level—scarcely that of subsistence." Conditions in the camps were generally appalling, and the death rates in them were considerably higher than in northern prisons: 41 deaths per 1,000 as opposed to 15 per 1,000 in the North, according to an 1882 survey (Cable 1969). Yet advocates of private correctional facilities today argue that history need not repeat itself and point to the substantial disincentives to degrading the conditions of confinement in prisons and jails. These include the possibility of losing the contract, increasing the risk of violence from disgruntled inmates, and increasing strife between labor and management, which makes day-to-day operations more difficult (McDonald 1990c). In addition, conditions will not be permitted by the courts to sink below minimum constitutional standards.

Critics of privatization argue that the demands for effective public regulation of private contractors create an additional cost to government that may offset whatever savings contracting produces (Keating n.d.). It is argued also that despite any short-run savings that may be reaped from contracting, these will be offset by the cost to governments of having to reconstitute a public correctional facility if the private sector goes bankrupt or pulls out of the business. Dependence on the private sector is seen as having a further risk: firms will "lowball" in their bids and then renegotiate reimbursement rates once they have captured the public correctional facility. Or they will become so en-trenched in a jurisdiction, especially if they own the facility, that po-tential competitors may be deterred from bidding (McDonald 1990c). (Public authorities could minimize the risk of lowballing, however, by requiring long-term contracts with fixed rates or formulas for increas-ing rates; dependence could also be avoided by not permitting the contractor to own the facility.)

B. Research on the Comparative Cost and Effectiveness of Privately Contracted Facilities

Few of these propositions have been evaluated systematically by researchers. Moreover, our capacity to draw strong conclusions about the cost-effectiveness of privately operated prisons and jails has been frustrated by several methodological difficulties.

The first is that different accounting rules are followed in the public and private sectors. Accounting methods developed for private firms are designed to value all inputs used for producing goods and services; a large proportion of costs incurred are thereby captured. In contrast, public accounting systems were designed not to monitor costs but to control the allocation of appropriated public funds through agencies and to detect misuse of taxpayers' money (Clear, Harris, and Record 1982; Leonard 1986). Two characteristics of these accounting proce-dures make cost estimation especially difficult in the public sector: the focus on the agency rather than the service delivered and the deficient treatment of capital expenses.

Counting only expenditures by corrections departments often results in an undercounting of the actual direct cost of imprisonment. In many jurisdictions, the costs of operating prisons and jails are borne by a number of different agencies and accounts (McDonald 1980, 1989). Employee benefits are often paid out of separate government overhead accounts and are not included in the correctional department's budget; medical care of inmates might be charged to the public health depart-ment, utilities to the department of public works, legal work to the attorney general or equivalent, and so forth. To identify all the "hid-

den" costs directly attributable to correctional operations, special studies are needed rather than relying simply on measures of costs based
on the correctional agency's budget or reported expenditures. For example, the average daily cost to the correctional department for impris-
oning one inmate may undercount actual direct costs by as much as
30–40 percent (McDonald 1980, 1989; Wayson and Funke 1989).

Different treatment of capital ·spending by public and private accounting procedures further frustrates comparison of costs. Whereas
private firms have adopted accounting conventions to spread expenditures for capital assets (buildings, land, equipment) throughout the
period of those assets' useful lives (so that the year-to-year cost of a
service includes some portion of the physical assets that are "consumed" in the production of that service), public accounting systems
make no such attempt. In the public sector, capital expenses are
counted only in the year they are made. Because no attempt is made
to spread these costs across subsequent years, it is impossible to determine how much it actually costs to deliver a service without conducting
an inventory and appraisal of existing capital assets. The commonly
cited costs of imprisonment by public agencies are therefore lower than
they would be if physical assets were capitalized.

Finally, if one is interested in comparing the relative cost efficiency
of public and private provision, it is helpful to know at what cost
private agencies deliver their services. However, what we typically
know is the *price* charged to government, rather than the actual cost to
the firm of doing business. From the taxpayers' point of view, this is
sufficient, for what matters most to them is the cost of the contracted
services to the government (i.e., the price it is charged). For analytic
purposes, however, it is helpful to know actual costs because firms
may offer the service at a price lower than their costs in order to gain
entry to the market, or their costs may in fact be much lower than
their prices.

A small number of studies have been published to date that attempt
to estimate the different costs of public and private provision of imprisonment, although most have not been able to overcome fully these
various methodological difficulties.

One of the first studies was Chi's 1982 report on work release centers
in Illinois. At the time of his study, the state Department of Corrections operated eleven centers directly and contracted with private firms
for seven. He calculated that the average daily cost per offender of
operating the state-run centers was $39.81, compared to $25 for the

contracted ones. He attributed this difference largely to private firms paying their employees 40–60 percent less and to uncounted subsidies by the private organizations. That is, these organizations received contributions of money and volunteered labor, which was not counted as a cost. Because little effort was made to impose consistent accounting rules for both public and private expenditures, and because the value of these subsidies to the private centers was not monetized, it is difficult to feel confident about the cost comparison reported in this study (Chi 1982).

Another study compared the cost of the Eckerd Foundation's operation of the Florida School for Boys at Okeechobee to the cost of another publicly operated training school (the Dozier School for Boys). The evaluation team from the National Institute of Corrections found that the state of Florida spent 4 percent less to operate Okeechobee than Dozier prior to transfer to Eckerd; in the year following transfer, the cost was 3 percent less. The team concluded that "the Eckerd Foundation achieved no significant reductions in operational cost" (Brown et al. 1985, p. xiii). Indeed, the team argued that the change from being 4 to 3 percent less expensive than Dozier was a mark of Eckerd's failure to reduce the cost of service: "Under the Foundation, Okeechobee became relatively more expensive to operate" (p. 67). This is not a fair inference. An inspection of one table in the report (p. 69) indicates that the per capita cost of incarceration increased at Ocheechobee over a three-year period, from $10,853 before transfer to $14,617 in the year following, whereas Dozier's per capita costs increased more rapidly, from $12,155 to $17,215. If one adopted this measure, one could argue that Eckerd did a *better* job of controlling cost increases than did the public administrators at Dozier over the three-year study period.

There were more serious problems in the analysis, beyond interpretation of findings. The evaluators did not report how they handled the possibility of inconsistent accounting procedures. They also appear to have explained away what other observers have seen as significant differences between Okeechobee's and Dozier's population and operation. For example, Roberts and Powers (1985, p. 99) call the evaluators' choice of Dozier as the comparison facility "the methodological equivalent of a 'shell game'" because they were not comparable. Finally, everybody agrees that the transition from public operation to private contracting was difficult (Brown et al. 1985) and a finding of no dramatic effect in the year immediately following the takeover should not surprise anyone.

In his study of public and privately operated custodial facilities for juveniles in the United States, Donahue (1990) calculated the average cost per resident during 1985 as $22,600 in the public facilities and $22,845 in the private ones—an insignificant difference. This study relied on data reported by public agencies, however, and does not seem to make adjustments for inconsistent counting rules in public and private organizations, which probably resulted in an undercounting of public agency costs.

In its 1985 study of privately operated detention centers, the Pennsylvania General Assembly's Legislative Budget and Finance Committee examined cost data provided by the U.S. Immigration and Naturalization Service and concluded that their average daily cost per inmate was 17 percent higher in the private facilities (Joint State Government Commission 1987). Once again, however, the consequences of inconsistent accounting procedures were not taken into account, and the findings should be viewed with skepticism.

Three other studies have attempted to impose consistent counting rules. Logan and McGriff (1989) studied expenditures for CCA's Silverdale Detention Center in Hamilton County, Tennessee. They estimated the various "hidden" costs that would be incurred if the county resumed responsibility for operations, including various costs that would be borne by other agency budgets and accounts, and some estimate of capitalized physical assets. They concluded that during fiscal years 1986 and 1988, the cost of private contracting was between 3 and 8 percent less than what the county would have had to pay if it operated the facility directly. They attribute this small difference to lower labor costs under private management. They report, however, that CCA improved conditions in the facility. If these benefits were indeed valuable, the private management's advantage in cost-benefit terms would be greater than a simple comparison of costs would suggest.

A study by the Urban Institute (1989) compared the costs of the Marion Adjustment Center, a private minimum-security facility under contract with the state of Kentucky, and a structurally similar facility operated directly by the state, the Blackburn Correctional Complex. The Urban Institute also studied two secure treatment facilities for serious juvenile offenders in Massachusetts, one public and the other private. In Kentucky, the private facility was found to be about 10 percent more expensive; in Massachusetts, private facilities were about 1 percent more expensive. Unfortunately, capital costs were not treated consistently. The costs of the private firms in both states included capitalized costs of physical assets, but these costs were omitted from the public costs. Lacking such information about the current value of existing assets, Hatry and his colleagues estimated what public costs would have been if the state had redesigned or reconstructed the Blackburn complex at current costs. They then concluded that government-run facilities would be 20–28 percent more expensive than private ones.

The third study that attempts to standardize accounting rules is my own examination of the costs of alien detention centers in the United States, both those operated directly by the INS and those operated by private firms under contract with the INS. Whereas an earlier study by the Legislative Budget and Finance Committee of the Pennsylvania General Assembly calculated that private centers were 17 percent more costly than public ones (Joint State Government Commission 1987), cost data provided to me by the INS indicated that the per diem cost of private detention was about 7–19 percent less expensive than government centers between 1984 and 1988 (McDonald 1990*b*). These cost figures were incomplete, however, because they did not include, on the public side, some estimate of the capital assets consumed, legal services, insurance and other liability costs, administrative overhead, and interagency costs. Whereas many more expenditures were captured in the private centers' cost data (or, more precisely, were reflected in the *prices* charged to the government), the cost of private imprisonment did not include a variety of "transaction costs" Williamson (1984) associated with contracting—for example, expenditures for government monitoring of the facilities, bidding, and contract negotiation. Had these costs been included, the spread between public and private costs would probably have been larger by some undetermined amount because the uncounted costs were probably larger on the public side (McDonald 1990*b*).

It is important to note, however, that the private facilities were occupied more fully than the public centers, which directly affects the measure of cost that was used here and in nearly all such studies: the per diem or per annum cost per inmate. Because daily per inmate costs are calculated by dividing total facility cost by the number of prisoner days, a facility having a higher occupancy rate will have a lower per inmate cost, other things being equal. If occupancy rates of the private and public centers had been the same, the apparent cost advantage of the private ones would have diminished substantially (McDonald 1990*b*).

A useful and fair comparison of costs should consider the benefits as well. Cost reductions alone should not be seen as a sufficient reason for preferring private over public provision, or vice versa. Unfortunately, very little has been done in the way of cost-benefit or cost-effectiveness analyses of public and private correctional facilities. The best attempt to consider both sides of the ledger is that by Hatry and his associates at the Urban Institute (1989)—the comparison of the Marion Adjustment Center and the Blackburn Correctional Complex. In addition to their cost analysis, they attempted to assess systematically the quality of services delivered in both facilities. The authors found that "by and large, both staff and inmates gave better ratings to the services and programs at the privately-operated facilities; escape rates were lower; there were fewer disturbances by inmates; and in general, staff and offenders felt more comfortable at the privately-operated ones" (pp. ES 6–7). They speculated that this may be due to the more youthful and less experienced (and less "burned out") staff at the private facilities.

Another attempt to assess the nature of services provided in private and public facilities is Logan's study (1991*a*) of the quality of confinement conditions, which did not attempt an analysis of costs. He studied two facilities: the private 200-bed New Mexico Women's Facility, operated by CCA in Grants; the same facility, operated by the state before it was turned over to the contractor; and a federal women's prison at Alderson, West Virginia, a larger 600-bed facility. He developed measures of several dimensions—what he termed security, safety, order, care, activity, justice, conditions, and management. The prisons were scored, using data drawn from institutional records and surveys of staff and inmates. Logan concluded that "by privately contracting for the operation of its women's prison, the State of New Mexico raised the quality of operation of that prison." Logan argues further that it is realistic to expect high quality from commercially contracted prisons, which he attributes to "(1) a well-designed facility; (2) greater operational and administrative flexibility; (3) decentralized authority; (4) higher morale, enthusiasm, and sense of ownership among line staff; (5) greater experience and leadership among the top administrators; and (6) stricter, 'by the book' governance of inmates" (1991*b*, p. 7).

This effort to measure the services systematically represents an advance, although one must raise questions about the generalizations Logan draws about public and private prisons. First, the comparison was a limited one, examining one prison before and after contracting for operation and only one other prison. Moreover, the comparison of subjective staff assessments of prison conditions before and after contracting may be confounded by a bias resulting from selection: many of the staff did not stay after the contractor assumed control. One must wonder if the decision to stay on also affected those employees' assessments of the privately operated prison. (Were those who stayed on more biased in favor of the contractor's operation, and were they likely to distort their perception in order to justify their decision to stay?) Moreover, the Alderson prison cannot be taken as representative of all public facilities, no more than a single contract facility in New Mexico can be seen as representative of all private prisons. In other words, Logan's comparisons provide too narrow an empirical foundation to support a general proposition about public and private provision of correctional services.

IV. The Legality and Propriety of Private Imprisonment

Some of the most interesting questions about privately operated correctional facilities are not about facts but about principles. Should private imprisonment be legally permitted? Is it constitutional? Even if it is deemed to be both constitutional and legal, should we encourage private firms, and especially for-profit ones, to confine individuals? Does it make good public policy to do so? If private imprisonment is permitted, should governments continue to be liable for contractors' actions, or is it acceptable that liability be delegated to private contractors along with management authority? With respect to private ownership of facilities that are leased to governments, should these arrangements be permitted? Or are they unwanted and unwise evasions of laws intended to keep public officials from "buying now" while passing the costs on to a later generation? Although there is no empirical research on these issues to review (because these are not empirical questions), these considerations are of great interest to policymakers.

In this concluding section, I examine three principal issues. The first is whether it is constitutional to delegate authority to operate prisons and jails to private parties. I am not a lawyer and cannot speak with authority about legal issues; my impression, however, is that the arguments attacking the constitutionality of private delegation are not compelling. The second issue is whether it is proper and desirable to delegate imprisonment powers, even if it is constitutionally permitted. This question is a tougher one, I think, because there are a number of good arguments against delegation and for continuing prison management as a public responsibility. My own policy preference is for the continued maintenance of dominant state responsibility for imprisonment. I see no good reason for the state shedding this responsibility completely to the private sector (although, it must be admitted, not even the most fervent advocate of privatization argues for the transfer of all prisons and jails to private jailers). However, I also see no compelling reason to prohibit privatization in all instances, especially if public authorities are unwilling or unable to provide adequate services. The third issue is whether governments should turn to the private sector to finance, construct, and own correctional facilities that are leased to the public authorities. Because these maneuvers constitute an end run around legal restrictions on debt creation and make it too easy to incur long-term obligations that will have to be paid by later generations, they seem unwise.

A. *Is Private Delegation of Correctional Authority Constitutional?*

In 1989 the American Bar Association's (ABA) House of Delegates passed a resolution urging jurisdictions to proceed "with extreme caution in considering possible authorization of contracts with private corporations or other private entities for the operation of prisons or jails . . ." (American Bar Association 1989). The report accompanying the proposed resolution argued that "there can be no doubt that an attempt to delegate total operational responsibility for a prison or jail would raise grave questions of constitutionality under both the federal constitution and the constitutions of the fifty states. The more sweeping the delegation, the more doubtful would be its constitutionality" (American Bar Association 1989, p. 3).

As I have argued elsewhere (McDonald 1990c), such doubts seem misplaced. No majority opinion of the Supreme Court has been troubled by the delegation doctrine since 1948. For fifty years, since *Carter v. Carter Coal Company*, 298 U.S. 238 (1936), the courts have allowed the federal government to delegate broad powers to private actors. At least at the federal level, concluded Lawrence (1986) in his review of the law of private delegation, "private exercise of federally delegated power is no longer a federal constitutional issue." Nor has delegation by state and local governments been seen as a federal constitutional issue since the 1920s.

Robbins (1988), the author of an ABA-sponsored report that was influential in the development of the resolution passed by the association, argued that federal courts "might apply more stringent standards of review to delegations that affect liberty interests than they do to those that affect property interests" (p. 39). But private bail bondsmen's powers to arrest and detain certainly affect liberty interests, and those powers have consistently been upheld. Similarly, private security guards are also permitted to detain persons forcefully, and this authority has been seen to pose no insurmountable constitutional problems (Shearing and Stenning 1981). Nor has any federal court found privately delegated imprisonment to be unconstitutional. In a 1984 case involving the delegation of federal detention powers to a private firm, *Medina v. O'Neill*, 589 F. Supp. 1028 (1984), the U.S. District Court for the Southern District of Texas was asked to decide whether the INS was liable for a prisoner's death caused by a private security guard. The plaintiff's attorney declared that the Constitution does not permit government to "retail out the detention of human beings." Chief Judge John Singleton agreed in part, holding that "detention . . . is the exclusive prerogative of the state" and that the private firm was providing a public function even though its employees were private individuals (Becker and Stanley 1985). Because detention powers were delegated to them by the INS, they were state actors, and the INS was liable for their actions. Although this case was not brought as a head-on challenge to the constitutionality of private imprisonment, the judge did not take this as an opportunity to rule that such delegation was unconstitutional.

Regarding delegation by state governments: There is no clear legal ban in state constitutions against private delegation of correctional authorities. Because established doctrine holds that state constitutions are limitations on power rather than grants of power (Lawrence 1986), state governments may take any action whatsoever in the absence of explicit prohibitions as long as it does not contravene the U.S. Constitution. Nonetheless, judges in state courts have ruled inconsistently on issues regarding private delegation of state powers (Lawrence 1986). To clarify this, legislatures in several states have passed laws authorizing delegation of correctional authority to private individuals or firms.

One of the other struts supporting the argument that private imprisonment is of questionable constitutionality is the proposition that "power over the conditions of confinement of individuals convicted of violating the criminal law is a core responsibility of government, one that cannot be left to the discretion of private parties," as the ABA resolution puts it (American Bar Association 1989, p. 3). Robbins (1988) argues similarly that incarcerating prisoners "is a power that states traditionally had to themselves," and that, "because this function is 'intrinsically governmental in nature,' the courts may distinguish private-prison operations on delegation grounds," (p. 43) thereby finding a way to treat such matters differently from other types of delegations found to be lawful.

This argument blurs the distinction between the power to *impose* imprisonment and the power to *administer* it (McDonald 1990c). The power to order imprisonment rests with the public authorities. Only governments may determine who will be imprisoned and for how long. This principle is not violated if the administration of the imprisonment sentence is delegated to a private firm. Nor does private delegation mean that power over the conditions of confinement is necessarily left to the discretion of private parties. Governments cannot abdicate their responsibilities. The courts have established that private imprisonment on behalf of government agencies constitutes "state action" and that governments retain the ultimate responsibility for what goes on in private facilities. Private facilities are required to comply with the same standards that apply to public ones. Delegating administrative authority for imprisonment does not free private firms to do what they want with the persons they hold. They must conform to law and established standards (Logan 1990; McDonald 1990c).

Moreover, the notion that imprisonment is a core responsibility of government, if what is meant is the actual power to administer imprisonment, runs counter to the historical record. It is true that governments have assumed near complete responsibility for administering prisons and jails, but, as discussed earlier, this was not the case in the nineteenth century. Nor has it been the case in juvenile corrections since the early 1800s. For many years, there has existed in the United States a variety of private halfway houses, work-release centers, other residential community correctional facilities for adult criminals, and secure facilities for juveniles, all of which involve the exercise of coercive detention power. It is fruitless to argue, it seems to me, whether this or that service is "intrinsically" governmental in nature. Instead, the significant question is whether the service *should* be exclusively, or predominantly, delivered by government. Resolution of this matter turns primarily on political philosophy.

B. Is Private Imprisonment Proper and Desirable?

Because no public authority has declared private imprisonment to be unconstitutional or illegal, the most salient question is whether it is good and desirable public policy to delegate powers to administer prisons to private agents. There is considerable controversy about this.

Some believe that privatizing imprisonment erodes civic values that should instead be shorn up (e.g., Robbins 1988; DiIulio 1990). DiIulio, for example, argues that the criminal law "is the one area where Americans have conceded to the state an almost unqualified right to act in the name of the polity, and hence one of the few places where one can discern an American conception of political community that is not a mere collage of individualistic and materialistic assumptions" (p. 176). To delegate responsibility for administering prisons to private individuals threatens to "undermine the moral writ of the community itself" (1990, p. 176).

Logan (1990), in contrast, argues that it is entirely proper to delegate correctional authority and that this violates no fundamental principle of the democratic state. According to classical theories of social contract on which our political order is founded, the state does not possess exclusive rights but derives them from individual rights. Consequently, "the state does not *own* the right to punish . . . . It merely *administers* it in trust, on behalf of the people and under the rule of law. Because the authority does not originate with the state, it does not attach inherently or uniquely to it, and can be passed along to private agencies" (Logan 1990, p. 53).

DiIulio (1990) and Robbins (1988) also argue that the legitimacy of governmental authority in inmates' eyes is weakened by having private (and especially for-profit) corporations administer imprisonment. Whether this actually occurs, however, is an empirical question that has not been studied. Moreover, it is reasonable to suspect that inmates' perceptions of legitimacy have more to do with conformity of the actions of the keepers to law and norms of fairness than with their status as public or private employees (Logan 1990; McDonald 1990c).

Others warn of private imprisonment because of other risks. The development of a self-interested private imprisonment industry may distort legislative policy-making regarding sentencing and confinement

(Schoen 1985; Tolchin 1985c). That is, private prison operators, whose business opportunities derive from a shortfall of cell space relative to demand, may organize themselves into a kind of "penal-industrial complex" that could lend powerful support to other lobbies pushing for tougher sentencing laws. But is this really likely to happen? With the private sector housing so small a proportion of the total number of prisoners behind bars, and with other forces pressing prison populations upwards, it is hard to see a need for private prison providers to lobby for a still more expansive use of imprisonment. Public employee unions are now extremely powerful lobbies in state and local governments, but they are not organizing to promote tougher sentencing laws. Moreover, attempts to sway considerations of sentencing policy by self-interested and profit-seeking prison operators will not be seen as legitimate.

Perhaps a more serious concern is the risk of creating incentives to sacrifice prisoners' interests and the interests of the larger society in having a humane penal system, in order to increase profits. There may be significant disincentives to counter this tendency. Even more important than these alleged disincentives, however, are the moral and legal constraints that are felt by prison operators, both private and public. During the past three decades, there has been a sea change in the moral and legal climate for imprisonment. The public is probably less tolerant of degrading prison conditions than it was during Reconstruction, when convict leasing—which often brought with it horrible conditions—was common. There is also little reason to believe that the courts would permit a return to nineteenth-century conditions. Convict leasing amounted to a continuation of slavery by other means, a practice ratified by rulings such as that made by a Virginia court in 1871, finding that a prisoner "is for the time being a slave of the state" *Ruffin v. Commonwealth*, 62 Virginia (21 Gratt.) 790, 796 (1871). Since the mid-1960s, we have witnessed what amounts to a revolutionary change in the rights accorded prisoners (Jacobs 1980; Bronstein 1980). In the absence of a profound counterrevolution, the courts will be no more forgiving of private contractors' performance than they are of public administrators'.

What of the worry that privatization will weaken public control over prison keepers and their performance? The reason for the worry is apparent: private facilities are legally separated from public authorities, and this barrier is bridged only by contractual agreements that are negotiated and put into writing. Because public managers are bound—and limited—by these contractual agreements, political leadership may have less flexibility in responding to circumstances not foreseen or adequately planned for, such as riots. In contrast, direct public administration may provide an unbroken chain of command between the officer who deals with inmates day by day and the highest public official in the government.

But direct public administration may not always provide this unbroken chain. In our federal system of government, political and administrative controls over correctional administration are sometimes fragmented. This is perhaps more characteristic of local jail administration, which is generally the responsibility of sheriffs, who are often elected officials not directly answerable to other county officials or to state officers. In such circumstances, contracting may *increase* a county board's control of a jail. Contractors may be more responsive to the boards, or their executives, than are sheriffs, who have their own independent power base. The necessity to write a contract also creates the opportunity to bind the contractor to perform certain desired tasks (such as facility renovation, or obtaining accreditation for the facility) and to provide certain services. County boards or executives do not have a comparable opportunity to bind elected sheriffs. A fair reading of events that led to the contracting of some county jails (e.g., Bay County, Florida, and Santa Fe, New Mexico) suggests that contracting was chosen by county commissioners and executives for the explicit purpose of enhancing their control (McDonald 1990c; Press 1990). In short: it is not self-evident that contracting necessarily diminishes public control of prisons and jails.

I find no compelling reason to conclude that private delegation of prison or jail operations is improper or inherently undesirable and that it should be discouraged as a matter of sound public policy. Nor do I think there are compelling reasons to discourage continued public provision of prisons and jails. My personal preference would be for a well-managed and humane public correctional system, but if public authorities in a particular state or county cannot or will not provide such a service, the private sector should be permitted to do so if it is willing, and it is fair that it should be rewarded for assuming the risk. Governments should "go private" as a last resort, and the higher value should be placed on the provision of humane conditions of confinement rather than on the public or private status of the keepers (McDonald 1990c).

C. Should Governments Rely on Nominally Private Correctional Facilities?

The use of privately owned but publicly operated facilities poses policy questions that are different from those raised in connection with privately operated ones. The most critical issue is whether public managers should be permitted to rely on private entities to undertake financing, thereby avoiding the conventional methods of financing capital construction.

The benefits of creative financing are clear. Public managers, pressed to build more prison cells, can obtain them more quickly this way than by waiting for voter approval of prison construction bonding proposals, and they can avoid hitting the limit on public debt (if those limits are being reached). Creative financing also allows acquisition of more prison space when voters reject proposals to build prisons by increasing public debt.

But there are several reasons to discourage these sorts of financing arrangements. The raison d'etre of such arrangements is to dodge the legal requirements for financing capital construction projects by incurring debt that taxpayers will have to repay. Indeed, some of the private entities that own prisons and jails are corporations set up by public officials for the sole purpose of accomplishing such a dodge, and these public officials constitute themselves as the corporation's directors. Such facilities are only nominally private.

The end result is that public debt is in fact incurred. Although an agreement to pay lease fees is not legally binding on future legislatures, or beyond the fiscal year during which the appropriation is made (because such an obligation would be considered a debt), the need to maintain good credit ratings and investor confidence creates a powerful incentive for governments to honor such agreements. To break such agreements imperils the ability to find investors for similar projects in the future.

Creative financing thereby avoids procedures that exist to ensure the fiscal accountability of public managers. It provides a means of relaxing fiscal discipline and makes it easier to satisfy all current demands for services while pushing off payments until later. By structuring lease payment schedules over decades, public managers thereby impose a costly burden on future generations of taxpayers. (For that reason, some wag has called debt financing "fiscal child abuse.") The cost of such financing is also higher. Investors must be paid at higher interest rates than is common for conventional, general obligation bonds issued directly by governments because there is a higher risk of nonpayment.

One expert on public finance, Herman Leonard, argues that we should neither endorse nor prohibit creative financing techniques on a priori grounds, but that we should evaluate how public officials manage public debt and quasi debt and how an informed public responds to their performance. "That will be the test of whether the privatization of prisons is an accountable response to public demands for more prison services or an unaccountable end run around legitimate scrutiny devices by hard-pressed public managers" (1990, p. 85). My own view is less agnostic. Questions of sentencing policy have tended, in recent years, to be uncoupled from considerations of scarce resources. Money spent for prisons and jails is not a free commodity, for this is money that cannot be spent to advance other public purposes. Because correctional expenditures have grown so rapidly during the past two decades, to the point where prison budgets are among the largest in state governments, it seems prudent to require public managers and the public to face directly the costs of penal policies as well as the hoped-for benefits. Practices that encourage easier spending, by deferring payments into the future, make it too tempting to uncouple sentencing policies from resource allocation questions.

REFERENCES

Alabama Penitentiary. 1882. *Report of the Inspectors.* Wetumpka: Alabama Penitentiary.

Allen-Hagen, Barbara. 1991. *Public Juvenile Facilities: Children in Custody, 1989.* Washington, D.C.: U.S. Department of Justice, Office of Juvenile Justice and Delinquency Prevention.

American Bar Association. 1969. *Standards Relating to Sentencing Alternatives and Procedures.* New York: Project on Standards for Criminal Justice.

American Bar Association, Section on Criminal Justice. 1986. "Report to the House of Delegates." Unpublished document. Chicago: American Bar Association.

―――. 1989. "Report to the House of Delegates." Unpublished document dated February 13. Chicago: American Bar Association.

American Correctional Association. 1991. *Directory.* Laurel, Md.: American Correctional Association.

American Federation of State, County, and Municipal Employees, AFL-CIO. 1984. *Passing the Bucks: The Contracting Out of Public Services.* Washington, D.C.: American Federation of State, County, and Municipal Employees, AFL-CIO.

American Hospital Association. 1990. *Hospital Statistics*. Chicago: American Hospital Association.

Bakal, Y. 1973. *Strategies for Restructuring the State Department of Youth Services*. U.S. Department of Health, Education, and Welfare, Office of Youth Development. Washington, D.C.: U.S. Government Printing Office.

Batten, Helen Levine. 1991. *Drug Services Research Survey: Provisional Report, Phase II*. Waltham, Mass.: Brandeis University, Bigel Institute for Public Policy.

Becker, Craig, and Amy Dru Stanley. 1985. "The Downside of Private Prisons." *Nation* 15(June):728–30.

Bernat, Betsy. 1991. (American Civil Liberties Union, National Prison Project.) Personal communication with author, September 27.

Bivens, Terry. 1986. "Can Prisons for Profit Work?" *Philadelphia Inquirer Magazine* (August 3), p. 4.

Bronick, Matthew J. 1989. "The Federal Bureau of Prisons' Experience with Privatization." Unpublished paper. Washington, D.C.: U.S. Bureau of Prisons.

Bronstein, Alvin. J. 1980. "Offender Rights Litigation: Historical and Future Developments." In *Prisoners' Rights Sourcebook, Volume II*, edited by Ira P. Robbins. New York: Clark Boardman.

Brown, Aaron A., Roy E. Gerard, Roberta L. Howard, Wallace A. Kennedy, Robert B. Levinson, Carol A. Sell, Paul A. Skelton, Jr., and Herbert C. Quay. 1985. *Private Sector Operation of a Correctional Institution: A Study of the Jack & Ruth Eckerd Youth Development Center, Okeechobee, Florida*. Washington, D.C.: U.S. Department of Justice, National Institute of Corrections.

Bureau of Justice Assistance. 1988. *Treatment Alternatives to Street Crime: TASC Programs*. Washington, D.C.: U.S. Department of Justice.

Bureau of Justice Statistics. 1986. "Jail Inmates, 1986." Washington, D.C.: U.S. Department of Justice.

———. 1989. "Children in Custody, 1975–85: Census of Public and Private Juvenile Detention, Correctional, and Shelter Facilities." Washington, D.C.: U.S. Department of Justice.

———. 1991a. "Prisoners in 1990." Washington, D.C.: U.S. Department of Justice.

———. 1991b. "Jail Inmates, 1990." Washington, D.C.: U.S. Department of Justice.

Butler, Stuart. 1985. *Privatizing Federal Spending: A Strategy to Eliminate the Deficit*. New York: Universe Books.

Cable, George. 1969. "The Convict Lease System." In *The Silent South*. Montclair, N.J.: Patterson Smith. (Originally published 1889.)

Camp, Camille G., and George M. Camp. 1984. *Private Sector Involvement in Prison Services and Operations*. South Salem, N.Y.: Criminal Justice Institute.

Carstens, C. C. 1915. "Report of the Committee: A Community Plan in Children's Work." Proceedings of the National Conference of Charities and Corrections. Chicago: Hildmann.

———. 1938. "The Proper Treatment of Delinquent Children." *Child Welfare League of America Bulletin* (October 4).

Chabotar, Kent John. 1985. "Financing Alternatives for Prison and Jail Construction." *Government Finance Review* 1(August):7–13.

Chaiken, Jan, and Stephen Mennemeyer. 1987. *Lease-Purchase Financing of Prison and Jail Construction*. Washington, D.C.: U.S. Department of Justice, National Institute of Justice.

Chi, Keon S. 1982. "Private Contractor Work Release Centers: The Illinois Experience." In *Innovations*. Lexington, Ky.: Council of State Governments.

Clear, Todd, Patricia Harris, and Albert Record. 1982. "Managing the Cost of Corrections." *Prison Journal* 62:3–63.

Coates, Robert B., Alden D. Miller, and Lloyd E. Ohlin. 1978. *Diversity in a Youth Correctional System: Handling Delinquents in Massachusetts*. Cambridge, Mass.: Ballinger.

Corrections Compendium. 1986. "Jail Inmates and Costs." 10(November):7, 12–14. Lincoln, Nebr.: Contact Center, Inc.

Corrections Corporation of America. 1985. "Proposal for State of Tennessee." Nashville: Corrections Corporation of America.

———. 1991. "1990 Annual Report." Nashville: Corrections Corporation of America.

Crew, A. 1933. *London Prisons of Today and Yesterday*. London: I. Nicholson & Watson.

Criminal Justice Associates. 1985. *Private Sector Involvement in Prison Based Businesses: A National Assessment*. Washington, D.C.: U.S. Government Printing Office.

DeWitt, Charles B. 1986. "Ohio's New Approach to Prison and Jail Financing." Research in Brief. Washington, D.C.: National Institute of Justice.

DiIulio, John J. 1990. "The Duty to Govern: A Critical Perspective on the Private Management of Prisons and Jails." In *Private Prisons and the Public Interest*, edited by Douglas C. McDonald. New Brunswick, N.J.: Rutgers University Press.

Donahue, John D. 1990. *The Privatization Decision*. New York: Basic.

Feeley, Malcolm M. 1991. "Privatization of Prisons in Historical Perspective." In *Privatization and Its Alternatives*, edited by William Gormley. Madison: University of Wisconsin Press.

Friel, Charles M., Joseph B. Vaughn, and Rolando del Carmen. 1987. *Electronic Monitoring and Correctional Policy: The Technology and Its Application*. Washington, D.C.: U.S. Department of Justice, National Institute of Justice.

Haas, James. 1986. Personal communication with author, December 18.

Hanke, Steve H., ed. 1987. *Prospects for Privatization*. New York: Academy of Political Science.

Harrington, Judy. 1987. "Adult Private Prison Will Teach 'Real World Job Skills' to Cons." *Denver Post* (January 10).

Herbers, John. 1987. "The New Federalism: Unplanned, Innovative, and Here to Stay." *Governing* (October), p. 30.

Hillsman, Sally T. 1982. "Pretrial Diversion of Youthful Adults: A Decade of Reform and Research." *Justice System Journal* 7:361–86.

Holdsworth, W. S. 1922–24. *A History of English Law*. Vol. 4, 3d ed. London: Cambridge University Press.

Hughes, Robert. 1987. *The Fatal Shore*. New York: Knopf.

Immarigeon, Russ. 1987. "Privatizing Adult Imprisonment in the U.S.: A Bibliography." *Criminal Justice Abstracts* 19:136–39.

Institute of Medicine. 1986. *Improving the Quality of Care in Nursing Homes*. Washington, D.C.: National Academy Press.

Jacobs, James B. 1980. "The Prisoners' Rights Movement and Its Impacts, 1960-80." In *Crime and Justice: An Annual Review of Research*, vol. 2, edited by Norval Morris and Michael Tonry. Chicago: University of Chicago Press.

Joint State Government Commission. 1987. "Report of the Private Prison Task Force." Harrisburg, Pa.: General Assembly of the Commonwealth of Pennsylvania.

Keating, J. Michael, Jr. n.d. "Seeking Profit in Punishment: The Private Management of Correctional Institutions." Washington, D.C.: American Federation of State, County, and Municipal Employees.

Klein, Philip. 1918. "A Contribution to the History of Correctional Institutions and Methods in New York State." Ph.D. dissertation, Columbia University.

Krisberg, Barry. 1987. "Preventing and Controlling Violent Youth Crime: The State of the Art." In *Violent Juvenile Crime: What Do We Know about It and What Can We Do about It?* Minneapolis: University of Minnesota, Hubert Humphrey Institute of Public Affairs, Center for the Study of Youth Policy.

Krisberg, Barry, Ira M. Schwartz, Paul Litsky, and James Austin. 1986. "The Watershed of Juvenile Justice Reform." *Crime and Delinquency* 32:5–38.

Law Enforcement Assistance Administration. 1977. *Children in Custody, 1974*. Washington, D.C.: U.S. Government Printing Office.

Lawrence, David. 1986. "Private Exercise of Governmental Power." *Indiana Law Journal* 61:649.

Lazar Institute. 1976. *Phase I Report, Treatment Alternatives to Street Crime (TASC) National Evaluation Program*. Washington, D.C.: Law Enforcement Assistance Administration.

Legislative Research Council, Commonwealth of Massachusetts. 1986. *Prisons for Profit*. Boston: Legislative Research Council.

Leiby, J. 1978. *A History of Social Welfare and Social Work in the United States*. New York: Columbia University Press.

Leonard, Herman B. 1986. *Checks Unbalanced: The Quiet Side of Public Spending*. New York: Basic.

———. 1990. "Private Time: The Political Economy of Private Prison Finance." In *Private Prisons and the Public Interest*, edited by Douglas C. McDonald. New Brunswick, N.J.: Rutgers University Press.

Lerman, Paul. 1982. *Deinstitutionalization and the Welfare State*. New Brunswick, N.J.: Rutgers University Press.

———. 1984. "Child Welfare, the Private Sector, and Community-based Corrections." *Crime and Delinquency* 30:5–38.

Lewis, Orlando. 1922. *The Development of American Prisons and Prison Customs: 1779–1845*. Albany, N.Y.: Prison Association of New York.

Logan, Charles H. 1989. "Privately Operated Prisons for Adults as of June 1989." Unpublished manuscript. Storrs: University of Connecticut, Department of Sociology.

————. 1990. *Private Prisons: Cons and Pros.* New York: Oxford University Press.

————. 1991*a*. "Well Kept: Comparing Quality of Confinement in a Public and a Private Prison." Unpublished report submitted to U.S. Department of Justice, National Institute of Justice.

————. 1991*b*. "Well Kept: Comparing Quality of Confinement in a Public and a Private Prison—Executive Summary." Unpublished report submitted to U.S. Department of Justice, National Institute of Justice.

Logan, Charles H., and Bill W. McGriff. 1989. "Comparing Costs of Public and Private Prisons: A Case Study." *NIJ Reports* 216:2–8.

Logan, Charles H., and Sharla P. Rausch. 1985. "Punish and Profit: The Emergence of Private Enterprise Prisons." *Justice Quarterly* 2:303–18.

MacAvoy, Paul W., W. T. Stanbury, George Yarrow, and Richard J. Zeck-hauser. 1989. *Privatization and State-owned Enterprises: Lessons from the United States, Great Britain and Canada.* Boston: Kluwer Academic.

McDonald, Douglas C. 1980. *The Price of Punishment: Public Spending for Corrections in New York.* Boulder, Colo.: Westview Press.

————. 1986. *Punishment without Walls: Community Service Sentences in New York City.* New Brunswick, N.J.: Rutgers University Press.

————. 1989. *The Cost of Corrections: In Search of the Bottom Line.* Washington, D.C.: U.S. Department of Justice, National Institute of Corrections.

————. 1990*a*. "Introduction." In *Private Prisons and the Public Interest*, edited by Douglas C. McDonald. New Brunswick, N.J.: Rutgers University Press.

————. 1990*b*. "The Costs of Operating Public and Private Correctional Facilities." In *Private Prisons and the Public Interest*, edited by Douglas C. McDonald. New Brunswick, N.J.: Rutgers University Press.

————. 1990*c*. "When Government Fails: Going Private as a Last Resort." In *Private Prisons and the Public Interest*, edited by Douglas C. McDonald. New Brunswick, N.J.: Rutgers University Press.

McKelvey, Blake. 1969. *American Prisons: A Study in American Social History prior to 1915.* Montclair, N.J.: Patterson Smith.

————. 1977. *American Prisons: A History of Good Intentions.* Montclair, N.J.: Patterson Smith.

Matheson, Scott. 1986. "Political Leadership in Juvenile Justice Reform." In *Youth Corrections and the Quiet Revolution*, edited by Lee Eddison. Minneapolis: University of Minnesota, Hubert Humphrey Institute of Public Affairs, Center for the Study of Youth Policy.

Mennel, Robert M. 1983. "Attitudes and Policies toward Juvenile Delinquency in the United States: A Historiographical Review." In *Crime and Justice: An Annual Review of Research*, vol. 4, edited by Michael Tonry and Norval Morris. Chicago: University of Chicago Press.

Miller, Alden D., Lloyd E. Ohlin, and Robert B. Coates. 1977. *A Theory of Social Reform: Correctional Change Processes in Two States.* Cambridge, Mass.: Ballinger.

Mullen, Joan. 1985. "Correction and the Private Sector." *Privatization Review* 1:12.

Mullen, Joan, Kent Chabotar, and Deborah Carrow. 1984. *The Privatization of Corrections.* Washington, D.C.: U.S. Department of Justice, National Institute of Justice.

National Center for Health Statistics. 1972. *Vital and Health Statistics.* Series 14(6):43. Rockville, Md.: National Center for Health Statistics.

———. 1974. *Vital and Health Statistics.* Series 14(12):49. Rockville, Md.: National Center for Health Statistics.

National Criminal Justice Statistics Association. 1987. *Private Sector Involvement in Financing and Managing Correctional Facilities.* Washington, D.C.: National Criminal Justice Statistics Association.

Pease, Ken. 1985. "Community Service Orders." In *Crime and Justice: An Annual Review of Research,* vol. 6, edited by Michael Tonry and Norval Morris. Chicago: University of Chicago Press.

Peterson, John. 1988. *Corrections and the Private Sector: A National Forum.* Proceedings of a conference. Washington, D.C.: U.S. Department of Justice, National Institute of Justice.

Poole, Robert W., Jr., and Philip E. Fixler, Jr. 1987. "Privatization of Public-Sector Services in Practice: Experience and Potential." *Journal of Policy Analysis and Management* 6:612–24.

Powell, J. C. 1970. *The American Siberia: Or, Fourteen Years' Experience in a Southern Convict Camp.* Montclair, N.J.: Patterson Smith. (Originally published 1891.)

President's Commission on Privatization. 1988. *Privatization: Toward More Effective Government.* Washington, D.C.: President's Commission on Privatization.

Press, Aric. 1990. "The Good, the Bad, and the Ugly: Private Prisons in the 1980s." In *Private Prisons and the Public Interest,* edited by Douglas C. McDonald. New Brunswick, N.J.: Rutgers University Press.

Pricor. 1988. "Second Quarter Report, 1988" (corporate report to shareholders).

Rich, Bruce. 1987. "State Government Joins Private Business to House Inmates." *Corrections Today* (August), pp. 60–62.

Robbins, Ira P. 1988. *The Legal Dimensions of Private Incarceration.* Washington, D.C.: American Bar Association.

Roberts, Albert R., and Gerald T. Powers. 1985. "The Privatization of Corrections: Methodological Issues and Dilemmas Involved in Evaluative Research." *Prison Journal* 65:95–107.

Rothman, David. 1971. *The Discovery of the Asylum: Social Order and Disorder in the New Republic.* Boston: Little, Brown.

Rutherford, Andrew. 1990. "British Penal Policy and the Idea of Prison Privatization." In *Private Prisons and the Public Interest,* edited by Douglas C. McDonald. New Brunswick, N.J.: Rutgers University Press.

Savas, E. S. 1982. *Privatizing the Public Sector: How to Shrink Government.* Chatham, N.J.: Chatham House Publishers.

Schmidt, Robert. 1987. Personal communication with author.

Schoen, Kenneth. 1985. "Private Prison Operators." *New York Times* (March 28).

Scull, Andrew T. 1984. *Decarceration: Community Treatment and the Deviant—A Radical View.* 2d ed. New Brunswick, N.J.: Rutgers University Press.

Shearing, Clifford D., and Philip C. Stenning. 1981. "Modern Private Security: Its Growth and Implications." In *Crime and Justice: An Annual Review of Research*, vol. 3, edited by Michael Tonry and Norval Morris. Chicago: University of Chicago Press.

Shichor, David, and Clemens Bartollas. 1990. "Private and Public Juvenile Placements: Is There a Difference?" *Crime and Delinquency* 36(2):286–99.

Steinberg, Allen. 1983. "From Private Prosecution to Plea Bargaining: Criminal Prosecution, the District Attorney, and American Legal History." Paper presented at the Philadelphia Center for Early American Studies Seminar, Philadelphia.

Stewart, James K. 1986. "Costly Prisons: Should the Public Monopoly Be Ended?" In *Crime and Punishment in Modern America*, edited by Patrick B. McGuigan and Jon S. Pascale. Washington, D.C.: Institute for Government and Politics of the Free Congress Research and Education Foundation.

Swartz, Thomas R. 1987. "A New Urban Crisis in the Making." *Challenge* 29(September/October):35–37.

Sweeney, Paul. 1982. "Vision Quest's Rite of Passage." *Corrections Magazine* 3(1):22–32.

System Science, Inc. 1978. *Final Report—Evaluation of TASC, Phase II*. Bethesda, Md.: Law Enforcement Assistance Administration.

Taft, Philip B., Jr. 1982. "The Fiscal Crunch in Private Corrections." *Corrections Magazine* 8(6):27–32.

Thomas, Charles. 1989. Personal communication with author.

Thomas, Charles W., and Suzanna L. Foard. 1991. "Private Correctional Facility Census." Unpublished document. Gainesville: University of Florida, Center for Studies in Criminology and Law, November.

Timko, Paul. 1991. Personal communication with the author, September.

Tolchin, Martin. 1985a. "Private Concern Makes Offer to Run Tennessee's Prisons." *New York Times* (September 13), p. A14.

———. 1985b. "Prisons for Profit: Nashville's CCA Claims Operations Aid Government." *Tennessean* (February 24).

———. 1985c. "Experts Foresee Adverse Effects from Private Control of Prisons." *New York Times* (September 17).

Touche Ross. 1987. *Privatization in America: An Opinion Survey of City and County Governments on Their Use of Privatization and Their Infrastructure Needs*. Washington, D.C.: Touche Ross.

Urban Institute. 1989. *Comparison of Privately and Publicly Operated Corrections Facilities in Kentucky and Massachusetts*. Washington, D.C.: U.S. Department of Justice, National Institute of Justice.

U.S. Bureau of the Census. 1950. *Institutional Population*. Washington, D.C.: U.S. Department of Commerce.

———. 1970a. *Historical Statistics from Colonial Times to 1970*. Series A 119-134. Washington, D.C.: U.S. Bureau of the Census.

———. 1970b. *1970 Census of the Population*. Washington, D.C.: U.S. Bureau of the Census.

———. 1970c. *Persons in Institutions and Other Group Quarters*. Washington, D.C.: U.S. Bureau of the Census.

————. 1987. *Biannual Census of Public and Private Juvenile Detention, Correctional, and Shelter Facilities* (1987 census). Washington, D.C.: U.S. Bureau of the Census.

————. 1989. *Biannual Census of Public and Private Juvenile Detention, Correctional, and Shelter Facilities* (1989 census). Washington, D.C.: U.S. Bureau of the Census.

U.S. House of Representatives. 1986. *Privatization of Corrections: Hearings before the Subcommittee on Courts, Civil Liberties, and the Administration of Justice of the Committee of the Judiciary, House of Representatives, Ninety-ninth Congress, First and Second Sessions on Privatization of Corrections, November 13, 1985, and March 18, 1986.* Washington, D.C.: U.S. Government Printing Office.

Wayson, Billy L., and Gail S. Funke. 1989. *What Price Justice? A Handbook for the Analysis of Criminal Justice Costs.* Washington, D.C.: U.S. Department of Justice, National Institute of Justice.

Wayson, Billy L., Gail S. Funke, Sally F. Hamilton, Peter B. Meyer. 1977. *Local Jails: The New Correctional Dilemma.* Lexington, Mass.: Lexington Books.

Williams, Hubert, and Patrick V. Murphy. 1990. *The Evolving Strategy of Police: A Minority View.* Washington, D.C.: U.S. Department of Justice, National Institute of Justice.

Williamson, Oliver E. 1984. "What Is Transaction Cost Economics?" Working Paper no. 1014 (May). New Haven, Conn.: Yale University, Institution for Social and Policy Studies.

Wines, E. C. 1874. "Annual Report of the Secretary." In *Transactions of the National Prison Reform Congress.* New York: National Prison Association of the United States.